INTERACTIVE QUALITATIVE ANALYSIS

To the students, who perpetually renew us.

To Oscar Mink, who understood from the first moment, who never failed to encourage, and who is our model of a scholar, a mentor, and a gentleman.

INTERACTIVE QUALITATIVE ANALYSIS

A SYSTEMS METHOD FOR QUALITATIVE RESEARCH

NORVELL NORTHCUTT
DANNY McCOY

SAGE Publications

International Educational and Professional Publisher

Thousand Oaks ■ London ■ New Delhi

For information:

Sage Publications, Inc.
2455 Teller Road
Thousand Oaks, California 91320
E-mail: order@sagepub.com

Sage Publications Ltd.
1 Oliver's Yard
55 City Road
London EC1Y 1SP
United Kingdom

Sage Publications India Pvt. Ltd.
B-42, Panchsheel Enclave
Post Box 4109
New Delhi 110 017 India

Printed in the United States of America

Library of Congress Cataloging-in-Publication Data

Northcutt, Norvell.
Interactive qualitative analysis: A systems method for qualitative research/Norvell Northcutt, Danny McCoy.
    p. cm.
Includes bibliographical references and index.
   ISBN 0–7619–2833–2 (Cloth)—ISBN 0–7619–2834–0 (Paper) 1. Social sciences—Research.
2. Qualitative research. I. McCoy, Danny. II. Title.
H62.N734 2004
001.4′2—dc22

                    2003020767

04   05   06   07   10   9   8   7   6   5   4   3   2   1

Acquisitions Editor:	Lisa Cuevas Shaw
Editorial Assistant:	Margo Beth Crouppen
Production Editor:	Melanie Birdsall
Copy Editor:	Sally M. Scott
Typesetter:	C&M Digitals (P) Ltd.
Proofreader:	Cheryl Rivard
Indexer:	Juniee Oneida
Cover Designer:	Edgar Abarca

Contents

Prologue

A True Story

High School With Ashtrays

The classroom looks and smells like a thousand others. It is a long rectangular prism infused with fluorescent light that makes skin look sallow and is transfused with the arid scent of 40 years of chalk dust and stiff new textbooks. The chalkboards are of a kind not seen much anymore; heavy black slate, too expensive for modern construction budgets. The visitor, alone in the room for the moment, picks up a piece of chalk and writes his name and contact information on the board. He smiles with a sensual satisfaction, known by any craftsman when using a quality tool, as the saturated crisp white letters appear at the point of contact between chalk and board.

A desk sits at the front, and writing chairs for 30 students are scattered about. Brushing the dust from his hands in a ritual movement, the visitor sets up a flip chart and then places a cardboard carton, his toolbox, on the desk. Inside the box are the tools of the Interactive Qualitative Analysis (IQA) researcher: rolls of masking tape, stacks of blank 5×8 cards, and three dozen marking pens. As he places the empty box out of sight underneath the desk, the first teacher walks through the door. The visitor quickly moves to the front of the classroom to introduce himself and to greet the instructors as they begin to stream into the room.

The classroom is located in one of the original buildings on the attractive campus of a community college, and the instructors, some two dozen of them, are as varied as human beings can be. They have been selected by the visitor to participate in this first phase of the study not because of their diversity but because they have some things in common: They all have long tenures at the college; they all teach subjects required by almost all degree or certificate programs; and finally, there are indications that most, perhaps all, are becoming increasingly frustrated with their jobs. They comprise, in IQA parlance, a *constituency.*

The visitor begins the session by explaining that he has been invited by a committee of faculty (all of whom are present in the room) to help the group explore the nature of faculty/student relationships. He then invites open discussion of this issue and keeps notes on the flip chart as a lively discussion ensues.

After 15 minutes of free-flowing discussion, most of which consists of testimony recounting incidents illustrating the "problem," speculation as to the causes and nature of the "problem," or proposed solutions to the "problem," the visitor exploits a brief pause in the conversation, which he notices has become more and more laden with emotion, to suggest a strategy. Referring to the many pages of notes on the flip chart, he proposes a question that seems to capture the essence of the conversation: *Why do so many students seem to have behavior and learning problems in the past few years?* The group quickly agrees that this is a fair description of the issue. The visitor then points out that the first step in what he introduces as the IQA process has been taken: an agreement on the nature of the issue. He then guides the instructors through the rest of the IQA process.

Generating Data on the Issue. Distributing the note cards and markers to the faculty, the visitor asks them to silently reflect on their thoughts and reactions to the discussion that has just occurred and to record each of these thoughts on a card. Participants are encouraged to do a "brain dump" or to *brainstorm,* and to not censor or edit their thoughts and reactions. The odor of marking pen ink fills the air. Approximately 200 cards are generated in less than 20 minutes.

Sorting the Data Into Categories of Meaning (Inductive Coding). With the help of some of the faculty, the visitor tapes the cards to a wall in a columnar display in no particular order so that everyone can read all of them. He then leads the group in a discussion of what is written on each card, encouraging the group to come to a shared understanding of the meaning of the thoughts or emotions represented by each card. At the end of this clarification stage, the faculty are asked to silently arrange the cards into groups based on any rubric or system of categorization that occurs to them. There is very little noise in the room, save for the sound of tape being pulled from the wall and footsteps as cards are shuffled from place to place. Some faculty take to the task immediately and proceed independently, while some hang back and wait to see what others are doing, becoming fully engaged only as the patterns begin to emerge.

Clarification of Meaning and Axial Coding. After about 30 minutes, the cards have been sorted into 15 categories. The visitor then asks the faculty members to examine each group of cards (an *affinity*) and discuss why these particular cards were placed together. This discussion leads to (1) a common understanding of the underlying meaning represented by the group of cards and (2) a name for the affinity determined by consensus.

As the discussion proceeds, cards are moved from one group to another, groups are refined and redefined, and subgroups of cards are recognized and named. By the end of this stage, the data represented by the 200 cards are reduced to 11 affinities, some with subaffinities, and each has a name that has a common meaning to all participants.

Theoretical Coding. After a lunch break, the faculty return to the classroom to find (on the wall facing the one containing their analysis so far) a circular array of just 11 cards. Each of the 11 has written on it the name given to that affinity. The visitor now asks faculty to think about the relationships among these affinities. He points out that there are 55 possible pairwise relationships, and a groan of mock dismay rises from the group, suggesting that the participants have worked through the classic first three stages of group activity—or forming, storming, and norming—and are eager to proceed to the fourth stage of performing. Despite the obvious enthusiasm of the group members, the visitor knows that he has a problem. Looking at his watch, he knows from experience that there is not time to do an exhaustive analysis on all 11 affinities, so he improvises a field experiment that will allow for greatest level of analysis in the time remaining. The group is asked to prioritize the 11 affinities by means of techniques borrowed from the Total Quality Management (TQM) literature. The process identifies 5 of the 11 as the most critical, so the visitor announces a reduction in the group's workload from 11 affinities to 5, and from 55 pairs to 10, which is received with cheers by the group. The visitor explains that each of the 10 pairs will be examined in terms of a possible direct influence between the affinities forming the pair, and he provides a protocol to guide and record the analysis. The faculty break into small groups to analyze the 10 pairs independently. Each small group attacks its assignment vigorously, writing examples (*if/then statements*) to share with the larger group.

Group Reality and the IRD. In less than an hour, the small groups reconvene to present to the others in a plenary session. The small groups discover that for most affinity pairs, their independent efforts have produced identical judgments as to the nature of the relationship between the affinities forming each pair. In the few cases where there is disagreement, the visitor facilitates a discussion and further analysis that quickly produces consensus. As the presentations progress, the visitor records the groups' judgments as to the nature and directionality of each of the possible 56 relationships on a tabular display on his laptop (the IRD, or Interrelationship Diagram) as well as the examples generated from the personal experience of group members. By the end of this stage, a consensus has been reached on all 10 pairs, and the group is ready for a break.

Representing Group Reality. During the break, the visitor uses a process called *rationalizing the system* to produce a group *mindmap* or *SID* (Systems Influence Diagram), which is a picture of the system that underlies the group's analysis. The group returns to find this picture displayed on a screen at the front of the room:

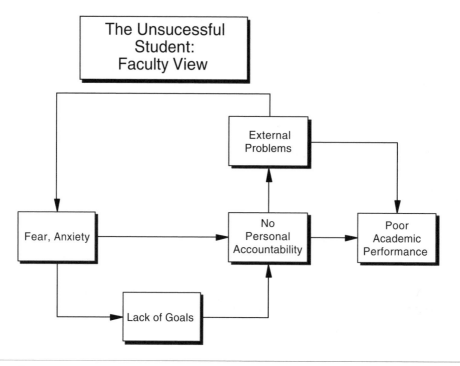

The Unsucessful Student: Faculty View

External Problems

Fear, Anxiety

No Personal Accountability

Poor Academic Performance

Lack of Goals

Figure 1

The visitor facilitates a group discussion, again using small groups reporting back in a plenary session, whose purpose is to bring to the surface a common understanding of the overall features of the system (its progression from drivers or primary causes to outcomes) as well as an understanding of how each affinity is related to, directly or indirectly, every other one. Notes on the discussion are recorded on a laptop and on the flip chart.

Interpreting Group Reality. With the day almost at an end, the visitor encourages faculty to *tour the system* by giving examples from their own experiences of how each link in the system behaves, and to exercise the system by comparing what the system suggests would happen in certain circumstances to the reality of their own experiences. The group's analysis is again recorded on a laptop and on the flip chart. Time runs out, but the group has managed to work through a complete iteration of the IQA process, albeit in less detail than desirable in a perfect world because of time limitations.

Later, the visitor wrote in his report of the day's activities:

At the beginning of the workshop, several instructors expressed a remarkably high level of frustration at their perceived failure to "connect with" students. One teacher captured the essence of their concern when she said, "I'm a good teacher, and I'm an experienced one. But *what used to work, doesn't.*"

He immediately recognized that this was the title of his report. In continuing his report, he wrote:

> By the end of the day, the facilitator noticed a reduction in frustration, and observed or heard many instructors indicating a different understanding of the situation that they could make use of in the classroom; for example, the system they developed suggests that poor academic skills cannot be addressed independently of a number of other factors. The faculty SID clearly reveals faculty's perception that fear (or frustration) on the part of the student leads to a lack of goals and to lack of personal accountability. This condition tends to exacerbate the already significant number of external problems (those outside the classroom), which has two effects: First, academic skills are degraded. But just as important, this network of causes and effects feeds back into fear, creating a vicious feedback loop. Faculty are beginning to understand that all these factors must be addressed from a systems point of view in order to treat the "symptom" of poor academic skills and inappropriate or obstructionist student behavior.

After working with faculty, the visitor, now more familiar with the terrain, understands that at least one other group or *constituency* must be heard from: students. After consultation with faculty and student support staff, students are partitioned into two separate constituencies, named privately by faculty cooperating in the study as "successful" students and those who are "clueless." Arrangements are made to identify representatives of both student constituencies through confidential faculty nominations, and two separate daylong student conferences on student life at the college are organized. At each of these conferences, in which students are told only that they have been nominated by faculty to participate in a student conference on issues of student life, the IQA procedure is implemented in a manner identical to that used with faculty, with the only difference being that the general issue is simply described as student life at the college. The pictures, or mindmaps, of the "clueless" and successful students are reproduced in Figures 2 and 3.

Days later, in his interpretation of the results of the student focus groups, the visitor wrote:

> Friday's group [those nominated in confidence as "clueless"], with some notable exceptions, was in what can only be called pain. Forgive the personal reference, but as an "uninvolved" facilitator, I found myself deeply moved on several occasions as the frustration and hurt bubbled up from the group. Friday's students [the "clueless" group] knew they were not accomplishing much at the college and were frustrated and angry at not being able to deal with the problems. The more insightful of the group acknowledged their own responsibility for their difficulties, but in general, the Friday group tended either to (1) blame their problems on external sources and

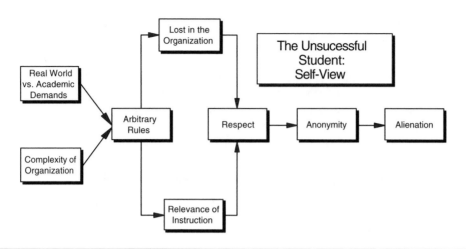

Figure 2

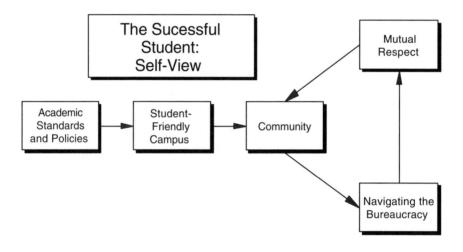

Figure 3

conditions, leading to acting out and to a confrontational relationship with the college; (2) refuse to acknowledge the severity of their academic problems [exactly the ones the faculty called "clueless" in their own focus group] and were invariably shocked when reality finally raised its ugly head; or (3) disengage from the situation by either not attending class or dropping out of school or even by leaving town altogether.

Drawing on language used by both students and faculty, the visitor suggested in his report an interpretive metaphor by which to understand the world of clueless students:

...the group tended toward a very consumerist view of their college experience, a view that faculty perceived very accurately by satirizing the student experience at the college as "McEducation." Time and again students implied they had paid for a "product," and the product was found not to be as represented. In this view, the students understood, at least at some primitive level, that they had a responsibility for their own success at the college; but when pressed, they tended to fall back into blaming external factors or, more frequently, in expressing a belief that they were, intentionally or not, misled about what would be the requirements for success. In the more extreme version of this perception, students come to regard themselves as victims of an oppressive and hostile system.

The visitor's report then focused on a description of the successful students and to a comparison of the two student groups:

The difference in atmosphere or emotional timbre between the two could hardly have been more dramatic. While a reading of the affinities generated by the Saturday [successful] group might suggest they were unhappy with their college experience, this was actually not the case at all. With some very few exceptions (notably, the semi-tongue-in-cheek "High School With Ashtrays" category, suggesting that the only difference in the way the college treated them versus the way they were treated in high school was that the college student lounge had ashtrays), all the discussion proceeded in a constructive manner clearly reflecting support and enthusiasm about their experiences at the college. Many of Saturday's group reported that their college experience was "the high point of my academic life." Clearly, the college is connecting at a deeply satisfying level with many successful students.

The two groups are different in another meaningful way. When interviewed about their view of education, their [successful students] outlook was dramatically different from the Friday group. Rather than the *consumer* outlook of the Friday group, the Saturday group saw their college life as more of a *partnership* between themselves and the college, and consequently were much less likely to blame, to disengage, to act out, or to flee. The Saturday group reported much the same kinds of problems in "negotiating" (their word) with the college as did the Friday group: lack of information, conflicting information, less than enthusiastic support from college staff, limited facilities, etc. *The lists of "problems" generated by the two groups are much more similar than they are different. But the Saturday [successful] group dealt with the college proactively and assertively, whereas the Friday [clueless] group dealt with these same problems passively and aggressively.*

The report elaborates on the theme by further contrasting and comparing the two student groups, drawing on the students' own words to provide an example:

Members of both groups were intimidated by the simple task of locating classes or support offices when they were new to campus. But where the Friday student was likely to become immediately frustrated and give up because of the lack of a clear map or a detailed list of instructions indicating what to do next, the reaction of the Saturday group was dramatically creative, as illustrated by the following quote from an employed mother of three when she described her first day at the college as she tried to get enrolled:

> I read stuff, and I asked questions, and if I couldn't get an answer, I just followed someone who looked like they knew what they were doing!

This comment was followed by laughter and knowing nods from the rest, and another woman reinforced the idea that resourcefulness was necessary to "navigate all the hoops and hurdles they place in your way." Standing up, she pointed to the chair she had just vacated. In a voice trembling with emotion, she made a brief speech that drew applause from the group:

> Every day I go to my job, where I iron clothes for three cents a pound, and I put my kids in daycare, and then I come here and I put my butt in that seat and I try to learn; and there's NO WAY you are going to keep me from graduating!

The report observes that by "you," she was not so much accusing the college of obstructionism as referring to the entire constellation of events in her life that required all her energy, resourcefulness, and just plain grit to improve her life.

Having interpreted the differences between the two student groups as revealed by an analysis of their group mindmaps or SIDs, the report then turns to the commonalities between the two:

> Both groups want to be respected as individuals and as persons of worth with responsibilities consistent with adult roles; both want, indeed demand, to participate in something larger than themselves, a college community to which they can contribute and which will support them in times of need and give them recognition when they succeed; both indicate that college support staff sometimes are less than helpful; both groups detested what they regarded as arbitrary classroom management, attendance, and grading policies; and both felt that the college was insensitive to their responsibilities and roles off-campus as parents, employers, employees, and adults for whom education was very important but who had to struggle to meet what seemed sometimes to be an overwhelming configuration of conflicting priorities in their lives.

A major tenet of IQA research is that comparison is fundamental to interpretation; therefore, explicit comparisons should be built into the design of a study from the beginning. The report addresses this issue in the context of a comparison of the two student groups:

> Commonalities and differences between the groups are equally important. For example, if only the Friday [clueless] group had raised the issue of arbitrary classroom management policies and had objected to linking grades to attendance rather than performance, one could reasonably argue that there is no compelling reason to consider changing these policies. But when both groups, successful and unsuccessful alike, make the same argument independently of the other, then the evidence suggests that either these policies ought to be examined in detail, or the message as to why certain classroom management and grading policies are in force is not getting through to the students.

After analyzing the commonalities and differences between the two student constituencies, the visitor's report compares faculty's perception of students: the mindmap of faculty concerning the issue they named "What Used to Work, Doesn't" to the student's mindmaps of their own experiences at the college. In a section titled "Faculty and Students: Two Different Worlds?" the report focuses the visitor's interpretive lens on the commonalities and differences of the different realities of teachers and students:

> *Did the faculty get it right?* Before the student groups were run, college faculty participated in their own focus group in which they arrived at a general consensus about why students were having difficulty. The resulting faculty SID [mindmap] of this issue portrays students who become victims of a pernicious feedback loop consisting of fear or anxiety leading to what instructors named a lack of goals and a lack of personal accountability vis-à-vis their responsibilities as a student at the college. This lack of accountability contributes (although certainly not exclusively) to "external" problems (problems not located specifically on the campus), which tend to feed back into fear and anxiety. These factors all operate, predictably enough, to produce poor academic performance. Faculty also "correctly" (i.e., their assessment was essentially identical to both student groups) perceived a common attitude among students that the college served up a mass-produced, low-cost, standardized product that many faculty referred to as "McEducation."
>
> So, did the faculty get it right? In examining all three focus groups' SIDs and supporting interviews, one must answer, "Yes, remarkably so." But two questions arise when comparing faculty to student data. First, what is the true nature of what faculty call *No Personal Accountability?* Second, can the college afford to regard *External Problems* as external?

Having raised two important ontological differences between faculty and students, the visitor's report then elaborates on each in turn by comparing faculty reality to student reality, using the students' mindmap to critique the faculty's:

The Nature of Student Accountability. The student focus groups provide useful insights into why students are "clueless." For example, one begins to understand how *policies whose intention is to increase student accountability (linking grades to attendance) can very well backfire and have the opposite effect.* There obviously is nothing wrong with attendance policies per se, but a student who is struggling financially, who doesn't know which questions to ask, who understands education to be more like a purchased product than anything else, and who is dealing with critical problems that may be "external" to the college but are absolutely at the core of his or her being is very likely to understand these policies more as a challenge or an insult.

The Nature of External Problems. Which brings us to the second critique that the student data provide for the faculty's perception: It is supremely ironic that at an institution that has "community" as its middle name, the essential feature of all these factors inhibiting student success is, at least in the eyes of a student, *a lack of community.* Which is not to say that the college is any more or less vulnerable to this condition than any other community college; indeed, this problem is common among "community" colleges if for no other reason than relatively few community colleges have the usual mechanisms to create community: On-campus housing, fraternities and sororities and highly active student groups, and big-time sports around which students can rally . . . are obvious examples. But such is the nature of many community colleges, which means that while "external problems" might be a useful administrative or organizational category, the college must nevertheless find a way to understand and address these "external" problems in a very internal way, because they are not external to the student, and therefore they cannot be external to our concerns as community college educators.

The report concludes with a prediction (or, more accurately, a scenario) and a re-emphasis on the necessity of understanding that what was originally understood by the college as a simple "symptom" is much more systemic in nature:

The Locus of the College Response. Recall that our problem originally presented as one of classroom management and student behavior: The title given to the faculty report, in the words of faculty themselves, was *What Used to Work, Doesn't.* By that appellation, faculty meant that students seemed to be changing in a way that made it more difficult to reach out to them in the classroom; students were "clueless," apathetic, not goal-oriented or accountable, and upon occasion even hostile and threatening.

It is probably true that the college's students are changing. But the implications of the focus group activities and interviews are compelling: If students are changing and the college does not, then *What Used to Work,*

Doesn't will continue to be the status quo. The locus of the problem, and therefore the response, cannot be just the classroom and the individual instructor. Simply changing classroom management policies will not work; indeed, such a change made in a vacuum will likely be counterproductive. As long as the problem is understood only within the narrow physical and intellectual confines of the image of a roomful of students, the results are predictable: continued student attrition, frustration, resentment; and, on the other side of the "partnership," instructor frustration and, ultimately, burnout.

The causes are multiple and systemic; so must be the response. What manifests as a classroom behavior problem may well have had its genesis during the first day on the college campus when, for whatever reasons, the student didn't know what question to ask, which didn't get answered, which resulted in the student not being identified as having potential problems, or equally likely, the student was placed in a remedial class for reasons he or she didn't understand. The response must be systemic and involves student services, notably admissions and financial aid, the administration, and all aspects of student life. Like all generalities, this admonition sounds suspiciously like a cliché, but it is nonetheless true. The college must find ways to foster and nurture a sense of belonging, a feeling of community within its student body transcending the boundaries separating student from student and student from staff and faculty. Individual instructors recognize this need at some deep level, and some are more adept than others are at creating community. But creating community, by its very nature, cannot and should not be left up to the efforts of lone creative individuals.

More specifically, both the focus group data and other evidence suggest that the college should bring its administrative guns to bear on the target of early assimilation of students into the college community; on early identification of students at risk—at risk for whatever reason without respect to the expedient but ultimately counterproductive categories of internal and external—and on early and probably massive intervention of those so identified (but, the student mindmaps tell us, the intervention must be a partnership rather than the standard allopathic medical model). The college can and should be a community of educational partners that is far superior to a high school with ashtrays serving up McEducation.

This is a true story illustrating one application of IQA, an approach to qualitative research grounded in systems theory whose primary purpose is to represent the meaning of a phenomenon in terms of elements (affinities) and the relationships among them. IQA exploits the traditional ethnographic tools of observation and interview, but it also combines these with others borrowed from market research, notably the focus group. IQA focuses not just on techniques of fieldwork, but also recognizes design, data collection, and especially analysis (hence the "A" in the name) as the handmaidens to interpretation. The story largely ignores the mechanics of how the IQA process works; rather, it emphasizes the

INTERACTIVE QUALITATIVE ANALYSIS

analytical and interpretational possibilities that emerge as a result of the systematic process so that the reader can get a glimpse of its potential.

This work attempts, first, to explicate a general systems theory that demonstrates how ontological, epistemological, and ethical issues are systemically related, the outcome of such a system being one's understanding of rigor; and second, to describe how that theory translates to research practice in terms of design, data collection, analysis, and interpretation. If this book accomplishes the first goal, readers will find the theoretical aspects of IQA to be based on clear assumptions and its internal logic to be coherent and consistent (which, as Gödel suggests, is about all one can ask of a theory[1]). If the second goal is reached, even readers who are oriented more toward results than theory will find IQA accessible (which may offend those who seem to regard research as a secret text to be shared with only the few who demonstrate the appropriate sensibilities) and intuitively appealing. In the words of one practitioner, "IQA seems to represent a much more contextualized approach to the problem under investigation than currently exists in the literature. That the results are sensitive to both similarities and differences across groups is great. This is what I need—to identify points where feelings/attitudes come together or move apart and the 'pathways' [*the links between affinities in a mindmap*] seem to fit this well." It is our intent that others will share in this assessment.

Coverage

This book focuses on an approach to qualitative research (Interactive Qualitative Analysis, or IQA) that attempts to integrate and reconcile some of the disjunctures in theorizing about the purposes and methods of qualitative research, and also describes a detailed, applications-oriented, systematic process by which data, analysis, and interpretation are integrated into a whole. The following is a brief overview of the structure of the book.

Rigor, as Lincoln and Guba (1985) well noted years ago, has to do with the "truth value" of research. Chapter 1 extends Kuhn's concept of a paradigm by the articulation of a general theory of rigor, represented as a system consisting of specific sets of relationships among ontological (What is real?), epistemological (How do we know?), and ethical (What is good?) elements. By combining systems theory with dialectical logic, a rationale for the locus of IQA on each ideological dialectic is presented, and concepts such as "validity" and "reliability" are defined in systems terms.

Because IQA uses the concept of a system as its basic method of representation, Chapter 2 is a primer in *systems theory*, which in turn is used to introduce the reader to the specific application of systems theory to qualitative research that is the focus of this book: the construction, interpretation, and comparison of *mindmaps* (systems representations of the way individuals or groups understand a phenomenon).

Chapter 3 describes the structure of a typical IQA study and places such a study in a larger epistemological context. The practical implications of the IQA theory of rigor are first developed in Chapter 4 into a method, represented as a *recursive system,* for thinking about or designing a qualitative study. Borrowing from the work of Foucault and others, the concept of a constituency or a group defined in terms of distance from, and power over, a phenomenon is articulated. The manner in which comparisons among constituencies determine research questions, which in turn comprises one's overall research objective, is also described.

The first section of the book (Chapters 1–4) lays out the theoretical rationale and foundation for the applied sections that follow, with Chapter 4 providing a transition from the strictly theoretical to the practical.

The next section (Chapters 5 and 6) describes how group processes adapted and extended from the TQM movement (or fad, as some cynics would have it) are used to create a picture of the phenomenological reality for a group. Chapter 5 introduces the building blocks of *mindmaps: affinities,* and then describes the group processes for identifying, clarifying, and describing affinities. In this chapter, the IQA theory of *coding* is introduced and situated within a wider epistemological context of the logical operations of *deduction and induction.* Chapter 6 describes how to go about creating the second component of a phenomenological system or *mindmap,* which is the set of relationships perceived by the group to exist between affinities. Chapter 6 completes the IQA theory of coding by introducing *theoretical coding,* the third and final level.

The third section (Chapters 7 and 8) is the individual analogue to the previous section, which is to say IQA methodology uses a consistent integrated approach to observation and analysis regardless of whether the reality to be represented is from the point of view of a group or an individual. Chapter 7 describes the protocols for conducting and analyzing an IQA interview, and Chapter 8 describes the protocol for coding the interview in order to develop a mindmap of, and in concert with, the individual being interviewed.

In the next section, Chapters 9 and 10 address the issues of *description* and *interpretation,* developing a theory of interpretation and articulating the theory to these issues. One of the major assumptions of IQA interpretive theory is that there is no such thing as pure description, if one understands description as having an element of meaning. All descriptions are, in some meaningful sense, interpretations. And furthermore, all interpretations involve comparisons, an idea obviously borrowed from Glaser's (1967) concept of *constant comparison.* Because the only question is whether comparisons are explicit or implicit, IQA theory encourages the researcher to make formal comparisons of mindmaps between, and among, individuals and groups, and provides procedures for doing so. Intersystemic comparisons are examined and related to the statistical concepts of variation and central tendency, and procedures for making intrasystemic comparisons are described as well. Chapter 11 provides some actual examples of IQA studies to demonstrate the interpretive potential of IQA methodology and to illustrate the variety of disciplines and topics for which the methodology is appropriate.

Editorial and Pedagogical Features

History will judge the impact of this book, but it seems fair to make the following assertions and observations:

1. There appears to be no other single work in the field of qualitative research methods that integrates a theory of epistemology with systems theory to produce an explicit set of protocols by which qualitative studies can be conducted and documented. This is not to say IQA theory came into being *ex nihilo*. The debt to numerous streams of inquiry and activity, notably concept mapping, grounded theory, Kurt Lewin's field theory, action research, systems theory (especially the man whom some call the father of systems theory, Ludwig von Bertalanffy), and many elements of the postmodern critiques of modern society, is acknowledged throughout the book.

2. The book attempts to provide a soft landing as the reader descends from theoretical heights to the often unforgiving ground of practicality. A general theory of rigor as an ideology is first developed; subsequently, the practical implications of the theory are pursued with fidelity. Later chapters contain *theoretical sidebars* or *lemmas* that are necessary to explain the rationale for certain analytical or procedural steps. For example, one such sidebar is a demonstration that all graphical representations of the same Interrelationship Diagram are topologically homologous. Readers oriented to theory may find these sidebars interesting to the point that, in the highest tradition of science, they do their best to refute them. Readers more interested in the practicalities of research can easily skip over these sidebars.

3. Beginning with Chapter 4, on research design, a case study is introduced, and this case is followed throughout the rest of the book. The case study allows the reader to examine the details and issues that arise as a study progresses from initial conceptualization to design to observation to analysis and, finally, to interpretation.

4. The text is accompanied by a set of interactive CD exercises carefully constructed to provide readers and students with summaries of the concepts in the text and, more important, with activities that require an application of specific IQA concepts. A parallel CD section containing relevant exercises accompanies each chapter. The general research audience can certainly derive a benefit from the CD exercises, as well as a little fun, but the CD is designed primarily to support instruction.

5. The organization of the book is itself the product of a systems analysis of the IQA process; that is, after the necessary introductory theoretical exposition, the organization of the book follows the IQA research flow.

6. Because of its original content and a subsequent need to name new concepts, the language of IQA is unfortunately littered with words and phrases that will be new to many readers or are used in a very specific or technical sense. The following list contains a few examples:

- ❖ Systems topologies and homologies
- ❖ Drivers and outcomes
- ❖ Topological zones
- ❖ Branching, recursion, and feedback
- ❖ Affinities
- ❖ Inductive, axial, and theoretical codes
- ❖ ARTs, IRDs, and SIDs
- ❖ Zooming in, zooming out, and looping
- ❖ Pareto Protocol

7. Finally, a note about the tone of the book and voice in which it is written is in order. A serious subject such as methods of qualitative research deserves a serious treatment, but it seems that many of the writers in this field confuse themselves with their subject. Much of the writing is terribly solemn, almost as if it were written, on the one extreme, in fear and loathing of punishment lest some heresy in the text be revealed. At the other extreme, some of the literature, especially the more theoretically or critically oriented, has the feel of pronouncements made *ex cathedra*. Either way, the result can be a text that is less than engaging. Inspired by postmodern sensibilities, we have attempted to engage the reader through the use of mild humor, irony, nonroutine sources of citation, interesting examples, and even occasional whimsy. This editorial voice stems from several decades of attempts to communicate concepts of research to graduate students, and from a belief that one need not take oneself too seriously even when dealing with a serious subject.

Audiences

The book has two audiences in mind: first, the practitioner and teacher of qualitative research, and second, but not secondarily, the student in a graduate-level qualitative methods class.

For its *primary audience,* the book is aimed at the graduate level—theoreticians, instructors, practitioners, and students alike. Those not terribly attracted to theory can skim through the first three chapters, taking the authors' word for it, and proceed immediately to the particulars of conducting an IQA study. Those more inclined to theory, however, are provided with the theoretical rationale, as well as sufficient references to set the context for IQA without pretending to be an exhaustive review of qualitative method. It is the authors' expectation that this book will be included on the required reading list (or at least on the supplementary list) of every graduate-level qualitative methods class in every university. Moreover, it is the authors' goal that within a decade of the book's first printing, IQA systems theory will be as well known and as frequently cited as grounded theory is at present.

Secondary audiences may very well include the following:

1. *Cognitive researchers,* especially those interested in concept mapping.

2. *Instructional designers* who can use the IQA process as the first stage in developing specifications and objectives for the instructional system. In fact, the instructional design for the accompanying CD was developed using the IQA research design process.

3. *Organizational researchers,* especially those interested in planning and organizational development, will find the IQA process to be something of a formalization, but also a significant extension, of many of the techniques they learned piecemeal as part of the TQM movement. In general, the IQA process can be used as a planning or visioning tool in any organization whenever there is a question about the nature of a phenomenon and a corresponding lack of understanding or agreement as to courses of action (a feature that should also make IQA attractive to those with an inclination toward action research). On the other hand, IQA is flexible enough to assist in providing quick, but insightful, answers to critical organizational problems. For example, the application of IQA to the problem of student misbehavior at a community college is recounted here.

As illustrated by the case study developed with each succeeding chapter, IQA has applications for qualitative *evaluation* of a wide variety of phenomena in a variety of disciplines.

Note

1. Kurt Gödel (1906–1978) was a mathematician whose Undecidability Theorem and Incompleteness Theorem, when taken together, suggest that a theory can be comprehensive or consistent, but not both.

Acknowledgments

Thanks are due to all those passing through the authors' research methods course who were either courageous or naïve enough to incorporate an untested methodology into their research projects, but especially to the original apostles who took the greatest risk: Cindy, LeeAnn, and Luke. Thanks also to the two Debras for providing editing, case material, interpretation, and insight. We believe the enthusiasm and dedication of these and dozens of other students will be justified.

Sage Publications would also like to acknowledge the following reviewers: William B. Kline, Ohio University; Alice McIntyre, Hellenic College; Justin M. Laird, State University of New York College at Brockport; and Jan Guidry Lacina, Stephen F. Austin State University.

Paradigm Wars 1

The Place of IQA

Particles and People: The Relationship of the Observer and the Observed

In their search for the fundamental elements of matter, physicists have uncovered or theorized a seemingly ever-expanding array of subatomic particles. These particles have certain quantum relationships to each other, but their states and behaviors seem quite literally to depend on the method of observation used by the physicist. Just as it is useful to think of matter as systems composed of elements (particles) and the relationships among them, systems of interest to the qualitative researcher may be represented as elements and the relationships among those elements.

The Paradox of Representation

In a striking parallel to the ethereal world of subatomic particles, the qualitative researcher finds that the nature of both elements and relationships depends on complex interactions between the phenomenon that the system represents and the purpose and methods of interpretation brought to the phenomenon by the researcher. This interaction between the observer and the observed creates a fascinating paradox. On the one hand, many different systems can be used to represent the same phenomenon or "object," depending on one's purpose and point of view. Translated into the language of postmodernism, the thesis of the paradox suggests that there are no universals or principles or grand *metanarrative*. On the other hand, seemingly disparate phenomena are often discovered to be fundamentally similar when analyzed from a systems point of view, a pattern that suggests there might indeed be underlying principles or metanarratives (see examples in

Chapter 2, on systems). This antithesis lends itself more to the worldview and language of positivism, or at least postpositivism, which presumes some reality independent of the observer and the existence of universals at some meaningful level, however contextual or restricted they may be. How does the researcher deal with this paradox?

Paradigm Wars

Only a finite number of ways exist for resolving a dilemma, which is one kind of paradox. Members of the academic intellectual community seem to have done what comes naturally, which is to choose one horn of a dilemma or the other and try to gore the other side with it. Thomas Kuhn (1970) offered an explanation (and popularized the use of *paradigm*) when he noted that researchers who espouse different epistemologies cannot directly confront the other's viewpoint because each springs from different values and perceptions. Because the beliefs and values on which interpretation is based are different, it is not surprising that one group finds the criticisms of the other to be "vicious, unjustified, and irrational" (Kauffman, 1993).

Because of these differing beliefs and values (a synonym for which is *ideology* and, depending on how far one pushes the concept, even *religion*), *Postmoderns* view The Others (to use Foucault's concept) as representing the forces of oppression and injustice, at worst, or simply quaint and out of touch, at best. *Postpositivists* regard The Others as nihilistic, albeit clever, scientific Luddites whose writings never rise above the level of investigative journalism.

A Framework for Discourse

Much, perhaps too much, has been written either in support of or to criticize those who hold one of the two views just described. Although our purpose is not to increase the body count in these wars, it is necessary to examine for a moment some important dimensions in which the two intellectual camps differ. This work chooses to go *through* the horns of the dilemma,[1] not so much by compromise but by a reconciliation based on a careful analysis of the contribution of both schools of thought. The graphic in Figure 1.1 summarizes these dimensions, and a brief discussion follows. In the interest of reconciliation, the order in which the elements of each pair appear has been scrambled; assigning elements to opposing paradigms is left as an exercise for the reader.

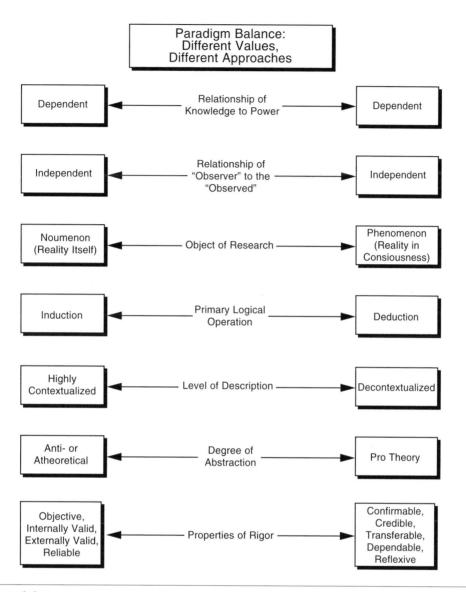

Figure 1.1

1. *Knowledge and Power.* The old saying that "knowledge is power" suggests that knowledge produces or results in power, which presumes that knowledge is "out there," a resource that can be gathered or mined or exploited. Recently, the reasoning behind the aphorism has been turned on its head. Foucault's investigations into the antecedents of the prison (Foucault, 1977) and the insane asylum (Foucault, 1965) suggest that knowledge is much more a result of power relationships than an antecedent. Foucault argued that knowledge is "stratified" by power relationships manifested in institutions into "regimes" that operate to define

what is "legitimate" knowledge. In other words, power and knowledge are inextricably linked into institutional regimes. What is regarded as legitimate knowledge (i.e., what is real) is influenced strongly by how power is distributed across institutional or other social structures. This argument stands in stark contrast to the opposing assumption that knowledge stands apart from power.

2. *The Observer and the Observed.* We have already commented on the parallels between observing both subatomic particles and people: The very act of observing has at the very least a potential for changing the nature of what we want to observe. This is not to say that researchers in the social sciences have only recently become aware of the phenomenon. Every introductory course in research methods in the social sciences mentions the Hawthorne Effect, the name given to a set of surprising results (that productivity increased despite obvious degradation in the physical surroundings) produced by Elton Mayo's 1927 study of worker productivity in Western Electric's Hawthorne plant (Street, 1994). It is only recently, however, that the Hawthorne study results have been interpreted as the result of a fundamental relationship between observer and observed rather than as a problem in experimental control or a lack of proper operationalization.

3. *The Object of Research.* Here we follow Husserl's (1965) lead in borrowing Kant's distinction between *noumenon* and *phenomenon*. This is the bedrock of the distinction between, for example, realism versus idealism, and, when the ontological distinction is applied to research paradigms, distinguishes between phenomenological approaches and more positivist ones. *Phenomenology,* as described by Merleau-Ponty (1967), privileges the nature of socially constructed meaning in its focus on *an inventory of consciousness.* More positivist paradigms focus on behavior more or less apart from the context of individual meaning.

4. *Primary Logical Operation.* Induction and deduction are the two *logical operators* of research, and different understandings of how research should be conceptualized (and, therefore, should be carried out) depend on one more than the other. Polkinghorne (1983) links deductive reasoning to positivism by arguing that under the rules of the positivist regime, induction is less valid than deductive statements because they represent only approximations. Who is to say, so this argument goes, that the very next observation might not contradict all the previous observations?

More phenomenologically oriented researchers (those who are more interested in *lived experience* rather than behavior per se or meanings defined by or attributed by the researcher) are prone to make much greater use of induction. Beginning with the classic work of Glaser and Strauss (1967), an entire industry has sprung up around the concept of Grounded Theory, whose reliance on induction is captured by the very motto of the Grounded Theory Institute: *Trust in Emergence.*[2]

5. *Level of Description.* Level of description is the extent to which description is contextualized. If one argues that there is no epistemological stance outside of experience, it follows that attempts to understand "meaning" must, first, be based on description—the most radical position here is that description (or narrative, if voice is regarded as a necessary component) is the only legitimate objective of research—and next, that description must be highly contextualized or situated within a particular life experience.

Decontextualized descriptions (see the later discussion of degree of abstraction) are viewed with suspicion if not as outright oxymorons. The role of operationalization is an excellent example of this paradigmatic distinction. An operational definition is, in one sense, a very specific and highly contextualized construct. Only by defining a construct in terms of measurable, or at least publicly observable, variables, it is reasonably argued, can reliable communication occur between different researchers who are interested in the same phenomenon. Paradoxically, the very process of operationalizing, at least when carried too far, results in a disconnect from the phenomenon to be studied. Defining intelligence, for example, as simply the score on a particular intelligence test is facile and disingenuous at best.

Then again, if symbols have no ultimate referents, then, with the possible exception of parties who share exactly the same worldview, communication would seem to be well nigh impossible. Postmodernists often reinforce this view; for example, a 2001 review in the *New York Times* literary supplement praises without apparent irony the communicative value of inarticulation in teenagers' speech. Apparently, the ubiquitous use of "like" ("It was, like, awesome!") is an indicator that teenagers, unlike their parents who are, like, annoyed by their children's misuse of the word "like," are more aware than their elders of the ultimate failure of language to communicate meaning.

Wordplay such as that in the previous paragraph is in itself an example of the different values placed on the degree of contextualization. If nothing else, deconstructionists, intellectual gunslingers who are the children of Jacques Derrida (1974), have sensitized us to the power of paradox, humor (especially wordplay), and metaphor. Although the question of whether deconstruction qualifies as a paradigm is still open, we can at least thank Derrida and like-minded writers for legitimating a sense of fun in the service of intellectual activity.

6. *Degree of Abstraction.* Desired degree of abstraction is a paradigmatic dimension closely related to both *level of description* and *primary logical function* (see the discussion that follows). Robert Hughes (1988), in his compelling history of the convicts who founded Australia, paints a compelling portrait of one use of abstraction. He examines The System, itself an abstraction for a constellation of policies and procedures resulting in the punishment and deportation ("transportation" was the euphemism of choice) of thousands of convicts:

> Few people want to take direct responsibility for hanging; *understandably, they prefer abstractions* [italics added]—"course of justice," "debt to society," "exemplary punishment"—to the concrete fact of a terrified stranger choking and pissing at the end of a rope. (p. 164)

Hughes's vivid description of the phenomenon of a man (and, less often, a woman) dancing at the end of both his life and a rope is in stark contrast to the abstractions of jurisprudence; this suggests that, at least in this case, abstraction serves to put psychological distance between the observer and the observed (note the link to an earlier item). Hughes buttresses his thesis by describing other punishments characteristic of The System:

> Likewise, the idea that flogging reforms the criminal was an abstraction. The realities of the lash were only apparent where the cat-o'-nine-tails met the skin. Neither the man inside the skin nor the other wielding the cat was apt to think that an act of reformation was taking place. What happened was crude ritual, a magical act akin to the scourging-out of devils. All punishment seeks to reduce its objects to abstractions, so that they may be filled with a new content, invested with the values of good social conduct. (p. 164)

Hughes spoke of abstractions in a particular context, but it seems fair to ask the extent to which a paradigm reduces its objects to abstractions. Note the connection in Hughes's dramatic examples of the abstraction/phenomenon dialectic to dimensions already listed, notably the *relationship of the observer to the observed* and the *relationship of knowledge to power*. Is not the person whose ribs are beginning to show white as the flesh is scourged away at the very center of the phenomenon of flogging? Should an examination of flogging give voice to the other prisoners who are forced to watch the ritual while silently thanking God it is not they who are being lashed? What about the mob that gathers, some of whom munch on small meat pies bought from vendors even as bits of bloody flesh fly through the air to land almost at their feet? What about the man who administers the punishment, or the person who gave the order and set the number of lashes? Or the provincial judge who provided the authority or the member of Parliament who voted in favor of the legislation codifying flogging? Whose voice will we privilege?

Note that these parties—later, we will call them *constituencies*—have been listed in a rough order. In terms of *distance from the phenomenon*, they are, arguably, listed from closest to most distant. In terms of power (over the flogging), they are again arguably listed in inverse order; a relationship between power and knowledge that represents a modest extension to ideas first articulated by Michel Foucault (1972). This relationship is important because it determines, at least in part, what kinds of questions the researcher asks about the phenomenon. For example, one researcher might choose to study the argot of the lower classes (class itself being a socially constructed invention of the era) used to denote capital punishment by hanging. According to Hughes, among the lumpenprole-tariats' many colorful ways to describe death by hanging were to "take a leap in the dark," "go up the ladder to bed," or to "stretch" or "squeeze," or, more bitterly humorous, to "loll your tongue out at the company."

Some investigators might study the meaning of hanging as reflected in official documents or statistics,[3] while others might be interested in ana-lyzing how hanging was related to other social constructs, such as social class or the rise of mercantilism. The symbolic or ritualistic facets of pub-lic punishment could very well be the focus in one study, while another might investigate the relationship between number of public hangings and the incidence of crime, and yet another might be interested in popu-lar beliefs about the relationship of hanging to crime.

The value placed on abstraction is a marker or a flag for the value placed on the purpose of theory in research. Some investigators eschew both theory testing and generation because they fear theorizing must inevitably lead to the objectification or oppression of humanity. By no means, how-ever, are all qualitative researchers anti- or atheoretical, as we have already seen in the example of grounded theory. Even though some may believe, as Margaret Wheatley (1999) so very well puts it in her interesting treatment of implications of the "new science" for leadership, that "there is no objec-tive reality out there waiting to reveal its secrets" (p. 82), it seems a step too far to then conclude, as Wheatley does, that "there are no recipes or for-mulas, or checklists or expert advice . . . nothing really transfers; everything is always new and different and unique to each of us" (p. 82).

To use a retort favored by the columnist George Will when he is con-fronted with an extreme or outrageous claim: "Well!" Even granting the lim-ited utility of universals, the breathtaking claim that everything is always new and different would seem to equate social or organizational researchers with ducks who, as a farmer characterized them, wake up in a brand-new world every morning. A duck is probably not the most flattering model for someone striving to learn more about the nature of the human condition.

7. *Properties of Rigor.* The ultimate outcome of the interaction of the six values just listed is one's personal definition of rigor or, to use a term coined by Lincoln and Guba in their seminal work (1985), the *truth value* of research. *Naturalistic Inquiry* suggested the "traditional" properties of rigor—objectivity, internal and external validity, and reliability—ought to be reconceptualized in the light of postmodern thinking and the concomi-tant rise (in 1985) in popularity of qualitative research. Lincoln and Guba proposed an approximately parallel set of desirable properties of rigor, which they called *confirmability, credibility, transferability,* and *dependabil-ity.* To this parallel list (see Figure 1.1), they added a final property that seems unique to qualitative or naturalistic inquiry called *reflexivity.* Reflexivity, as it has come to be understood, proceeds from Heidegger's

(1889–1976) existential investigations into the nature of observation, being, and time.[4] Heidegger (1927) suggested that the very process of investigation is itself reconstitutive of meaning. The practical application is that researchers must of necessity approach their work from some viewpoint that is part of their being. As their work proceeds, however, Lincoln and Guba exhort the researcher to move toward self-disclosure, which they call *reflexivity*. Largely due to the influence of *Naturalistic Inquiry*, reflexivity has become arguably the *sine qua non* of qualitative research writing, leading skeptics to question whether "confessional writing" simply lends a false air of authenticity to the writing or leads to textual radicalism (Seale, 1999), both of which impair critical analysis.

More Than a Laundry List

We have hinted that the seven paradigmatic dimensions represent more than just a "laundry list,"[5] a series of items that have in common only the fact that they all belong to some set—dirty items of clothing—and have been thrown into the same bag. Rather, the seven are related to each other in consistent and meaningful ways, which is to say they form a system. In Interactive Qualitative Analysis (IQA) parlance, the seven dimensions are "affinities." Now it is time to see how the affinities configure into a system.[6]

Revisiting Kuhn

Recalling Kuhn's assertion that the components of a paradigm are *beliefs and values*, this system suggests that our personal understanding—beliefs—of what is real influences our preference—values—for ways of knowing; this, in turn, determines our judgment of what differentiates good research from bad or, more generally, what differentiates true claims from false claims. This system suggests that one's definition of *rigor*, which is to say one's judgment of the truth value of a particular research approach, is first influenced by ontological considerations. How one views the relationship of power and knowledge, the observer to the observed, and the very object of research all interact to create a personal definition of reality for each researcher. This loop in turn influences the analysis/ discourse (epistemological) loop, which is also composed of three interactive elements or preferences: (1) the role of theory, (2) the extent to which description should be contextualized, and (3) the role of induction versus deduction. The result is a personal definition of rigor.[7]

The most concise name for what the two feedback loops represent is *ideology:* a closely organized system of beliefs, values, and ideas. Our personal ideological system, whether articulated or not, determines what we believe to be relevant or irrelevant, useful or useless, liberating or oppressing, orthodoxy or anathema. We are all ideologues, to which Jerry Seinfeld would add, "Not that there's anything wrong with that!" Ideology is only one name given to the way humans bring meaning to what otherwise would be a chaos of random disconnected events.

The Problem With Zealots

It is easy to forget, however, that the finger pointing at the moon is not the moon; that the signifier is not identical to the signified. The name we give to one who carries ideology too far is *zealot*. Although we may admire the integrity and courage of those first-century Jews who fanatically resisted Roman rule at Masada, and to whom we owe the current meaning of the word, it is instructive to also remember that the Zealots of Masada committed mass suicide, if Flavius Josephus is to be believed.[8] Regardless of Josephus's veracity, the etymology of zealot is instructive and cautionary. Epistemological zealotry tempts us first to try to destroy our opponents and, failing that, to then destroy ourselves (and now we take the metaphor too far in a fit of zealous enthusiasm) by being hoisted on our own petard.

Discourse and Dialectics

Modern public discourse has become, to put the matter mildly, extremely polarized, with both camps attempting, to use a term that came into vogue among political campaign managers in the 1980s, to *demonize* the other. The pragmatic reason for this tactic is that it seems to work, at least under certain conditions. There is, however, a certain logic underlying the politics of polarization, which is not difficult to understand. Consider the following collection of aphorisms:

- ❖ For every action there is an equal and opposite reaction. (Isaac Newton)
- ❖ We're right, they're wrong. (James Carville, *The War Room*, 1984)
- ❖ Daniel-san, must talk. Man walk on road. Walk left side, safe. Walk right side, safe. Walk down middle, sooner or later, get squished. (Mr. Miyagi to Daniel Larusso in *The Karate Kid*, 1984)

❖ If you don't stand for something, you'll fall for anything. (Anonymous)

❖ East is East, and West is West, and never the tween shall meet. (Rudyard Kipling)

What, other than whimsy, do these aphorisms have in common? First, they are all concerned with opposites, and second, these opposites reflect a *Western* conceptual duality inherited originally from the Greeks (notably Aristotle), then ingrained into Western minds by the Scholastics of the thirteenth century (notably Thomas Aquinas) and reinforced during the Age of Reason.

Aristotelian Logic

We owe much to the collection of treatises (Aristotle) in which *The Stagarite* first defined what are now called *variables* and that formalized the logic of the deductive syllogism. Of particular relevance are his three laws of argument:

1. *Identity.* X is X, which is to say that X has "substance" and can be identified as such. For example, the concept of "fish" has substance. We can point to a creature and identify it as such.

2. *Contradiction.* Both X and not X cannot be. The creature cannot be both fish and not fish (say, fowl).

3. *Excluded Middle.* Either X or not X must be. The creature swimming in the water must be either fish or fowl.

The modern, especially someone unfamiliar with the arcania of logic, is likely to dismiss these statements as either irrelevant or obvious, which is exactly the point: In what is now more than two thousand years, these assertions, which in contrast to Aristotle's day were the subject of analysis, dialogue, and argument, have become part of the perceptual *ground* of our being, unarticulated assumptions about the way things work that are such an integral part of our everyday ontology and epistemology that we can hardly conceive of alternatives.

Aquinas and the Scholastics

The Dumb Ox (as Aquinas was known when he was young) and his less famous contemporaries profoundly influenced the way we view today's world in many ways, only two of which we will mention here. First, they rediscovered, revived, and ultimately persuaded the Church hierarchy (which, in the Middle Ages, also enjoyed near-hegemonic secular authority) that Aristotelian logic was a legitimate tool for the understanding of God. Second, the Scholastics inadvertently established the foundation for today's physical sciences in successfully arguing[9] for *natural philosophy,* which insisted that since God's mind was revealed in nature, the laws of nature (God, to the medieval mind) could be revealed by observation of the natural world.

Looking back through a millennium of history, we struggle to grasp what the fuss was all about, and we tend to dismiss this era as irrelevant or simply quaint. The ideas for which both women and men died while tied to a burning stake are now so embedded in our worldview that we regard them as *natural,* which is to say they have been *reified.* Who, for example, would seriously challenge the notion that conclusions must be consistent with observations? Yet this assumption is no more natural than the idea that salamanders spring from the cold hearth ashes or that the succubus seduces men while they sleep.

The Limitations of Logic

Aristotelian (or Newtonian) logic has served us well, especially in the physical sciences and their technological progeny. The problem arises when values and beliefs (meaning) become the subject of scientific inquiry. Aristotle's three laws are of limited utility in discourse about values, and indeed are prone to serious misuse. The problem lies in the seduction of the following syllogism:

1. Value A is good.

2. Value B is the opposite of Value A; therefore . . .

3. Value B is bad.

The attraction of this syllogism is that it produces clear, albeit stark, results. If democracy is good, then socialism and certainly communism are bad; if individualism is good, then collectivism is bad; if human rights are good, then any action that limits freedom of action is bad. Recall the list of beliefs (assumptions about the nature of reality) and values (epistemological and ethical preferences) relevant to research paradigms in Figure 1.1. The temptation to demonize, or at least marginalize, someone whose beliefs and therefore values are at the opposite end of the continuum is very strong.

A Dialectical Alternative

The theory outlined in Figure 1.2 suggests that values, like emotions, are not directly malleable. It is difficult to address emotions directly, but emotions can be accessed through the mediation of cognitive activities. Values are also difficult to access directly but can be changed by changing the way we view reality. Furthermore, dialectical logic, or at least the IQA version of dialectical logic, is an excellent tool for analysis and discourse as an alternative to the (mis)use of Newtonian logic. Consider the following quotes and contrast them to the ones given earlier:

❖ My father says there's only right and wrong—good and evil. Nothing in between. It isn't that simple, is it? (Elsa in *Ride the High Country*, 1962)

❖ Want him to be more of a man? Try being more of a woman. (Coty perfume ad, circa 1975)

❖ I have become what I have beheld, and I am convinced that I have done no wrong. (Elliot Ness in *The Untouchables*, 1987)

❖ There are trivial truths, and there are great truths. The opposite of a trivial truth is plainly false. The opposite of a great truth is also true. (Niels Bohr)

❖ The opposite of a correct statement is a false statement. But the opposite of a profound truth may well be another profound truth. (Niels Bohr)

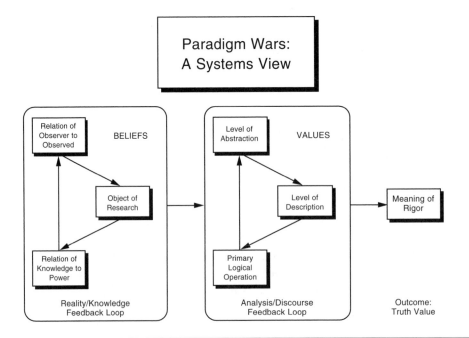

Figure 1.2

Elsa, although uneducated and certainly unschooled in formal logic, intuits that the opposite of a good thing is perhaps not a bad thing. The Coty slogan, in a tone of detached irony so characteristic of postmodern culture, suggests that an increase in one variable will paradoxically result in an increase in its opposite. Elliot Ness, speaking in David Mamet's poetic rhythms, suddenly apprehends one of the great ironies of human existence: His actions are indistinguishable from those of his *bête noir,* Al Capone. Niels Bohr used this same logic to distinguish between *trivial truths* and *great truths,* or between statements that are merely *correct* and those that are *profoundly true,* and plainly stated that there was a different system of logic at work between the two.

Here are some examples of Bohr's trivial truths:

❖ The opposite of hot is cold.

❖ The opposite of long is short.

❖ The opposite of fast is slow.

But what does Bohr mean by *profound truths?* And by what process does the opposite of a profound truth also take on the value of *true?* Consider the following list and think about the opposites of each of these terms before you read further:

What is the opposite of . . .

❖ Thrift?

❖ Innovation?

❖ Rights?

❖ Peace?

The typical responses given to these questions by the authors' graduate students in classes over the years have been:

❖ Thrift: Not Thrifty or Waste or (rarely) Profligacy

❖ Innovation: Routine or Uncreative

❖ Rights: Repression

❖ Peace: War

Notice that the students' level of analysis was clearly at Bohr's *trivial* level. They invariably looked for an opposite that is simply the negation of the concept, and since each of the four values was presented to them as desirable, they searched for an opposite (without prompting by the instructor, by the way) that was an undesirable.

There is another way to think about values (or beliefs), and dialectical reasoning is the basis for it. *Dialectics* is a term often misunderstood and misused, most often as a synonym for logical argument of any kind. As a formal tool of rhetoric (another word whose real meaning has been lost), a *dialectical argument* is one in which an interlocutor, when interrogating his opponent, presumes that the opponent's statements are true and uses those statements in support of his own argument. Here, we use the word more in the philosophical sense, influenced first by the Hegelian[10] construction of reality as a dynamic consisting of the interaction between two opposites, leading to an understanding of history as thesis-antithesis-synthesis; and second, by Marx's and Engels's translation of Hegel's ideas into less mystical terms. Our interest here is neither history nor social theory, so in the interests of brevity and relevance, we rewrite Engels's Laws of Dialectics (Engels, 1878) for our purpose as follows:

❖ A good thing, when taken to the extreme, becomes a bad thing.

❖ The opposite of a bad thing is a good thing, therefore . . .

❖ A good thing has as its opposite another good thing.

Let us apply this syllogism to the examples of *trivial* analysis given just above.

Thrift, taken to the extreme, becomes stinginess, and, even more to the extreme, results in deprivation of one's own basic needs. The opposite of this (the *cure*, in spiritual terms) is *generosity*, both to oneself and to others. Therefore, the opposite of thrift is generosity, and both are good (if balanced by the other).

Innovation (in an organization), taken to the extreme, results in unpredictability; and to even more of an extreme, chaos. The opposite of chaos is *order*. Therefore, the opposite of organizational innovation is order (i.e., policies and regulations), and both are good if balanced by the other.

Citizens of the United States have *rights*. But untrammeled freedom of individual action leads to selfishness, which leads to anarchy. Anarchy must be counteracted by a sense of *responsibility* for the other, individually and as a group. Therefore, the opposite of rights is responsibility, and both are good if balanced by the other.

Peace is a desirable social condition. But extreme pacifism leads to lack of action, which leads to oppression. The opposite of oppression is *justice*, which suggests that both peace and justice are opposites that are part of a greater reality.

The Ideology of IQA

Dialectical logic is one of the major underpinnings of IQA, which is fanatical only in its opposition to zealotry. This assertion may be taken to be

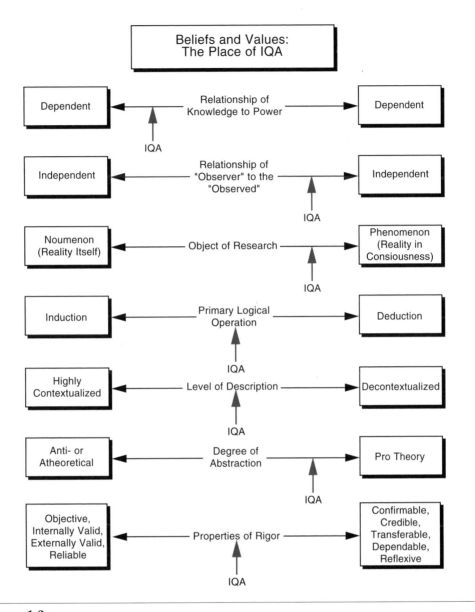

Figure 1.3

paradoxical, which it is; or humorously, which was the intent; or seriously, which was also the intent. This foundation in dialectics has both theoretical and practical implications. The practical implications will be discussed later in the context of coding data (in particular, axial coding). An important theoretical implication is that IQA strives to represent a balance with respect to the ideological dimensions of research paradigms that have already been introduced. Figure 1.3 locates IQA, at least approximately, on each of the dimensions.

Beliefs and Values Redux

The following is a discussion of each of the locations of IQA on the ideological dimensions:

1. IQA presumes that *knowledge and power* are largely *dependent;* that power influences which knowledge is determined to be relevant and irrelevant, important and unimportant. The methodology reflects this assumption most obviously in its conception of *constituencies* as an important component of the research design phase, and also by including planned comparisons of the conceptual maps (mindmaps) among constituencies. *Constituency* is a term deliberately selected because of its political flavor. One of the two criteria for selection is the degree of power that a constituency has over the phenomenon to be investigated.

2. IQA presumes that the *observer and the observed* are *dependent* (or perhaps more accurately, interdependent). Many qualitative studies, while espousing a desire to capture the meaning of a phenomenon from the *subject's* point of view, nevertheless rely on methods of *data collection* and *analysis* that are essentially positivist; that is, the very terms imply a separation between the subject of the research and the researcher. IQA begins by challenging two common assumptions, apparently borrowed without much thought from the positivist paradigm, of much qualitative research: (1) that data collection is separate and distinct from analysis and (2) that only the researcher is qualified to *interpret the data.*

3. The *object of research* in IQA is clearly *reality in consciousness* (the phenomenon) rather than reality itself, a construct that IQA contends is far too elusive for any one research study, or perhaps even for the human mind. IQA therefore uses *distance from the phenomenon* as the second of two criteria for constituency selection, and formal comparisons among constituencies are made along these two criteria. Furthermore, the use of group processes as a *data collection device* presumes that the researcher can gain useful insights into a socially constructed reality, as reported by members of the group, while the use of follow-up interviews is designed to both elaborate and contrast individual meanings to that of the group.

4. IQA insists that *both deduction and induction* are necessary to the investigation of meaning. Participants themselves are first asked to induce categories of meaning (induction), then to define and refine these (induction and deduction), and finally to investigate deductively the relationships of influence among the categories. These three stages of data production/analysis (IQA contends that there is no great difference between these two, that they both are interpretation) correspond to the three formal classes of analysis of coding: *emergent, axial,* and *theoretical.*

5. IQA contends that *decontextualized* descriptions are useful and possible (see item 6) as long as they are backed up or grounded (to use a term from grounded theory) by highly contextualized ones, and as long as the process by which the text was decontextualized is *public, accessible,* and *accountable.* While admitting the danger of decontextualization and abstraction, IQA makes the judgment that there is a difference between research and storytelling. Although stories can be told with great insight and art, it is the responsibility of the researcher to help the reader understand what the story is about; what it means in some larger context.

6. Largely as a result of its stance vis-à-vis level of description (pro decontextualization) and primary logical operation (both induction and deduction), IQA is clearly *favorable to theory,* both from the point of view of inducing theory and of testing it. The *mindmap* of a group or an individual is, in fact, a *theory* by the classic definition: (Campbell & Stanley, 1963) a set of relationships from which hypotheses can be deduced. The theory, however, is a theory in perception or the mental model[11] of a group or an individual with respect to a particular phenomenon, rather than one imposed by previous findings or by researchers' theorizing. IQA chooses not to call this representation a "theory" (although it is) primarily because we have discovered that the appellation creates a roadblock to communication, especially with some of our colleagues who are more inclined to positivism,[12] although it fits Campbell and Stanley's definition perfectly.

7. The arrow placing IQA on Figure 1.3 has been placed in the middle of the last (Properties of Rigor) dimension, not because we disagree with Lincoln and Guba's (1985) alternative ways of thinking about rigor, but because we contend that the *traditional* concepts of validity and reliability still are useful ones, whatever words we use to describe them. The operational definition of *internal validity* is *the extent to which a System Influence Diagram (mindmap) is consistent with the individual hypotheses comprising it,* and the IQA definition of *external validity* is *the extent to which mindmaps constructed by independent samples of the same constituency on the same phenomenon are similar.* Concerning reliability (or dependability, if one prefers), we have presented the same issue statement, a description of the phenomenon to be analyzed, to succeeding cohorts of doctoral candidates for several years, and the mindmaps so far are distinguished more by their similarity than their differences, in terms of both their elements and the relationships among elements. Is this not the essence of temporal stability, which is one meaning of reliability? The principles of IQA certainly support constructs such as credibility, transferability, and dependability, while highlighting (if not quantitatively) the concepts of validity and reliability through public, accessible, and accountable procedures.

Looking Back and Looking Forward

The understanding of what constitutes good research, or, for that matter, what is research at all, is fundamentally an ideological system composed of the seven elements described in this chapter. The elements are much more than a simple list, but interact with each other in meaningful ways. The elements of one's belief system (relation of knowledge to power, relation of the observer to the observed, and the object of research or the "thing" to be investigated) form the ontological base. Upon this base rests our epistemological values, or preferences for ways of knowing, which again is a feedback loop consisting of three elements: level of abstraction, level of description, and primary logical operation. These two loops interact to create a personal (and often unarticulated) meaning of rigor.

Later we shall see that one characteristic of feedback loops is their "momentum," which is to say that once a loop is set in motion, it tends to become ever more resistant to outside influences; or in the jargon of IQA, to "go negative," to spin ever faster in ever-decreasing concentric circles of ever-decreasing radii, a condition that obviously must reach some limit (usually a negative one, hence the name). This systems understanding of the meaning of rigor is quite consistent with Kuhn's observation that researchers with different epistemologies and ontologies have difficulty in understanding each other's viewpoints.

Neither Kuhn's "separate universes" viewpoint nor Lincoln and Guba's re-interpretation of the classical dimensions of rigor is the last word, however. A systems perspective strongly suggests that reconciliation is not only possible but also desirable for some research purposes. The next chapter begins to build a base for this argument by introducing systems theory and describing the nature of systems.

Notes

1. A tactic that some regard as cheating, or at least, spineless. But Gödel's (1906–1978) Incompleteness Theorem, in a refutation of Bertrand Russell and Alfred North Whitehead's attempt to develop a strictly deductive mathematical system, demonstrates that there are any number of propositions not derivable from the axioms of a system that nevertheless are true within the system. Gödel's work suggests that Aristotle's law of the excluded middle is perhaps not so clearcut as it appears.

2. Web site: *www.groundedtheory.com.*

3. Hughes observes that the official language of hanging in eighteenth-century England was both abstract and suggestive of high purpose. Contrast the following examples to the ones already given: The executed were "launch'd into Eternity" or "suffered the ultimate exaction of the law."

4. This is the authors' attribution; Lincoln and Guba might disagree.

5. Laundry lists seem to be a favorite form of discourse in qualitative studies, the notable exception being *true* grounded theory studies.

6. In the interests of reflexivity, we disclose that the systems representation that follows is, in fact, a product of the IQA process itself; that is, the IQA process was used to construct a theory of meaning by articulating the nature of both the affinities comprising research paradigms and the relationships among them.

7. A good test of the IQA ideological system would be to see how adequately permutations of extremes on the three beliefs and three values described in Figure 1.1 map onto known research approaches; that is, this system ought to generate a taxonomy of research methods. Although we will leave this as an exercise for the reader, an insightful and humorous hint for how to accomplish such a task can be found in Sutherland, S. (1990). Choose Your Method. *Nurses Notes* 22(2): 121.

8. See *www.ccel.org/j/josephus* for the complete works of Josephus, translated by William Whiston. But also see an example of modern attempts to debunk the Masada Myth: Ben-Yehuda, N. (1995). *The Masada myth: Collective memory and matchmaking in Israel.* Madison: University of Wisconsin Press.

9. But not without losses: For example, Peter Abelard (1079–1142), of Abelard and Heloise fame, was convicted of heresy for his radical contention that "theology is the handmaiden of knowledge" in a trial conducted by a relentless protector of the Pope's authority, Bernard of Clairvaux. Abelard would have suffered the same fiery death as many of his contemporaries had he not died first under the protection of Peter the Venerable of Cluny. For a fascinating fictionalized account of these ideological battles, read Umberto Eco's (1980) excellent murder mystery, *The Name of the Rose.*

10. Hegel, G. W. F., 1770–1831. A good commentary on Hegel's ideas can be found in Houlgate, S. (1991*). Freedom, truth and history: An introduction to Hegel's philosophy.* London and New York: Routledge. Also, see the Hegel Society of America's Web site: *www.hegel.org.*

11. For an excellent treatment of mental models, see Jonassen, D. H. (1995). *Operationalizing mental models: Strategies for assessing mental models to support meaningful learning and design-supportive learning environments.* Available at *www-csc195.indiana.edu/csc195/jonassen.*

12. A highly respected colleague was introduced to mindmaps as a dissertation committee member on an IQA study. After raising several objections to the candidate's use of the word *theory* in the dissertation defense to describe the representation of a focus group's analysis—after all, theorizing is something that only theoreticians do—he finally reluctantly conceded, but whispered only partly in jest: "Theorizing by committee! What are we coming to?"

Systems as Representations 2

In for a Dime, In for a Dollar

Before devolving into a sterile seminar on semantics, philosophy posed the three great questions of human existence: (1) What is real? (2) How do we know? (3) What is good (or beautiful)? While postpositivists attempt to divorce ethics (or aesthetics) from ontological and epistemological issues, postmoderns, in their concern for giving voice to the marginalized and their distrust of anything smacking of universalism, totter on the brink of solipsism. Neither of the extremes just described is willing to follow their dime ante with a dollar raise, so numerous theories of truth, or "belief policies," are competing for the researcher's attention and fealty. As was argued in Chapter 1, one's understanding of rigor in qualitative research or what constitutes "good" qualitative research depends first on one's understanding of the nature of truth itself. Before examining systems as representations of reality, let us discuss different theories of truth.

Theories of Truth. Lynn Bauman (*www.praxisofprayer.com/*) has developed a very clever set of metaphors illustrating different theories of truth. The list that follows is taken from Bauman's materials:

1. *The Tightrope Theory.* Truth is a tightrope, and there is only one tightrope. To know truth is to walk a narrow, dangerous way; and one false step leads to disaster.

    a. Truth is inherently difficult to find.
    b. There is only one truth and few are capable of finding it.

2. *The Dungeon Theory.* Those who have not come into the light of truth are forever locked in a dark dungeon. Only those who, typically by

virtue of extraordinary talent or effort, have received the light can unlock the door to the dungeon.

    a. The dungeon doesn't seem all that bad to people who live in it because they know nothing else; it is their home, and home may be elaborately furnished with markers of culture and learning, but all this is an illusion.

    b. Any attempt by those in the dungeon to explain the "outside" is either a misimpression, self-deception, or an outright perversion.

3. *The Round Table Theory.* All claims to truth are equally valid, so we all sit like King Arthur's knights at a table, which has no head. Unlike Arthur's knights, however, the rules for who sits at the table are ambiguous.

    a. Tolerance is the highest value at the table.

    b. Dialogue among different perspectives is necessary to discover mutuality.

    c. No one has hegemony over the truth, but each needs to hear the truth of the other to approach wholeness.

4. *The Gunslinger Theory* (which Bauman calls *the Potshot Theory*). There is no truth, for whatever is "pointed to" (signified) is just another target for the gunslinging skeptic to be shot down with a dismissive, "See! There's nothing there!"

    a. Truth is a human fabrication and, therefore, an illusion.

    b. All claims to truth are false.

    c. An annihilating skepticism is the only intelligent response to any truth claim.

5. *The Film Theory.* Truth is a human projection of the stories we tell about our existence. Humans make up their own meaning by means of these stories.

    a. All truth is relative, but some truth is better than others in the sense that it is more adaptive according to some utilitarian criteria.

    b. Most of us live any number of stories, but usually only one at a time, because it's confusing to see two pictures simultaneously on one screen.

    c. Some stories are dull and some are beautiful, but all are made up in the imagination of humanity.

6. *The Graduation Theory* (or *the Developmental Theory*). Various kinds, and multiple levels, of truth exist, but each level leads to a higher and more complex level. Both individuals and societies grow by mastering the issues at each level.

a. The lowest levels include the narrower and more restricted modes of understanding.

b. The middle levels require greater degrees of intellectual discipline and involve more developed linguistic and rational skills.

c. The high levels express forms of greater wholeness or synthesis and are connected in patterns of great complexity.

7. *The Crown Jewel Theory.* There is one highest form of truth by which all other truths, as lesser "jewels" but jewels nonetheless, are judged and evaluated. Each jewel has its place in the crown, but all are not of the same value, nor do they possess the same place or play the same role.

a. The highest truth can be known, but in some traditions it is a gift bestowed or a grace given.

b. Each truth has value, though all truths are not equally valuable; yet they all fit together to form the crown.

c. The relative value of a truth can be verified in the light of the highest truth.

Bauman was thinking of religious philosophies when he developed his metaphors, but one can find vibrant resonance in his list in the more secular intellectual foundations of modern qualitative research. In particular, the Round Table, the Gunslinger, and the Film metaphors, by whatever name, are common themes in current research literature. The values implied by much postmodern research seem to rest on a combination of the Round Table (all claims are valid), the Gunslinger (deconstructionists come immediately to mind), and the Film (emphasis on meaning through storytelling). The great irony, though, is that the very moment these values are canonized, the acolytes immediately begin to behave as if they were walking on a metaphysical tightrope. They are transmogrified into secular Gnostics who regard those in disagreement as either prisoners in an ontological dungeon or as epistemological troglodytes. In doing so, the keepers of the faith deny the basic tenets of their own secular religion (too much of a good thing is a bad thing; see Chapter 1).

Dialectics, Paradoxes, and Systems. In Chapter 1, we presented the paradox of representation, and we reaised the question of how the researcher deals with this paradox. Ontological and ethical (or aesthetic) issues arise from the dialectical nature of reality and aesthetics; therefore, the locus of reality is not strictly external to the observer, but neither is reality simply a matter of choice. Truth lies in the ability of the observer to discern (a term used here almost in its theological sense) the dialectical interaction of representation and phenomena to achieve a worthwhile goal or to address an important problem. *Truth,* by which is simply meant *a useful way to think about reality,* is a dialectic created by the dynamic interaction of the two components of the paradox. This work seeks, through a systems approach, to exploit the most useful features of this dialectic. Let us look at some examples of systems as representations.

Corvettes, Golden Means, and Fibonacci Numbers

Take the case of a new automobile body design, for example. To the design engineer, the object consists of elements such as symmetry, curves, lines, ratios, perspective, unity and variety, texture, color and contrast, to name only a few. All of these stand in a pattern of relationships to each other. A common design objective (later we will call this an *outcome*) is *unity*. The designer uses various combinations of the elements just mentioned in different relationships to each other to achieve a unified *look*. The relationships are the aesthetic principles that either explicitly or implicitly work together (and oftentimes in contradiction) to achieve a particular aesthetic effect.

THESIS: ONE PHENOMENON, DIFFERENT REPRESENTATIONS

How can such a slippery concept as beauty be represented as a *system?* In our car example, the design engineer understands that changing the curve of the windshield may require a change to the curve of the rear window because the first change impacts the symmetry or the relative proportions of the parts of the car in relation to the overall aesthetic effect. Changing the curve of the rear window may demand a change to the rear fender design, which may create a need to change the look of the front end, and so on. The elements and relationships all form a dynamic system in which a change in either an element or a relationship will likely produce changes in many or all of the other elements. This dynamism results from the designer's desire to create a unity that constitutes a particular *look*.

The car is something quite different to the mechanical engineer. The elements are the propulsion system, the power train, and the chassis that carries these elements. Each of these elements is related to each other in terms of stresses, forces, structural properties of materials, velocities, and the like. A decision to shorten the stroke of the pistons may require different structural materials in the piston itself or in the cylinder, which may in turn have effects throughout the whole propulsion system, the power train, and the chassis.

The term *automobile* clearly refers to something quite different to the two engineers, which is to say that the system is not the automobile, just as the finger pointing to the moon is not the moon: The signifier is not the same as the signified. Rather, a system is a way we choose to represent the auto. Systems are representations, which implies that we choose the system we use to represent a particular reality.

ANTITHESIS: DIFFERENT PHENOMENA, SAME REPRESENTATION

In opposition to different representations of what, in some meaningful sense, is the same reality (the Corvette, or more accurately, the aesthetic appeal of the Corvette), we give just one example of different phenomena that have an identical systemic foundation.

Phenomenon 1: Old Greek Geometers. Pythagoras (circa 582–580 BCE) first constructed a geometric figure called the Golden Mean or the Golden Ratio, in which the perfect or most aesthetically pleasing rectangle (a system composed of the elements, length and width) is defined by a certain proportion between the elements (the mathematical relation between the elements, in this case, the irrational number Ø [phi] approximated by the number 0.618). This is a simple system, consisting of the two elements (length and width) and a relationship between the length and the sum of the length and width.[1] To Pythagoras, the Golden Proportion was one example from geometry of how numbers themselves represented the ultimate in proportion, order, and harmony, that is, the ultimate aesthetic principle.

Phenomenon 2: Old Italians and Rabbits. Leonardo of Pisa, better known as Leonardo Fibonacci (c. 1140–1270), was one of the foremost mathematicians of his day. Among other contributions, we owe our current use of the decimal system of notation to Fibonacci. It is not Fibonacci's work in decimals that we are interested in here, however, but in his famous Rabbit Problem. Fibonacci, never one to take himself too seriously, wrote many works in recreational mathematics, an activity that might strike many modern readers as an oxymoron but that was hugely popular among the elite of the Italian Middle Ages. Fibonacci proposed the following problem to entertain the titled nobility of Pisa:

1. Begin with two newborn rabbits, one male, the other female.

2. Rabbits can reproduce at the age of one month.

3. Rabbits gestate for one month.

4. Rabbits will give birth every month.

5. Rabbits always give birth to one male rabbit and one female rabbit.

6. Rabbits never die.

Fibonacci then posed this question: How many male/female rabbit pairs are there after one year (12 months)?

Fibonacci demonstrated that the Rabbit Problem could be represented by a series (in our language, a system) consisting of numbers in which each term is the sum of the previous two: For example, the first few terms of a Fibonacci series are: 1, 1, 2, 3, 5, 8, 13, 21, 34, 55, 89, 144, 233, . . .

What is the connection to Greek geometry and principles of aesthetics? It is not clear that Fibonacci himself made the connection, but certainly by the time Eduard Lucas (1842–1891) named the series in honor of Fibonacci, a very interesting relationship was well known among mathematicians: the Golden Ratio, which could be constructed only geometrically by the Greeks of Pythagoras' time (because the concept of an irrational number had not yet been either created or discovered, depending on one's ontological perspective), was the limit of the series formed when one divides each term of a Fibonacci series by the previous one. How is it that a mathematician creating mathematical recreations about rabbits stumbled onto a fundamental ancient Greek principle of visual aesthetics?

Phenomenon 3: Spirals and Numbers in Nature. Most people think daisies are pretty. It turns out that the seeds in the center of a daisy are arranged in a Fibonacci spiral, and it also turns out that daisies tend to have 34, 55, or 89 petals, numbers that should be familiar by now. Many other flowers (buttercups, coreopsis, black-eyed susans) have petals whose numbers are found on the Fibonacci series. The spirals on a pineapple and the chambers of the many-chambered nautilus (widely regarded as an object of natural beauty) are arranged in a Fibonacci spiral. Pinecones are arranged into two sets of Fibonacci spirals, one clockwise and the other counterclockwise.

Reification, Reality, and Social Construction

The ancient Greeks, in the process of inventing the modern notion of numbers, regarded numbers as the very essence of harmony and order. Centuries later, mysterious patterns, such as the ones just described, led to mystical and magical practices, such as numerology that exists even today. We give these examples not to support the idea that numbers themselves have magical properties, but to make the point that the Corvette is one way of thinking about beauty, while a Fibonacci series is another way. The Corvette is an example of one phenomenon, or reality, that can be usefully represented by many different systems. But the Fibonacci series (a system) seems to underlie many apparently different phenomena, many of which have an aesthetic appeal to humans. So, it seems reasonable to ask: Is beauty strictly in the eye of the beholder (is it strictly socially constructed, with no reference to external reality or universal principles), or are there universals that exist independent of the observer that have something to do with aesthetic appeal?

Now we must abandon our critique of aesthetics to those more competent and return to the idea of systems as representation. The same system can be used to represent many different phenomena or *realities*. Qualitative researchers tend to choose either the thesis or the antithesis of this epistemological dialectic (perhaps without thinking) and reject any paradigm that proceeds from different assumptions. Humans construct their reality in social settings, and qualitative researchers are not immune from one of the primary mechanisms—*reification*, or *treating an abstraction as if it were concrete or tangible*—by which reality is socially constructed. Some qualitative researchers (e.g., phenomenologists and, to some extent, critical theorists) are leery of "theorizing" in the sense of using qualitative research to explicate general principles, and they have good reasons for being so. On the other hand, other researchers espouse qualitative techniques primarily for the purpose of creating theory, albeit contextualized to different extents. From a systems point of view, both paradigms have merit. Both, if carried to an extreme, have serious limitations.

This chapter, then, is about systems: how to conceptualize phenomena as systems, how to represent different phenomena with different systems, and how to recognize the systemic parallels or similarities that undergird different phenomena. First, we examine some basics of systems theory.

Understanding a System

Systems have two components: *elements* and *relationships among the elements*. The elements may be as disparate as physical objects (parts in a manufacturing process, for example), mathematical constructs (acceleration, profit, loss, or IQ, for that matter), or, for the purposes of this approach to qualitative research, categories of meaning.

Understanding a system means:

- ❖ Identifying the elements of the system
- ❖ Describing the relationships among the elements
- ❖ Understanding how the elements and relationships dynamically interact to result in different *states* of the system, which implies
- ❖ *Interpretation.* What is the nature of the unity represented by the system?
- ❖ *Making intrasystemic inferences.* What are the logical effects of changes of state of some elements on others?

❖ *Making extrasystem inferences.* Analyzing the effects of outside influences (interventions) on the system—What may we logically expect the effects of extrasystemic effects to be?

The three major inquiries above apply to a single system. By *single system,* we mean the *systemic representation of a phenomenon from one person's or group's* (later on, we will call these *constituencies*) *viewpoint.* If we have more than one system, a fourth very useful inquiry is possible:

❖ How do two (or more) systems compare in terms of elements and relationships, and what are the interpretive implications, both intra- and extrasystemic, of the comparison?

Research Questions and Systems

It might be useful at this point to restate the preceding section, which describes the issues that may be addressed through systems representation of phenomena, in more conventional language. If we have only one system, two research questions are possible:

1. What are the components of the system?

2. How are the components related to each other?

If we have a minimum of two systems, then a third question can be asked:

3. How do the systems compare?

Note that the three questions are in a requisite sequence. One cannot answer a question about relationships without having first identified the things (components) that are in relationship to each other. Neither can the third question be answered unless the first two have been addressed with respect to at least two systems.

What Is Research?

Research, in the context of this work, means *any activity that can answer at least one of the three overarching research questions.* Note that this definition makes no distinction between qualitative and quantitative. The researcher who uses factor analysis is no different from one who induces themes from interview data in that both are addressing question 1 above.

A historian who attributes the decline of the Roman Empire to certain factors and the survey analyst who notices a strong correlation between conformity and influence are identical in that they are addressing question 2. And the behavioral psychologist who uses standard practices of experimental design to study resistance to extinction associated with different schedules of reinforcement is structurally identical to the anthropologist who makes cross-cultural comparisons of courtship rituals.

Systems Topology

Once the elements of a system are defined, and once the nature of the relationships among elements (meaning of the arrows) is defined, systems differ primarily only in their structure (systems topology), which is composed of two features: branching and recursion (feedback loops):

No Branching. The simplest systems are strictly *linear,* which is to say that *one element always leads to another, regardless of the condition of the previous element.* For example, there is one, and only one, path through the system. Figure 2.1 shows the simplest system of all.

Figure 2.1

This system captures the logic of the simplest true experiment in which treatment and control groups are compared on some element of interest. In classical experimental research language, A represents the independent variable (*cause*), the arrow represents a presumed cause-and-effect relationship, and B represents the dependent variable (*effect*).

Branching. Most systems, on the other hand, are considerably more complicated, not only in the number of elements but in the number of possible paths through the system. Figure 2.2 is an example.

This system differs from the first not only in the number of elements but also in the number of relationships that connects the elements. *Branching,* in classical computer programming terminology, refers to a choice of paths depending on a logical test. We appropriate the term here to mean simply *more than one possible relationship emanating from an element without demanding a formal logical test.* For example, in Figure 2.2, A directly influences the states of B, C, and D.

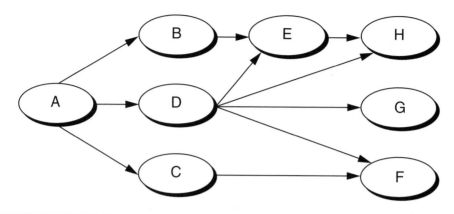

Figure 2.2

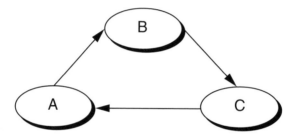

Figure 2.3

Recursions or Feedback Loops. The second structural feature is the presence or absence of feedback loops. *Feedback,* in the general systems sense, *is present when there is a relationship from an element later in the system back to one earlier in the system.* *Later* refers to elements residing in the Outcome Zone, either intermediate or primary, while *earlier* refers to elements residing in the Driver Zone, either intermediate or primary. (See the zone diagram shown later in Figure 2.5.) To be precise, this kind of relationship is *recursive,* but the most common name for recursive relationships is *feedback loop.* Recursive relationships result when a relative outcome *feeds back* or influences the state of an element that is a relative driver.

Feedback Loops. Figure 2.3 shows an example of a system with feedback but no branching. Note that this is the simplest feedback loop, which requires a minimum of three elements.

In this system, note that there is one, and only one, arrow emerging from each element, which is an indicator of a lack of branching. Feedback is created by the influence of C (a relative *outcome* of the system) on A (a relative *driver*), creating a loop among the three components. Note also that the so-called reflexive relationship, in which A and B (to take any pair

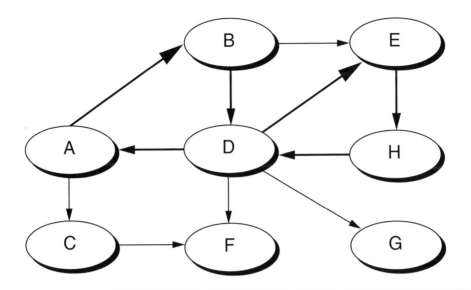

Figure 2.4

as an example) are both simultaneously drivers and outcomes of each other, is considered to be a *non sequitur* in that a "double-headed arrow" between two components indicates a relationship that does not follow from the premises of systems theory. IQA uses the concepts of direct and indirect relationships, combined with recursion, to elaborate the "true" nature of relationships that are, on the surface, reflexive or bidirectional.

Members of a focus group might very well argue that A influences B, or conversely, that B influences A, and both arguments might be equally compelling. As we will see in later chapters, this situation is almost certainly indicative of a feedback loop containing at least a third element that is not yet recognized by the group. In Figure 2.3, A directly influences B, but B indirectly influences A through the mediation of C, which feeds back to A. If C's relationship to A and B is unrecognized, it is entirely understandable that the relationship between A and B would seem to be bidirectional. The same can be said for B and C (if A is undetected) and A and C (if B is undetected).

Branching With Feedback. The most complex system is one that contains both branching (multiple arrows emerging from at least one element) and feedback (an arrow emerging from a relative outcome back to a relative driver). The diagram shown in Figure 2.4 is an example of a system with both feedback and branching.

The system obviously has branches. Elements A and B both have multiple arrows emerging from them, which is to say they influence more than one other element of the system. Feedback also is a characteristic of this system. A-B-D-A is one such loop, as is D-E-H-D. So is A-B-E-H-D-A. On the other hand, B-D-E is not a feedback loop because there is no way to start at one of these three elements and return to that same element.

Drivers and Outcomes

An important implication of understanding elements and relationships in this way is that we may speak of elements as relative *drivers* and *outcomes*. A driver is a relative *cause* (more accurately, an influencer) and has more arrows going "out" than "in"; an outcome is the converse. Furthermore, it is useful to distinguish between primary and secondary drivers and outcomes. Primary drivers have arrows "out" but none "in," while primary outcomes have arrows "in" but none "out." Secondary drivers have both "in" and "out" arrows, but relatively more going "out"; secondary outcomes are the converse. In other words, the elements are arranged from left to right (or in some dimension) beginning with the drivers and ending with the outcomes.

Topological Zones

Systems may be organized or rationalized according to different sets of rules, depending on the purpose of the research. The objective of rationalization is to sort out the elements into a series of *zones*. A *topological zone* or, more simply, a *zone*, is *a region of a system in which the elements have similar characteristics of influence.*

The number of zones we choose to represent a system is somewhat arbitrary, but the definition of a system demands at least two because there must be at least two components in a system. The classic experiment, in which the effect of one independent variable (driver) on one dependent variable (outcome) is an example of the simplest two-zone, two-element system. It is convenient, although somewhat arbitrary, to speak of four topological zones:

1. *Primary Drivers.* Elements in this zone are the *fundamental causes* or *sources of influence* in the system. Diagrammatically, these elements have arrows going out, but none in.

2. *Secondary Drivers.* Elements in this zone are influenced by those in the primary zone, but elements in this zone are nevertheless relative *causes.*

3. *Secondary Outcomes.* Elements in this zone are influenced by secondary drivers, but in turn influence the primary outcomes.

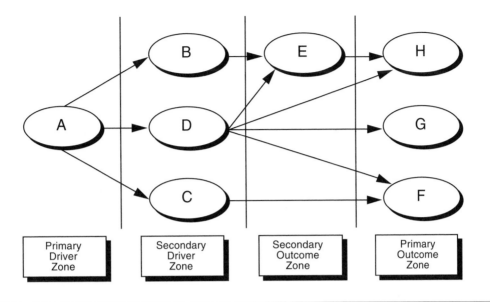

Figure 2.5

4. *Primary Outcomes.* Elements in this zone are strictly outcomes (with the exception of feedback loops, to be discussed later). These elements have arrows going in, but none out.

In Figure 2.5, we see that

1. A is a primary driver.

2. B, C, and D are *secondary drivers.* They are driven by A, but in turn drive E, F, G, and H.

3. E is a *secondary outcome* because it is driven by B and D, and drives H in turn.

4. F, G, and H are *primary outcomes* because they drive no other elements in the system.

Comparing the Two Models: Ritz Crackers and Coffee Cups

The *topology* of a system refers to *the pattern of links among elements in a system.* As long as the pattern of links is not changed or broken, transformations to a system do not change its essential topological character. Before comparing the topologies of the two different systems above, let us

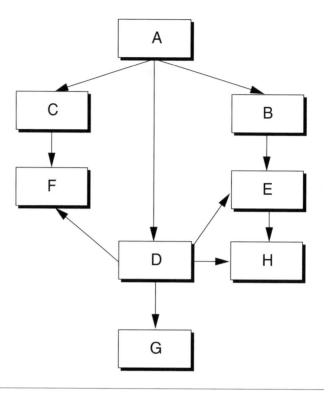

Figure 2.6

first examine the topologies of two everyday objects: a handleless coffee cup (a mug) and a Ritz cracker.

Think of both objects as being infinitely plastic, or moldable. We can do anything we want to the objects as long as we do not tear the object or, in more technical terms, *introduce a discontinuity*. Now, can we transform a Ritz cracker into a coffee mug without changing its topology (without introducing a discontinuity)? Imagine pressing down with your thumb on the center of the Ritz cracker. Because it is elastic, a bulge will form, and the more we press, the greater will be the bulge. Like a potter working clay, we can imagine shaping the Ritz cracker until it forms a cylinder, which in fact is our desired coffee mug. Yet we have never torn the cracker, and so we have left the topology of the cracker unchanged.

A superficial examination of the two systems shown here, in Figures 2.2 and 2.6, may lead one to conclude that these are two different systems; after all, they look quite different. However, they are identical topologically. You may confirm this by tracing the relationships (the arrows) and noting that they are identical in the two models. The two models look different because we have imposed a process called *Rationalizing the Model* on the first to produce the second. More will be said about rationalizing models later, but for the moment, the important point is that rationalization does not disturb the basic topology of the model, and by inference does not injure or degrade the essential nature of the system.

Epistemological Acrobatics: Zooming In, Zooming Out, and Looping

The example of the automobile illustrates three other features of systems that are worthy of mention at this point.

First, we note that any (or practically any) system is really a system of systems. To put it another way, almost any interesting system is composed of subsystems, each of which has its own elements and relationships. An interesting consequence of this notion is that no matter how we define a particular system, we can *zoom in* on one element of the system to discover a micro system within that element, or we can *zoom out* to discover that this system is an element within a larger macro system. From the researcher's point of view, this is the most important consideration when defining one's objectives, and it is one way to distinguish among the different approaches to social research. (Another way is to note the level of abstraction that is characteristic of a particular approach, but more on that later.) Figure 2.7 shows an example of a system within a system.

Second, the automobile design example shows how the finished system (the automobile) is a product or, more accurately, an interaction or a vector of systems that often have competing demands or objectives. The final system always reflects the systemic influences on the choices made by the designers. The Corvette is seen as a thing of beauty to most people, even to those who have no particular interest in cars. Not only is it beautiful, it is also a performance auto, meaning it is both nimble and quick. On the other hand, the Corvette is not the preferred mode of transportation as a family automobile, or as a long-distance tourer for a tall person, for reasons that are obvious to anyone who has ever sat in one. The final system that represents the Corvette is a product of trade-offs and interactions between the two major subsystems of engineering and design, with the outcomes of performance and aesthetic appeal clearly winning out over alternative ones such as comfort, practicality, efficiency, and cost of maintenance. One could argue that a work of industrial art, such as the Corvette auto or the Ducati motorcycle or Frank Lloyd Wright's Hollyhock House, is a "successful social dialectic" in that each represents a unity (the dialectical reconciling of opposites) of functional beauty (or of beautiful function, depending on one's biases).

The third interesting feature of systems is *recursion* or feedback, which is the fascinating tendency of elements that are relative outcomes or effects

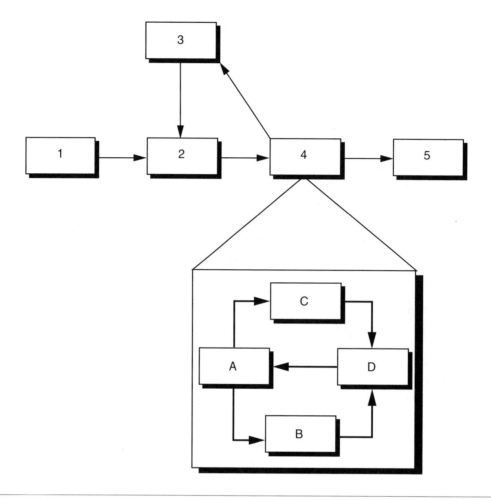

Figure 2.7

in the system to feed back or to influence elements that appear *earlier* in the system (relative causes). In our Corvette example, the choice of a particular exhaust system may influence the design of the induction system (the way the engine mixes fuel and air for ignition). The induction/exhaust example illustrates how a relative outcome (the need to dispose of products of incomplete combustion in the cylinder) can influence a relative cause (the need to feed a proper mixture of fuel and air to the cylinder) through a chain of events.

In a similar way, we observe that feedback loops (recursions) are typical of social systems, and quite often they offer the key to understanding the often-puzzling dynamics of these systems. Later on, the reader may notice a similarity between the way we represent systems and a quantitative technique called *path analysis* or *structural modeling*. There is a similarity, but there are important differences, only one of which we mention now. The primary limitation of structural modeling, other than the obvious ones of depending on quantitative data and *a priori* theorizing, is that the models are *one way*. The implication of these models is that certain inputs at the beginning of the model will inevitably produce certain results, subject to the error contained in the model itself, and subject to the extent to which influences outside the model are constrained.

But even if a structural model has no error, and even if forces outside or unaccounted for by the model are controlled, the path analytic approach suffers from its essentially deterministic nature; it cannot explain, for example, as we so often notice in the real world, why things suddenly spin out of control despite apparently good inputs, or, alternatively, why good results are almost inexplicably obtained from bad inputs. The answer, we think, lies in the recursive nature of social systems, which implies that an adequate methodology must account for these. Later, in Chapter 6, we will discuss not only how feedback loops can be identified but also how to exploit the nature of the relationships in a system to envision or create recursions in order to build feedback loops that have predictable results.

Making Sense of Systems: A Preview of Rationalization

Rationalization is a *set of rules*, independent of the nature of the elements of the system, *by which elements are first sorted into zones and then connected with the minimum number of relationships consistent with the data.* The details of rationalization must be delayed until Chapter 6. For the time being, it is sufficient to describe the goals of rationalization:

1. *Comprehensiveness.* In system terms, this means that all elements relevant to the phenomenon are identified.

2. *Complexity.* The system should represent fairly the complexity of the phenomenon. In system terms, complexity is represented by the degree of interrelationships among elements.

3. *Parsimony or Simplicity.* Following the admonition of William of Occam, IQA adheres to the principle that, all other things being equal, the simpler of two representations is the better. Note that complexity and parsimony are to some meaningful degree opposites, which suggests that good systems are successful trade-offs between complexity and parsimony.

4. *Visual Interpretability.* The final representation in IQA is a picture or a diagram, and we have already discussed how systems with the same

topology (by inference, the same phenomenological structure) can look radically different. Some representations communicate more to the eye than others do.

Rigor and the Nature of Qualitative Research

The IQA definition of research and the rules for constructing a system (rationalization) have important implications that deserve mention at this point. First, defining research as an activity that answers any one of the three possible questions about systems suggests not only what is research but also what is not. Journalism and storytelling would not seem to qualify (which is not to say they are not useful or even scientific activities in some sense) as research because of the de-emphasis on abstraction, which is the *sine qua non* of identifying elements of a system. Proponents of extreme phenomenological approaches who eschew abstraction as a legitimate activity (or who purport to, at least) and who would strongly object to including investigation of relationships as part of a formal definition of their craft would be eliminated for similar reasons.

IQA also has a distinct position on the meaning and utility of rigor in qualitative research, which is different from some schools of qualitative thought. *Rigor* as used here refers to procedures for both data collection and analysis that (1) are public and nonidiosyncratic; (2) are replicable within reasonable bounds; and (3) do not depend (especially for analysis) on the nature of the elements themselves; that is, the IQA rules for constructing a system are independent of the content or nature of the elements themselves. Another way of putting this third point is that two different analysts, presented with the same set of focus group data, will produce system representations that are topologically identical by adhering to the rules for rationalization, regardless of either the analysts' biases or the meaning of the elements. To summarize, rigor in qualitative research is achievable. It is relevant. And it is a good thing. We respectfully disagree with those who suggest rigor is an irrelevant construct, or with those who try to finesse the issue through redefinition, and especially with those who contend that discourses on rigor serve only to oppress and subjugate.

IQA addresses these issues not only by allowing the "subjects" of research to identify both the elements and relationships among elements themselves but also through application of rules for rationalization, along with some guidelines for visual representation, to produce three different versions of each system: Cluttered (high in complexity but low in simplicity), Uncluttered (high in simplicity but low in complexity), and Clean (simplicity is highlighted and complexity is represented but in the background). For example, Figures 2.8, 2.9, and 2.10 show the Cluttered, Uncluttered, and Clean versions, respectively, of the same system.

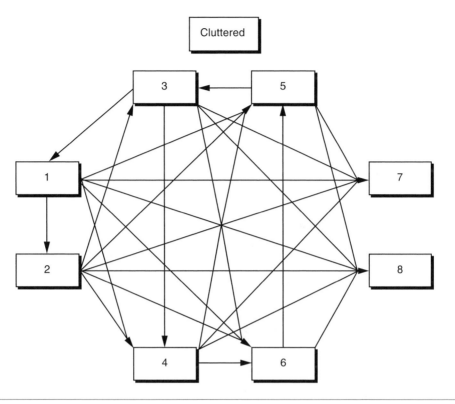

Figure 2.8

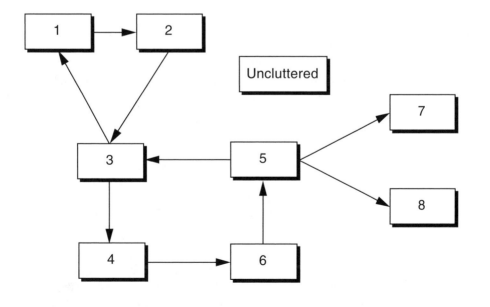

Figure 2.9

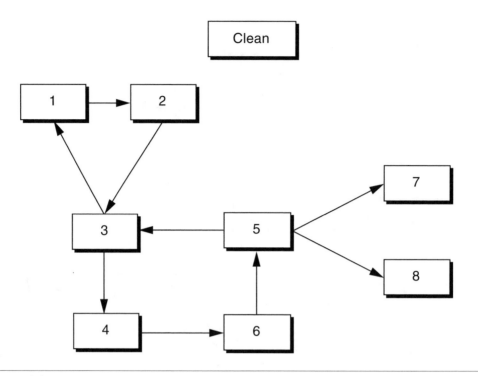

Figure 2.10

IQA Systems

To return to our example of automobile design, the term *automobile* refers to something quite different to the two engineers, which is to say that the system is not the automobile. Rather, a system is a way we choose to represent the auto. Systems are representations, which implies that we choose the system we use to represent a particular reality.

We will focus on *social systems,* defined here as *systems in which human interpretation of meaning is involved.* Just as physical systems are composed of elements and relationships, so are social systems. The elements of social systems are characterized only by their diversity. They may be psychological or unique to the individual (emotional states, for example); or they may represent organizational or institutional features (the way in which a graduate course is structured); or they may represent interactions between the individual and some social structure, such as an organization (student/ faculty relationships).

While the elements are as varied as the different ways humans have of making meaning, the relationships among these elements have a remarkable consistency. Meaning, for our purposes, is translated roughly as, *What makes things happen, and why?* Although there are many possible relationships that have interest to the social sciences, we will define relationships as those of perceived cause and effect, or influence, among the elements. In addition, the purpose of our approach is to describe both the elements and the relationships of social systems in such a way as to delineate the patterns of influence among the elements. The product of an IQA study is a visual representation of a phenomenon prepared according to rigorous and replicable rules for the purpose of achieving complexity, simplicity, comprehensiveness, and interpretability.

Note

1. See *http://library.thinkquest.org/27890/mainIndex.html* for an excellent discussion of theory and applications of Fibonacci series.

IQA Research Flow 3

Bricolage or Petit Point?

Denzin and Lincoln, in the introduction to what is surely the best single source of readings on epistemological and methodological issues in qualitative research (Denzin & Lincoln, 2000, pp. 4–6), offer the metaphor of the *bricoleur* or quilt maker (or one who creates montages or, even more broadly, an epistemological Jack-of-All-Trades [Levi-Strauss, 1966]) for the role of qualitative researchers, especially those who see the primary responsibility of research as one of interpretation. Interactive Qualitative Analysis (IQA), through systematic facilitation of group processes and by means of similarly systematic representation of the discourse created by the group, offers one way to create such a quilt of meaning. The quilt (*bricolage*) metaphor is a dialectical one and is consequently cautionary as well as prescriptive. The danger is fixating on the stitches to the extreme of doing intellectual petit point, rather than creating a larger work that is quite possibly not as detailed. While small pieces of embroidery can indeed be works of art, IQA's focus is more on the quilt.

The purpose of an IQA study is to allow a group to create its own "interpretive quilt," and then to similarly construct individual quilts of meaning: Together, the two levels of meaning are used by the investigator as the foundation for interpretation. The quilt is represented as a system of patches (affinities) held together by stitches (relationships among affinities). In plain language, an IQA study prompts the participants to examine these issues with respect to a phenomenon important to them:

- ❖ What does this mean to you?
- ❖ What led to this?
- ❖ What are the results?

43

The Researcher's Footprint

No matter the paradigm (positivist, postpositivist, constructionist, interpretivist, poststructuralist, critical theory, to name but a few variations), the responsibility of the investigator is threefold:

- ❖ To interpret
- ❖ To ensure that the ground of interpretation provides as much epistemological traction as possible
- ❖ To tread softly on that ground

Researchers leave tracks at the moment the very first inchoate questions enter their minds, but IQA provides a set of data "collection" and "analysis" protocols that are designed to minimize erosion. Participants have a remarkable degree of freedom within a framework provided by the facilitator (which itself is typically developed in consultation with knowledgeable participants); participants themselves perform the first steps of analysis by organizing their discourse into categories of meaning called *affinities;* and participants themselves take the analysis even further by articulating their own perceived relationships of influence among the affinities. The first responsibility of the researcher is to create a process that will invite the group members to produce the most "data" while minimizing the influence of the process on the content. The researcher's role then moves from designer to facilitator, teaching the group members the process and guiding them to generate and analyze their own data with minimal external influence.

Overview of the IQA Research Flow

Figure 3.1 shows a diagram of the flow of a typical IQA project.

IQA research flow has four distinct phases: research design, focus group, interview, and report; therefore, the remainder of this book is organized around these four phases. Before examining each of the four, it may be useful to discuss in some detail the components of each phase as well as the details of how the phases interlock to form a complete study.

Chapter 4, on IQA research design, provides a series of tools to help articulate problems of interest, to identify constituencies that have an interest in the problem, and to state research questions that are implied by the problem statement. IQA then uses focus groups to identify the "quilt pieces" (affinities) of a system or systems that will ultimately represent the group's experience with the phenomenon. The group next identifies the "stitches," the relationships among each of the affinities. Using a set of protocols or rules stemming from IQA systems theory, a system is drawn that represents a "mindmap" of the group's reality.

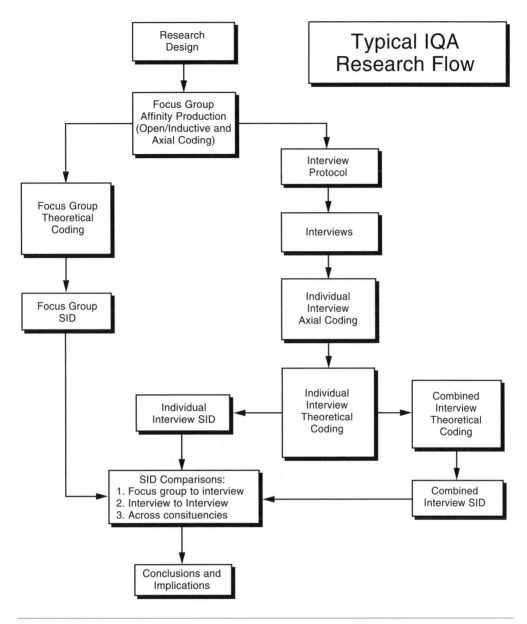

Figure 3.1

Affinities defined by the group are then used to develop a protocol for interviews, which are invaluable to further explore the meanings of the affinities and their systemic relationships. A comprehensive system diagram is developed from the interviews to explain the phenomenon. The final report allows the researcher to describe the affinities and their relationships, to make comparisons among systems and individuals, and to make inferences (predictions) based on the properties of the system(s). The following is a summary of each of the major stages in the research flow.

IQA Research Design. IQA research design starts with what is traditionally called a "problem." By "problem," we mean nothing more dramatic than an issue someone thinks is either interesting or needs attention. Often at this stage, a solution to some perceived problem is sought, but it is difficult to articulate what the problem really is. By its very nature, the problem is not clearly defined at this point. Rather than simply demanding *ex cathedra* that the problem be made explicit on the one hand, or simply hoping that a well-defined problem will somehow rise from the chaos of our activity on the other, IQA research flow presumes that ambiguity is a characteristic of the early thinking about a project and deals with this ambiguity, reducing it with every recursion around the IQA design cycle. IQA research design starts with the vague problem and seeks to identify those who have something to say about the problem. For each constituency—a group of people who have a shared understanding of a phenomenon— two questions are asked: How close is this constituency to the problem, phenomenologically speaking, and how much power does this constituency have over the phenomenon? From this analysis, a tentative selection of constituencies is made.

Once constituencies are identified, then the question becomes, What issue should this constituency examine? Different constituencies are selected because they have different perspectives (either in terms of the lived experience with the phenomenon or power over it), and therefore may respond to different facets (issues) of the phenomenon.

Once a tentative issue has been defined for each constituency, research questions may be addressed. Again, IQA systems theory offers a template for the design: Any IQA study answers at most three "generic" (standard inquiries possible of any system) research questions. If the study has only one constituency, the first two are as follows:

1. What are the components of the phenomenon?

2. How do the components relate to each other in a perceptual system?

If more than one constituency comprises the study, a third systemic inquiry is possible:

3. How do the systems compare, in terms of components, intrasystemic relationships, and intersystemic relationships?

Research questions are then tested for adequacy against two criteria, stated as the following questions:

1. What problem do these questions, taken as a whole, address (what is the current problem statement)?

2. Is this the problem we should be addressing?

IQA research design is complete when the answer to question 2 is affirmative.

Group Realities: IQA Focus Groups

IQA studies usually begin with a *focus group*, which is a group of people who share some common experience, work or live within some common structure, or have a similar background. This definition suggests that the researcher should think first about commonalities rather than differences when designing the composition of the group; IQA focus groups are formed with groups of individuals who may certainly have varied opinions and experiences with the system under study but who more critically share a common perspective.

Identification of Factors (Affinities). The first step for an IQA focus group is silent brainstorming. During this phase, a focus group is asked to write their experiences about the subject on note cards, one thought per card. After producing as many cards as they can, the focus group is asked to tape the cards along a wall. The facilitator reads each card and the group comes to a consensus as to the meaning of the card in the clarification of meaning activity, during which the foundations are laid for constructing, through discourse, a shared reality among group members. The facilitator then asks the group to silently organize the cards into groups of meaning, an activity referred to as *inductive coding*. Grouping is followed by the affinity naming and revision phase (*axial coding*), which consists of giving a name to the group (affinity) and sorting any cards that may have been miscategorized into the proper group.

Identifying Relationships Among Factors. With the affinities clearly defined, the group is asked to analyze the nature of relationships between each of the affinities. They are given some rules: analyzing all possible pairs (only three possibilities; either A $\rightarrow$ B, B $\rightarrow$ A, or no relationship). They are asked to record their responses in an Affinity Relationship Table, which is a matrix containing all the perceived relationships in the system. IQA provides a variety of protocols for building the group Interrelationship Diagram (IRD), which contains all the information required to produce the group (or individual) mindmap.

Constructing the IRD. The focus group investigates links between the affinities by developing propositions (statements of cause and effect) from their own data. This activity, called *theoretical coding*, creates an extended reality for the group through further discourse. Again, IQA provides a number of protocol variations for this stage of analysis. Using a forced directional choice in a specific order, focus group participants determine if there is a direct cause/effect relationship or if no relationship exists. The goal is to identify the skeleton of a "theory in perception." Theoretical coding of the affinities results in an IRD, a table that represents all the relationships among the affinities.

Constructing the SID. The System Influence Diagram (SID), also called a *mindmap,* is a visual representation of an entire system of influences and outcomes. The graphic representation of relationships paints a vivid picture of system dynamics for both investigator and participants, and lends itself readily to analyzing how modifications might change the nature of the system.

As a visual representation of the mindmap developed from the data, the SID is roughly analogous to a set of *qualitative structural equations* or as a *path diagram;* however, it is distinguished from traditional path diagrams in that recursion or feedback loops are allowed. The SID is a visual representation of the "theory in perception," grounded in the specific experiences and logic of the participants.

IQA Interviews

The IQA interview is a semistructured interview. It is designed to capitalize on the consistency afforded by highly structured interviews and the level of detail offered by open-ended or emergent interviews. The interview questions are designed and based on the affinities and subaffinities developed by the focus group members. An IQA interview protocol is designed to achieve specific objectives, each of which relates directly to the research questions of the study. In particular, IQA interviews serve to:

❖ Add richness and depth description of the meaning of affinities that is not possible with a focus group alone

❖ Allow for individual mindmaps, which can be used in a debriefing session as an interpretive aid to the investigator

Interview Analysis. Analysis of an IQA interview proceeds exactly parallel to the manner of focus group protocol. For each of the affinities, the interview respondent is asked three kinds of questions, as stated earlier:

❖ What does this mean to you?

❖ What led to this?

❖ What are the results?

In a manner analogous to the focus group's activities, the interview transcript is coded both axially and theoretically as follows:

Individual Interview Axial Code Table. The Individual Interview Axial Code Table (ACT) is the primary documentation for all utterances that illustrate the range of meaning of each affinity for each respondent. The researcher identifies axial codes by noting key words or phrases that describe or illustrate an affinity. This text is then documented for easy retrieval in the ACT. Quotes relating to a specific affinity can be cut and pasted into the ACT, along with the line(s) of the transcript that were the source of the axial quote. There will usually be multiple axial quotes for any given affinity; each quote is represented by another row in the ACT.

Individual Interview Theoretical Code Affinity Relationship Table. The Theoretical Code Affinity Relationship Table (TCT) is the primary documentation for all utterances that illustrate the manner in which the affinities are related for each respondent. The researcher also identifies, through a formal line of questioning in the second phase of the IQA interview, *theoretical codes,* which *illustrate a relationship between two or more affinities.* The relationship reported by the respondent (using the same rules as the focus group) is recorded by placing the appropriate arrow in the TCT, which documents both the direction of the relationship and the example or line of reasoning given by the respondent. Additionally, the interview transcript should be examined for statements that illustrate a link between affinities. Additional relational quotations (offered without prompting) may be found in the axial interview and should be placed in the table. The transcript line should be recorded in the table.

Composite SID. Using the same procedure used to develop a focus group SID, an IRD and SID can be created for each respondent. Once all interviews have been coded, the data from the interviews are summarized to create a combined SID that represents a composite of the individual's experience with the phenomenon. A count of each theoretical code is entered into the Combined Interview Theoretical Code Frequency Table. Because individual respondents may have defined relationships differently, and may in fact disagree about the direction of a relationship, IQA provides a protocol (the Pareto Protocol with MinMax Criterion, discussed in detail in Chapter 6) to constructing a composite SID from individual interview SIDs.

IQA Results

The IQA systems approach is designed to be of the greatest possible assistance in interpretation. The focus group is used to identify the affinities, each of which is well documented as part of the focus group protocol. Interviews then expand on the descriptions of the affinities. Because the primary result of an IQA study is a picture of a system or systems, it is no accident that the process that produced these systems is designed to aid in the writing process. The typical IQA report accomplishes three goals:

1. It names and describes the elements of the system.

2. It explains relationships among elements of a system (system dynamics).

3. It compares systems.

Elements. In order to set a base for systems analysis, each affinity is identified and discussed in detail. Included in such a discussion are succinct and relevant quotes from the interviews that help illustrate the range of meaning for each affinity. Affinities comprising the system are described largely in the participants' own words.

Relationships. The SID is presented and readers are given a "tour" through the system in which the relative influence of each affinity on others is portrayed in a systemic context; once again, the words of participants are used to illustrate the behavior of the systemic links, to "ground" the abstract representation that is the SID in the data of the participants' words and descriptions.

Comparisons. Comparisons can be made at two levels: A qualitative analogue to the statistical concept of variation is possible by comparing individual mindmaps to each other and to the composite; and a qualitative analogue to post hoc group comparisons is possible by comparing the composite mindmaps of different constituencies. These two interpretive protocols are the logical results of the dialectical nature of IQA research, as revealed in the following:

1. Individuals are unique in meaningful ways. Individual perspectives or voices are important and should not get lost in our attempt to find patterns. However . . .

2. Patterns or commonalities in perceptions do exist within constituencies. These patterns or abstractions are useful for both theoretical and practical purposes. Furthermore . . .

3. Comparison is the primary method of interpretation, both from the participant's point of view and from the investigator's. IQA focus group and interview protocols are designed to encourage constant comparison by the participants; for the investigator, the following comparisons are provided by following the IQA research design process:

❖ Among individuals within and across constituencies (comparing individual mindmaps to each other and to composites)

❖ Comparisons among constituencies (comparing composites)

What Is and What If. A mindmap or SID, whether it is the map of a group's or an individual's perception, is a system or a model, and systems are made to be "exercised." Systems may be exercised (or scenarios may be cast) in three basic ways:

1. We may ask the model to "predict," based on its internal logic, the ultimate state of the outcome affinities given known states of its antecedent affinities.

2. We may do the opposite, which is to ask what antecedents might, by the logic of the system, lead to a particular state of its outcomes.

3. We may ask what might be the effect of extrasystemic influences or those forces not named or accounted for in the system.

In other words, IQA methodology allows for a representation of both individual and group realities, comparisons of which allow the researcher to ask the two great interpretive questions: "What is . . . ?" and "What if . . . ?"

IQA Research Design $\Large 4$

Thinking About the Problem

Where Do I Start?

Thinking about the design for a study typically (although not always—more on that later) begins with a *Problem Statement*, which at the early stages of design may be no more than a vague concern, a desire to know more about an ill-defined and poorly understood phenomenon, or a need to correct or ameliorate a situation, the nature of which is not fully circumscribed. This initial lack of clarity is probably the most difficult hurdle for researchers to overcome, and the literature from both the quantitative and qualitative streams tends to give this element of research design less than meticulous attention, as illustrated below.

An Epistemological Dialectic

At One Extreme. Through the mid-1980s, influential quantitatively and positivist-oriented writers stressed the necessity for a clear problem statement; some even suggested criteria:

> It is not always possible for a researcher to formulate his problem simply, clearly, and completely. He may often have only a rather general, diffuse, even confused notion of the problem. . . . Nevertheless, adequate statement of the research problem is one of the most important parts of research. . . . Bearing this difficulty in mind, a fundamental principle can be stated: If one wants to solve a problem, one must generally know what the problem is. (Kerlinger, 1985, p. 16)

One paragraph later, Kerlinger continued:

> A *problem,* then, is an interrogative sentence or statement that asks: What relation exists between two or more variables?

By equating the problem with a research question, Kerlinger's definition, while succinct, quickly leads the researcher into an epistemological swamp. How can a problem, such as *Why are people dropping dead in the streets?* be the same as a research question, which Kerlinger insists must point to a relationship between variables, such as *Are they dropping dead because of bad water, or an airborne hantavirus, or due to the recent nuclear blast?*

In The Middle. Kerlinger, like many of his contemporaries, did not offer much guidance as to exactly how to achieve these criteria. More current writers, reflecting the influences of postmodernism and the rise of qualitative approaches to research, are hardly more helpful. For example, Rubin and Babbie (1993), in their excellent overview of methods for social research, dispensed with the issue of the problem statement as follows:

> *Problem Formulation.* A difficulty is recognized for which more knowledge is needed. A question, called the research question, is posed. The research question and its inherent concepts are progressively sharpened to be made more specific, relevant, and meaningful to the field. (pp. 91–92)

The obvious difference in understanding between the two sources is Kerlinger's insistence on operationalization and on defining research strictly as an investigation of relationships between variables (which would no doubt make anthropologists and ethnographers uncomfortable), while Rubin and Babbie take a less restrictive approach. However, the two conceptions of the nature of the problem statement are more similar than different with respect to one very important feature: *They both link the problem statement directly to the research question or questions.* Therein lies the rub.

The Other Extreme. More ethnographically oriented writers on research methods seem almost to finesse the problem statement issue, and many choose not even to use language such as *problem statement* or *research question.* Take, for example, Bogdan and Biklen's (1992) introductory paragraph in their chapter on research design:

> We have a friend who, when asked where she is going on vacation, will tell you the direction she is traveling and then concludes with, "I'll see what happens as I go along." Another friend makes detailed plans, with all the stops . . . and routes set in advance. "Design" is used in research to refer to the researcher's plan of how to proceed. *A qualitative researcher is more like the loosely scheduled traveler than the other* [italics added]. (pp. 58–60)

Bogdan and Biklen, after having given the reader due notice that their approach to research design demands adaptability and flexibility, introduce their version of Glaser and Strauss's (1967) famous *constant comparison* theory of qualitative research design. By way of illustration, they describe a hypothetical researcher's *first day in the field,* portions of which are quoted below:

> Mary Schriver is about to arrive at an elementary school to begin a rather lengthy study [about what, we do no yet know; and as it turns out, neither does Mary] using the constant comparison method [more on this in a moment]. While she has no investment in any specific topic, she is interested in teachers. . . . Her plan is to start there [with teachers] and see what develops. . . . She is struck immediately [we do not know why; perhaps neither does Mary] by how much of the talk that goes on is about other people: Teachers talk about students, other teachers, and administrators. The tone of the talk varies from humor to anger, and some of the conversations halt when certain people enter the room. . . . From then on, Mary concentrates her data-collecting activities on incidents of gossip. . . . She listens to those conversations. (pp. 58–60)

Although Mary Schriver's approach to research design may strike some (a funding agency interested in a particular problem, or company struggling with how to improve communication among employee groups, for example) as a bit too ill-defined and a bit too reliant on the capabilities of the researcher, it is clear that Mary is using some set of recursive heuristics that she herself may not be able to articulate clearly. How would she answer the question, "Why did you suddenly choose to focus on teacher talk?"

Synthesis, Not Compromise

Recursive heuristics simply means that Mary Schriver uses her observations to inform her focus (mediated by her experience, training, and personal inclination) to inform her observations to inform her focus in a recursive loop that could either get tighter and tighter or even send her off in an unexpected direction. A structure underlies these radically different views of research design, but it is apparently hidden to those who insist there is only *one* way to think about, and to do, research. This structure ultimately has to do with the interaction between the general purpose of the research, the conditions under which the purpose is or should be explicit, and the resulting implications for observation and analysis.

The interaction among the problem statement, research question (or more likely a *set* of research questions), and observation is arguably the single most difficult concept for novice researchers to understand. One might also conclude that the topic is most poorly taught in graduate research courses, no matter what their epistemological bent. The relationship is not, as Kerlinger (1985) seemed to suggest, linear and direct (the research questions somehow flow deductively from the problem statement). Neither is the relationship, as Rubin and Babbie (1993) implied, recursive and direct; which is to say that each feeds back to the other. Rather, as Mary Schriver seems to have intuited, the relationship is both indirect and recursive. But as we have already seen, Mary can't seem to tell outsiders what the components are that make up the indirect relationships. The source of confusion lies in an insufficiently elaborated epistemological theory concerning the relationship of the problem statement to the set of research questions. In the sections that follow, such a theory is proposed.

Research Design as a System

If the collection (or generation, or creation, depending on one's point of view), analysis, and interpretation of qualitative data can be approached from a systems point of view, it follows that the question of how to think about doing qualitative research can itself be the subject of an Interactive Qualitative Analysis (IQA) systems analysis. Figure 4.1 shows a system representing the major design considerations in a qualitative study and the relationships among them.

Touring the System: An Example

Previously, we met Mary and analyzed the manner in which she developed her research focus. Now, meet Debra (D) as she meets with her dissertation research advisor (A) for the first time. The transcript of the session that follows is interspersed at strategic points by an analysis of the interaction between A and D.

A: So, tell me about your dissertation ideas. You're in human resources, right?

D: Yes, but more so in organizational development. We do a lot of specialized training that is a lot more like coaching than training, using materials that we develop in the context of a specific work situation.

A: And you are interested in doing your dissertation research in that area?

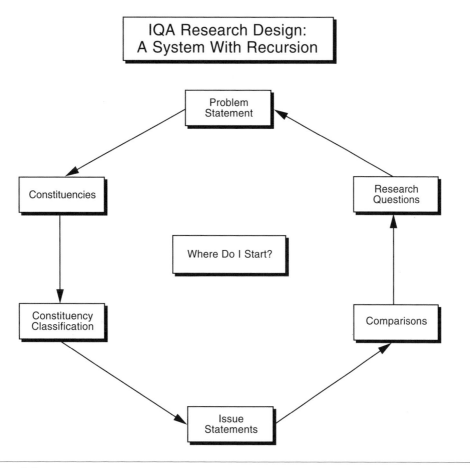

Figure 4.1

D: Yes . . . maybe . . . I'm not really sure. You read the papers, so you know that like many other high-tech companies, we've had several rounds of layoffs, and because of the nature of my job, I've gotten really interested in how people react to being laid off.

A: So you're interested in studying how people react to being laid off?

D: Well, that's just an example. I think I want to study something more interesting than that.

A: By "more interesting" you mean . . . ?

D: I've noticed that no matter what the situation, some people seem to have more of a sense of efficacy than others. The way people deal with layoffs is simply one example.

A: Give me some more examples of efficacy.

D: Take learning a new computer task, for example; or a new office procedure. Some people seem to just naturally be more confident about dealing with change than others.

A: Which is what you're calling "efficacy."

D: Yes, exactly. I've seen research lately that says the typical employee is going to have to retrain—completely overhaul themselves—three times in a career. I'm interested in how an organization can help people adapt to change.

A: That sounds like the beginning of a study.

D: Yeah, but what do I do now? I don't really know where to start.

A: Here's a suggestion: Take a minute, and then just give me a short statement describing what you want to study. Don't worry about editing or censoring the statement; just give me a brain dump.

D: *(Sits a moment with her eyes closed)* I want to know why some adults weather change better and believe in their ability to learn new skills or requirements when others don't.

Reflections on Dialogue 1. D's situation is typical of many researchers at this stage of her thinking. Her training and experience has led her to a reasonably well-articulated statement of the problem, considering the early stage of her thinking. In his mind's eye, A visualizes a quick-and-dirty systems analysis of D's current problem statement, which is represented in Figure 4.2.

Note that this simple system is A's mindmap, not necessarily D's. D's use of the conjunction "and" between the two affinities is represented in A's mind by a relationship, the direction of which is ambiguous at this point; A suspects, however, that in D's mind the picture, looks more like that shown in Figure 4.3.

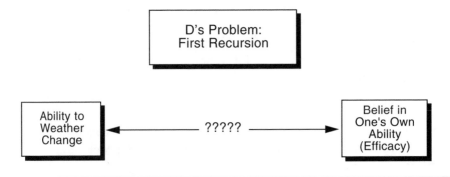

Figure 4.2

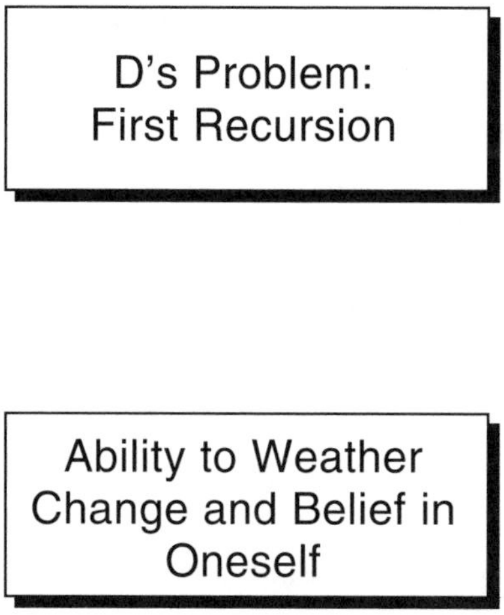

```
┌─────────────────────────────┐
│                             │
│        D's Problem:         │
│      First Recursion        │
│                             │
└─────────────────────────────┘
```

```
┌─────────────────────────────┐
│                             │
│      Ability to Weather     │
│    Change and Belief in     │
│          Oneself            │
│                             │
└─────────────────────────────┘
```

Figure 4.3

A's first goal is to help D clarify the meaning of the word "and" in her current problem statement. The dialogue proceeds as A begins to lead D through the IQA system of thinking about research design:

A: OK, that sounds like a good start to me. Now, tell me: Who do you think has something to say about this situation?

D: *(Hesitating, a bit taken aback)* What do you mean?

A: You're interested in people's ability to adapt to change and also in something you're calling efficacy. You want to do a study on this topic, right?

D: Right.

A: And you're going to have to gather some information about this topic, right?

D: You mean, like interviews or fieldnotes, or are you talking about a lit review?

A: No, let's not worry about all those details now. Ask yourself this question: Who has something to say about the topic?

D: Oh, well . . . lots of people. Everybody does, in some sense.

A: Yes, but you can't talk to everybody and finish your study in your lifetime, can you? Try to be a little more specific.

D: I'm thinking about the people laid off at the company. Some people are dealing with it much better than others.

A: So, people who have been laid off might be a way to think about the problem. Now, who else? Who has something to say about the problem?

D: When I finish this study, I want to be able to tell companies something useful about how to help employees adapt to change . . . so . . . managers are important, because they directly supervise people. Also, HR [human resources] generalists are important, as are a number of other people—exit interviewers, because they hear the stories of people who got laid off, and career center employees.

A: Career center?

D: The company has contracts with career centers that provide counseling, placement, and retraining resources to people who have been laid off.

A: We're almost out of time, so I want to give you an assignment for our next planning session. First, I want you to develop a list of the groups that, in the best of all possible worlds, you would want to talk to about this problem. Then, I want you to order the list in two different ways: first, by distance from the phenomenon.

D: Distance? You mean . . . ?

A: Who's at the very center of the thing you want to study from an experiential point of view?

D: People who have been laid off, I guess.

A: That sounds right to me. Now, of all the people you've mentioned in the last hour, who's the furthest?

D: (Laughs) I suppose that would be the executive officers who get bonuses if they lay off enough people to bring the company stock price up.

A: Fine, so you have two extremes. Put the others in between in some order that makes sense to you.

D: OK, how do I construct the other list?

A: Use the same groups, but this time, order them in terms of how much power they have over the phenomenon. For example, who has the most power?

D: Well, it depends on how you look at it, but the executive leadership makes all the major decisions about layoffs.

A: And the least . . . ?

D: (Laughs again) The people who get laid off, I suppose.

A: Very well. Bring me the two lists at our next session, and we will see what happens. Oh, one other thing. For each group, write an issue statement.

D: I thought the issue statement is the purpose of my research. Isn't that what we've spent an hour talking about?

A: They're related, but here's a way to think about issue statements: Visualize yourself standing in front of each of the groups on your list. What single issue would you want each of them to talk about? Suppose you had the opportunity to run a focus group of some people who have been laid off at the company. What do you want them to talk about?

D: I want to know how they have dealt with being laid off—what they've done, what they've experienced, how they feel, what their emotions are. I want to know what the experience means to them.

A: Good enough. But you wouldn't ask the question in exactly the same way if you were talking to, say, exit interviewers, would you?

B: No, obviously not. I'd ask exit interviewers to tell me about what people who have been laid off say to them in the exit interviews.

A: Now you've got the idea. See you tomorrow.

Reflections on Dialogue 2. A is pointing D toward the *first* (the adjective is a bit misleading in the context of a completely recursive system such as IQA research design) steps in developing a strategy and related tactics for her study. D will develop a list of constituencies—groups of people who experience the phenomenon differently, but in some meaningful way. Then, she will order the list, first, by distance from the phenomenon and second, by power over the phenomenon. After developing the two different orderings of the list, she will write a question that summarizes what she wants to know from each group.

D will certainly run into problems in completing her assignment, but A chooses not to try to resolve these for her. The recursive journey A is sending D on, when used with reasonable fidelity and intellectual honesty, tends to be self-correcting, which is to say internal ambiguities and contradictions are exposed in successive trips around the hermeneutical circle.

Theoretical Sidebar: Dialogue, Demonizing, and Discourse. The recursive IQA design process is a formalized version of what is commonly called "critical thinking." The researcher, in effect, participates in a systematic internal dialogue, moving around the hermeneutical circle until he or she is satisfied with the answers to the questions that have been raised. The direct analogue to this internal process in public discourse is called *dialogue.* Dialogue between competing or different perspectives—political dialogue—has classically been identified as a hallmark of democracy, and as the most effective method for identifying the greatest social good as well as ways and means to achieve that good. The postmodern concern for inclusiveness and with power structures as manifested by class, race, and gender, while laudable, has had the perverse effect of minimizing or even eliminating certain kinds of public or political discourse; every astute politician (or doctoral candidate) knows that certain topics are beyond the pale and simply must not be discussed, thereby proscribing any public critical thinking about the topic. The regime of political correctness, albeit well-intentioned, is not without its social penalties; it must be held at least partially responsible for the popularity of political "spin" and of demonizing the opposing side.

To return to the dialogue between D and A, note the advice that A did *not* give D. He did not tell her to stop everything and go to the library or get on the computer and read everything that has been written about efficacy or about job layoffs or any of a dozen other topics implied by D's problem statement. Scholarship is always important, and certainly at some point, D should be very aware of the current state of research, both theoretical and applied, that is relevant to her problem. But since her problem is still somewhat vague at this point, such activity, at least as a major emphasis, is premature.

Nor did A insist that D start forming research questions immediately. As a matter of fact, the business of research questions, while critical, is the *last* issue A and D will address. The issues involved with defining meaningful constituencies, stating questions to be asked of constituencies (which are not identical to research questions), and analyzing the meaning of comparisons among constituencies all precede the formulation of research questions.

The dialogue between advisor and student continues the next day:

A: So, how goes the business of constituencies and ordering and issue statements?

D: Not well. Things got really confusing. I think I have a mess on my hands.

A: That's not so unusual. Show me your list of constituents.

D: *(Hands it over)* I ordered them by power first and noticed a lot of interesting distinctions. But I got in trouble when it came to distance, and I'm afraid some of these don't make much sense.

A: *(Notices that there are more than two dozen items on the list. His eyebrows go up.)*

D: What?

A: So you're going to get information from more than two dozen groups? That might take some time. Plan to spend the rest of your life on this study, do you?

D: Yeah, I know. So what does all this mean? Are you telling me this study can't be done?

A: Well, a large number of constituencies present obvious logistical problems, but it's not necessarily a deal killer. I'm more concerned with something else for the time being. In my experience, a long list like this indicates conceptual problems.

D: Tell me about it.

A: Actually, why don't you tell me about it?

D: As I looked at this last night, it almost seemed as if I needed two lists.

A: And what's the difference between the two? Can you give me an example?

D: These two [points to items "Efficacious employees" and "Noneffi-cacious employees"] seem different from these ["People who deal with change well" and "People who don't"], but yet they seem the same.

A: Do me a favor. Read your problem statement to me again.

D: I want to know why some adults weather change better and believe in their ability to learn new skills or requirements when others don't.

A: Look at the conjunction in your problem statement. What does that word mean?

D: "And" means "and." It means "in addition to" or "plus."

A: You're talking about parallel construction in grammar, right? Like dogs and cats, this and that, Butch Cassidy and the Sundance Kid?

D: *(Hesitates)* Yes, but it means something different in my problem statement, I guess.

A: I guess so, too. What does the word mean in your case? Rewrite your problem statement by using some word other than "and."

D: I suppose it means, "Some adults weather change better *because they* believe in their ability to learn new skills or requirements."

A: I think you're right. So actually, your study is very easy; as a matter of fact, you don't have to do any interviews or focus groups or look at any documents or do any observations at all. Your study has already been done.

D: By someone else?

A: Not at all—by you. Your problem statement says that the reason why some people weather organizational change better than others is because they are more efficacious. Your problem statement contains both the question and the answer, what's known in mathematics as a tautology. End of story.

D: So that's why I had trouble with one list in terms of distance? Because I'm interested in two things: change and response to change?

A: I believe so *[hands her his sketch of "D's Problem: First Recursion"; Figure 4.2]*.

D: Why didn't you tell me this earlier?

A: Because my job is to help you teach yourself how to think about research design. You don't really want to suffer through a three-hour session with me every time you want to do a new study, do you?

D: *(D is far too tactful to run the risk of offending a member of her committee, but unknowingly makes a moue.)*

A: *(Ignoring D's sour face)* I don't know how to do that by just laying out what I think are the answers to questions you haven't yet discovered. I tried laying on of hands for a while, and that worked OK, but I got calluses.

D: *(Ignores A's egregious joke)* But even if I divide my list into two, one dealing with organizational change, and the other with efficacy, it still has a lot of constituents.

A: Just so. Let's take a look at what might constitute the bare bones of your study. You believe that a sense of efficacy is key to weathering organizational change, right? In other words, you already have developed at least the beginnings of a theory. Basically, you want to describe "efficacy" in some meaningful and rich way, don't you?

D: So, I should look at people who've been laid off and see how efficacious they are?

A: Can you identify an efficacious person?

D: Sure. They're the ones who don't just sit home watching TV and getting depressed after the layoff. They go to the career centers, or start calling their network of friends and associates, or even use the layoff as an opportunity to reevaluate their lives. Maybe all I have to do is talk to these people.

A: Certainly you should. But suppose you did have a very clear picture of how these people process and understand what is certainly a traumatic experience. How do you know that this has anything to do with efficacy, and more to the point, how do you know that people who don't do these proactive things after getting laid off won't describe and, by inference, understand the situation in much the same terms?

D: Well, I guess I don't. You're telling me I should do a comparison?

A: I'm saying a comparison, if you found significant differences in the way the two constituencies understand being laid off, would go a long way toward helping you give some real understanding of what you mean by "efficacy."

Reflections on Dialogue 3. As A expected, D did indeed experience problems in developing her constituency list. A exploited this difficulty to help her clarify her problem statement. A's goal was twofold: First, he wanted to help D realize that problem statements almost always imply relationships (one is tempted to remove the "almost," but in the spirit of dialectical analysis, dogmatism is always avoided—usually). Second, D and A moved to the issue of comparisons, which is the only—oh, very well, just a very good way—to understand the nature of relationships. In suggesting that D compare two groups of people who have been laid off, A is preparing D to think about research questions (the derivation of which, once appropriate comparisons have been identified, becomes relatively routine) and preparing the ground for the *last* stage or, more accurately, the last stage in the first of however many recursions are needed, of research design.

D: If I understand correctly, the logic behind the comparison is that I can infer that the differences in the meaning of being laid off between the two groups are due to efficacy?

A: Well, that's what you expect will happen, but you should be open to the distinct possibility that other components of meaning—we call them "affinities"—will emerge from the data. I believe some of them you will recognize as being part of what you're calling efficacy, but it's entirely likely that others will have much to do with extrapersonal influences, such as social support. That's the beauty of an emergent approach to research: You don't have to make all of your predictions in advance, and you shouldn't. Can you live with that?

D: Certainly. But where do my research questions come from?

A: Straight from your comparisons. Actually, in any IQA study, and in much qualitative research, there are only three "generic" research questions: the first two are intrasystemic and the third is intersystematic.

D: Pardon me?

A: You'll get more details later, but basically, what I'm suggesting you do after defining your relevant constituencies is, first, to allow each constituency to identify the components of what you are calling "efficacy." Behind this activity—called affinity production—is the research question, "What are the components of the phenomenon?"

D: I understand. And the second?

A: Once you've identified the components, it's reasonable to ask the question, "How do these relate to each other?" which is exactly the question answered by a mindmap. It is literally a picture of the mental model of a particular constituency, represented as a system of perceived cause-and-effect relationships.

D: So, the first generic question has to do with describing the elements of the system for a given constituency; the second has to do with the system in which those elements relate to each other; and the third has to do with comparison of different constituencies' systems.

A: Now you're getting the idea. In many ways, the third research question, "How do the mindmaps of different constituencies about the same phenomenon compare to each other?" is the most interesting. In your case, comparing different constituencies' understanding of the meaning of being laid off will probably give you the best insight into efficacy and, very likely, other related components that you haven't even conceptualized yet.

Reflections on Dialogue 4. D has been introduced to the three general forms of research questions that can be addressed by an IQA study:

1. *What are the components of meaning of a phenomenon?* These are called *affinities* in an IQA study. They are the basic building blocks, the elements, of the system that is used to represent the mental map—the picture of meaning—that is a primary product of an IQA study.

2. *How do these affinities relate to each other in a system of perceived influence or cause-and-effect (What is the constituency's mindmap?)?* A system consists of elements (affinities, in the case of IQA) and relationships among them. The relationships are deduced (theoretically coded) by the participants themselves in a process facilitated by the researcher.

3. *How do the mindmaps of constituencies who differ either in terms of experiential distance from, or power over, the phenomenon compare?* It is primarily through the comparison of different constituencies' mindmaps that the researcher gains insight into the meaning of a phenomenon. The assumption underlying this claim is that reality, or meaning, is socially constructed, and that two important factors of social construction are (1) the extent to which a constituency directly experiences the phenomenon (distance) and (2) the extent to which a constituency has power over the phenomenon.

D: Wait a minute. I understand the first two research questions, but why is the third necessary? Why can't I just draw a mindmap for people who deal with being laid off proactively and be done with it?

A: You can, and a lot of research is conducted exactly that way. Actually, a lot of research just answers the first question. Qualitative researchers identify some group of interest, interview the members of the group, do a thematic analysis—we call them affinities—and they're done. That's all right, but let me answer your question with another question.

D: Fine. I'm listening.

A: There's a concept in quantitative research called "discriminant validity" . . . where are you going?

D: *(Walking out the door)* I'm an interpretivist, not some antediluvian positivist. I'm not going to let you poison my mind with outmoded, irrelevant, maybe even immoral positivist quantitative propaganda.

A: Wait and hear me out. You can leave if you don't like what you hear.

D: *(Reluctantly returns to her seat and sits in silence)*

A: I promise not to say either "discriminant" or "validity" ever again. Now . . . suppose I wanted to describe excellent high-tech companies. I identify a group of excellent companies by criteria everybody agrees on; then I study them. I interview. I run focus groups. I observe. Then I synthesize a list of factors all these companies have in common. Suppose one of these is teamwork. What should a reasonable person conclude from my study?

D: That a company ought to use teamwork if it wants to be excellent.

A: A reasonable conclusion, although no thoughtful person would argue that simply having teamwork guarantees excellence. But let me ask you a question: How do you know that lousy companies don't use teamwork?

D: *(Hesitates)* Well, we can assume . . .

A: But as far as your study goes, how do you know?

D: I suppose I really don't.

A: And you don't know because . . . ?

D: Because I didn't study lousy companies.

A: And it would be a stronger argument if you could demonstrate that excellent companies use teamwork and lousy companies don't, wouldn't it.

D: Yes, I suppose it would, although we still can't guarantee that teamwork leads to excellence.

A: Certainly. Now, you're trying to do something a lot more interesting and a lot more challenging than describing what makes for a profitable company. You're trying to understand, from the participant's point of view, why it is that some people deal with traumatic episodes well and, by implication, why others don't. So how should your design reflect this purpose?

D: By comparing those two different people.

A: I agree. Just because we're interpretivists and interested in meaning doesn't mean we can't use some basic principles of research design.

D: Good enough. All I have to do is run a couple of focus groups and do some interviews of two constituencies.

A: Again, that would be all right. But you can do better than just all right. You're interested in making some practical suggestions to organizations about what to expect and how to deal with the issues that are bound to arise in the course of layoffs, aren't you?

D: Of course. I even thought that I might make a career of consulting with companies based on my research findings.

A: Not a bad idea. But if all your findings are just from the point of view of people who have been laid off, isn't that a pretty restricted perspective? Think about distance and power.

D: So, I should talk to some people at the company who deal with layoffs?

A: I think so. You mentioned exit interviewers and counselors at the career centers. These two constituencies are one step removed from the phenomenon, but I suspect they would bring very important insights to your problem statement.

D: I do mindmaps not only for proactive and nonproactive laid-off employees but for exit interviewers and career center counselors as well?

A: Think about the analytical possibilities. You have four different mindmaps. How many two-way comparisons are possible?

D: (Writes the numbers 1 through 4 on a list) I can compare 1 to 2, 1 to 3, 1 to 4, 2 to 3, 2 to 4, and 3 to 4. That makes a total of six.

A: Right. Now, notice that one of these is "intrasubjective" [1 to 2], one is "intraorganizational" [3 to 4], and the other four are "interactions" between the subjective [the point of view of the people closest to the phenomenon; i.e., those who have been laid off] and the organizational [the point of view of representatives of the organization] aspects of your study.

D: I see. My problem statement resolves to these six comparisons, each of which represents a research question. I can use the subjective-organizational-interaction categories to organize my write-up.

A: Excellent. Actually, all we're doing is using the logic behind a factorial analysis of variance design in which we look for main effects and interactions. . . . Oops, I'm sorry. Did I say that out loud? I know, I promised not to use any quantitative language. Please don't leave. Maybe we can continue tomorrow? Hello?

(Door slams)

Reflections on Dialogue 5. In arguing for multiple comparisons, A reflects the assumption of IQA that reality or meaning is socially constructed, and that the researcher's purpose is to (1) capture these multiple meanings at both high and low levels of abstraction, and then to (2) compare and contrast these meanings. Careful consideration should be given to defining the relevant constituencies, using distance and power as criteria. As many meaningful comparisons as are feasible should be made. *Feasible* is an important word, if for no other reason than that the number of potential comparisons increases rapidly (actually, binomially) with the number of constituencies.

Table 4.1 shows this relationship for the first 10 possibilities.

Mathematicians will recognize this relationship as a kind of *mathematical progression,* specifically the one generated by the binomial function. It's not necessary to know this equation, because the number of possible comparisons can easily be determined by simple enumeration. More

Table 4.1

Number of Constituencies	Possible Comparisons
1	None
2	1
3	3
4	6
5	10
6	15
7	21
8	28
9	36
10	45

Table 4.2

Some Constituencies for D's Study: Distance and Power Analysis		
Constituency	Distance	Power (dealing with being laid off)
1. Laid off—proactive	Immediate	Presumably higher than constituency 2, subject to empirical verification
2. Laid off—passive	Immediate	Presumably lower than constituency 1, subject to empirical verification
3. Exit interviewers	One level removed	Low
4. Career center counselors	Two levels removed	Low, but higher than constituency 3

Table 4.3

Comparisons in D's Study	
1 vs. 2	Intersubjective or emic
3 vs. 4	Interorganizational or etic
All others (1 vs. 3–4, 2 vs. 3–4, 3 vs. 4)	Interaction of emic and etic

NOTE: The "emic" and "etic" constructions, which are roughly analogous to Lincoln and Guba's (1985) "ideographic" and "nomothetic" dimensions, are not suggested as universal dimensions arising from the constituency analysis for all studies. The dimension(s) on which constituencies may be arranged depends on the nature of the study.

important is the analytical difficulty presented by a large number of comparisons. The prospect of making a coherent presentation of 45 comparisons (10 mindmaps) is quite daunting, at least for most mortals. This is why A encourages D to conceptualize ways to organize the comparisons. In D's study, considerations of distance and power lead to a loose, but useful, taxonomy of the comparisons into these categories. Tables 4.2 and 4.3 summarize D's design in its current formative stage.

Power/distance analysis offers the researcher a way to judge the potential utility of a constituency for a given problem statement. For example, there would seem to be little to be gained by including a constituency in a study that was both far removed from the phenomenon and had little power over it. The inclusion of particular constituencies is never cut-and-dried, however, especially if the problem statement has an organizational or institutional aspect. The researcher quite often finds that those farthest from the lived experience of the phenomenon of interest are those with the most power over it, which means that constituency selection often involves trade-offs, not to mention a careful consideration of one's philosophical inclinations vis-à-vis the proposed research. A rock-ribbed phenomenologist, for example, might not be at all interested in constituencies that have power over the phenomenon but are at a distance from it. On the other hand, a critical theorist whose interest is in highlighting oppositions, conflicts, and contradictions (one could easily take this kind of approach to D's study) can hardly afford to ignore the power dimension when thinking of constituencies.

Final Reflections

IQA research design is not conceived of as a linear get-it-right-the-first-time process; rather, it is circular in nature, as implied by the process graphic, which is shown once more here, in Figure 4.4.

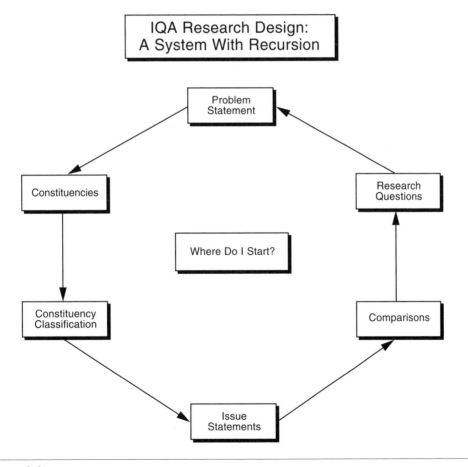

Figure 4.4

While going in circles is a metaphor for getting nowhere, the recursive feature of IQA design allows for successive refinements of each of the following:

Constituencies. "Constituency" is a term reflecting both an interest (perceptual or phenomenological distance) and power over the phenomenon, which is at the center of the problem statement. Who has something to say about the phenomenon? Who can do something about the phenomenon?

Classification of the Constituencies. Regardless of the researcher's epistemological inclinations, sorting out the constituencies in terms of both distance from and power within the phenomenon is a useful design exercise. Some researchers are more interested in distance, others in power; both interests are valid. Distance and power analysis, when used as a component in the system above, helps to ensure consistency among the purpose of the study, the field methods, and the analytical procedures. Does the study address the purpose the researcher wants it to address?

Issues. Different constituencies have different perspectives on the same phenomenon, so the issue statement must be meaningful to each. The issue statement is quite simple and is always a variation of *Tell me about . . .*, but it must be presented in terms that are real to a given constituency.

Comparisons and Research Questions. Comparisons generate research questions. As mentioned before, there are three universal research questions. If only one constituency is involved, two, and only two, questions can be answered from a systems point of view: (1) What are the components of the phenomenon? and (2) How do the components relate to each other as a perceptual system? If more than one constituency comprises the study, a third systemic inquiry is possible: (3) How do the systems compare, both in terms of components, intrasystemic relationships, and intersystemic relationships? By addressing the three research questions, the researcher finds meaning in the constituencies' multiple meanings.

Congenital Deformities. Many studies are congenitally deformed in one of two ways:

1. The research questions can't be answered by the data or observations either because the wrong observations were made or because the data cannot be analyzed in a manner relevant to the questions.

2. The research questions can be answered, but nobody cares.

Avoiding Analytical Disconnects. Any experienced researcher can articulate research questions. Developing research questions that adequately address a more transcendent problem, however, is much more difficult. It is remarkably easy to complete a study based on research questions that seemed perfectly adequate at the time but turned out to be superficial and irrelevant after all was said and done. This unfortunate situation is a result of an analytical disconnect between problem statement and research questions, which in turn is a result of misunderstanding the multi-element recursive nature of the system that represents research design.

Following the IQA research design cycle with fidelity, scholarship, and intellectual honesty reduces the likelihood of either of these congenital defects. Research questions comprise the problem statement, and it is at this point that the power of the IQA hermeneutical circle becomes evident.

Induction, Deduction, and Recursion: Getting It Right. Forming the original version of the problem statement is largely *inductive* or, if you will, intuitive, which is one reason why many writers do not have much to say about how to form problem statements. Another reason for the paucity of comment on this topic in the literature is that the recursive interaction between induction and deduction in the research design process seems to be largely unrecognized. By the time one reaches the stage of generating research questions, *deduction* is the primary analytical tool. Generating (a term that implies a machinelike "grinding it out," which is a fair way to characterize deduction) research questions once constituencies have been defined is deductive, which is to say a fixed number of constituencies always results in a given number of comparisons. Which is *not* to say that all possible comparisons are equally attractive to the researcher. At this point, the researcher shifts back into inductive mode and selects, by whatever intuitive criteria, the comparisons that seem most appropriate to satisfying that feeling of unease that created the original version of the problem statement. Having selected a set of comparisons, which directly reflect a set of research questions, the researcher then asks two critical questions:

1. If I answer these research questions, what purpose will be served (what problem statement is addressed by these questions)?

2. Is the answer to the first question satisfactory to me and to members of my discipline?

If the answer to the second question is "no," and usually it is during early recursions through the cycle, then the researcher proceeds around the cycle again, *but starting with the revised problem statement that was the answer to question 1.* With successive recursions, the vague outcome, which the researcher (like D in our dialogues) intuited in the first place, should become more and more precise. Each new (and, one hopes, better) version of the problem statement demands that we reconsider the other elements: constituencies, power and distance, issues, comparisons, and research questions. Successive recursions around the cycle, each of which produces a new problem statement, must ultimately produce one of two conditions: Either the researcher is satisfied with the design or the researcher drops out of the cycle and goes on to other activities, such as resuming relationships and getting a life.

Theoretical Sidebar: Aesthetics and IQA. The positivists, in their desire to be more scientific than the scientists, may have erred in attempting to divorce issues of knowing from issues of value (specifically, axiology and aesthetics). IQA presumes that these dimensions of meaning are inextricably interwoven and, as usual, takes a systems view. This view is best illustrated by telling a story:

In the fall of 2003, the very successful southwestern artist Amado Peña spoke on the topic of creativity to a group of doctoral candidates in the Community College Leadership Program (CCLP) at the University of Texas at Austin. In the ensuing discussion session, many of the students asked variations of Cole Porter's question: "How do you do that voodoo that only you do?" Rather than responding, as many creative people would, with a roll of the eyes and a shrug to indicate the futility of answering such an obtuse question, Peña, a teacher to the bone, engaged the students in a long and spirited dialogue about the nature of creativity and, in doing so, revealed a very succinct and coherent value system that underlies his body of work. The author, a silent participant in this discussion, conducted a real-time affinity analysis of Peña's comments and discovered that the artist continually asked himself two questions during the process of producing a painting:

1. Do I think this idea (or painting, as the work progresses) is good, never mind what anybody else thinks?

2. Will this painting, when viewed by others, bring them joy?

Peña's theory of aesthetics is a breathtakingly elegant dialectic: He is no precious self-absorbed tortured artist, because he is always thinking of those who view his work. On the other hand, he is no hack who paints anything that will sell, because he is always interrogating himself about the quality of the work judged by his own lights.

Perhaps Peña was simply being polite when asked if these two questions summarized his aesthetic theory, but he seemed to agree enthusiastically, and one presumes the analysis at least did no great violence to his ideas. In responding to the analysis, Peña made his position clear: "If, at any point in the process, the answer to either of these questions is 'No,' then I improve it [the work] or move on to something else."

The "Peña Aesthetic Decision Tree" is analogous to the two questions the IQA research design process poses at the end of every recursion. Like

Peña, the researcher asks two questions of value (or of "beauty" in the intellectual sense), suggesting that the gulf between research, especially in the design stage, and art is not so great after all.

CASE EXAMPLE

In this and subsequent chapters, case material will be provided so that by the end of the book, an entire project will have been designed, implemented, and documented. The case study in each chapter is designed to demonstrate a particular stage of an IQA study. Each chapter covers, in detail, the section of the research flow just outlined.

Background

By the fall of 2001, the concept of IQA had matured to the point that a text containing theoretical and applied material, and an integrated set of interactive instructional materials on CD-ROM, were ready for more extensive field testing. Prior to this time, IQA concepts were presented using traditional techniques, such as lectures, demonstrations, small-group work, and case studies. Little or no use had been made of communications technology such as email; nor was the course organized to exploit the capabilities of current technologies, such as office productivity applications (Microsoft Word and Excel with associated graphics capabilities), specialized concept-mapping software (Inspiration), statistical software (SPSS), or interactive computer-driven instructional software. In other words, as is often the case, the course had evolved rather than developed.

The IQA course—offered to doctoral students as a research methods course in the College of Education at the University of Texas at Austin—was designed and constructed on systematic principles of instructional design. Briefly, the features of the new version of the course were as follows:

1. Goals and student performance objectives were written first, along with ways to measure performance and to give students feedback regarding progress.

2. Activities and evaluation materials were developed next. The nature of a particular activity determined whether it would be included in the text itself or would be presented as an interactive computer-mediated exercise on CD-ROM.

3. Material for the textbook was subsequently written to coordinate with the performance objectives and the activities. The text contained

both theoretical or conceptual sections, as well as "how-to" chapters that
were primarily expository or demonstrative in nature. Applications of the
IQA theory or procedures requiring step-by-step development and feedback
to the student were assigned to the interactive CD-ROM system.

4. All materials in prototype form were available the first day of the
IQA class for fall 2001, including a detailed instructor manual with lesson
plans for each of the 15 sessions, multimedia presentations, classroom
activities, and testing exercises. Students were provided with a draft of the
text and an interactive CD-ROM.

The Problem: First Recursion

The initial description of the purpose of the study was as follows: *To
develop and field-test an integrated IQA curriculum.*

Identifying Constituents: First Recursion

The following potential constituencies were identified:

❖ Administrators
❖ Instructional designers
❖ Students
❖ Teachers

A closer look suggested that subgroups were necessary to help define
the constituents. They were identified as follows:

❖ Administrators
  – Department heads or principals

❖ Instructional designers
  – Who design courses for an instructor to teach
  – Teachers who design their own courses

❖ Students
  – Who have taken a traditional course
  – Who have taken an instructionally designed course

❖ Teachers
  – Who teach with a traditional class style
  – Who teach from an instructionally designed instructor manual

Constituencies were then classified along lines of power and distance
from the phenomenon as shown in the following Power/Distance Analysis
(see Table 4.4).

Table 4.4

Constituency	Continuum
Students	Closest to the phenomenon Least power to effect change Receivers
Instructional Designers	Some distance from the phenomenon Some power to effect change Mediators
Teachers Administrators	Farthest from the phenomenon Most power to effect change Creators

Identifying Issue Statements: First Recursion

The next step was to identify issue statements that could be asked of each group that would reflect some light on the problem.

❖ Administrators
   – Tell me about resources devoted to instructional design of curriculum.
   – Tell me about students who go through traditional classes.
   – Tell me about students who go through instructionally designed classes.
   – Tell me about teachers who teach traditional classes.
   – Tell me about teachers who teach instructionally designed classes.

❖ Instructional designers
   – Tell me about designing courses.
   – Tell me about designing multimedia integrated courses.
   – Tell me about how you design your class (teachers).
   – Tell me about traditional classrooms.
   – Tell me about students who have gone through a multimedia integrated course designed by you.
   – Tell me about students who have gone through a traditional course designed by you.

❖ Students
   – Tell me about your experience in the class.

❖ Teachers
   – Tell me about your class.

Identifying Comparisons: First Recursion

If provided with all of the necessary resources, including unlimited time, each constituency would have been analyzed and compared to all the others. Because neither time nor resources were unlimited, the first question to be addressed was, "If I could talk to only one group, to whom would I talk?" Because the first recursion of the problem statement implied a comparison, it became clear that a two-constituency design would be required at a minimum. Students in a traditional classroom, and those in an instructionally designed course, are closest to the phenomenon and would probably have the most insight into the phenomenon. Administrators, though they would have something to say about the matter, are far removed from the classroom and may not be the best option to address the problem.

Because it appeared that a two-student constituency design was the best compromise, the first research question seemed clear: *What are the differences between how students perceive their experiences in the traditional class and in the instructionally designed course?*

Other questions could have been addressed had it been possible to include other constituencies in the design. Research question possibilities included:

- ❖ How do instructional designers and teachers differ in their approach to developing courses?
- ❖ How do teachers perceive support from administrators and how do the administrators categorize their support?
- ❖ Do teachers who teach with one method have different experiences than those who teach with the other?

Identifying Research Questions: First Recursion

A study involving two student constituencies, one participating in a technology-integrated IQA curriculum and the other in a more traditional approach to teaching IQA, yielded four research questions, as follows (recall that systems theory suggests that we can ask questions about elements and relationships of a system and can compare systems if we have more than one constituency):

1. What factors comprise students' perceptions of, and reactions to, the IQA course?

2. How do these factors relate to each other in a perceived system of influence or cause and effect?

3. How does the individual's experience compare to that of the group as a whole?

4. How do the two groups' experiences compare to each other?

The Problem: Final Recursion

The goal was not just to outline a research method but also to develop a curriculum with the students' needs in mind, one that contained both theoretical and applied material. Those interested in theory could delve into the more esoteric sections, but those not so theoretically inclined could still benefit from the chapters that were more oriented to the "nuts and bolts" of research. Students completing the text, CD, and classroom exercises should have a thorough understanding of the mechanics of IQA, as well as a foundation in the concepts of research. Students should feel comfortable with the method and should see utility in IQA and relevance to their academic and professional careers. Therefore, a usability study was designed to evaluate the effectiveness of the course and the course materials (by no coincidence, this design also provided an excellent dissertation topic). All of these considerations, enlightened by the original version of the purpose and the "generic" systemic research questions, led to a final set of research questions:

1. Can IQA be applied to instructional systems evaluation, and what would be the nature and conclusions drawn from such an evaluation? In other words, if IQA were as robust a concept as claimed, could IQA itself be used to evaluate a course whose subject is IQA?

2. Would students exposed to two different approaches to teaching IQA have different experiences in learning how to do IQA research, and what are the implications of any such differences for the instructional design of the course?

3. No matter the method of instruction, what do students think of IQA as a research methodology?

In the fall of 2001, two sections of the IQA course were offered; one was taught the usual way by the instructor (except that the draft text materials comprised the text for the course); the other (taught by the same instructor) used the integrated system just described. IQA itself would be used as the evaluation process to examine differential experiences between the two classes; that is, IQA (as a research process) would be used to evaluate IQA (as an instructional offering).

The Problem Statement: Final Recursion

The purpose of this study, as reflected in the threefold problem statement just given, was:

1. To develop a systematic description from the students' point of view of participation in two different modes of presentation in a graduate qualitative research methods class (IQA)

2. To determine the feasibility and utility of using the IQA approach as a method of evaluating instructional design

Summary

By recursing through the IQA research design process (see Figure 4.1), a large number of constituencies were reduced to two student groups based on the results of a power/distance analysis and in consideration of logistical constraints. Reducing the number of constituencies and the accompanying issue statements also changed the number and nature of comparisons, which in turn affected the research questions, which in turn resulted in a revised understanding and description of the problem statement. This case will continue at the end of the next chapter.

Group Reality 5

System Elements

Interactive Qualitative Analysis (IQA) data collection/analysis techniques originated from Total Quality Management (TQM) techniques, which were designed to capture knowledge from organizational members to solve problems and improve industrial processes. A major TQM assumption is that people who are closest to the job best understand what is wrong and how to fix it. Similarly, IQA data collection techniques assist members of a group close to a phenomenon of interest in describing and labeling their experiences, and in articulating perceived relationships among these experiences to produce a *theory in perception* or a *conceptual map*[1] (collective, in the case of a focus group, and individual, in the case of an interview), which is a systems representation of how a person or a group understands a particular phenomenon. This system consists of categories of meaning called *affinities* and the perceived causal relationships among the affinities.

Affinities: The Building Blocks of Mindmaps

The first step in creating a mindmap is to assist the focus group members in organizing their thoughts into a manageable number of categories or *affinities—sets of textual references that have an underlying common meaning or theme,* synonymous to *factors* or *topics.* During affinity production, the constituents are given an opportunity to reflect on their experiences and then express their thoughts and feelings. The thoughts of the group as a whole are combined and organized into common themes or affinities by the group itself with the aid of a facilitator. The group collectively names the affinities and helps the researcher create a detailed written description or definition of each affinity. The goal is to produce the smallest number of affinities with the greatest amount of detail or "richness."

Affinities and Variables: A Rough Analogy

Similarities. An affinity is similar to the quantitative concept of a variable: Both are homogeneous—they are reflections of one thing or construct. Both have a range, which is to say that just as a variable must exist in at least two states in order to vary, an affinity must have a range of meaning in order to be useful. As a consequence, an affinity should have, within the limits of practicality, only one unit of analysis: An affinity should be about people, apples, or alligators, but not people, apples, and alligators.

Differences. The analogy between affinities and variables breaks down when pressed too far. The first difference between the two is created by the need to operationalize variables; affinities, being conceptually "looser" than variables but by the same token more robust, do not labor under the constraints of the strict rules of operationalization and measurability. As a consequence, affinities do not suffer nearly as much from the single greatest limitation on variables created by the need to operationalize. Variables often are "trivial" signifiers in that they contain too little of the construct to be signified and too much of other constructs that have little or nothing to do with the signified. Because they are constructed of the thoughts and by the words of those close to the phenomenon of interest, affinities tend to be richer and more meaningful.

A second and perhaps even more significant distinction between affinities and variables is *the ability of affinities,* in concert with a systems understanding of relationships, *to represent dialectical unities,* a task at which variables fail miserably. Variables represent simple monotonic relationships quite well; indeed, many affinities are of this kind: For example, "Emotions" may be understood by a focus group as running the gamut from unpleasant to pleasant, or from maladaptive to adaptive, or along any useful continuum. If it were feasible to operationalize this affinity, a variable would result.

On the other hand, many categories of meaning are not well represented by simple bipolar monotonic constructs, an argument that anthropologists, ethnographers, and other kinds of qualitative researchers have effectively made time and again. For example, *Growth,* in the sense of intellectual growth, could be conceptualized as a simple variable, however elegantly operationalized, ranging from some low value to a high value. But a focus group of graduate students may (as one group in the case study of this text did), through their analysis and discussions, come to realize that they constructed *Growth* as a dialectic consisting of two opposites, both of which were essential to the unity of meaning they called *Learning*. The students named the opposites *Confusion* and *Clarity*. They came to understand that *Confusion* was necessary for *Clarity*, which in turn was necessary to prepare for the next state of *Confusion*. Recursion (not iteration, mind you, which implies no interaction between the two opposites or simply going in circles) from *Confusion* to *Clarity* to *Confusion* and back again was, they recognized, the very process of *Growth*. Therefore, the focus group constructed an affinity called *Growth*, which was composed of two dialectically opposite subaffinities, *Confusion* and *Clarity*.

One might argue that growth, considered in light of this discussion, is nothing more than a variable ranging from *Confusion* at one pole to *Clarity* at the other. Such a metaphor misses the point by implying that in order to grow, either *Confusion* (or, less intuitively, *Clarity*) must be maximized at the expense of the other. The dialectical representation of *Growth*, however, suggests that for *Growth* to occur, there must be a constant and dynamic interaction or tension between the two polar opposites comprising the greater unity; furthermore, just as one force is at its greatest, it sows the seeds of its opposite.

To summarize the example, the contrasting representations of *Growth* as a variable on the one hand and as a dialectic on the other may be diagrammed, as shown in Figure 5.1.

The arrow is the understanding if *Growth* is represented by a *variable;* the dialectical symbol below the arrow is the understanding of *Growth* if it is represented as an *affinity*. The dialectical diagram is hardly original to this book; it is obviously a simple adaptation of the ancient Yin-Yang mandala that has been used by Eastern philosophies for millennia to represent reality.

This chapter outlines and describes how focus group processes are used in IQA to identify the elements of a systemic portrait of a particular group reality. Protocols for data collection or construction (depending on one's epistemological inclination) are outlined. A second section on group data analysis or coding follows that describes IQA group coding protocols and situates these procedures within a specific epistemological theory.

The Power of Naming: Constructing Affinities

The listing that follows provides a concise overview of these steps involved, from the facilitator's point of view, in constructing affinities. The process is covered in detail in the ensuing sections of this chapter.

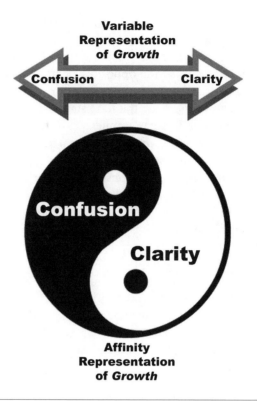

Figure 5.1

ACTIONS

.   **Prerequisites (see Chapter 4)**

1. Draft research questions.

2. Produce an issue statement.

3. Identify the focus group.

4. Gather tools (see list on page 85).

During the Focus Group

5. Convene the group and conduct an orientation.

6. Conduct the warm-up exercise and state the issue.

7. Facilitate the silent nominal process.

8. Tape all the cards to the wall.

9. Facilitate the clarification of meaning.

10. Ask the focus group to silently cluster cards by theme.

11. Guide the affinity analysis.
    a. Facilitate affinity naming.
    b. Facilitate inductive, axial, and theoretical coding.
    c. Facilitate procedures for attaining consensus as needed.

12. Document affinities and subaffinities.

TOOLS

1. 5 × 8 index cards (about 25 per participant)

2. Marking pens for each participant

3. Masking tape

4. Available wall space or bulletin boards

5. Tape recorder, tapes, and batteries

Designing the Focus Group

Focus Group Equals Constituency. IQA studies usually begin with a focus group. As stated in Chapter 3, a focus group is a group of people who share some common experience, work or live within come common structure, or have a similar background; this implies that the researcher should think first about commonalities rather than differences when designing the composition of the group.

Two Different Masters. Too often the purpose of a focus group, which is to capture the perception of a phenomenon by a group of people who all have something important in common vis-à-vis the phenomenon (i.e., a constituency), is confused with the purpose of random sampling, which is to obtain a representative sample of a highly variable population. The two are usually at odds, and the researcher who tries to satisfy the demands of both masters at the same time will satisfy neither. Once constituencies have been defined, consideration may be given to random sampling, but only after the first master has been well served.

Preparing for Comparing. IQA focus groups are formed with groups of individuals who may certainly have varied opinions and experiences with the system under study, but who more critically share a common perspective (see the discussion of distance and power as the defining characteristics of a constituency in Chapter 4). For example, if distance and power analysis suggests that gender is an important factor in the construction of the phenomenon, then it would be a mistake to run a single focus group with both men and women. Although affinities and relationships can surely be articulated by such a group, the "system" that results will very likely be ill-defined, consisting of turgid affinities and feeble links between the affinities that result from an attempt to achieve compromise between two different realities. A much better strategy would be to run two different focus groups by gender, presenting the same issue to each, and then to compare the two systems. This second approach is much better justified from a theoretical point of view in two ways:

1. The concept of a constituency suggests that representatives of different constituencies should not be aggregated because of differences in either distance from the phenomenon or power over the phenomenon.

2. Comparison, as grounded theory reminds us time and again, is our primary process for constructing meaning, both as a "subject" and as a researcher. IQA takes this presumption seriously by encouraging as many formal comparisons of systems as is appropriate.

Invidious and Insidious Comparisons

It is on the issue of comparisons that many of our students balk. Some contend that comparisons are nothing more than a manifestation of Foucault's concept of The Other and therefore inevitably result in the marginalization or subjugation of one group by the other. Other students are more interested in "pure description" and are disturbed by the prospect that formal comparisons will take them too far afield from their desire to describe a phenomenon in rich detail. Yet others are troubled because the business of formal systemic comparisons simply strikes them as too positivistic and, therefore, hopelessly naïve.

Beware the Stealth Comparison

With the possible exception of the accusation of naïveté, these reservations are understandable and have merit. The reply to these and similar concerns, however, is that although IQA comparisons are arguably invidious (depending on their use), they at least are not insidious. All description points to other descriptions, which, in turn, point to others. In other words, meaning comes from comparisons, whether implicit or explicit. In a very real sense, there is no such thing as "pure" description, and those who make such a claim are simply and perhaps unknowingly substituting implicit comparisons for explicit. Even granting the rather extreme premise that all comparisons are invidious, are not insidious comparisons even more dangerous?

Some Practical Design Suggestions. Focus group representation should include 12 to 20 members who have the following characteristics:

- ❖ They are *information rich,* possessing knowledge of, and experience with, the issue.
- ❖ They have the ability to reflect on the question and to transfer those thoughts into words.
- ❖ They have the time and inclination to participate in the study.
- ❖ They are homogeneous with respect to important dimensions of distance and power.
- ❖ They can respect and practice group dynamics—they are neither overpowering nor too timid to speak.

Although the researcher may be tempted to use fewer than 12 participants in a focus group, usually because of logistics of getting certain groups together or the constituent base is very small, every attempt should be made to avoid using smaller focus groups. Smaller groups are not as serious a problem during affinity production but can skew data when it comes theoretical coding. Theoretical coding will be addressed in detail in Chapter 6, but note that a focus group of five participants would mean that one person can influence the data by 20 percent.

Another important aspect of focus group development is that of time. The typical IQA focus group session will take three to four hours to complete. As noted earlier, it is vital to recruit constituents who understand, and will commit to, this time demand. Convincing 12 or more people to gather for more than three hours is not always an easy sell. But the work put into the front-end recruitment and confirmation of participants pays off in spades during the affinity production phase. It is helpful for the researcher to illustrate the "what's in it for me" incentive to potential focus group members during the recruitment process.

Focus Group Facilitation: Preparing to Conduct a Focus Group Exercise

In the case study introduced earlier, a problem was identified, constituencies were determined, and relevant questions for the constituencies were written in the form of issue statements, setting the stage for affinity production and analysis. During the focus group process, the group discusses the issue openly and in considerable depth, so the researcher/facilitator is too busy to take many notes. An assistant facilitator is useful to help with the logistics of the process, and tape-recording the sessions is recommended as well. The facilitator should come to the focus group with preprinted forms and tables used to organize and code data. These materials will be discussed in detail in the next chapter.

With the focus group formed, the researcher introduces the group to the nature of the research and to the problem statement. The researcher should put the group at ease by briefly explaining the process through which they are about to participate. The focus group must be made aware that they are free to express their thoughts without penalty, their identity will be protected, and no reprisals will occur due to their participation. The researcher should make clear to the group how the tape recorder will be used to prepare a transcript, how the transcript will be used, and how confidentiality will be protected.

Warm-Up Exercises: Some Variations

The warm-up exercise is designed to clear the mind of all thoughts except the issue at hand, and to prime the group participants' thoughts about the issue statement. The facilitator presents the issue statement to the group members and then gives them a reasonable time to consider the topic by engaging them in a warm-up exercise. Warm-ups may be modified to fit individual situations, but we have found several variations to be useful:

Standard Warm-Up. Following a procedure that is typical of more "traditional" focus group protocols, the facilitator leads a group discussion about the issue. Depending on the issue, a list of subissues or important questions may be used (much like a standard focus group protocol) to generate discussion. The facilitator may record key concepts or phrases that come up in the discussion on a flip chart. As sheets are filled with remarks, they become a reference to be used as a reference by group members during the silent nominal phase that follows.

Context-Specific Visual Stimuli. Floyd-Bann (2001), in her investigation of the influence of media on body image, used images of female models taken from women's magazines to serve as a stimulus for discussion and reflection prior to the nominal group process. The same stimulus and discussion protocol was used to produce and compare mindmaps of women who were at risk for eating disorders to those who were not, and to draw inferences about how the two groups arrived at radically different meanings from media messages about body image (note the use of a formal comparison, which is highly desirable).

Ambiguous Visual Stimuli. Another useful variation of the warm-up exercise is borrowed from the use of projective techniques in psychotherapy such as the Rorschach and the Thematic Apperception Test. In this alternative, about a dozen color photographs of people in different situations are mounted on a board (or shown on a large slide), and participants are asked to select a picture in response to a question posed by the facilitator and to discuss why they selected the picture. The pictures themselves are relatively ambiguous, which is to say they are simply selected at random from magazines or other media. Participants project their meaning onto the picture they select and, in the process of describing why they picked a particular picture, generate thoughts, reflections, and images that serve as grist for the nominal process mill. An example: Kallendorf and Speer (Delta Associates, 1995), in a proprietary study of the communications patterns of an orthopedics manufacturing company, presented a display containing a dozen pictures of ordinary people in everyday communications activities to a cross-section of employees, who were then asked to identify two pictures: the one most representing communication at the company and the one least representing communication at the company. Results were tallied (there was remarkably little variance), and focus group participants explained their choices and discussed them with others. In a subsequent meeting with upper management, the same process was followed. After the executives had discussed their choices, the results from employees, together with examples of the explanations given by them, were shown for the first time to the executives.[2]

Guided Imagery. It has often been said that we experience and understand life as drama. Consequently, this variation exploits the human capability of constructing narratives as a way to understand experience. Guided imagery is valuable in evoking affective dimensions of the phenomenon, and is especially appropriate when the issue statement can be portrayed as a scenario or in episodic form. Participants are asked to close their eyes and relax by taking deep breaths and putting aside thoughts about the day. The facilitator then "tells a story" that portrays the issue in episodic form and invites participants to recall their experiences relative to the issue, reminding them to remember the words, phrases, mental pictures, or other memories of experiences. For example: In his investigation of the meaning of health and development to college freshmen, Laird (2001) first showed the focus group several slides containing descriptions of the components of health, such as mental, emotional, and social. He then showed a slide displaying behaviors relevant to health, such as drinking, smoking, and exercise. Participants were then taken on a "mental tour" of their first-semester college experience, starting with the first day they arrived on campus, and given several moments to reflect on their mental and emotional state early in their first semester and to think about the impact these new experiences had on their health. Using major milestones in academic life (midterms, big football games, etc.), he continued the tour through the second semester (the current semester for the students), asking them to recall incidents, people, and places that influenced their health and to think of ways they may have changed "when it comes to your health and 'you' as a person."

Architecture and Warm-Ups: The Same Principles Apply

The manner in which the issue statement is presented to the group must be considered in the light of the research purpose and questions, but the Guided Imagery variation has been found to be quite successful in practice. The following are some suggestions for the facilitator that are relevant to all the variations but pertain to the Guided Imagery protocol in particular:

1. The facilitator must be familiar enough with the phenomenon prior to convening a focus group so that a chronology (or the major structural features) of the phenomenon can be presented in a short time (typically not longer than five minutes) in language that makes sense to the participants. Preliminary interviews by the facilitator may be required. For example, in preparing for a focus group of seminary students on the issue of their concerns about their first pastorate, the author interviewed two experienced pastors and two current seminary students about the structure, timing, and events of the seminary experience leading up to the first pastorate position. This material was formatted into a chronology that took the participants (none of whom had yet finished seminary) on a mental "tour" of the latter years of seminary and subsequently through a hypothetical "First Call," which is the seminary term for the first job offer from a congregation to a new graduate.

2. The purpose of the Guided Imagery form of the issue statement is to help participants clear their minds and focus on the phenomenon. The Guided Imagery exercise is not an extensive interview protocol; nor is it an opportunity for the facilitator to engage in a long lecture on the subject.

3. When in doubt, the facilitator should error on the side of ambiguity and generality rather than in the direction of specificity.

4. The tone should be neutral. The facilitator should avoid "leading" characterizations, either positive or negative, as part of the Guided Imagery.

5. In developing the Guided Imagery form of the issue statement, the facilitator should follow the advice of Mies Van Der Rohe: "Less is More."

A sample of how to conduct this exercise is shown in Table 5.1.

Table 5.1 Sample Guided Imagery Warm-Up Exercise

Brief summary. In a few minutes, I am going to ask you to tell me about your experience with *the phenomenon.*

- ❖ To begin, try to get as comfortable as you can.
- ❖ Close your eyes.
- ❖ Putting aside your thoughts of the day, take a deep cleansing breath.
- ❖ Now imagine yourself *in the environment of the phenomenon.* (long pause)
- ❖ See yourself engaging in the activities of *the phenomenon.* (long pause)
- ❖ Notice your surroundings. (long pause) Looking around you, take in the sights and sounds that are associated with being *in the environment of the phenomenon.* (long pause)
- ❖ Allow yourself to become aware of your environment with all of your senses.
- ❖ Focus on what it feels like to be totally absorbed *in the environment of the phenomenon.* Be there in your mind. (long pause)

Now, tell me about *the phenomenon.*

Reflect on all the thoughts you had concerning *the phenomenon.*

Write these thoughts down on the cards.

Write one thought or one experience per card, using words, phrases, sentences, or pictures.

Brainstorming the Rudiments of Meaning

Following the warm-up exercise, the facilitator invites focus group members to participate in a group brainstorming session. Group processes encourage the maximum production of individual thoughts, feelings, and ideas, yet create a coherent group construction disparate these individual realities.

Individuals silently "brainstorm" by writing individual thoughts and reflections on index cards. The group is given time (approximately 10 minutes) to record these thoughts in single words, short phrases, or even diagrams that come to mind regarding the issue statement. Each participant is given a black marker and approximately 25 5 × 8 cards, and asked to write down one thought per card. Focus group members are encouraged to produce as many cards as they wish.

Silence and privacy reduce undue influence by peers in the focus group or by the facilitator. It is important that the process is conducted in silence so that discussion does not influence individual responses. This prevents hierarchical influences and domineering tendencies by members of the focus group, and thus ensures authenticity and individuality of thoughts and reflection about the issue statement.

THE FACILITATOR SHOULD:

❖ Provide suggestions that participants refrain from censoring their thoughts or responses, and help them feel that they are in a comfortable and safe environment, easing the task of the data production and participatory research. Examples of suggestions include, "All thoughts are OK." "Don't analyze; just write." "No one will criticize your thinking."

❖ Provide directions, such as, "Write as many thoughts from your experience as you can, one per card until you have exhausted your ideas or until I ask everyone to stop."

❖ Monitor the group, calling an end to the process when it appears the participants have had an opportunity to generate a *satisfying* number of responses. There is no prescribed time for the silent nominal process. When they have stopped writing, it is time to proceed to the next step.

ADVANTAGES OF THE SILENT BRAINSTORMING PROCESS INCLUDE:

❖ Minimizes group pressure to respond in an influenced, rather than authentic, manner.

❖ Provides introverts with private time to think and generate ideas in the group processes.

❖ Generates a large amount of data, as opposed to verbal brainstorming, which often causes a group to follow a single train of thought or conversation.

DISADVANTAGES OF THE SILENT BRAINSTORMING PROCESS INCLUDE:

❖ Extroverts who do not do their best thinking silently may be frustrated at this first stage.

❖ Group members may feel vulnerable due to the lack of conversation cues.

❖ A leader skilled in facilitation is required, especially after the first round of card generation during the naming and coding phases.

Facilitator's Role and Functions

The primary role of the facilitator is to serve as a process guide focusing the group on the work of creating and organizing the ideas created during the brainstorming session. In order to accomplish this, the facilitator performs myriad functions including, but not limited to, the following:

- ❖ Sets the brainstorming agenda, proposing a series of steps toward the end product
- ❖ Manages the discussion, adhering to time constraints by pacing the discussions
- ❖ Remains neutral, maintaining objectivity while keeping to the background
- ❖ Intervenes only in the process, not content, and has no vested interest in the outcome
- ❖ Promotes understanding among members of the group
- ❖ Maximizes full participation, drawing out responses
- ❖ Minimizes dominance and interruptions of team members
- ❖ Develops trust and rapport
- ❖ Maintains focus and minimizes disruptive side discussions
- ❖ Demonstrates professionalism and tact
- ❖ Steers the group in a positive direction, showing knowledge of the process
- ❖ Displays a sense of humor

It becomes evident that a group facilitator should be competent in the skills of organization, listening, observation, analysis, systems thinking, questioning and probing, and using good judgment and discretion during the process. Kayser (1995) summarizes the role of the facilitator quite succinctly:

> In the purest sense, when wearing the "facilitator's hat" an individual acts as a neutral servant of the people. By that I mean the person focuses on guiding without directing; bringing about action without disruption; helping people self-discover new approaches and solutions to problems; knocking down walls which have been built between people while preserving structures of value; and, above all, appreciating people as people. All of this must be done without leaving any fingerprints. (p. 12)

Clarification of Meaning

After the silent nominal group process, the focus group members are instructed to tape the index cards on the wall in rows and columns where everyone can view them. During the course of a group discussion, the facilitator guides participants in clarifying their understanding of the responses on each card to eliminate any ambiguity and vagueness associated with the meanings of the words or phrases.

The data clarification process continues as the research facilitator, or one of the group members, reads each response out loud for the entire group to consider. The purpose is to arrive at a socially constructed, shared meaning of each card among members of the group. The purpose is also to reduce any vagueness or ambiguity associated with the meaning of the words or phrases on the cards. Each participant of the focus group reflects on every card to achieve clarity and consensus on the meanings of the words. Even though each card was written by an individual, the anonymous author has no more claim to the meaning of the card than any other group member does; therefore, anyone in the group can offer an opinion about the meaning of a particular card.

After the clarification conversation, the participants may choose to add more reflections and thoughts to the original body of index cards. The facilitator encourages any further production of responses and a second clarification discussion, if necessary, to ensure that the responses reflect the individual and shared experiences of the group members relative to the issue statement.

ADVANTAGES OF THE CLARIFICATION PROCESS:

❖ The discussion creates a more full-bodied understanding of the written comments and a shared understanding of the responses.

❖ The discussion engages participants who need to interact to gather their thoughts and prompts additional data to be produced.

DISADVANTAGES OF THE CLARIFICATION PROCESS:

❖ Individuals who are attached to specific definitions can disengage if the group constructs a different understanding of a response.

❖ Participants may grow impatient and begin clustering ideas prematurely.

Affinity Analysis:
The Logic of Inductive and Axial Coding

Because IQA analysis derives from a formal epistemological theory, we must leave the practical world for a moment and first examine some concepts underlying the IQA focus group procedure. After the following sidebar, we will resume the discussion of conducting a focus group.

Theoretical Sidebar: A Definition of Coding. IQA focus groups begin to analyze the data generated during brainstorming in three successive and recursive steps:

1. *Clarification,* in which the group adopts a shared meaning for each card

2. *Clustering,* in which cards with similar meanings are arranged into groups and given names

3. *Refining,* in which the names given to groups of cards (affinities) are critiqued by members of the focus group in the context of the other affinities. Often, affinities also are broken down into sub-affinities at this stage.

These three processes are known collectively as "affinity analysis" and involve the first two (of three) kinds of IQA coding. Coding is a common process in qualitative research, but it can be mysterious to the novice researcher, which is not surprising considering that many sources don't ever seem to define the term.

Coding is the name given by qualitative researchers to describe *the way in which text is represented by abstractions.* Coding demands both induction and deduction, but this requirement is not often evident in many discussions of coding; rather, it almost seems as if many qualitative researchers are wary of using the language of logic, perhaps fearing that if they do, their colleagues will label them with the red "P" of positivism.[3] Nevertheless, both logical operations are unavoidable in qualitative analysis (and synthesis), which is exactly the point: Although many researchers use the word "analysis" to represent the entire range of intellectual activity comprising critical thinking, both deduction (analysis, approximately) and induction (synthesis, also approximately) are appropriate at different stages of research.

If anything distinguishes the qualitative researcher from other breeds, it is their concern for how humans make meaning, which suggests that one's coding system ought to be consistent with one's theory of meaning. John Dewey (1910) long ago quite effectively expressed the relationship between logical processes and meaning:

The characteristic outcome of thinking we saw to be the organization of facts and conditions, which, just as they stand, are isolated, fragmentary, and discrepant, the organization being effected through the introduction of connecting links, or middle terms. The facts as they stand are the data, the raw material of reflection; their lack of coherence perplexes and stimulates to reflection. There follows the suggestion of some meaning, which, if it can be substantiated, will give a whole in which various fragmentary and seemingly incompatible data find their proper place. The meaning suggested supplies a mental platform, an intellectual point of view, from which to note and define the data more carefully, to seek additional observations, and to institute, experimentally, changed conditions. Back and forth between facts and meanings. *There is thus a double movement in all reflection:* movement from the given partial and confused data to a suggested comprehensive (or inclusive) entire situation; and back from this suggested whole—which as suggested is a meaning, an idea—to the particular facts, so as to connect these with one another and with additional facts to which the suggestion has directed attention. *Roughly speaking, the first of these movements is inductive; the second deductive.* A complete act of thought involves both—it involves, that is, a fruitful interaction of observed (or recollected) particular considerations and of inclusive and far-reaching (general) meanings (*italics added*).

The postmodern reader might squirm a bit at phrases such as "the facts as they stand" and "to institute, experimentally, changed conditions," but we have to remember that Dewey wrote this in 1910 and was not the beneficiary of today's enlightened critical analysis. Yet Dewey got it right when he contended that "a complete act of thought involves both [induction and deduction] . . . a fruitful interaction of observed (or recollected [or reconstructed]) particular considerations and of inclusive and far-reaching (general) meanings."

The Double Movement. One could hardly find a better definition for two of the three kinds of IQA coding activities. Analysis of data actually begins with its technical opposite—synthesis or inductive coding, that first action in Dewey's "double movement." This is then followed by analytical or axial coding, which is primarily deductive in nature. Both of these interact recursively, mediated by that mysterious and wonderful thing we call the human mind. IQA, in a sense, simply imposes a public structure onto the recursive cycle of meaning, not with the purpose of limiting human freedom or oppressing or subjugating or marginalizing or even establishing epistemological hegemony, but simply so that the researcher can examine, describe, interrogate, reflect on, and enter into dialogue with others about the meaning of phenomena. The only significant extension to Dewey's ideas represented in IQA is the notion of tearing down, or at least rendering more transparent and semipermeable, the epistemological and metaphysical wall between researcher and researched. Figure 5.2 illustrates

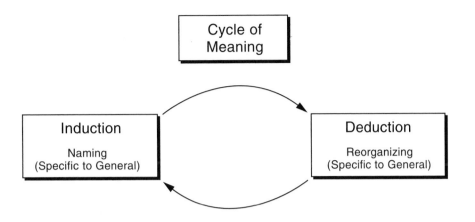

Figure 5.2

the relationship between induction and deduction as they interact to help form meaning.

The Middle Terms. One more variation on Dewey represented in IQA methodology is perhaps worthy of mention, which is the third level of IQA analysis. Dewey anticipates the formal IQA process of theoretical coding when he talks about "connecting links" or "middle terms." He embeds these references within his discussion of induction and deduction; however, it is not completely clear from Dewey's treatment if the "middle terms" can be identified by one logical process or the other, or whether both are required. Closer reading suggests that Dewey is saying that the middle terms require both logical operators, and IQA agrees. A more detailed discussion of theoretical codes[4] is reserved for the next chapter.

Back to the Focus Group

Upon completion of the clarification of meaning, focus group partici-pants are invited to recognize themes or communalities within their many responses. The purpose of affinity analysis is to cluster or categorize the cards via as-yet-unarticulated, but nevertheless meaningful, criteria. Qualitative researchers use several names for this process (although it seems not to have occurred to them that the participants in the research may be at least as qualified as they are to accomplish this first stage of analysis): *Open or emergent* and *inductive* coding are the more common names. We will use these terms synonymously but prefer *inductive* because this term refers most directly to the logical operation most fundamentally involved in this early stage of analysis.

Inductive coding, therefore, seeks to identify affinities; *axial coding* refines, reorganizes, and describes the range of meaning of each affinity within the context of the others. Categories and topics begin to emerge, but categories, topics, meanings, ideas, and the like, may change or alter during the coding process.

Inductive Coding

Participants are all asked to silently (1) review all of the cards on the wall and (2) group them into similar themes/affinities. Participants are instructed to cluster and group the cards silently into whatever categories they believe the cards belong. The participants are informed not to defend their categorization of the card(s), but various participants may move the card multiple times. If a participant believes that a card belongs in one column as opposed to another column, he or she moves the card. The participants move, sort, and shift the cards into a cluster group until everyone is satisfied with the categories or groups. When the majority of the ideas have been clustered, the facilitator assists the participants in identifying an appropriate label for each cluster or affinity, and further to identify labels for subcategories within each affinity. The intent of this process is to categorize data into thematically organized groupings, referred to as *affinities.*

The facilitator must be especially alert during this exercise. There will be much activity, and some people will tend to withdraw while others take leadership roles almost competitively. The facilitator will need to guide the group process to encourage everyone to participate, answering questions and helping the group clarify the themes as they proceed. There is no prescribed time for the grouping process. When the group seems to have hit a stopping point, it is time to move to the next step.

Axial Coding

Axial coding seeks to name, reorganize, clarify, and refine the affinities. While the first kind of coding is, as the name implies, almost exclusively inductive, axial coding cycles back and forth from inductive to deductive. Once the affinities are refined and often reorganized by the group participants, they are encouraged to narrow down the meanings of the affinities and their categories. Major categories of affinities are reviewed and then may be combined or divided into hierarchical systems of subaffinities.

Once again, this process is achieved through group discussion and consensus. The descriptions are refined and narrowed by the group until each

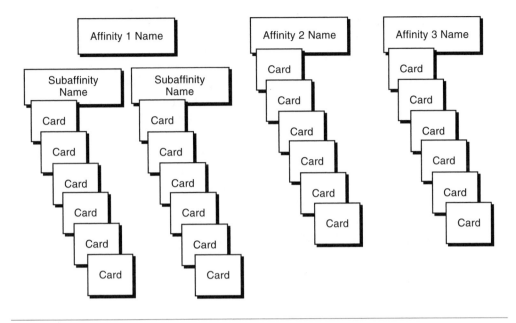

Figure 5.3

participant agrees that the definition accurately reflects the meaning of the affinity. Affinities are given titles, as determined by participants, that accurately reflect the meaning of the affinity. These titles are documented on header notepads and placed at the top of each vertical column. An example is provided in Figure 5.3.

A well-identified affinity has several characteristics:

❖ It is *not* a person, a place, or a physical thing (except, perhaps, metaphorically); rather, an affinity describes constructs or characteristics of categories of meaning.

❖ It is homogeneous—it is about *one construct* rather than a mixture of topics.

❖ It is easy to define. If it is difficult to name or points to several different things, most likely it is a mixture.

❖ On the other hand, it should have a range of meaning within this definition. Take care not to confuse values or polarities with affinities. For example, rather than having two affinities such as *Positive Emotions* and *Negative Emotions,* one affinity *Emotions* suffices.

❖ It has context (relationship) to other things, but affinity descriptions should not depend on definitions that point to other affinities within the system; for example, do not include theoretical codes within axial ones.

Affinity Descriptions

After each affinity has been named and possibly further divided into subaffinities, the facilitator's task is to define the affinity using the data to capture its meaning. Gathered from the cards and affinities produced, as well as from transcripts of the group discussion, the researcher (or even better, the participants) write(s) a paragraph description representing the general content of the affinities. A paragraph for each affinity and subaffinity is also written. Paragraphs should be descriptive and should be "grounded" in the text through reference to specific quotes or examples.

Affinity descriptions should provide in-depth coverage of the range of data included. Each description should contain four basic elements:

- ❖ Detail

- ❖ Contrast (what the affinity is not)

- ❖ Comparison (how it is different from other related affinities)

- ❖ Richness (elaboration and examples)

During this process, the meanings of each affinity and subaffinity are thoroughly articulated so that the full range of data is incorporated in each. The researcher can get creative with the paragraphs and the descriptive titles. Word play and humor can be effectively and appropriately used if they are grounded in the participants' reality, although care must be taken to avoid an overuse of idiosyncratic language or terms whose meaning may be obvious to the group but do not communicate to a larger audience. In other words, although the research is serious, the presentation does not have to be dull. "Description," whether conducted by the participants or by the researcher, is by its very nature interpretive. In particular, the facilitator/researcher should be sensitive to the use of metaphoric language by participants. It is appropriate to use a metaphor if it will enable the participants and the researcher to *make sense of the data,* moving the coding to a higher level. In addition, the use of simple graphics can enhance depictions of how subaffinities are related to each other and to the umbrella affinity under which they appear.

It is important that each affinity is described clearly and directly, remaining faithful to the language used by focus group members and following the sense of what participants were saying. Members of the focus group may participate in this activity. Alternatively, the facilitator may complete this step individually. Participant input, however, can be key if further clarification is necessary.

Facilitation Guidelines: Flags for the Facilitator

Facilitation in any context, but especially in an IQA setting, is more art than science, so there is no official laundry list of procedures or rules for the IQA facilitator that guarantees success. However, what follows is a brief list of "flags" in the group's discourse that should immediately attract the facilitator's attention. The suggestions that follow are obviously influenced by our personal experiences with focus groups; however, a major theoretical influence has been the work of Lawrence-Lightfoot and Hoffman Davis's (1997) work on portraiture, and, more generally, Denzin's (1989) discussion of interpretive biography.

1. *Recurrences and Patterns.* The facilitator should listen for recurrent key words, phrases, or patterns of discourse and point these out to the group for verification or confirmation, and to explore the meaning of these with the group.

2. *Metaphors and Other Symbolic Language.* Metaphorical or "colorful" terms should always gain the facilitator's attention. Again, the purpose is to explore the meaning of the metaphor and to bring in variation and depth to the language. The facilitator should not assume that the meaning of the metaphor is shared by all or even understood by all. It is not unusual that the same metaphor may have entirely different meanings to different group members

3. *Institutional or Cultural Rituals.* "Rituals," despite the esoteric connotations of the word, are often so commonplace and seemingly banal they escape the attention of the facilitator, which is a great loss because exploration of these rituals can provide a great depth of meaning to the problem statement. For example, in a study of the first-year experiences of doctoral students at a West Coast university in a cohort program designed to allow mid-career professionals to continue their jobs while going to school, many focus group members wrote "Fireside Chats" and "Poker in the Dorm" on their cards during the silent nominal process. These two cards referred to, respectively, a formal feature of the cohort program and another entirely informal one, both of which turned out to have great significance in the participants' narrative about the significant dimensions of their experience.

THEORETICAL SIDEBAR: THE FIRST BUREAUCRAT

Make for thyself a definition or description of the thing which is presented to thee, so as to see distinctly what kind of a thing it is in its substance, in its nudity, in its complete entirety, and tell thyself its proper name, and the names of the things of which it has been compounded, and into which it will be resolved.[5]

In Chapter 1, we examined the importance of ideology to a personal definition of rigor, and we subsequently discussed the critical role that one's ontological stance plays in shaping ideology. Before returning to the practicalities of facilitating the nominal group process, it may be helpful to elaborate a bit on the ontological position of IQA.

In the first of the two Genesis creation stories, God creates by naming, then delegates the power to name to Adam, a bureaucratic action demonstrating the ancients' awareness of the surpassing power of naming. To name is to presume a great deal about the nature of reality, and the debate over the nature of reality has continued for millennia and no doubt will continue for many more. The current manifestation of the debate pits "realists," meaning approximately the "scientific" logical positivist view that reality is what it is and, by implication, external to the observer, against those variously styling themselves as "constructionists," "deconstructionists," "subjectivists," "antirealists," "interpretivists," or "postmoderns." The latter contend there is no such thing as the world in itself, but that all this talk about "reality" is just that—talk. In this view, words refer only to words and sentences to other sentences; no matter how deeply we pursue the words and sentences, we never find a signified that truly is in and of itself.

Obviously, the postmoderns have the upper hand at the moment in the humanities in general, and in qualitative research in particular,[6] but by no means is the argument now settled, nor is it likely to be settled in the future. We may expect the debate to continue and we may also expect to see one side or the other in a position of power over the other at different points in history. This ebb and flow is a result of the dialectical nature of both history and reality itself. The ontological position of IQA is, to restate what has been said earlier, a bit to the left (toward constructionism) of Philip Kitcher's (2002) "modest realism," who articulates an ontology of "good sense" by recognizing that both sides of the argument have merit (when not carried too far).

THE POWER OF NAMING: CODING HINTS FOR THE FACILITATOR

Within this context, the following practical suggestions for facilitating the group nominal process are offered:

1. One affinity is too few; 20 are too many. One is too few because the objective is to break down the issue statement into components. On the other hand, 20 affinities create a system of potentially 190 pairwise relationships; experience suggests that this is an overwhelming analytical task for a focus group to accomplish in a reasonable time.

2. Look for similarities in names among the original list of affinities. Similar names may indicate that ostensibly different affinities are better

conceptualized as different "values" or points in the range of meaning of a larger affinity.

3. Look for differences in the names. Two names are different either because (1) they really represent different meanings or (2) they are polarities of the same affinity. Facilitators should be sensitive to this dialectical paradox.

4. Conceptual overlap among affinities, which indicates a lack of homogeneity or conceptual messiness, should be minimized. Affinities that are difficult to name (e.g., point to more than one category of meaning) probably should be subdivided.

5. Avoid defining affinities in terms of other affinities; that is, do not let the group proceed to theoretical coding prematurely. Affinity descriptions and names should, to the greatest extent possible, stand alone.

6. Coding is not like lunch. Eat dessert first by naming the easy or more obvious affinities first and use this foundation to build the group's work on the more difficult affinities.

Systems and IQA Focus Group Protocols

Recall that for a particular system, two inquiries or research questions are possible: *What are the elements of the system?* and *How do these elements relate to each other?* This chapter has described the protocols involved in answering the first of these two questions and has presented a theoretical rationale for the procedures. Using a nominal group process, the elements of the system, called "affinities," that represent the reality of a group with respect to a particular issue (the "phenomenon") are articulated and refined through a cyclical application of induction and deduction, operationalized via the IQA *inductive* and *axial coding* protocols.

The third research question concerns relationships among affinities. Articulating relationships is a deductive process operationalized in the IQA *theoretical coding* group protocol, which is the topic of the next chapter. The following continuation of our case study illustrates nominal group technique, inductive and axial coding, and affinity documentation.

CASE EXAMPLE

Fifty-one doctoral students (24 in the Tuesday traditional class and 27 in the Wednesday multimedia integrated class) from a variety of departments at the University of Texas at Austin (UT) participated in the study.

Students were assigned more or less randomly, subject to the necessity to accommodate individual schedules and program requirements, to one of two sections of the IQA class. The major exception to random assignment to the two classes was represented by seven Community College Leadership Program students who participated in a cohort or "block" program that prevented their taking the course on one of the two nights the course was offered. (These seven were all assigned to the Wednesday class.) By random choice, the Tuesday night class was selected for the traditional approach and the Wednesday class was selected for the technology-supplemented integrated approach. After several recursions through the IQA research design process (see Chapter 4), a four-part research question was developed to address the problem statement: *What are the differences between a traditional and a technology-integrated instructionally designed course?*

1. What factors comprise students' perceptions of and reactions to the IQA course?

2. How do these factors relate to each other in a perceived system of influence or cause and effect?

3. How does the individual's experience compare to that of the group as a whole?

4. How do the two groups' experiences compare to each other?

By midterm, members of both classes had read and discussed a draft of the IQA text and had conducted a brief IQA study. Each class was convened as a focus group to identify affinities comprising their experience with the course.

Index cards and Magic Markers were passed out to each table. The focus group was informed about the nature of research, told of the interest in their experiences in the class, and assured that this process would identify a rich detail of common themes to their experiences.

Participants were asked to close their eyes and relax by taking deep breaths and putting aside thoughts about the day. They were asked to reflect on their experiences in the class. What thoughts and emotions were involved? What memories did they have? What were their impressions of the course? They were then given the issue statement, *Tell me about your experiences in the class.* Table 5.2 shows the focus group warm-up exercise used by the facilitator.

The guided imagery process continued for about five minutes. The participants were asked to reflect on their experiences to date. Emphasizing that they would be allowed to brainstorm without the penalty of

Table 5.2

You have spent the past two months in the IQA pilot course. We need your help in making this course the best it can be. In a few minutes, I am going to ask you to tell me about your experience with the course.

- ❖ To begin, try to get as comfortable as you can.
- ❖ Close your eyes.
- ❖ Putting aside your thoughts of the day, take a deep cleansing breath.
- ❖ Now imagine yourself in this class from the first class day through last week. (long pause)
- ❖ See yourself engaging in the activities of the class. (long pause)
- ❖ Notice your surroundings. (long pause) Looking around you, take in the sights and sounds that are associated with being in class. (long pause)
- ❖ Allow yourself to become aware of your environment with all of your senses.
- ❖ Focus on what it feels like to be totally absorbed in the class. Be there in your mind. (long pause)

Now, tell me about your experience with the course [the issue statement].

Reflect on all the thoughts you had concerning the course.

Write these thoughts down on the cards.

Write one thought per card.

censorship, the group was asked to think of words, phrases, mental pictures, or memories of experiences in the course from their first class meeting up to, and including, the present class.

The group was asked to take a dozen or so cards and a pen in order to write their experiences on a card. They were told to write one experience per card, with no right or wrong answers, using words, phrases, or sentences to describe what they had experienced. They were asked to write on their cards in silence. It did not matter what others were writing. Information about their own experiences was needed. They were assured that whatever they wrote on the card would stay confidential; all cards would be lumped together so the author would not be known. There was no limit on how many cards they could make. When they appeared to be done, a few students were asked to collect the stacks of cards, mix them up to ensure anonymity, and tape them to the wall in no particular order.

The Tuesday night traditional course produced the cards shown in Table 5.3, organized in alphabetical order.

(Text continues on page 110)

Table 5.3

- 7–10 P.M.—a little late in the evening
- A linear process
- Able to share thoughts freely
- Achievable
- Active participation in every class is possible. That helps my attention span
- After gathering data, I will be prepared to finish last 2 chapters
- All homework has a valid purpose/learning goal
- Appreciate flexible setup
- Appreciate the extra class for mindmapping
- Appreciated the use of Inspiration to develop mindmap "practical"
- Are students missing out on non-IQA qualitative methods?
- Assignments—some parts confusing at times
- Bad
- Building confidence to carry out research
- Building peer relationships
- Builds my repertoire of research—I will use parts of IQA, but I will not use all
- Camaraderie
- Caring instructors
- Causes reflecting on own dissertation
- Class "connected" some quantitative to qualitative research. (Nice blend)
- Class assignments and readings directly applicable to dissertation
- Class cuts into late hours—cannot focus at the end of class
- Class size is too large but instructor style can accommodate it
- Class time enjoyable
- Clear instructions
- Collaborative
- Collaborative learning works great in this class
- Comfortable
- Comfortable asking questions

- Computers
- Concrete
- Confidence building
- Confused but interested
- Confusing
- Constructive group discussion
- Continued contact through email
- Could use a little more group work on initial coding steps
- Data collection
- Did not understand last week's grid calculations (frequency tables)
- Difficult to read (text)
- Difficulty in finding redundant links
- Difficulty with spatial reasoning on mindmaps
- Discussion encouraged
- Do not love the very guided interview, although easy to code
- Do not understand all components of IQA
- Doing IRD and SID can be tedious
- Doing rather than lecturing
- Easy to understand but not easy to do well
- Effective scaffolding (instructional design)
- Effective use of email for communication
- Email sent out on a regular basis
- Encourages self-motivation
- Enjoyed the IQA Web research exercise—good approach to reading on topic
- Enlightening [2X; stated on two cards]
- Entertaining
- Enthusiastic instructors
- Established some good bonds
- Excellent facilitation by the professor
- Exciting—possible dissertation method
- Feedback on homework would be useful

- For once, I can see the light at the end of the tunnel
- Frequent heavy email
- Friends help and support a lot
- Frustration in learning
- Frustration learning to use Macs
- Frustration over not understanding some parts
- Frustration with people who did not do the readings or who were not paying attention
- Fun 2X
- Fun with friends
- Good communication (email)
- Good design and planning of class activities
- Good email
- Good info but too much at once
- Good instruction
- Good instructor
- Good interviews
- Good people
- Good research
- Good step-by-step explanation
- Good support
- Good use of technology
- Graphic organizers are helpful to draw out themes and relationships
- Great instructors
- Great use of examples
- Group work
- Happy to use and learn new technology software [Inspiration]
- Hard to understand
- Healthy class environment
- Helpful instructors
- Helpful to work on assignments in class
- High-energy professor
- High-tech
- Homework—tasks and amount are reasonable
- How credible is this process? 2X
- How do I connect this to my area of interest?
- How is IQA perceived outside this class (in the academic world)? 2X
- How is this relevant to me?
- Hunger! Especially at around 8 P.M.
- I am still not sure about making interpretations, but I do know how to construct the research packet
- I can do this!!!
- I do not feel that I have a good understanding of qualitative methods, only IQA
- I feel like I get it!
- I liked being able to focus on learning and not on a grade
- I look forward to this class. I am interested
- If/then statements tedious
- Instructor cared that whole class "got it"
- Instructor focused on learning and comprehension
- Instructors provided adequate feedback
- Instructors respond quickly to email
- Interactive
- Interesting 3X
- Interesting how information connects
- Interesting process
- IQA is practical, makes sense, answers real questions
- IQA seems like squeezing qualitative into quantitative study
- Is there anything else besides IQA we need to know in the field of qualitative research?
- It all seemed to make sense, until I went home and tried to do it on my own
- It is late! I am sleepy driving home
- Laborious process
- Learn by doing
- Learned a lot
- Learning by applying concepts
- Learning is definitely taking place here
- Like the mindmap drawing—fun

(Continued)

Table 5.3 (Continued)

- Like using software [Inspiration]
- Logical format
- Logical method of qualitative research
- Looking forward to the CD
- Lots of good modeling of procedures helped me understand how IQA works
- Lots of lines and arrows
- Love being able to email assignments
- Manageable workload 2X
- Material presented in orderly, relevant manner
- Meeting new people
- Methodical
- Mind-boggling
- Mindmaps are fascinating
- Mindmaps turn "words" into something visual
- Mixed feelings about the amount of structure in the method
- More quantitative than first thought
- More than I expected
- Much like using TQM tools
- Need more reference texts . . . not just Web
- Needed a little more help in transitioning from saturated SID to unsaturated (additional write-up helped)
- Needs explanation of methods
- Needs more lab time instruction
- Needs other qualitative perspectives incorporated
- New email assignments, i.e., "ask a buddy to review," are not easy for people who do not always have access to computers
- New friends
- New software [Inspiration]
- New technique of research
- No pressure to learn
- Nonstressful
- Not clear how "no relationship" should be talked about
- Not clear understanding of IQA
- Not enough clarification
- Not enough info on the technology part
- Not enough time to learn Inspiration adequately
- Not much reading. Which is so different from other courses
- One of the best classes so far
- Organized 2X
- Other research method?
- Peer interaction increased our understanding
- Practical hands-on 3X
- Practical nature of class for dissertation purposes is great
- Prefer quantitative research—cleaner
- Prepared to write dissertation
- Process can be utilized with low-performing schools
- Professor and assistant work hard! Thank you.
- Professor great with graduate/adult pedagogy
- Professor has exceptional patience: He answers questions, even the redundant ones
- Professor is very good at explaining ideas
- Prompt feedback on assignments
- Provides another option for research
- Qualitative background reading challenging to get in through self-study on Web
- Questions answered
- Realize IQA could be useful "not just stats or quant."
- Reasonable, interesting reading
- Reassuring to know there doesn't have to be one right answer
- Relationships are very subjective— any thought pulled from the air would suffice
- Reliable method

❖ Removed my fear of working with numbers
❖ Repetitive
❖ Research questions added value to practice
❖ Rushed
❖ Sad to give up learning other models in qualitative research
❖ Scary walking to my car in the dark
❖ Simplifies a complicated process
❖ Skills not taught for mastery
❖ Slow pace
❖ Small focus groups are more manageable
❖ Small gaps between process steps
❖ Some challenge in distinguishing axial and theoretical codes
❖ Some topics were taught less or more thoroughly
❖ Sometimes I wonder if the class is too focused on IQA
❖ Sometimes the work feels repetitive
❖ Speed of class seemed slow at times, we could cover material in less time
❖ Structure
❖ Structure makes analysis more manageable
❖ Structured qualitative process
❖ Subjective but it will help me come up with things to write about in chapter 5 of dissertation
❖ Supportive environment with hand-over-hand support when needed from instructors
❖ Supportive instructors
❖ Tag team instruction helpful (multiple sources of info)
❖ Teachers easily accessible for clarification of subject matter
❖ Teamwork
❖ Tedious recording of numbers and arrows
❖ Tense
❖ That mindmap stuff confuses me

❖ The cause could really be the effect. The effect could really be the cause
❖ The class is always too cold
❖ The design is VERY theoretical
❖ The email updates and assignments are useful
❖ The hands-on approach really helped me grasp concepts
❖ The mindmapping program was challenging—the support was provided so that I was able to master it
❖ The pace works—slow but steady
❖ The step-by-step examples in the readings have been great
❖ The structure part 1 & 2 is perfect for a research class
❖ The teaching method was systematic, which made it easier to learn
❖ Theory: COME ALIVE actually doing work with model
❖ Time-consuming process
❖ Time in class not used wisely all the time
❖ Tired
❖ Tired after late night classes
❖ Too many affinities to deal with
❖ Too much information to digest in a short time
❖ Topics organized well (sequential)
❖ Transition from the saturated SID to unsaturated SID difficult
❖ Trusting environment
❖ Understanding of subject matter
❖ Use of email to class and feedback is useful
❖ Useful process
❖ Very applicable
❖ Very helpful TA
❖ Want to know more (other methods)
❖ We could sometimes make better use of class time (allow less outside chatter)
❖ Web assignment hard to engage in, not immediately or directly tied to IQA

(Continued)

Table 5.3 (Continued)

- ❖ Well organized
- ❖ Will modify IQA to fit my needs if I decide to use it
- ❖ Wish I knew what department, goals, etc., everyone has
- ❖ Wishing for more time in class to do mindmap/SID

- ❖ Working with technology was liberating
- ❖ Worry over getting a complete grasp of how to do a mindmap/SID (anxiety)
- ❖ Would be better with whole book

The Wednesday night instructionally designed, multimedia integrated course produced the cards shown in Table 5.4, also organized in alphabetical order.

With the cards taped on the wall, each focus group was then asked to quickly and silently read the cards. When the group was finished, the facilitator went up to the wall and read each card aloud. The group was asked if each card made sense. If a card was unclear, the author or another member was asked if he or she wanted to explain what was meant. Usually the author had no hesitation in coming forward to clarify the meaning.

When they were done, the group was asked to, again silently, begin to move the cards into columns. The cards in the columns were to have a similar theme. If anyone disagreed with where a card had been moved, they were to feel free to move it to another column. This went on for several minutes until the group felt that each card was in place. Some members of the group seemed to get a little frustrated when a card that they had placed was moved. They were asked not to talk about where their cards should go. If a card's meaning and placement was ambiguous, it was cleared up in the next step.

After the cards were placed and meanings were clarified, the group was given an opportunity to write out any new cards that might have come to mind after reading what the others wrote. Several new cards were produced and the authors were asked to tape them in the appropriate columns.

The facilitator began with the column that seemed to be the easiest to name and asked the group to give it a name. A new card reflecting the name was placed above the column. The facilitator progressed through each column until all had been named. The facilitator then instructed the group to examine the clusters of cards and to see if any might be the dialectic of a higher theme; for example, *love* and *hate* might be opposites, but they fall under a higher theme of *emotions*. When several columns were combined under one newly named category, the original columns became *subaffinities* of the new affinity. Each card was then reexamined to see if it had been miscategorized and now belonged in one of the newly named columns. If categories seemed to be overly complex, the group was

(Text continues on page 113)

Table 5.4

- 10 P.M. is late for me
- Adding info in digestible chunks
- Allow sharing of ideas
- Am being patient with a "class under construction"
- Am I going to be ready for advanced qual?
- Am learning to manipulate software, which is fun
- Analyze
- Anticipating with interest
- Anxiety
- Applicable
- Apply knowledge
- Assessable, helpful
- Assignments on email confusing
- At times tiring
- Being surprised by my understanding
- Beneficial
- Build the system around professor's style
- CD-ROM
- Celebrating a birthday
- Challenging [2X; stated on two cards]
- Challenging but good to feel like I can do this—not like I am drowning
- Challenging concepts
- Collaboration
- Concentrating (thoughtful)
- Confused
- Confusing
- Constantly had in the back of my mind the ? (how) does this apply to my dissertation
- Co-teaching seemed disjointed sometimes
- Critical to transformation process
- Crowded room
- Crowded table
- Did not feel as though I had a grasp on variations of qual despite the CD
- Different research method
- Diligent
- Directive
- Disarming process
- Discover
- Dissertation method
- Easy to follow—process, material
- Elements and relationships
- Email
- Email needs more descriptive subject lines to identify and sort
- End of long day
- Engaged teachers
- Engaging
- Enjoy
- Enjoy professor's humor
- Enjoyable
- Enjoying the technology part of the class
- Everyone engaged
- Excited at the prospects
- Exciting
- Exhausted after class
- Experiencing learning
- Exploration
- Feel like a guinea pig
- Focused learning
- Focused teaching
- Friendly communication
- Friendly people
- Friends
- Frustrated
- Frustrated by too many questions from students
- Frustration (mindmaps)
- Fun 5X
- Fun class
- Fun time, good humor
- Gave me hands-on experience for qualitative data analysis
- Glad to have the professor for an instructor
- Good communication (email)
- Good exposure (first time) to actual research
- Groundswell of data
- Handouts, resources
- Hands-on
- Hard chairs

(Continued)

Table 5.4 (Continued)

❖ Having fun with new computer program [Inspiration]
❖ Healthy discussion
❖ Help ever present
❖ Helpful instruction
❖ High energy
❖ Humorous
❖ I can do this!
❖ I can see IQA in my dissertation
❖ I get it!
❖ Incremental
❖ Information overload
❖ Informative
❖ Insightful
❖ Inspiration 3X
❖ Inspiration program was great
❖ Inspires curiosity logically sound theory
❖ Inspiring class
❖ Intellectually challenging
❖ Interactive class made learning meaningful
❖ Interactive classroom discussion
❖ Interactive technology
❖ Interesting 4X
❖ Interesting material
❖ Interesting software
❖ IQA is a mixed approach to data analysis
❖ Is this [IQA] useful for my dissertation?
❖ It all comes together
❖ Lack of knowledge with Macs
❖ Late at night
❖ Laughing
❖ Leading edge (innovative)
❖ Learned a lot about IQA
❖ Learned something new 2X
❖ Learning how to match IQA to dissertation study very helpful
❖ Learning a lot
❖ Learning experience
❖ Learning to think about things differently
❖ Lightbulb moments

❖ Like doing project-based work but would have preferred choosing my own project
❖ Liked having a CD to consult
❖ Liked interviews
❖ Liked lab days
❖ Logical and sequential process
❖ Looking forward to coming to class
❖ Lost and found
❖ Lots of details
❖ Lots of information
❖ Lots of new information
❖ Lots of people
❖ Love it
❖ Loved CD
❖ Loved use of motivation to learn more than assigned
❖ Mac lab (positive extension of the class)
❖ Make me think a lot about qualitative research
❖ Many new acronyms
❖ Material uncomfortable at times
❖ Mind on fire
❖ Model for dissertation research
❖ More confident about dissertation
❖ New experience
❖ New ideas 2X
❖ New information
❖ New people
❖ New way of looking at things
❖ No paper!
❖ Note-taking
❖ OK to disagree—not so zeroed in on the #1 right answer
❖ Open discussion
❖ Openness to share
❖ Organized approach
❖ Participant
❖ Participation by students
❖ Patient professor
❖ Physically uncomfortable
❖ Powerful process
❖ Practical, hands-on

- ❖ Process easy
- ❖ Process oriented
- ❖ Processing
- ❖ Productive
- ❖ Professor's sense of humor
- ❖ Promptness to help
- ❖ Qual is cool
- ❖ Quantifying the qualitative paradigm
- ❖ Question how to use practically
- ❖ Relaxed pace
- ❖ Relaxing
- ❖ Repetition
- ❖ Requirement (course)
- ❖ Research
- ❖ Rewarding
- ❖ Ruled out a qualitative dissertation
- ❖ Sharing ideas
- ❖ Socially fun
- ❖ Something new
- ❖ Sometimes trying to stay alert
- ❖ Spaced out or inattentive at times (fatigued)
- ❖ Strain-free allows for learning
- ❖ Structured 3X
- ❖ Struggling to get clarification
- ❖ Supportive
- ❖ Supportive classmates
- ❖ Synthesis 3X
- ❖ System
- ❖ Systems were familiar info
- ❖ Technical aspect
- ❖ The last part was much easier than the first part (to follow)
- ❖ Theory to the people
- ❖ Thinking in-depth, thoughtful
- ❖ Thought provoking
- ❖ Tiring at times
- ❖ Too many attachments to emails
- ❖ Uncertainty in process
- ❖ Understanding 2X
- ❖ Unfamiliar topic
- ❖ Unique professor
- ❖ Usage of Inspiration
- ❖ Use of technology
- ❖ Useful
- ❖ Useful syllabus
- ❖ Using new technology (challenging)
- ❖ Very cool process
- ❖ Very interesting
- ❖ Very sequential
- ❖ Visual application
- ❖ Wanted more homework and testing of some kind
- ❖ Well organized 2X
- ❖ Will I know enough to really use this later?
- ❖ Written text was awesome

instructed to see if subcategories were necessary. Each column was then rearranged to reflect the subcategories. Each subcategory was also given a name. Once the cards had been arranged and affinities named, the affinity production exercise was complete.

Later that evening the researcher typed up the cards and affinities. The typed affinity list was sent to the respective groups. They were asked to write a paragraph describing each of the affinities and subaffinities. The result was a wide range of rich descriptions for each affinity from which one master write-up was pulled together that described the affinities for both classes. *Note:* If the focus group had not been available to contribute to the write-up, the facilitator would have completed it. The following is the affinity write-up.

Focus Group Affinity Write-Up

As we've already discussed, two separate focus groups were convened and asked about their experiences with the IQA class for which they had spent the previous two months. The Tuesday class had been taught using traditional methods of instruction, readings followed by lectures, and discussions. The Wednesday course was an instructionally designed multimedia integrated course, which used readings and an interactive CD-ROM, followed by structured multimedia lectures and collaborative group discussions.

When asked, "Tell me about your experiences with the course," each class generated more than 250 responses in the form of a word, phrase, or sentence on 5 × 8 cards. The cards were then sorted by themes, and these themes, called affinities in IQA, were named by the groups.

The Tuesday group produced the following affinities:

1. Collaboration

2. Communication

3. Comprehension
   - ❖ Understanding
   - ❖ Difficulties

4. Course Structure
   - ❖ Design
   - ❖ Pace
   - ❖ Scope

5. Emotional Environment

6. Instructor

7. IQA as a Method
   - ❖ Applicability
   - ❖ Process

8. Learning Resources

9. Peer Relationships

10. Physical Environment

The Wednesday group produced the following affinities:

1. Application Toward Dissertation

2. Classroom Climate

3. Cognitive Reaction (Dialectic)
    - ❖ Confusion
    - ❖ Clarity
    - ❖ Growth

4. Collaboration

5. Course Structure

6. IQA Process

7. Physical Environment

8. Teacher Style

9. Technology

Because each member of the groups was a student learning the IQA process, they were asked by the instructor to produce an affinity write-up. The affinity write-up takes into account the cards generated in each affinity and any discussion that occurred during the focus group session. The instructor then compiled one large affinity write-up from responses developed by the students.

TUESDAY NIGHT EXPERIENCE WITH THE IQA COURSE

1. Collaboration

Collaboration represented the affinity that the focus group described as important to understanding Interactive Qualitative Analysis (IQA). Some group members indicated that group discussions and working in teams enhanced their learning experiences and kept them motivated. Other members pointed out that interacting with members of the class helped facilitate their learning. Some group members described the class as interactive, an atmosphere where sharing and discussion is encouraged. Questions and answers between the teacher and the students also contributed to the collaborative aspect of the course. It is clear that everyone in the group agreed that the class involved, and even encouraged, group collaboration and discussion.

The collaborative experiences in the Tuesday night class were clearly seen as an important aspect of the learning experience. This affinity reflects both the usefulness of the established group work, as well as some areas where students feel that additional peer interaction is desired. Qualitative research requires some level of interaction and involvement with people, whether via individual interviews or group work, so it seems only natural that a class on *Interactive Qualitative Analysis* should involve "collaborative learning" and "group work." Most students seemed to enjoy and benefit from the "constructive group discussion" and "peer interaction." The affinity also includes the acknowledgement that collaboration is valued and encouraged by the class leaders as a learning tool.

Collaboration seemed to be well received as the popular teaching method used in the IQA class. Discussions among each group helped negotiate understanding of the lesson for students. The class setup led to collaborative learning and, in fact, encouraged the teamwork process. Although there was much collaboration among groups, some of the groups did not really interact with each other. Some felt that they would have liked to have a better idea about everyone's goals. Yet the group as a whole felt strongly that there was much collaboration throughout. Collaboration, when implemented well, leads to a better understanding of IQA concepts.

Table 5.5 Collaboration

❖ Collaborative
❖ Collaborative learning works great in this class
❖ Constructive group discussion
❖ Could use a little more group work on initial coding steps
❖ Discussion encouraged
❖ Good design and planning of class activities
❖ Group work
❖ Interactive
❖ Peer interaction increased our understanding
❖ Teamwork
❖ Wish I knew what department, goals, etc., everyone has

---

2. Communication

This affinity reflects the students' positive response to easy access of the instructor through email. The teacher emailed the class on a regular basis to inform students about assignments, deadlines, clarification of the lesson or homework, or interesting information regarding research or understanding. Students submitted completed assignments, posted questions, and requested clarification and verification from the teacher. The use of email as the almost-standard means of communication was welcomed by the majority of students. Students spoke of convenience, usefulness, and prompt feedback regarding email contact with the instructor. Some described the use of email as a communication tool as "effective," "good," and "loved being able to email assignments." Others described the use of email as "useful," "frequent," and a "good way to communicate."

The instructors made good use of email to keep students abreast of assignments and instructions, as well as to provide feedback and advice. Busy graduate students greatly appreciated the ability to stay connected with their instructors and classmates, and email provided a convenient communication conduit. The fact that a busy professor would take the time to promptly respond to students' email encouraged the trust and goodwill that characterized this class.

The group believed that communication was a prerequisite to understanding the information conveyed by the instructor(s) in class as well as the homework assignments. The group also maintained that communication inside and outside of class (including emails) enabled them to access assignments more easily.

Communication also carried some negative aspects, as some students believed the emails were too frequent or cited that not all in the class were privy to the frequent use of a computer.

Table 5.6 Communication

- ❖ Continued contact through email
- ❖ Effective use of email for communication
- ❖ Email sent out on a regular basis
- ❖ Frequent heavy email
- ❖ Good communication (email)
- ❖ Good email
- ❖ Instructors respond quickly to email
- ❖ Love being able to email assignments
- ❖ New email assignments, i.e., "ask a buddy to review," are not easy for people who do not always have access to computers
- ❖ Prompt feedback on assignments
- ❖ The email updates and assignments are useful
- ❖ Use of email to class and feedback is useful

---

3. Comprehension

Students' assessments of their understanding/mastery of the IQA research method varied from one extreme to the other on a comprehension spectrum. *Comprehension* describes the affinity used to relate two sub-affinities, those of *understanding* and *difficulties*. The subaffinity *understanding* conveyed the belief that students are truly learning in the class and are thrilled that they are both able to do the tasks and can achieve their end goals. It also conveyed some frustration in the ability to understand but not use the tasks as well as a student would have liked. Meanwhile, *difficulties* as a subaffinity described the confusion and frustration some students have in comprehending IQA and many of its individual parts. In some instances, students cited that the model was too difficult to comprehend or that there was not enough time to fully comprehend the model in the time allotted in class. Along with the frustration, it appeared that some students had anxiety that is reflected in this affinity.

Understanding. Many students readily grasped the concept of IQA and found its components "easy to understand" and "achievable." They seemed proud of their accomplishments and the amount they learned, and in many cases were invigorated by the method. Some students expressed excitement that this course had helped them believe that they "can do this!!!"—with "this" referring to conducting research and finishing their dissertations. Student felt that they could do the work and that they learned a lot.

The group described "understanding" as being able to thoroughly know meaning of the material presented in class. They also contended that their grasp of the material helped them to feel confident that they could progress and succeed in the class. Grasp of the general IQA concept made people feel enlightened and confident that the method was achievable.

Difficulties. This subaffinity reflects the confusion and frustration felt by some of the students as they tried to master the various components of the IQA research methodology. The difficulties set in during the process of practicing IQA. Unclear assignments, Interrelationship Diagram (IRD)/ System Influence Diagram (SID) grid making, mindmap drawing, and the limited time to digest all information contributed to students' anxiety and created obstacles to full comprehension of the course. These students experienced "frustration over not understanding some parts" of IQA, especially in regards to drawing the mindmaps and making interpretations of the subsequent relationships, feedback loops, and the like. Although there was much communication, and it seemed easy to understand, once the group was on its own, the difficulties began. The relationships on the tables were difficult to figure out and the mindmapping was extremely confusing. The group as a whole agreed that the process taught was achievable. However, some of the members of the group felt that there was not enough clarification in certain areas, leaving some gaps for the group to fill. The redundant links were difficult to find for some and made it mind-boggling as to how to accomplish a product that would be of benefit to the research.

Some students who expressed feelings of accomplishment attributed their classmates' frustrations to inadequate preparation for class in terms of the readings, practice assignments, and participation in extra labs for mindmapping. However, even these IQA enthusiasts shared the initial feeling that "it all seemed to make sense, until I went home and tried to do it on my own." They all agreed that mastery of the IQA method takes a lot of hands-on practice, which some students do not have the time or resources to do diligently.

Table 5.7   Comprehension

Understanding

- ❖ Achievable
- ❖ Easy to understand but not easy to do well
- ❖ I can do this!!!
- ❖ I feel like I get it!
- ❖ Learned a lot
- ❖ Learning is definitely taking place here

Difficulties

- ❖ Assignments—some parts confusing at times
- ❖ Confused but interested
- ❖ Confusing
- ❖ Did not understand last week's grid calculations (frequency tables)
- ❖ Difficult to read (text)
- ❖ Difficulty in finding redundant links
- ❖ Difficulty with spatial reasoning on mindmaps
- ❖ Do not understand all components of IQA
- ❖ Frustration over not understanding some parts
- ❖ Graphic organizers are helpful to draw out themes and relationships
- ❖ Hard to understand
- ❖ I am still not sure about making interpretations, but I do know how to construct the research packet
- ❖ IQA is practical, makes sense, answers real questions

[On occasion, a card or two will not make it into the "right" category. The category can still be identified by the other cards in the group. A researcher may choose to let the card remain where it is or move it to an appropriate category later. It is probably best to move the card, but not doing so would have little effect in the overall study because a full study using interviews will only be focused on the affinity names and not the individual cards.]

- ❖ It all seemed to make sense, until I went home and tried to do it on my own
- ❖ Lots of lines and arrows
- ❖ Mind-boggling
- ❖ Needed a little more help in transitioning from saturated SID to unsaturated (additional write-up helped)
- ❖ Needs more lab time instruction
- ❖ Not clear how "no relationship" should be talked about
- ❖ Not clear understanding of IQA
- ❖ Not enough clarification
- ❖ Not enough info on the technology part
- ❖ Reassuring to know there doesn't have to be one right answer
- ❖ Relationships are very subjective—any thought pulled from the air would suffice

(Continued)

Table 5.7 (Continued)

- ❖ Skills not taught for mastery
- ❖ Some challenge in distinguishing axial and theoretical codes
- ❖ The cause could really be the effect. The effect could really be the cause
- ❖ The mindmapping program was challenging—the support was provided so that I was able to master it
- ❖ Too many affinities to deal with
- ❖ Too much information to digest in a short time
- ❖ Transition from the saturated SID to unsaturated SID difficult
- ❖ Understanding of subject matter
- ❖ Web assignment hard to engage in, not immediately or directly tied to IQA
- ❖ Worry over getting a complete grasp of how to do a mindmap/SID (anxiety)

4. Course Structure

Students identified *Course Structure* as an affinity to describe the aspects of *design, pace,* and *scope* of the course. The group believed that the structure of the course was what provided the access to learning. Design emphasized how course structure (flexibility, use of collaboration, encouraging self-motivation, clear examples) enhanced learning. With regard to *design,* there were many positive elements to the course structure cited by students, including the connection of the course tasks to the "real world" of qualitative research. Other examples given included the practical and logical nature of the course and the ability to do "hands-on" work on assignments outside of and in class with a reasonable workload. The course appeared to exceed students' expectations in the context of order and relevancy. *Pace* addressed students' perceptions of how quickly or slowly class time moved. With regard to pace, there were mixed reviews; some believed that more material could be taught in the same amount of time, while others complained about the lack of time to master certain aspects of IQA. *Scope* was the students' concern that the course focused solely on IQA and did not address other qualitative methods of research.

Design. Students seemed to truly appreciate the opportunity to "learn by doing." Graduate courses inherently require a great deal of reading that is not applied in the classroom setting. These students were relieved to have a lighter reading load, supplemented with practical "active participation" that afforded the opportunity to learn "by applying concepts." Many students applauded the structure and organization of the course, particularly how it was broken into Part I (instructor-led complete IQA study), and Part II (students followed the steps demonstrated in Part I while conducting all parts of a new study). One student summed up the enthusiasm for the course design with the comment: "Theory: COME ALIVE actually doing work with model."

The design aspect focused on the active participation of students, hands-on learning, well-structured assignments, and effective scaffolding that help build students' confidence and understanding of IQA. Students seemed to welcome the learning-by-doing aspect of the course and found the course load manageable. Design descriptions such as "clear instructions," "active participation in class is possible," and "encourages self-motivation" were named as factors that positively affected learning. Design helped them to learn the material. They pointed out that all of the assignments, both in and outside of class, were tied to the instructor's learning goals set for the class. Moreover, the group mentioned that the way that the class was organized helped to create an environment conducive to learning.

Pace. The pace of the course was defined in terms of the in-class and out-of-class progress. Pace was used to represent the time spent on the material from class meeting to class meeting. In-class instruction included lectures, interactions between the teacher and the students, and progress on the lessons. The out-of-class aspect refers to the time and effort it took to complete the assignment or to master a computer skill. Students' responses seemed to suggest that the class time could be better managed. There was downtime during the in-class discussion—not all members of the class were involved. On the other hand, there was not enough time to give explanation of and feedback on the out-of-class course assignments— some felt rushed.

There were some extreme views regarding the pace of the class activities. A few students felt rushed because there was too much information given at once, while more students expressed some frustration at the slow pace, the repetition, and the feeling that "time in class [was] not used wisely all the time." Some students attributed this slow pace and repetition to a lack of preparation on the part of a few classmates. In addition, the instructor had to repeat himself numerous times because of "outside chatter" that can slow down the pace of a class. In general, it seems that most students agreed that IQA is a "time-consuming process" and the "slow, but steady" pace was appropriate. The group realized that the speed at which the material was presented affected their ability to learn the material.

Scope. Scope addressed the students' concerns that IQA was the only method taught during the course. Scope also questioned the credibility of IQA as a process and its acceptability in the academic community. Though students were informed on the first day of class that the course would cover only IQA and was not a survey research course, some seemed to question if they were "missing out on non-IQA qualitative methods."

Table 5.8   Course Structure

Design

- ❖ Active participation in every class is possible. That helps my attention span
- ❖ All homework was a valid purpose/learning goal
- ❖ Appreciate flexible setup
- ❖ Class "connected" some quantitative to qualitative research. (Nice blend)
- ❖ Clear instructions
- ❖ Do not love the very guided interview, although easy to code
- ❖ Doing rather than lecturing
- ❖ Effective scaffolding (instructional design)
- ❖ Encourages self-motivation
- ❖ Great use of examples
- ❖ Helpful to work on assignments in class
- ❖ Homework—tasks and amount are reasonable
- ❖ Learn by doing
- ❖ Learning by applying concepts
- ❖ Logical method of qualitative research
- ❖ Lots of good modeling of procedures helped me understand how IQA works
- ❖ Manageable workload 2X
- ❖ Material presented in orderly, relevant manner
- ❖ Methodical
- ❖ More than I expected
- ❖ No pressure to learn
- ❖ Not much reading. Which is so different from other courses
- ❖ Organized 2X
- ❖ Practical hands-on 3X
- ❖ Qualitative background reading challenging to get in through self-study on Web
- ❖ Small focus groups are more manageable
- ❖ Some topics were taught less or more thoroughly
- ❖ Structure
- ❖ Tag team instruction helpful (multiple sources of info)
- ❖ The hands-on approach really helped me grasp concepts
- ❖ The structure part 1 & 2 is perfect for a research class
- ❖ The teaching method was systematic, which made it easier to learn
- ❖ Theory: COME ALIVE actually doing work with model
- ❖ Topics organized well (sequential)
- ❖ Well organized

Pace

- ❖ Good info but too much at once
- ❖ Not enough time to learn Inspiration adequately
- ❖ Repetitive
- ❖ Rushed
- ❖ Slow pace

❖ Sometimes the work feels repetitive
❖ Speed of class seemed slow at times, we could cover material in less time
❖ The pace works—slow but steady
❖ Time-consuming process
❖ Time in class not used wisely all the time
❖ We could sometimes make better use of class time (allow less outside chatter)
❖ Wishing for more time in class to do mindmap/SID

Scope

❖ Are students missing out on non-IQA qualitative methods?
❖ How credible is this process?
❖ I do not feel that I have a good understanding of qualitative methods, only IQA
❖ IQA seems like squeezing qualitative into quantitative study
❖ Is there anything else besides IQA we need to know in the field of qualitative research?
❖ Needs explanation of methods
❖ Needs other qualitative perspectives incorporated
❖ Other research method?
❖ Sometimes I wonder if the class is too focused on IQA
❖ Want to know more (other methods)

5. Emotional Environment

Students in the course ran the gamut of emotions in the affinity of *Emotional Environment* with most students finding the environment comfortable, free, enlightening, and "healthy." There was an overwhelming sense that the classroom environment—established from day one by the enthusiastic, caring instructor—was "healthy" in that the students were allowed to "share thoughts freely" and "focus on learning and not on a grade." The majority of the students felt comfortable, relaxed, and able to have fun while learning an intense research methodology. Most students agreed with the comments that the instructor had created a "trusting environment" that allowed them to build confidence in their ability to conduct research.

Emotional Environment represented the affinity that the group said they needed in order to succeed in the class. They pointed out that a positive, healthy learning environment helped them feel comfortable, which led to confidence in their ability to learn. The emotional environment influenced student learning. Most students thought the course was fun, enjoyable, and entertaining, and said it built confidence. There was a general sense that the course focused more on learning than on grades, which created a healthy and open setting for the knowledge to be acquired.

There were some mixed feelings about the learning process. A few commented that the environment was frustrating or tense. Interestingly, one student's card read "bad," which the group did not relate to at all. Someone suggested that maybe he or she meant "bad as in good," as used in the pop culture. Because no one spoke up to the contrary, in the jovial nature of the class, the students agreed to that connotation. The negative aspects were often cited in one-word explanations such as "bad," whereas the positive aspects outweighed the negative in verbiage, with students reporting specific aspects they enjoyed such as "focusing on learning and not on a grade" and by one-word exhortations such as "comfortable." A prevailing attitude of a lessening of negative aspects that were anticipated at the beginning of this research-focused course could generalize this affinity.

Table 5.9   Emotional Environment

- Able to share thoughts freely
- Bad
- Building confidence to carry out research
- Class time enjoyable
- Comfortable
- Comfortable asking questions
- Confidence building
- Enlightening 2X
- Entertaining
- Frustration in learning
- Fun 2X
- Healthy class environment
- I liked being able to focus on learning and not on a grade
- I look forward to this class. I am interested
- Interesting 3X
- Like the mindmap drawing—fun
- Nonstressful
- Removed my fear of working with numbers
- Tense
- That mindmap stuff confuses me
- Trusting environment

---

6. Instructor

Words used repeatedly to describe the professor were "great," "enthusiastic," "caring," "supportive," and "high-energy." He and the graduate assistant were commended for their enthusiasm, accessibility, and "hard work" in their efforts to make sure that the "whole class 'got it.'" Students commented that the instructor was caring, patient, and took time to help students understand concepts. Furthermore, the instructor created a positive environment for learning.

The instructor was instrumental to the learning process. They mentioned that the instructor played a key role in making them feel like they possessed the ability to learn. Some members asserted that the instructor's teaching style helped them to feel free to ask questions, and he guided them through the learning process in a supportive way. The group believed that the instructor was the one responsible for facilitating the learning.

Clearly, the professor was an overwhelmingly positive force in this class and that is captured in the affinity of *Instructor*. Only one negative comment, that about a desire for more feedback on homework, is to be found in this area, and words such as "caring," "patient," and "thank you" are peppered in between comments about "good" or "great" support, instruction, helpfulness, and accessibility. One student exclaimed that this was "One of the best classes so far." It is obvious in this affinity that students were more than pleased with the instructor personally and professionally by their comments in this affinity.

Table 5.10 Instructor

- ❖ Caring instructors
- ❖ Class size is too large but instructor style can accommodate it
- ❖ Enthusiastic instructors
- ❖ Excellent facilitation by the professor
- ❖ Feedback on homework would be useful
- ❖ Good instruction
- ❖ Good instructor
- ❖ Good support
- ❖ Great instructors
- ❖ Helpful instructors
- ❖ High-energy professor
- ❖ Instructor cared that whole class "got it"
- ❖ Instructor focused on learning and comprehension
- ❖ Instructors provided adequate feedback
- ❖ One of the best classes so far
- ❖ Professor and assistant work hard! Thank you.
- ❖ Professor great with graduate/adult pedagogy
- ❖ Professor has exceptional patience: he answers questions, even the redundant ones
- ❖ Professor is very good at explaining ideas
- ❖ Questions answered
- ❖ Supportive environment with hand-over-hand support when needed from instructors
- ❖ Supportive instructors
- ❖ Teachers easily accessible for clarification of subject matter
- ❖ Very helpful TA

7. IQA as a Method

IQA as a Method is the affinity the focus group used to describe the actual material or method of qualitative research that was being studied in the course. Two subaffinities, those of *applicability* and *process,* make up the affinity of *IQA as a Method.* The subaffinity of *applicability* is used to explain either the usefulness of the course in the fulfillment of students' research needs, such as for their dissertation, or was used to ask the question of how it is useful and/or of relevance to a student's research needs. Most students were quite satisfied that the IQA method would be of immediate or future use to them, while a few dissenters were not so sure if this was the method for them and wondered if other methods would be more suitable. *Process* refers to the notion that students either found IQA's methodology "logical," "concrete," "fascinating," and "interesting," or they found it "laborious," "tedious," with some "small gaps." Many students found similarities between this method with others (such as TQM), and some found it more theoretical and able to be incorporated with quantitative methods than they expected.

Applicability. IQA has inspired many of the students to reflect on their dissertations with a renewed spirit that has allowed them to "see the light at the end of the tunnel"—the tunnel leading to completion of the doctoral program. Many students expressed that they found the IQA method "very applicable" and will use it, or part of it, in their dissertation study. The aspect of learning IQA that students truly appreciated was how it fits into the layout of the dissertation. Through these discussions, they learned about the framework of a dissertation, and lo and behold, the daunting task lost some of its mystique.

A few students conveyed a disappointment in not learning other qualitative methods, perhaps not realizing that some components of IQA are generally applicable to all qualitative research. Some members questioned whether the IQA method would have a practical use for their dissertations. Students seemed to enjoy the systematic processes of learning IQA but were baffled sometimes by the new software, or frustrated by the time-consuming aspects of the exercises. Students' experiences with these processes led to the consideration of how well IQA applies to their research for their dissertations, and whether the scope of the course was comprehensive. Students generally thought that IQA was a useful tool. However, the sole focus on IQA left some students wondering if other qualitative methods should have been included in this course. Although the method was seen as a valuable tool, some of the group members felt that they missed out on other methods of qualitative research.

Process. IQA is a very structured approach to qualitative research—an attribute that most students appreciated. A few students mentioned that the linear, systematic process "simplifies a complicated process" and made the analysis of interview data "more manageable." A few expressed dissatisfaction with the structure of the method, especially the interviews, but most preferred the structure and felt that it gave a bit more credence to qualitative data gathering. Most agreed that the mindmaps were fascinating and added an interesting component to a study, but some were concerned with the subjective interpretations of the unsaturated SIDs. As with any qualitative method, this interpretive component made some students question the reliability and the perception of IQA in academia. Whether the members described the IQA process as laborious or fascinating, they all felt that the IQA method involves a systematic process.

Table 5.11 IQA as a Method

Applicability
- ❖ After gathering data, I will be prepared to finish last 2 chapters
- ❖ Builds my repertoire of research—I will use parts of IQA, but I will not use all
- ❖ Causes reflecting on own dissertation
- ❖ Class assignments and readings directly applicable to dissertation
- ❖ Exciting—possible dissertation method
- ❖ For once, I can see the light at the end of the tunnel
- ❖ How is this relevant to me?
- ❖ Practical nature of class for dissertation purposes is great
- ❖ Prepared to write dissertation
- ❖ Process can be utilized with low-performing schools
- ❖ Realize IQA could be useful "not just stats or quant."
- ❖ Reliable method
- ❖ Sad to give up learning other models in qualitative research
- ❖ Subjective but it will help me come up with things to write about in chapter 5 of dissertation
- ❖ Very applicable
- ❖ Will modify IQA to fit my needs if I decide to use it

Process
- ❖ A linear process
- ❖ Concrete
- ❖ Data collection
- ❖ Doing IRD and SID can be tedious
- ❖ Good interviews
- ❖ Good research

(Continued)

Table 5.11 (Continued)

- ❖ Good step-by-step explanation
- ❖ How credible is this process?
- ❖ How do I connect this to my area of interest?
- ❖ How is IQA perceived outside this class (in the academic world)?
- ❖ If/then statements tedious
- ❖ Interesting how information connects
- ❖ Interesting process
- ❖ Laborious process
- ❖ Logical format
- ❖ Mindmaps are fascinating
- ❖ Mindmaps turn "words" into something visual
- ❖ Mixed feelings about the amount of structure in the method
- ❖ More quantitative than first thought
- ❖ Much like using TQM tools
- ❖ New technique of research
- ❖ Prefer quantitative research—cleaner
- ❖ Provides another option for research
- ❖ Research questions added value to practice
- ❖ Simplifies a complicated process
- ❖ Small gaps between process steps
- ❖ Structure makes analysis more manageable
- ❖ Structured qualitative process
- ❖ Tedious recording of numbers and arrows
- ❖ The design is VERY theoretical
- ❖ Useful process

8. Learning Resources

This affinity represents all the possible tools used to reinforce the learning of the IQA method and other information in the course. Learning resources helped students understand and apply the IQA method. While the instructor was a resource for information, so were the technology, software, and the IQA book draft given to the students during each class meeting. *Learning Resources* was the affinity used to describe how the resources helped, or hindered, the learning process in the course. Some members agreed that learning resources were helpful and practical. Other members described the affinity as frustrating.

The text was also included in this affinity with positive statements about its "step-by-step" examples and reasonable and interesting reading, as well as negative comments about its not being a book and its not being sufficient. Readings in general were helpful, but students seemed insecure without a core textbook for this course and unsure about using the Internet research resources as the basis for theoretical reading. Students did not have to purchase a book, and other learning resources were provided by the instructor. A few students expressed a desire for more textual reference material, but most were pleased with the chapters from the soon-to-be-published book and the technological resources.

Learning resources played an important role for students in their learning of the IQA model. Students appreciated the use of computers and the software called Inspiration and appeared to enjoy the "liberating" use of technology in the class. A few students were frustrated by the use of unfamiliar technology, but overall, students enjoyed and looked forward to the further use of technology. Many enjoyed being introduced to the *Inspiration* software, though some experienced "frustration" with technology. Most enjoyed conducting Web research to learn more about different aspects of qualitative research and learning to use Inspiration software to create mindmaps. The use of computers, new software, and Internet research were parts of the learning resources perceived as important by students. Although technology can be challenging sometimes, most students seemed to agree that the learning process and the support from the instructor helped ease the anxiety.

Table 5.12   Learning Resources

❖ Appreciate the extra class for mindmapping
❖ Appreciated the use of Inspiration to develop mindmap "practical"
❖ Computers
❖ Enjoyed the IQA Web research exercise—good approach to reading on topic
❖ Frustration learning to use Macs
❖ Good use of technology
❖ Happy to use and learn new technology software [Inspiration]
❖ High-tech
❖ Like using software [Inspiration]
❖ Looking forward to the CD
❖ Need more reference texts . . . not just Web
❖ New software [Inspiration]
❖ Reasonable, interesting reading
❖ The step-by-step examples in the readings have been great
❖ Working with technology was liberating
❖ Would be better with whole book

9. Peer Relationships

The friendships formed in the class constitute the affinity known as *peer relationships.* This affinity describes the supporting bonds of and fun times had with others in the class. The class provided a chance to meet new people and build on old friendships. There was a general feeling that the people in the class were "good people." Because class activities required collaboration and encouraged participation, many people made friends with persons they never knew before. The help and support of these friends made the class enjoyable and facilitated learning. The group believed that a by-product of the instructional set-up of the course allowed for discussion, collaboration, and interaction. Students considered the class to be conducive to building rapport among classmates, and they felt that the supportive relationships provided a positive social backdrop for learning.

However, this affinity also is made up of the negative belief that some peers were not on task and were keeping the class from moving along more rapidly, such as students who did not do the readings or who were not paying attention. Peer relationships then created frustration.

Table 5.13   Peer Relationships
❖ Building peer relationships
❖ Camaraderie
❖ Established some good bonds
❖ Friends help and support a lot
❖ Frustration with people who did not do the readings or who were not paying attention
❖ Fun with friends
❖ Good people
❖ Meeting new people
❖ New friends

10. Physical Environment

This affinity includes the classroom environment and time of day that the class was taught. The course was tiring because it ended late in the evening. Some students worked all day and found it hard to concentrate late in the evening. Adding to the difficult circumstances was the overcrowded classroom and uncomfortable chairs. The awkward room conditions prevented some students from staying alert and may have hindered their understanding of IQA research. At times, some of the things that required deep thought may have contributed to the fatigue. Group members felt that the physical conditions and physical exhaustion contributed to problems with attentiveness. This led to some group members trying to stay alert.

Table 5.14   Physical Environment

❖ 7–10 P.M.—a little late in the evening
❖ Class cuts into late hours—cannot focus at the end of class
❖ Hunger! Especially at around 8 P.M.
❖ It is late! I am sleepy driving home
❖ Scary walking to my car in the dark
❖ The class is always too cold
❖ Tired
❖ Tired after late night-classes

WEDNESDAY NIGHT EXPERIENCE WITH THE IQA COURSE

1. Application Toward Dissertation

Being exposed to IQA as a research methodology helped students make choices about future approaches to their own dissertations. Students expressed a newly minted confidence in their ability to complete a dissertation. Some of these same students anticipated using IQA as their dissertation research methodology. The comfort level was more evident because some were more confident about how to apply IQA to their topic. Some liked the IQA course and were able to evaluate whether or not qualitative research applied to their topic. In addition, the practical use of IQA with hands-on experience was an effective application. The introduction to IQA led to an epiphany for most students. It helped many of them answer the question, "How shall I conduct my own dissertation research?" The responses were mainly positive, and participants felt more confident about their dissertation because of their new level of knowledge. There was excitement for research as students pondered the new knowledge that could be gained through the IQA research method.

The importance of the dissertation to the doctoral students was evident. The capacity to connect or apply the learning to prior and future learning was well documented to enhance student success with complex learning. The answer to the question of how the IQA process would apply to the dissertation became evident and students stated that it was helpful to clarify some of the methodology aspects for writing the dissertation. The underlying theme appeared to be confidence-building experience—a positive reaction to the learning and the clarification of the looming question(s) the students had about the research and dissertation process.

Students were embarking on the final leg of their PhD: the start of the dissertation. Clearly, the prospect of the dissertation was on their minds. The results seemed to be skewed toward using IQA as opposed to not using it. The most confident respondents expressed the opinion that IQA will be the model for their qualitative research. Several others began in the cognitive stage: "this is new knowledge, can I apply it to help me?" and then moving to "yes, I believe I can." Some students ruled out qualitative research. Some did not perceive the IQA model as relevant at all to their research. For others, this introduction to qualitative research methods triggered a decision not to do a qualitative dissertation.

Table 5.15   Application Toward Dissertation

- ❖ Apply knowledge
- ❖ Constantly had in the back of my mind the ? (how) does this apply to my dissertation
- ❖ Dissertation method
- ❖ Excited at the prospects
- ❖ I can see IQA in my dissertation
- ❖ Is this [IQA] useful for my dissertation?
- ❖ Learned a lot about IQA
- ❖ Learning how to match IQA to dissertation study very helpful
- ❖ Makes me think a lot about qualitative research
- ❖ Model for dissertation research
- ❖ More confident about dissertation
- ❖ Productive
- ❖ Qual is cool
- ❖ Question how to use practically
- ❖ Research
- ❖ Ruled out a qualitative dissertation

---

2. Classroom Climate

This affinity represents how the group felt about the classroom as a learning environment. Because of the professor's unconventional approach to classroom instruction, most group members perceived the classroom as an enjoyable, open learning environment that engendered a willingness to participate in IQA exercises. A high level of student engagement was evidenced by the description of high interest and anticipation. Several group members simply described the class as fun, noting the humor that was injected in every class. Cohorts, making up the majority of the class, were another reason given for the camaraderie in the class as two group members commented on the support of classmates.

This affinity glowed with positive responses. The range of feelings for the classroom climate ran between "interesting," "exciting," "love it," "relaxing," "inspiring," and "rewarding." Several comments were made regarding IQA as interesting, which made for healthy class discussions. The class was described as enjoyable or socially fun, meaning there was an atmosphere that was open to both communication and humor. People (students and instructor) were described as friendly, and course materials as interesting. The class was inspiring because the instructor provided an atmosphere that was open for sharing. This openness also promoted relaxed course content and decreased the stress that students felt about IQA research. Finally, students felt that their classmates were supportive of learning, which led to openness to sharing, and interest in qualitative research.

One might assert that this is a distribution with a strong central tendency. The results all appear to be clustered around a mean (so to speak) of contentment and happiness. The fact that the instructor's birthday was celebrated in class made the list. This in itself reveals some of the novelty of the class. The word *friend* appears twice and *fun* appears three times. Clearly, students enjoyed attending the class. In fact, one student comment noted the "strain-free" environment. The conclusion was that the class was fun and resulted in the making of new friends.

Had students been spending Wednesday evenings in the Garden of Eden? Students left no doubt the classroom climate had been positive. They described the environment as "friendly," "supportive," "interesting," "fun," "relaxing," and "full of good humor." Student feedback on the classroom environment reflected a *positive unity*—the reference to the Garden of Eden was not intended to be ironic.

Table 5.16   Classroom Climate

- ❖ Anticipating with interest
- ❖ Celebrating a birthday
- ❖ Engaging
- ❖ Enjoy
- ❖ Enjoyable
- ❖ Exciting
- ❖ Friendly people
- ❖ Friends
- ❖ Fun 5X
- ❖ Fun class
- ❖ Fun time, good humor
- ❖ Humorous
- ❖ Inspiring class
- ❖ Interesting 4X
- ❖ Interesting material
- ❖ Laughing
- ❖ Looking forward to coming to class
- ❖ Love it
- ❖ Openness to share
- ❖ Relaxing
- ❖ Rewarding

(Continued)

Table 5.16 (Continued)

❖ Socially fun
❖ Strain-free allows for learning
❖ Supportive
❖ Supportive classmates
❖ Very interesting

3. Cognitive Reaction (Dialectic)

This affinity describes the reactions of students confronted with a large amount of information and new learning. The responses that are described illustrate a wide range of personal conditions that range from frustration to clarification to personal growth. Students were frustrated, confused, and anxious when confronted with uncertainty and overwhelming amounts of new information. At the same time, students experienced "lightbulb moments" when they were comfortable and felt successful with the learning. Students also described the growth experience of self-improvement through new learning that is deep and thoughtful. The group discussed several cognitive issues that are labeled *cognitive reaction.* These cognitive issues were divided into three subaffinities: *confusion, clarity,* and *growth.*

Confusion. Because of the newness of IQA as a research tool (and a way of thinking!) to most of the group, various approaches were taken to resolve the conflict. A majority of the group expressed confusion over the IQA as a process, noting that the material was "uncomfortable." Still others expressed feeling anxiety, simply frustrated by the material or the mindmaps or questions from students, or feeling like a test subject. One group member noted a struggle to get clarification of the IQA process, *while some others felt the quantity of information overloaded them.*

This affinity reflects the confusion some students may have had because of the anxiety and uncertainty of the process. Some students did not understand the qualitative research despite the CD and tutorial sessions. Some of the students were confused and frustrated because of the mindmaps and being given a lot of information. Sometimes, it was too much information for students to process, and the material was uncomfortable at times. Also, a source of concern for the students was whether or not they would know enough to use this method later in their dissertation. The focus group reported anxiety and confusion about IQA methodology possibly because of information overload. Students had difficulty understanding mindmaps and other materials because they were not able to apply them to future dissertation and research activities.

Clarity. The clarity subaffinity demonstrated many group members' experience with "getting" IQA as a research method. Moments of "eureka!" were discussed, while others felt comfortable with the process all along. The comments were stated with excitement: "I can do this," "I get it," and "it all comes together." Although not all group members enjoyed this clarity, the group expressed enjoying the process of learning something new and being able to see the relevance of IQA.

Growth. Perhaps clarity of IQA research leads to the subaffinity growth. There are rewards with growth, including new ideas, enhanced cognition, and a motivation to learn. Exploration of new concepts motivated students to new experiences and growth. The growth subaffinity dealt with group members' perception of intellectual growth regarding IQA. Although most of the discussion was the growth associated with learning something new, one student expressed the growth of looking at something new, while another felt as if he or she had a "mind on fire." The group's feelings in this seem to be driven by the exposure to a new idea and trying to intellectualize its purpose.

Cognitive reactions establish a dialectic with the subaffinities of *confusion* and *clarity,* providing a thesis and an antithesis that result in a synthesis of another subaffinity, *growth.* Confusion, frustration, and information overload can be followed by lightbulb moments. A lightbulb moment can in turn lead to a recognition that the student's intellectual journey has resulted in real personal growth. Dialectic suggests reasoning by dialogue. The dialogue moves from "struggling in confusion" to "I get it," about as far apart as two emotions could be. This dialogue suggests that perhaps some of the class was "there" while the others were still struggling to apply the concept. The class seemed to perceive the benefit of the analytic method of IQA. This suggests that those who needed help were more than ready to continue to pursue the study of IQA. The metaphor of an athlete in training is applicable here—"no pain, no gain." A student can struggle to get clarification (*confusion*), then be surprised by the level of new understanding (*clarity*), and finally recognize that learning to think about things differently leads to *growth* (Table 5.17).

Table 5.17 Cognitive Reaction (Dialectic)

Confusion
- ❖ Am I going to be ready for advanced qual?
- ❖ Anxiety
- ❖ Confused
- ❖ Confusing

(Continued)

Table 5.17 (Continued)

- ❖ Did not feel as though I had a grasp on variations of qual despite the CD
- ❖ Feel like a guinea pig
- ❖ Frustrated
- ❖ Frustrated by too many questions from students
- ❖ Frustration (mindmaps)
- ❖ Information overload
- ❖ Lots of information
- ❖ Material uncomfortable at times
- ❖ Struggling to get clarification
- ❖ Uncertainty in process
- ❖ Will I know enough to really use this later?

Clarity

- ❖ Being surprised by my understanding
- ❖ Challenging but good to feel like I can do this—not like I am drowning
- ❖ Discover
- ❖ I can do this!
- ❖ I get it!
- ❖ Insightful
- ❖ It all comes together
- ❖ Learned something new 2X
- ❖ Lightbulb moments
- ❖ Lost and found
- ❖ Understanding 2X

Growth

- ❖ Beneficial
- ❖ Diligent
- ❖ Experiencing learning
- ❖ Exploration
- ❖ Learning a lot
- ❖ Learning experience
- ❖ Learning to think about things differently
- ❖ Loved use of motivation to learn more than assigned
- ❖ Mind on fire
- ❖ New experience
- ❖ New ideas 2X
- ❖ New people
- ❖ New way of looking at things
- ❖ Something new
- ❖ The last part was much easier than the first part (to follow)
- ❖ Thinking in depth, thoughtful

4. Collaboration

This affinity consists of ways collaboration was used in the class. According to the focus group, the class allowed sharing of ideas. In addition, friendly communication with students and instructors encouraged healthy discussion. The interactive class made learning meaningful. Open classroom discussion allowed sharing of ideas for the students to build on ideas. Students endorsed the collaborative teaching strategies used in the IQA course. The open atmosphere made it possible to share ideas, discuss different points of view, and collaborate with others in a friendly fashion. *Collaboration* as an affinity reveals a basic positive unity in student attitudes, as does the affinity on *Classroom Climate*. Students valued the opportunity to collaborate.

The classroom environment allowed for the sharing of ideas through collaboration and communication with other students. Intellectual classroom discussion promoted more meaningful forms of learning the IQA method. The group seemed comfortable with one another. "Sharing" appears twice in the list, as does "interactive." The class seemed to thrive on the interactive nature of the group learning experience. These responses, coupled with the positive comments in the learning environment, suggest that the class was ready to tackle new ideas as a group.

The importance of collegial interaction is related in this affinity. Students not only enjoyed the healthy discussion and active sharing of ideas in the class, but they also found the discussions relevant to making the learning more meaningful. The sharing of ideas and collaborative interaction contributed to the learning. This affinity centered the class's ability to share ideas in a friendly way. As mentioned in the *Classroom Climate* affinity, healthy discussions were a part of the class that fostered this collaboration. Because IQA is by definition interactive, the group mentioned that this allowed for meaningful learning, which led to open discussions and sharing of ideas.

Table 5.18   Collaboration

- ❖ Allow sharing of ideas
- ❖ Collaboration
- ❖ Friendly communication
- ❖ Healthy discussion
- ❖ Interactive class made learning meaningful
- ❖ Interactive classroom discussion
- ❖ Open discussion
- ❖ Sharing ideas

5. Course Structure

The affinity course structure functions as a continuum, with most students providing positive feedback about elements of course structure and a few making suggestions for improvement. The course was described as "focused learning," "structured," "directive," "well organized," and "taught at a relaxed pace." Students expressed appreciation for handouts, the written text, a useful syllabus, and no paper requirement. One student characterized the course as "under construction"; another wanted to do an IQA research project of his or her own design. The sprinkling of terms like "practical," "useful," "digestible," and "relaxed" suggests that the students were quite satisfied with the course structure.

The class seemed to appreciate the open-ended nature of the course. Comments like "not zeroed in on one answer" indicate that the class enjoyed the additive structure of the class. Each class session built upon the next, as evidenced by comments like "well organized" and "gave me hands-on experience." The students praised the organization and structure of the course. It appears that they appreciated that the instructor knew where he was headed. This affinity describes a respect for a carefully

---

Table 5.19   Course Structure

- Adding info in digestible chunks
- Am being patient with a "class under construction"
- Directive
- Focused learning
- Gave me hands-on experience for qualitative data analysis
- Handouts, resources
- Hands-on
- Like doing project-based work but would have preferred choosing my own project
- Lots of details
- Lots of new information
- No paper!
- Note-taking
- OK to disagree—not so zeroed in on the #1 right answer
- Organized approach
- Participant
- Participation by students
- Practical, hands-on
- Quantifying the qualitative paradigm
- Relaxed pace
- Requirement (course)
- Structured 3X
- Useful syllabus
- Wanted more homework and testing of some kind
- Well organized
- Written text was awesome

structured, organized course that provided the previously described "information overload" in "digestible chunks." Appreciation was expressed for the organization that focused on practical, hands-on activities, and available resources. The course requirement for a project, rather than a paper, was noted. The pace of the learning was described as relaxed, although other references were made in regard to the rigor of the learning.

This affinity was critical in the students' view of how they felt about the course. Students were encouraged to participate and they were not admonished for incorrect answers. Although there was an abundance of new information, the pace was relaxed and a useful syllabus guided the students. The students felt that they received a lot of information, such as handouts and the IQA CD. The use of written text was beneficial to the students. The course was structured with a lot of new information but it was acceptable to disagree, and emphasis is not so much on the number one answer. An interesting paradox was given by a student who requested *more* homework and testing.

6. IQA Process

Many different aspects of group members' reactions to IQA as a process were found in this affinity. The affinity describes the group's reaction to IQA as a new tool for research. Members saw the IQA method as "challenging," both intellectually and mechanically, "informative," "easy to follow," "analytical," "sequential," "thought provoking," "useful," "well organized," and "applicable" to their own research. Others viewed IQA as "critical to the transformation process," "repetitive," and "process oriented"; while one member saw it as "disarming," referring to the way it allowed group members to open up about various issues. Another member echoed this sentiment when observing how everyone was engaged in the process. One member saw IQA as good first exposure to doing real research.

References were made to the challenging and thought-provoking nature of the material. Yet it was noted that the process was designed to be easy to follow and understandable. The idea that the process was applicable to the doctoral studies (i.e., dissertation) surfaces again in this affinity. Students referred to the significance of the high level of participant engagement through interviews, the mixed use of data, and the "groundswell of data." There was expression of positive feelings about IQA as an experience for doing real research, including the use of terms, acronyms, and visual applications.

Many steps are needed to complete a useful IQA study. The process involved engaging everyone in the class, and the instructor successfully accomplished this during in-class focus group activities. This type of research was described as intellectually challenging because it inspires curiosity and thought through its useful application to research. A groundswell of data results when it is completed logically, sequentially, and incrementally. The IQA process was data based and challenging for some.

To some students, this process was applicable and critical to transformation process. It was a different type of research method for some, but the material and process were easy to follow. The IQA process is incremental in that the researcher using the process knows what to do after finishing the previous step, and it allows the researcher the opportunity to organize data

Table 5.20   IQA Process

- ❖ Analyze
- ❖ Applicable
- ❖ Challenging 2X
- ❖ Challenging concepts
- ❖ Concentrating (thoughtful)
- ❖ Critical to transformation process
- ❖ Different research method
- ❖ Disarming process
- ❖ Easy-to-follow process, material
- ❖ Elements and relationships
- ❖ Everyone engaged
- ❖ Good exposure (first time) to actual research
- ❖ Ground swell of data
- ❖ Incremental
- ❖ Informative
- ❖ Inspires curiosity; logically sound theory
- ❖ Intellectually challenging
- ❖ IQA is a mixed approach to data analysis
- ❖ Leading edge (innovative)
- ❖ Liked interviews
- ❖ Logical and sequential process
- ❖ Many new acronyms
- ❖ New information
- ❖ Powerful process
- ❖ Process easy
- ❖ Process oriented
- ❖ Processing
- ❖ Repetition
- ❖ Synthesis 3X
- ❖ System
- ❖ Systems were familiar info
- ❖ Theory to the people
- ❖ Thought provoking
- ❖ Understanding
- ❖ Unfamiliar topic
- ❖ Useful
- ❖ Very cool process
- ❖ Very sequential
- ❖ Visual application
- ❖ Well organized

easier. Furthermore, the IQA process is more efficient in use of time by analyzing data more efficiently. IQA as a research method provides a vocabulary for student evaluators. It is a qualitative research methodology, but student evaluations of the process sounded like evaluations of a scientific process; for example, IQA is a "logical and sequential process."

Comments like "critical," "useful," "engaged," and "incremental" suggest that the instructor struck gold in light of the earlier comment that this is a "class under construction." The class enjoyed the analytical approach, noting that everyone was engaged. The process was seen as "powerful," "useful," and "well organized."

7. Physical Environment

This affinity includes the classroom environment and time of day that the class is taught. As with the Tuesday night focus group, the students in the Wednesday night group found that the course was tiring because it ended late in the evening. (It is interesting that the two classes, while working independently on the same topic, often came to the same conclusions. One of the purposes of this experiment was to show how two similar constituencies actually do produce similar results when working independently.) Some students worked all day and found it hard to concentrate late in the evening. Adding to the difficult circumstances was the overcrowded classroom and uncomfortable chairs. The awkward room conditions prevented some students from staying alert and may have hindered their understanding of IQA research. At times, some of the things that required deep thought may have contributed to the fatigue. Group members felt that the physical conditions and physical exhaustion contributed to problems with attentiveness. This led to some group members trying to stay alert, while one simply admitted to being "spaced out" at times.

Table 5.21   Physical Environment
❖ 10 P.M. is late for me
❖ At times tiring
❖ Crowded room
❖ Crowded table
❖ End of long day
❖ Exhausted after class
❖ Hard chairs
❖ Late at night
❖ Lots of people
❖ Physically uncomfortable
❖ Sometimes trying to stay alert
❖ Spaced out or inattentive at times (fatigued)
❖ Tiring at times

Those that felt compelled to write about the environment did so in the negative. Their reactions were that students were tired and exhausted at the end of a day, probably beginning their day around 6:00 A.M. This is in contrast to the responses about the friendly communication. Could *Collaboration* and *Physical Environment* be mutually exclusive affinities? Perhaps they are. These responses represented the feelings of some in the group who were simply too tired to pay attention at the late hour of the class. Perhaps there is a link from here to the one-third who expressed confusion in their *Cognitive Reaction*. Clearly, the crowded room and the late hour caused some respondents trouble when learning IQA.

Negative reactions of students to the classroom's *Physical Environment* can be contrasted to positive reactions provided in *Collaboration*, *Classroom Climate*, and *Teacher Style*. Fatigue and discomfort affected student performance. A move to limit class size and change the location of the classroom and the hour at which the course is offered could address student concerns.

8. Teacher Style

Teacher Style represents the affinity the group described as being important in the IQA course. Overwhelmingly positive, the group noted the professor's helpfulness, humor, energy for the topic, and patience with students' confusion. One member felt as though the system (probably the IQA process) was built around the professor's style. Another group member felt the co-teaching style was disjointed at times, while another was glad to have the professor. The teaching style of the instructor was "assessable and helpful," with encouraging questions and written communication. The instructor was very knowledgeable in the IQA process.

Table 5.22 Teacher Style
❖ Assessable, helpful
❖ Build the system around professor's style
❖ Co-teaching seemed disjointed sometimes
❖ Engaged teachers
❖ Enjoy professor's humor
❖ Focused teaching
❖ Glad to have professor for an instructor
❖ Help ever present
❖ Helpful instruction
❖ High energy
❖ Patient professor
❖ Professor's sense of humor
❖ Promptness to help
❖ Unique professor

The professor was seen as an accessible, friendly instructor who encouraged discussion outside of the class as needed. His teaching style included humor, patience, high energy, and engagement of discussion. His students were glad to have him as an instructor because his style promoted a greater understanding of IQA research. The instructor was well prepared, which helped students to feel comfortable in class, thereby enhancing their learning.

The comments on *Teacher Style* echoed the positive comments in *Course Structure*. The style of the teacher was appreciated. The high energy and helpful manner of the instructor elicited comments numerous times. The class seemed to have encountered a professor with a different teaching style than what they had been experiencing.

9. Technology

Technology was a critical affinity for the group as they saw this as either an "inspiring" way to approach the course or had trouble with some technical aspects of it. The use of technology to supplement class materials was challenging yet enjoyable. Although challenging, the integration of

---

Table 5.23   Technology

- ❖ Am learning to manipulate software, which is fun
- ❖ Assignments on email confusing
- ❖ CD-ROM
- ❖ Email
- ❖ Email needs more descriptive subject lines to identify and sort
- ❖ Enjoying the technology part of the class
- ❖ Good communication (email)
- ❖ Having fun with new computer program (Inspiration)
- ❖ Inspiration 3X
- ❖ Inspiration program was great
- ❖ Interactive technology
- ❖ Interesting software
- ❖ Lack of knowledge with Macs
- ❖ Liked having a CD to consult
- ❖ Liked lab days
- ❖ Loved CD
- ❖ Mac lab (positive extension of the class)
- ❖ Technical aspect
- ❖ Too many attachments to emails
- ❖ Usage of Inspiration
- ❖ Use of technology
- ❖ Using new technology (challenging)

technology seemed to be meaningful and satisfying. The comments varied from "assignments on email confusing" to "liking the lab and CD." The students seemed to enjoy the technology side of the class. Some enjoyed the tinkering aspect, while others found it frustrating. Overall, the responses to the technical side of the class were positive, suggesting that this method was readily accepted by the students. Technology clearly enhanced the collaborative nature of the class and promoted understanding of IQA research. Group members who saw the technology as a tool enjoyed the Inspiration software used to draw mindmaps, appreciated the email communications, and saw the Mac lab work as a positive extension of the class.

The IQA CD was noted for its consultative function. The CD ROM included exercises and software that made learning easier and promoted the use of a skill that is highly regarded. The CD-ROM was helpful as a practice tool and as a resource. The Inspiration program was great and helped to facilitate the learning process for students. In addition, the Inspiration CD was user-friendly for students to work on the exercises that the instructor discussed in class.

The answers seem divided in terms of students enjoying the technology. Some became frustrated with the emails. This is not unexpected in trying out a new teaching technology. Most students appreciated the classroom communication via email. The email needed to have more descriptive subject lines in order to identify assignment and information. The email communication was a good way for students to stay informed of class information. Those members who did not share their fellow group members' enthusiasm for technology saw emails assignments as confusing, whether they contained one assignment or too many assignments, or simply needed more descriptive subject lines.

The use of a variety of technologies and technical applications challenged students. Lab days were well received. The classes taught in the Mac lab were a positive extension of the class, although some students had difficulty using Macs. Because most of the group was familiar with PCs, some members expressed a lack of knowledge with Macs and their frustration in using them. Some had trouble with using the computers because of general lack of knowledge and experience.

In this chapter, we discussed the theoretical foundation for IQA group processes and gave examples of how to put this theory into action. We introduced a theory of coding; in the case example, we showed in detail how to use group processes to accomplish the first two (inductive and axial) coding tasks. Chapter 6 extends the theory to the third task (theoretical coding) and embeds this theory of coding within the larger context of systems.

Notes

1. Another less reverent term is "mindmap."

2. It may not surprise students of organizational communication to learn that the perspective of executives was dramatically different from that of employees, and also that the executives were shocked to see evidence that they were so "out of touch" with the way employees viewed communication at the company.

3. The justifiable postmodern sensitivity to the limitations of logic is often carried too far, resulting in researchers who have little or no formal training in logic of any kind.

4. Apologizing in advance for sexist language, we often call the theoretical code the *Queen of Codes* in the sense that, like the queen on a chessboard, the theoretical code is extremely powerful in revealing the structure of relationships among affinities.

5. Marcus Aurelius, *Meditations,* circa 167 A.C.E. Translation by George Long, found at The Internet Classics Archive: *http://classics.mit.edu/Antoninus/ meditations.html.* Accessed August 29, 2002.

6. Although we may look back at September 11, 2001, as a watershed moment in the debate: After all, who would have predicted the dramatic and sudden rehabilitation of two quintessential Dead White Males, Mark Twain and Sinclair Lewis?

Group Reality 6

System Relationships

Ghosts of Vienna. Mindmap is the Interactive Qualitative Analysis (IQA) vernacular for the very useful notion of mental models, which has found application in a variety of contexts over the past 60 years, and as a subject of formal logic for close to 80 years. In 1922, after having studied under Bertrand Russell, Ludwig Wittgenstein wrote a work that attracted the attention of what has become known as *The Vienna Circle,* to which is attributed the paradigm called *logical positivism.* In *Tractatus,* Wittgenstein (1922) highlighted the importance of semantics and semiotics[1] to the study of the mind by arguing that the shape of ideas in the mind and the relationship of words in a sentence are identical in form with the structure of reality or state of affairs they represent. Postmodern writers, obviously uncomfortable with the claims of logical positivism about the nature of reality, revise Wittgenstein's proposition by de-emphasizing, if not eliminating, the reference to reality as an absolute. For example, Johnson-Laird (1983) strongly evokes the ghost of Wittgenstein by suggesting that sentences are components of mental models and that a mental model created by a discourse exhibits a structure that corresponds directly to the structure of the world *described by the discourse* (italics added). Notice that Johnson-Laird is not making a claim that the structure of the sentences ultimately forms a map of reality, but that the structure is a legitimate map of the discourse itself, a thesis that Wittgenstein would likely characterize as tautological. Nevertheless, the work of Johnson-Laird and others[2] is an important component of the IQA approach to analysis of relationships, even as the dialectical nature of reality and language ensures a continuing debate.

Minds, Computers, and Systems. Beginning with Kenneth Craik's (1943) view that the brain builds internal models of the world by creating internal representations of phenomena that are linked by symbolic processes, the idea of mindmaps (in our language, *systems consisting of concepts and relationships among these concepts*) has created both controversy and a wide variety of applications. Some cognitive psychologists insist that mental models should be constrained to discourse about only thinking and reasoning.[3] A brief description of some of these applications follows.

Cognitive Psychology

The work of Johnson-Laird has already been mentioned, but Fodor's (1975) *mentalese* also deserves our attention. Fodor's earlier work stressed the comparison of the mind to a computer and indeed has been called a computational theory of the mind, a proposition that has been the source of some controversy. Our interest, however, is more in Fodor's understanding of mental representation as a language of thought—what he calls *mentalese*—and his contention that all knowledge is represented syntactically.

Cybernetics

The term *cybernetics* is used here to denote human-computer interaction, or what those in the trade call the *interface*. Indeed, there are journals dedicated to this topic,[4] all of which are heavily influenced by the concept of mental models. In particular, cognitive models have been developed that are used to create interfaces and tutoring systems.

Instructional Technology

David Jonassen (1995), in an online paper presented to the Computer Support for Collaborative Learning Conference, emphasized the importance of theorizing about mental models to developments in instructional technology and design. Jonassen identified several *constructivist learning environments* in which mental models can play an important role, and he argues that "higher order . . . learning outcomes can best be operationalized and predicted by assessing and understanding learners' mental models of the problem or content domain being learned."

Textual Analysis

Mental models are at the foundation of efforts to determine the causal structure of texts. Extending the scope of content analysis, Carley and Palmquist (1992)[5] have done some intriguing work combining both qualitative and quantitative approaches (notably the use of cluster analysis on qualitatively induced data) that they call *Map Analysis:* mental maps or network maps developed from texts that contain both concepts and relationships among concepts.

Assumptions About Mental Models

Controversies and legitimate disagreements exist about the very meaning of (let alone the proper construction of) mental models, yet certain common assumptions are prevalent among those in the mental model business. In the interest of laboring in the vineyard rather than spending time putting an ever-finer edge on our intellectual shears, IQA shares these assumptions to a large extent. Carley and Palmquist first outlined the assumptions in their 1992 work, and Jonassen's (1995) summary follows.

- ❖ Mental models are representations.
- ❖ Language is the key to understanding mental models.
- ❖ Mental models can be represented as networks of concepts.[6]
- ❖ The meanings for the concepts are embedded in their relationships to others.
- ❖ The social meaning of concepts is derived from the intersection of different individuals' mental models.[7]

What Is Theoretical Coding?

The purpose of IQA is to draw a picture of the system (System Influence Diagram or SID) that represents the perceptual terrain or the *mindmap* of a group with respect to a phenomenon represented by the issue statement. The SID is a picture drawn using a set of rules for rationalization on a summary of the theoretical codes called an Interrelationship Diagram (IRD) produced by the focus group. *Theoretical coding* refers to ascertaining the perceived cause-and-effect relationships (influences) among all the affinities in a system. In the focus group setting, this is accomplished by facilitating a systematic process of building hypotheses linking each possible pair of affinities. The group IRD summarizes the results of group theoretical coding.

All possible direct links between the affinities are investigated by developing hypotheses grounded in the data. IQA provides focus group participants with a formal protocol to determine whether or not there is a direct influence between every possible pair of affinities in the system. If so, the focus group then determines the directionality of influence. The goal is to identify the underlying (and generally hidden) structure of the group mindmap, which is summarized in a SID.

Issues in Theoretical Coding. Three issues must be resolved in the design of an IQA study with respect to theoretical coding. These are posed in the following questions.

1. What level of detail is desired in constructing each perceived relationship?

2. How will the group be organized for analysis of relationships?

3. How will a group composite (the system that represents the entire group) be constructed?

Notice that the first two issues concern the manner in which the theoretical codes are created. The third issue concerns the manner in which the codes are summarized as a prerequisite for creating the group IRD (prerequisite for rationalizing the system into its final representation, the SID). The sections that follow address two options for each of the three issues.

Issue 1: Level of Detail

Level of detail refers to the *extent to which the reasoning of the members of the focus group is documented.* Participants are encouraged to give examples supporting the relationships they perceive among affinities. These examples, which are valuable later to "ground" interpretation in the experiences of the participants, may be documented in natural language; for the sake of consistency and clarity, however, participants are taught to translate their logic into more formal logical discourse described in the following sections.

Hypothesis-Building Protocol. The preferred form of analyzing relationships among affinities is the "If . . . , then . . ." or hypothetical construction. Hypotheses are recorded on a protocol called the Affinity Relationship Table (ART). The investigator has a choice of level of detail at which to document the hypothesizing activity of the focus group; again, this choice must be made in light of both logistical considerations and the purpose of the research. Focus group participants may produce either a "simple" ART or a "detailed" one. The two differ in whether examples are given by the group members of their reasoning and documented on the ART protocol. Both kinds are discussed here.

SIMPLE ART

The Simple ART is the "quick and dirty" protocol for theoretical coding and should be used only if time constraints are severe. Simple ARTs document the direction of relationships but provide no detail by way of examples for the relationships. Table 6.1 is an example of a Simple ART that represents, for illustrative purposes, a system of only six affinities and is a facsimile of the actual working form that would be used by a focus group doing theoretical coding on a six-affinity system. Provided on all forms is a space reserved for the placement of affinity names. Because no affinity is more important than another, it is recommended that affinities be placed in alphabetical order. The affinity number does not represent any value placed on the affinity but is simply a quick reference for each affinity.

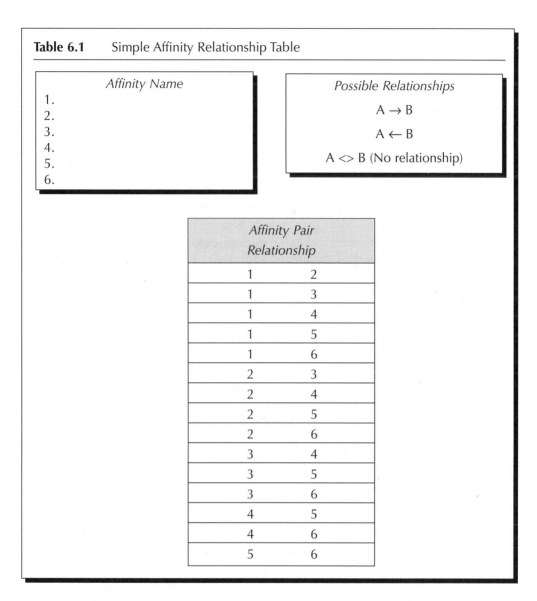

Table 6.1   Simple Affinity Relationship Table

Affinity Name	Possible Relationships
1.	A → B
2.	A ← B
3.	A <> B (No relationship)
4.	
5.	
6.	

Affinity Pair		Relationship
1	2	
1	3	
1	4	
1	5	
1	6	
2	3	
2	4	
2	5	
2	6	
3	4	
3	5	
3	6	
4	5	
4	6	
5	6	

Each focus group member is asked to determine the nature of the relationship between all possible pairs of affinities. For any two affinities A and B, there are only three possible relationships: Either A directly influences B, or B directly influences A, or there is no direct influence between A and B. These *Rules for Hypothesizing* are summarized as follows:

For any 2 affinities A and B, either

A → B (A influences B)
A ← B (B influences A)
A <> B (No relationship)

If, for example, a focus group member determines that affinity 2 influences affinity 1, a left arrow is placed between the pair. The member continues theoretical coding until the form is complete.

The Simple ART is quick and easy for the focus group to fill out. After an explanation of the rules of coding and an explanation of cause-and-effect logic, participants may be left on their own to fill in the arrows showing relationships. Although the Simple ART produces all the coding needed for a mindmap, volume and detail of data are sacrificed in the interest of time. The Simple ART contains no insight into the reasoning of the participant. The use of the Detailed ART overcomes that issue but at a cost of additional time for the focus group. By completing the hypothesis section of the table, participants have an opportunity to test their logic and reasoning by writing down specific examples from their experiences. The Detailed ART creates an audit trail—a record of the reasoning and examples taken from the experiences of the participants.

DETAILED ART

Table 6.2 is an example of the Detailed ART. Each focus group member (or subgroup) is asked to determine the nature of the relationship between all possible pairs of affinities as in the previous table. The Detailed ART requires more time than the Simple ART because participants are asked to write a statement—preferably in hypothesis form for consistency and clarity of logic's sake—that reflects their experiences and that supports the cause-and-effect relationship recorded for the affinity pair, that is, an example of the relationship that is "grounded" in the individual or subgroup's experience.

Each individual or small-group member (dyad or triad) is given a form on which to record the hypotheses. Members of the focus group are encouraged to explore the relationship between each pair by constructing a hypothesis in the form, "If . . . [cause; independent variable], then . . . [effect; dependent variable]." The facilitator guides participants' analyses by instructing them to break down each analysis into two steps. For example, if the pair under consideration consists of the affinities *Expertise in My Field* and *Empowerment,* then the facilitator gives instructions to participants, as shown in Table 6.3.

Issue 2: Organizing the Focus Group

The next issue to be addressed is how to organize the group for filling out ARTs. Asking each member to fill out an individual ART will result in a greater volume and range of data. If there are 15 focus group members,

Table 6.2	Detailed Affinity Relationship Table

Affinity Pair Relationship		Example of the relationship either in natural language or in the form of an IF/THEN statement of relationship.
1	2	
1	3	
1	4	
1	5	
1	6	
2	3	
2	4	
2	5	
2	6	
3	4	
3	5	
3	6	
4	5	
4	6	
5	6	

Table 6.3	Relationship Analysis (Theoretical Coding) Steps

Analytical Task	Facilitating Instructions
Step 1. Is there a direct relationship?	You have spent some time in identifying and talking about the meaning of *Expertise* and *Empowerment*. Now, think about the two affinities in relationship to each other. Do you feel there is a direct connection between the two?
Step 2. If the answer to the above is *Yes,* what is the direction of the relationship?	Now that you have decided there is a connection, write a hypothesis based upon our discussion that illustrates the direction of the relationship between *Expertise* and *Empowerment*. Make the hypothesis as specific as possible.

then there will be 15 separate pieces of code for each affinity pair and 15 separate explanations for the codes if the Detailed ART is used. On the other hand, if that same 15-member group were organized into five groups of three members each, each triad would discuss the direction of the relationship and come to a consensus on the direction. They would discuss and write a hypothesis to explain the relationship. This organization creates five relationship codes and five explanations, which is only one-third of the amount of data produced by the first approach.

To reiterate: Regardless of the chosen level of detail, ARTs may be produced by each member of the focus group, or the focus group may be organized into subgroups with two or three members. Individual ARTs are useful in that they are, in effect, an extension of the silent nominal process and make it possible for drawing a mindmap for each individual in the focus group. Alternatively, subgroups may produce a single ART, a structure that produces only one mindmap per group. Choice of organizational structure is determined by the need to produce the greatest volume of data within the time constraints unique to a particular situation. The following is a discussion of the implications of several variations in organizing the group and selecting a theoretical coding protocol.

1. Each participant works independently in *independent coding* by following the two-step analytical process for each pair using a worksheet tailored to the particular number of affinities produced by the group. If the participant feels there is a direct relationship, he or she writes a formal "If/then" hypothesis in the appropriate cell, making the hypothesis as specific ("grounded") as possible. The researcher is available as a resource making group-generated details of the affinities available to individuals as they work their way through the affinity pairs. The researcher also checks the deductive logic of each hypothesis as it is produced in order to make sure that the syllogism represents what the participant meant to say. Hypotheses are then posted for examination by the total group. This approach requires the most time and the most facilitation. If the group is large—approximately 15 people—two facilitators will probably be needed. On the other hand, the output from this protocol is certainly largest in volume and variety. For example, if everyone agrees that a relationship exists between a given affinity pair (and they often do), then 15 hypotheses will be created; all of this, taken in total, illustrates in great variety and depth the nature of the perceived link between the pair.

2. *Dyad coding* is faster than the first variation because participants are grouped into pairs. Each pair of participants conducts the analysis of all possible relationships among affinities. The two dyad members discuss each possible relationship and come to agreement as to whether or not there is a relationship and, if so, what is the direction? As a team, they write hypotheses that illustrate the relationships and submit them for examination by the entire group.

3. *Triad coding* is similar to coding in dyads, but the total group is subdivided into groups of three. If the triad cannot come to consensus on the nature of a relationship, majority vote rules.

4. *Variations 1–3 combined* with partialling out subsets of potential relationships to individuals or small groups can be used if time or other constraints limit the researcher's contact with the focus group. For example, suppose a focus group of 14 participants identifies a system with 12 affinities. The task is to determine the total possible number of direct relationships and then allocate subsets of these more or less equally to individuals or to subgroups. The combinatorial expression $n!/r!(n-r)!$ expresses the total number of potential direct relationships, where n is the number of affinities and r always equals 2, because we are looking for direct relationships. The expression evaluates as

$$12!/(10!2!) = \frac{12!}{(10!)(2!)} = \frac{132}{2} = 66,$$

which can be an intimidating workload for a focus group, especially if time is limited.

For efficiency, the 66 potential relationships can be partialled out among individuals, dyads, or triads as shown in Table 6.4.

Table 6.4	Possible Focus Group (14 members): Organization for Theoretical Coding of a System With 12 Affinities
Focus Group Structure	*Theoretical Code Quota*
Individual members	All members get 4 each, remaining are analyzed by the 10 members who finish first.
Dyads	7 dyads get 9, remaining are analyzed by the 3 dyads who finish first.
Triads	4 triads and 1 dyad get 13 each, remaining is analyzed by the group finishing first.

5. If the need for documentation and volume is low and the total number of relationships to be coded is small, the focus group may code in a *plenary session*. In this variation, the entire focus group is asked to consider each affinity pair, and a vote is conducted with a show of hands. The simple majority vote used in creating the democratic composite is quick and requires little effort. With a show of hands, the facilitator records the direction of the relationship identified by the majority. If time is available, the facilitator can quickly create an IRD and draw the SID in "real time," which gives the focus group an opportunity to react to their own mindmap.

6. If the group is not too large, acceptable results can be obtained by the researcher's facilitation of a group discussion on each potential pair, informally (without the use of majority voting) assisting the group to arrive at *consensus*. Care must be taken with this approach not to let the most voluble members drive the analysis. Attention must also be given to documenting the verbal examples of hypotheses given by group members in the course of analysis.

7. Under extreme conditions, the researcher may be forced to take a more traditional approach to coding, in which the participants do no examination of the relationships among affinities at all, but analysis is conducted *ex post facto*. Although this variation is better than nothing (especially considering the tentative nature of focus group SIDs—remember, the focus group SID should be validated and elaborated on by interview theoretical coding), it is clearly inferior in terms of quality and richness because another "filter" (the researcher) has been interposed between the participants and the data.

Issue 3: Creating a Group Composite

Selecting a protocol for representing the consensus or the "preponderance" of the group's analysis of relationships is similarly independent of level of detail or focus group organization. Two variations in developing a group composite are presented. The *Pareto Protocol* is a statistical method, while the *Democratic Protocol* is a group process method.

FOCUS GROUP THEORETICAL CODING: PARETO PROTOCOL

A reasonably rigorous and powerful technique for achieving and documenting the degree of consensus in a focus group is based on the Pareto Principle, named after the nineteenth-century economist Wilfredo Pareto (1843–1913) and popularized among management and systems theorists by Joseph Juran (1988). Pareto wrote of the "trivial many and the significant few" in his analysis of productivity and economics. The principle has been used in quality management to help focus priorities by providing an easy-to-remember rule of thumb. Put in systems terms, the Pareto Principle states that *something like 20% of the variables in a system will account for 80% of the total variation in outcomes* (such as productivity or profit). Other (sometimes tongue-in-cheek) incarnations of the Pareto Principle are:

1. Addressing the most troublesome 20% of your problem will solve 80% of it.

2. In any organization, 20% of the personnel will cause 80% of your headaches.

3. Eighty percent of all work that is completed is really the result of 20% effort.

4. Twenty percent of all potential solutions will solve 80% of the problem.

Whether the split is 20/80 or 70/30 or some other ratio depends on the nature of the system, but the essential utility of the Pareto Principle is this: A minority of the relationships in any system will account for a majority of the variation within the system. Depending on the variation of theoretical coding used, it is quite likely that there will be some disagreement among either individuals or subgroups about the nature of a given relationship. IQA uses the Pareto rule of thumb operationally to achieve consensus and analytically to create a statistical group composite. The *Pareto Cumulative Frequency Chart* provides an efficient and—to group members who find themselves in an initial stage of disagreement—satisfying method for achieving consensus.

The Pareto Composite will require more of the facilitator's time, but the focus group can be dismissed upon completion of the ARTs. The Pareto Composite requires an exact count of each relationship code but has distinct benefits in that it takes into account close votes and identifies conflicting relationships not addressed in a simple vote. Details of the Pareto Protocol are best left to the case material, but the following is a brief example of the technique. Frequency of each relationship is determined and recorded on a spreadsheet (Microsoft Excel is an excellent tool) by tallying all of the relationships from the ARTs. The total number of "votes" (we omit the quotes from now on) for each relationship is calculated, and the relationships are sorted out in descending order. Cumulative percentages are then calculated for each relationship, which is to say a Pareto Chart is constructed. The cumulative frequencies are used for two purposes:

1. To determine the optimal number of relationships to comprise the composite system. "Optimal" is used in the sense that the researcher's goal is to use the fewest number of relationships (for parsimony's sake) that represents the greatest amount of variation (for the sake of comprehensiveness and richness). Relationships that attract a very low percentage of votes are generally excluded from the group composite.

2. To help resolve ambiguous relationships, which are relationships that attract votes in either direction.

Table 6.5   Frequencies in Affinity Pair Order

Affinity Pair Relationship	Frequency	Affinity Pair Relationship	Frequency
1 → 2	1	2 → 6	3
1 ← 2	18	2 ← 6	0
1 → 3	3	3 → 4	1
1 ← 3	15	3 ← 4	0
1 → 4	3	3 → 5	0
1 ← 4	1	3 ← 5	18
1 → 5	1	3 → 6	1
1 ← 5	11	3 ← 6	1
1 → 6	1	4 → 5	2
1 ← 6	12	4 ← 5	1
2 → 3	20	4 → 6	3
2 ← 3	0	4 ← 6	17
2 → 4	3	5 → 6	2
2 ← 4	16	5 ← 6	15
2 → 5	13		
2 ← 5	3		
		Total Frequency	**185**

Continuing the six-affinity example discussed previously, assume that each member of the focus group has completed an individual ART. The first step in calculating frequencies is to record the total number of votes for each relationship pair in affinity order.

Table 6.5 shows that a total of 185 votes were cast for a total of 30 (30 permutations of 6 things taken pairwise[8]) possible relationships. Notice that some relationships received no votes at all: Every member of the group (20) voted for other relationships; and some relationships attracted a split vote.

The next step is to sort the relationships in descending order of frequency and to calculate cumulative frequencies and percentages in terms of both the total number of relationships (30) as well as the total number of votes (185, which is a proxy for the total variation in the system).

Table 6.6 contains the same frequencies as Table 6.5, but it has been sorted in descending order of frequency. Four columns have been added (again, Microsoft Excel is an excellent tool for this task) as follows:

Table 6.6	Affinities in Descending Order of Frequency With Pareto and Power Analysis					
Affinity Pair Relationship	Frequency Sorted (Descending)	Cumulative Frequency	Cumulative Percent (Relation)	Cumulative Percent (Frequency)	Power
1. 2 → 3	20	20	3.3	10.8	7.5
2. 1 ← 2	18	38	6.7	20.5	13.9
3. 3 ← 5	18	56	10.0	30.3	20.3
4. 4 ← 6	17	73	13.3	39.5	26.1
5. 2 ← 4	16	89	16.7	48.1	31.4
6. 1 ← 3	15	104	20.0	56.2	36.2
7. 5 ← 6	15	119	23.3	64.3	41.0
8. 2 → 5	13	132	26.7	71.4	44.7
9. 1 ← 6	12	144	30.0	77.8	47.8
10. 1 ← 5	11	155	33.3	83.8	50.5
11. 1 → 3	3	158	36.7	85.4	48.7
12. 1 → 4	3	161	40.0	87.0	47.0
13. 2 → 4	3	164	43.3	88.6	45.3
14. 2 → 6	3	167	46.7	90.3	43.6
15. 4 → 6	3	170	50.0	91.9	41.9
16. 2 ← 5	3	173	53.3	93.5	40.2
17. 5 → 6	2	175	56.7	94.6	37.9
18. 4 → 5	2	177	60.0	95.7	35.7
19. 1 → 2	1	178	63.3	96.2	32.9
20. 1 ← 4	1	179	66.7	96.8	30.1
21. 1 → 5	1	180	70.0	97.3	27.3
22. 3 ← 4	1	181	73.3	97.8	24.5
23. 3 → 6	1	182	76.7	98.4	21.7
24. 3 ← 6	1	183	80.0	98.9	18.9
25. 4 ← 5	1	184	83.3	99.5	16.1
26. 1 → 6	1	185	86.7	100.0	13.3
27. 2 ← 3	0	185	90.0	100.0	10.0
28. 2 ← 6	0	185	93.3	100.0	6.7
29. 3 ← 4	0	185	96.7	100.0	3.3
30. 3 → 5	0	185	100.0	100.0	0.0
Total Frequency	**185**				

❖ *Cumulative Frequency.* Entries in this column contain the running total or cumulative frequency. Each entry is the frequency of votes cast for an affinity pair added to the previous total.

❖ *Cumulative Percent (Relation).* This is a cumulative percentage based on the number of total possible relationships, in this case, 30; that is, each relationship represents 1/30 or approximately 3.3% of the total possible number. This cumulative percentage is one of two factors in the Power index.

❖ *Cumulative Percent (Frequency).* This is a cumulative percentage based on the number of votes cast (185). Each entry is the percentage of votes cast for an affinity pair added to the previous total.

❖ *Power.* Power is an index of the degree of optimization of the system and is simply the difference between Cumulative Percent (Frequency) and Cumulative Percent (Relation).

The MinMax Criterion. The last two columns of the Pareto table are the keys to deciding which relationships should be included in the group IRD. Because the relationships are displayed in decreasing order of frequency, the question is one of where to set a cutoff point; to put the matter another way, how to decide which relationships to exclude from the group IRD. Obviously, relationships such as the ones numbered 27 through 30 in Table 6.6 should be excluded, because they attracted no votes at all. But how should a cutoff point be determined for affinities that attract relatively few votes? The decision involves optimizing a trade-off between two criteria: The composite should account for maximum variation in the system (cumulative percent based upon frequency) while minimizing the number of relationships in the interest of parsimony (cumulative percent based on relations).

Accounting for Maximum Variance. True to Pareto's concept, we find that relatively few of the possible 30 relationships account for most of the variance; for example, the first six relationships (20% of the total) account for well over half (56%) of the variation in the system, and the first 10 (33% of the total) account for 84% of the total variation.

Maximum Variance: Frequency. Figure 6.1 illustrates the variance accounted for by each succeeding relationship.

Minimizing the Number of Affinities: Power. Figure 6.2 contains the power analysis for the system.

Power reaches a maximum at 10 relationships, which accounts for 84% of the variation in this system; therefore, 10 relationships would be a defensible choice for inclusion in the group IRD because it is an optimal number in the sense of the MinMax criterion.

Maximizing Variance

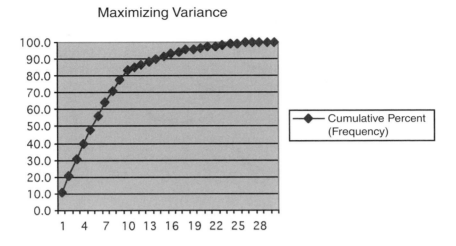

Figure 6.1

Power Analysis

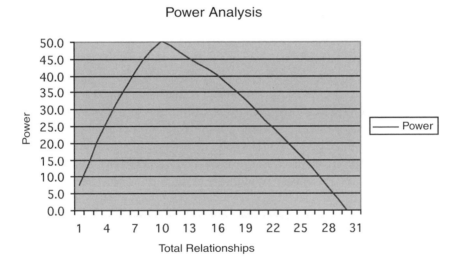

Figure 6.2

THEORETICAL SIDEBAR: AMBIGUOUS RELATIONSHIPS

Before returning to the practicalities of doing theoretical coding, it is useful to develop the theory of theoretical coding a bit more at this point, especially in light of what has been called "ambiguous" relationships and their importance to the identification of feedback loops. Assume that a focus group has written a number of hypotheses arguing that affinity A influences affinity B (A → B). Another set of hypotheses argues the

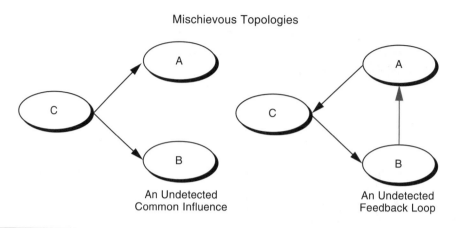

Figure 6.3

opposite, that B → A. When submitted to the Pareto Chart, the argument is not resolved: The top 20% contain hypotheses that argue for both directions, and both sets seem equally plausible.

What to do? The key to the puzzle lies in a realization that this kind of argument is surely the result of failure to identify at least one other affinity that somehow intervenes between, or interacts with, both A and B. In other words, the most plausible explanation is that the group has identified a direct relationship between affinities A and B when the relationship is, in fact, indirect. Let us look at the topologies of the simplest system that can produce this ambiguity, one involving only three affinities: A, B (the ones that are involved in the ambiguity), and a third, affinity C. Only two topologies are consistent with the ambiguity, as illustrated by Figure 6.3.

A Mischievous Topology: The Undetected Common Influence. If both affinities A and B are the result of a common affinity C, then they will covary in some meaningful way. This configuration (the topology on the left) is one plausible explanation for the argument about the direction of the arrow between A and B. Because the focus group, at least at this point in the process, is not aware of the common influence of C on both A and B, it is not surprising that there will be ambiguity during the hypothesizing phase of the project about the relationship between A and B.

Even More Mischief: The Undetected Feedback Loop. Suppose that A, B, and C are related to each other as indicated by the topology on the right. This is the very picture of the simplest kind of feedback loop, in which each affinity has an influence on the other two in the system. At first glance, one might conclude that the feedback loop topology supports those who argue B → A, because the arrow obviously emerges from B and terminates at A.

But A influences C, which in turn influences B, so A influences B indirectly; therefore, if C is excluded from the argument, we are likely to find equally compelling hypotheses supporting both directions A → B and B → A.

Exploiting Ambiguous Relationships. An ambiguous relationship, then, is really not so ambiguous at all. When there are compelling hypotheses pointing in both directions, IQA systems theory suggests that only two conditions can reasonably account for the ambiguity. This is not to say that all ambiguous relationships are simple three-affinity systems. Many more than three may be involved. Nevertheless, we can exploit the knowledge that the ambiguity is probably produced by either some common affinity in a subsystem involving at least three affinities, or by the linking of the two affinities in question in a feedback loop involving, again, at least three affinities.

This goal is accomplished by modifying the rule for hypothesizing by coding the ambiguous relationship with the highest frequency with the appropriate arrow and coding the relationship with the smaller frequency with a question mark (?). In other words, these ambiguous relationships are put into "suspension" until a picture of the system (the SID) is created based on the unambiguous relationships. If examination of the SID reveals that the ambiguous relationship is part of a subsystem that is one of the two mischievous kinds just described, then the SID accounts for the ambiguity and nothing else need be done. On the other hand, if the two affinities in question are not related either through a common affinity and are not part of a feedback loop, then the researcher must either reanalyze and rehypothesize with respect to at least some of the affinities, or the researcher must admit that the relationship is still ambiguous and a special effort must be made to resolve the ambiguity in the interview phase of the study. This issue will be addressed again in detail in Chapter 8.

Too Many Notes? In Milos Foreman's 1984 film *Amadeus,* the royal *kappelmeister,* when asked his opinion of Mozart's latest work, dismisses it with the best one-liner in cinematic history: "Too many notes." Two alternatives to each of three protocols produce eight variations, which may indeed seem to be too many. Following is an alternative procedure and a further analysis of the relationship of the eight variations to each other.

FOCUS GROUP THEORETICAL CODING: DEMOCRATIC PROTOCOL

An alternative to the Pareto Protocol is to use a simple majority vote while in the focus group to determine the direction of each relationship. For each potential combination there are three options: A influences B, B influences A, or there is no relationship. The option attracting the plurality of votes is recorded in the ART. Those relationships that attract

Table 6.7

<table>
<tr><td colspan="3">Affinity Name</td><td colspan="3">Possible Relationships</td></tr>
<tr><td colspan="3">1.
2.
3.
4.
5.
6.</td><td colspan="3">A → B

A ← B

A <> B (No relationship)</td></tr>
</table>

<table>
<tr><td colspan="6" align="center">Theoretical Code Frequency Table</td></tr>
<tr><td>Affinity Pair Relationship</td><td>Frequency</td><td>Theoretical Code</td><td>Affinity Pair Relationship</td><td>Frequency</td><td>Theoretical Code</td></tr>
<tr><td>1 → 2</td><td></td><td></td><td>2 → 6</td><td></td><td></td></tr>
<tr><td>1 ← 2</td><td></td><td></td><td>2 ← 6</td><td></td><td></td></tr>
<tr><td>1 → 3</td><td></td><td></td><td>3 → 4</td><td></td><td></td></tr>
<tr><td>1 ← 3</td><td></td><td></td><td>3 ← 4</td><td></td><td></td></tr>
<tr><td>1 → 4</td><td></td><td></td><td>3 → 5</td><td></td><td></td></tr>
<tr><td>1 ← 4</td><td></td><td></td><td>3 ← 5</td><td></td><td></td></tr>
<tr><td>1 → 5</td><td></td><td></td><td>3 → 6</td><td></td><td></td></tr>
<tr><td>1 ← 5</td><td></td><td></td><td>3 ← 6</td><td></td><td></td></tr>
<tr><td>1 → 6</td><td></td><td></td><td>4 → 5</td><td></td><td></td></tr>
<tr><td>1 ← 6</td><td></td><td></td><td>4 ← 5</td><td></td><td></td></tr>
<tr><td>2 → 3</td><td></td><td></td><td>4 → 6</td><td></td><td></td></tr>
<tr><td>2 ← 3</td><td></td><td></td><td>4 ← 6</td><td></td><td></td></tr>
<tr><td>2 → 4</td><td></td><td></td><td>5 → 6</td><td></td><td></td></tr>
<tr><td>2 ← 4</td><td></td><td></td><td>5 ← 6</td><td></td><td></td></tr>
<tr><td>2 → 5</td><td></td><td></td><td></td><td></td><td></td></tr>
<tr><td>2 ← 5</td><td></td><td></td><td></td><td></td><td></td></tr>
</table>

very few or no votes are excluded from the ART. This protocol is faster, but much cruder, than the Pareto approach; probably it should be used only when the primary purpose of the focus group is simply to produce an affinity list rather than to conduct an extensive group analysis of the systemic relationships among the affinities.

The frequency of each relationship can be recorded in a table such as the one shown in Table 6.7. The form allows the facilitator to quickly record the vote on each relationship as well as the theoretical code assigned to each pair of relationships.

Steps and Variations for Focus Group Theoretical Coding

IQA focus group theoretical coding consists of two steps: first, creating a set of descriptions of relationships among the affinities in a system (hypotheses), and then summarizing these into a singular group composite description. Two variations are possible for each of the two steps:

HYPOTHESIS BUILDING: PRODUCING RELATIONSHIP STATEMENTS (ART)

1. Individual Construction—(simple or detailed)

2. Subgroup Construction—(simple or detailed)

HYPOTHESIS SUMMARY: PRODUCING A GROUP COMPOSITE (IRD)

1. Pareto Composite

2. Democratic Composite

DEFINITIONS

❖ *Individual Construction.* Each focus group member completes an ART independently of others.

❖ *Subgroup Construction.* Focus group members complete ARTs in subgroups, consulting within the group.

❖ *Pareto (or Statistical) Composite.* Tallies of relationships in ARTs are arranged in descending order of frequency, and the Pareto Principle is used to identify relationships to be represented in the SID.

❖ *Democratic Composite.* Individual or subgroup nominees for relationships are presented to the entire focus group. The focus group votes each nominee up or down.

Table 6.8

Protocol Variation	Focus Group Time Required	Analysis Quality and Richness
1. Independent coding followed by frequency tally.	Longest	Highest
2. Independent/dyad/triad coding combined with partialling out relationship subsets among individuals or groups followed by majority vote.		
3. Researcher leads group discussion followed by informal consensus.		
4. Ex Post Facto Researcher Analysis. Participants do no theoretical coding at all. Researcher conducts theoretical coding after focus group creates and defines the affinities.	Shortest	Lowest

Time available with the focus group is a major determinant of choice of protocol. Table 6.8 describes some group theoretical coding protocol variations ranging from those that consume the most time (generating the most systematic, real, and deep analysis) to those requiring the least time (but result in a less rich/less deep analysis).

Design Considerations

Focus group protocol depends on the purpose of the research as well as administrative and logistical constraints. How much time is available? How rich in description is the study to be? Will interviews be conducted, or is the focus group data sufficient to meet the goals of the study? It is the authors' view that to get the richest study one must complete the entire IQA process, yet it is naïve to think that all researchers and constituencies will have the time and resources to complete such an in-depth study. The goals of the research may require a quicker approach in lieu of depth. Table 6.9 outlines the advantages available with each variation on the protocol.

Table 6.9	Design Considerations for the Protocol Variations	
	Shortest Time Required to Produce an IRD	*Greatest Volume or Richest Detail of Data Produced*
Simple ART	✓	
Detailed ART		✓
Individual Coding		✓
Subgroup Coding	✓	
Democratic Composite	✓	
Pareto Composite		✓

Focus Groups and Follow-Up Interviews

Other than the issues described previously, a very important consideration for the design of the focus group is whether interviews will be conducted as a follow-up activity (one that is strongly encouraged). Focus groups serve primarily as the "front end" for interviews in the IQA process. The affinities created by the group are the foundation for the interview protocol. Each interview also has a theoretical section, analogous to the theoretical coding activity of the focus group, in which those being interviewed systematically analyze the relationships among affinities from their individual perspective; in other words, the IQA focus group and the IQA interview have a parallel structure. IQA interviews produce a richer, more robust picture of the phenomenon than a focus group alone.

If interviews produce a better mindmap than a focus group, why even create a focus group SID? The answer lies in the use of the focus group to inform the development of the interview protocol. The focus group SID is useful in sharpening and clarifying the meaning of the affinities. Vaguely defined affinities frequently create irregularities or paradoxes in the ensuing SID; for example, an affinity may have no relationship to any other affinity and therefore sits "outside" the system. Another common marker for ill-defined affinities is the inability of the focus group to understand or explain a particular relationship when presented with the group SID. Rather than regard the focus group SID as "flawed," this situation actually is an opportunity to refine and reorganize the affinities with the assistance of the group. Left unattended, these issues likely will surface in the interviews; for example, respondents might tell the researcher that two affinities have the same meaning to them. Without the benefit of a focus group SID, several interviews are often conducted before the structural flaw in the interview is recognized. By examining the SID before going into the interviews, the researcher has a better chance of avoiding such issues.

Theoretical Coding for Follow-Up Interviews. A simple SID is all that is needed if one is going on to conduct follow-up interviews. The use of the Simple ART is the fastest method for the creation of the SID because all that is needed is a general idea of what the relationships are without dedicating a great deal of time to the process (the interviews will more than make up for the time). After the focus group has had time to think about and record their codes (in groups or as individuals), a simple majority vote is taken. The researcher records the results in an ART. The majority vote decides the direction of the relationship. With this, the researcher is ready to create an IRD and a SID. If a more rigorous SID is required, individual ARTs should be considered. These ARTs are collected by the researcher and a Pareto Composite is developed.

Focus Group–Only Research

Even though the IQA process is designed to incorporate interviews, limits on resources such as time may prevent interviewing. Useful studies can be conducted without interviews, but this is not the optimal situation and is discouraged. Extra care taken with the focus group can produce a good study, albeit not as rigorous and descriptive as a full IQA study.

The affinity production phase is important, with or without the interview phase. The facilitator must be aware that the complete description of each affinity will come only from the cards generated by the participants. For this reason, the meaning of each card must be clear to the researcher, and care must be taken to ensure all cards have been properly classified.

The SID from a focus group–only study should be as fully detailed as possible. The Detailed ART is preferred because it provides examples necessary to understanding and interpreting the relationships identified by the focus group and allows for the construction of individual mindmaps. In order to gather as much data as possible, participants should complete individual ARTs, which provide for a wider range of variation in the explanations. Finally, the Pareto Composite SID is preferred because of the higher level of detail provided.

Summary of Theoretical Coding Protocols. Selection of a protocol for group theoretical coding is an important aspect of IQA research design; group theoretical coding is driven by the trade-off between focus group time available and the goal of rich description. Regardless of the manner in which the group theoretical codes are constructed, however, the final output is always a standard display of the codes called an IRD—the Interrelationship Diagram. The following section will describe the process for creating a focus group IRD.

Theoretical Sidebar: Cause and Effect: Fear and Loathing. Before continuing with the process for recording the group's analysis of relationships, the issue of discourse about cause and effect should be addressed. Earlier, it was pointed out that some students may balk at the prospect of conducting formal comparisons between focus groups (and later, between individuals). IQA's insistence on using the "positivistic" language of cause and effect can be another ideological barrier. Many students seem to agree with Edgar Allan Poe's fashionable postmodern skepticism (but they overlook the great poet's self-mocking tone) when he says, "I am above the weakness of seeking to establish a sequence of cause and effect, between the disaster and the atrocity."

Although a skepticism about the power of logic and an associated reluctance in attributing effects to causes in any research design other than a true experiment is certainly healthy, IQA is closer to the argument expressed by another Dead White Male, Ralph Waldo Emerson, than to Poe:

> Punishment is a fruit that unsuspected ripens within the flower of the pleasure, which concealed it. Cause and effect, means and ends, seed and fruit, cannot be severed; for the effect already blooms in the cause, the end preexists in the means, the fruit in the seed.

Emerson's immediate referent is the nature of pain and pleasure, but more generally he is describing the dialectical nature of reality and how we construct that reality through a system of perceived causes and effects. The great transcendentalist has more to say about the nature of cause and effect:

> Skepticism is unbelief in cause and effect. A man does not see, that, as he eats, so he thinks: as he deals, so he is, and so he appears; he does not see that his son is the son of his thoughts and of his actions; that fortunes are not exceptions but fruits; that relation and connection are not somewhere and sometimes, but everywhere and always; no miscellany, no exemption, no anomaly,—but method, and an even web; and what comes out, that was put in.

Almost a century and a half later, Emerson's claim that "what comes out, that was put in" seems uncomfortably deterministic. Surely, given what we now know about the relationship of power to knowledge, there are cases in which fortunes are the exception rather than the fruit. Nonetheless, if we take Emerson's dialectic as a description of the way people think about reality, his point is well made. We construct reality, not exclusively but importantly, in terms of cause and effect. We must—else our individual worlds would be chaotic jumbles of actions unrelated to consequences, what Emerson called "miscellanies and anomalies." The thankfully brief popularity of applying chaos theory to human systems notwithstanding, the purpose of IQA is to represent the structure that people impose on life's miscellanies and anomalies.

Creating a Group Composite: The IRD

Creating an IRD is the first step in a general process called *rationalizing the system*. Output of the focus group hypothesizing activity is summarized in an IRD: a matrix containing all the perceived relationships in the system. The IRD displays arrows that show whether each affinity in a pair is a perceived *cause* or an *effect*, or if there is *no relationship* between the affinities in the pair. The IRD is created by placing arrows into the table, thereby showing the direction of the relationships. An arrow pointing from A to B (A → B) indicates that A is the cause or influencing affinity and that B is the effect or influenced affinity.

Table 6.10 is an example of an IRD that represents, for the purposes of simplicity, a system of only six affinities. The forms provided here are facsimiles of the actual working forms that would be used by a focus group doing theoretical coding on a six-affinity system. Each participant is given a form identifying the affinities and the rules for relationships.

Arrows point only left or up, and each relationship is recorded twice in the IRD in a manner not unlike double-entry bookkeeping. For example, if a relationship was determined between 1 and 2, it might be noted as 1 ← 2 and read as *2 influences 1*. Two arrows would be placed in the IRD to represent the relationship. Notice how the arrow in both cases points away from 2 and toward 1. All relationships are recorded in the table in this manner.

Table 6.10

Tabular IRD									
	1	*2*	*3*	*4*	*5*	*6*	*Out*	*In*	Δ
1		←							
2	↑								
3									
4									
5									
6									

Example: Suppose the six-affinity system was analyzed by the focus group as summarized in Table 6.11.

Table 6.11	Focus Group Affinity Relationship Table
Affinity Pair Relationship	*Example of the relationship either in natural language or in the form of an IF/THEN statement of relationship.*
1 ← 2	
1 ← 3	
1 → 4	
1 ← 5	
1 ← 6	
2 → 3	
2 ← 4	
2 → 5	
2 <> 6	
3 <> 4	
3 ← 5	
3 <> 6	
4 <> 5	
4 ← 6	
5 ← 6	

The blank IRD for a six-affinity system looks like Table 6.12.

Table 6.12									
Tabular IRD									
	1	*2*	*3*	*4*	*5*	*6*	*Out*	*In*	*Δ*
1									
2									
3									
4									
5									
6									

Relationships from the ART are recorded in the table. Each relationship is recorded twice, once with an up arrow and once with a left arrow, as shown in Table 6.13.

Table 6.13

	1	*2*	*3*	*4*	*5*	*6*	*Out*	*In*	Δ
1		←	←	↑	←	←			
2	↑		↑	←	↑				
3	↑	←			←				
4	←	↑				←			
5	↑	←	↑			←			
6	↑			↑	↑				

Tabular IRD

The arrows are then counted to find the value of *delta* (Δ), thereby completing the table (see Table 6.14). The rules for calculating delta are:

Table 6.14

Tabular IRD

	1	*2*	*3*	*4*	*5*	*6*	*Out*	*In*	Δ
1		←	←	↑	←	←	1	4	−3
2	↑		↑	←	↑		3	1	3
3	↑	←			←		1	2	−1
4	←	↑				←	1	2	−1
5	↑	←	↑			←	2	2	0
6	↑			↑	↑		3	0	3

❖ Count the number of up arrows (↑) or *Outs*.

❖ Count the number of left arrows (←) or *Ins*.

❖ Subtract the number of *Ins* from the *Outs* to determine the (Δ) *deltas*.

❖ Δ = *Out − In*.

The table is then sorted in descending order of delta (see far-right column, Table 6.15).

Table 6.15

	1	2	3	4	5	6	Out	In	Δ
			Tabular IRD: Sorted in Descending Order of Δ						
6	↑			↑	↑		3	0	3
2	↑		↑	←	↑		3	1	2
5	↑	←	↑			←	2	2	0
3	↑	←			←		1	2	−1
4	←	↑				←	1	2	−1
1		←	←	↑	←	←	1	4	3

Determining Drivers and Outcomes

The value of delta is used as a marker for the relative position of an affinity within the system. Affinities with positive deltas are *relative drivers* or causes; those with negative deltas are *relative effects* or outcomes. The Tentative SID Assignments Table (shown in Table 6.16) represents the initial placement of affinities for the SID.

An affinity marked by a high positive delta or number resulting from many *Outs* but no *Ins* is a *Primary Driver:* a significant cause that affects many other affinities but is not affected by others. The *No Ins Rule* states that any affinity with no *Ins* is always a Primary Driver.

The *Secondary Driver* is a relative cause or influence on affinities in the system. It is identified when there are both *Outs* and *Ins,* but there are more *Outs* than *Ins.*

Quite often affinities have equal numbers of *Ins* and *Outs,* indicating a position in the middle of the system; this suggests the metaphors of "circulator" or "pivot" in the final representation of the system. *Circulators/ Pivots* occur when there are equal numbers of *Ins* and *Outs.*

The *Secondary Outcome* reveals a *Relative Effect.* It is identified when there are both *Ins* and *Outs,* but there are more *Ins* than *Outs.*

An affinity marked by a high negative number that results from many *Ins* but no *Outs* is a *Primary Outcome:* a significant affect that is caused by many of the affinities, but does not affect others. The *No Outs Rule* states that any affinity with no *Outs* is always a Primary Outcome.

On occasion, an IRD will present itself where all *Ins* or *Outs* have a value other than zero. This does not mean that there is no primary driver or outcome. Instead, it indicates that that affinity is a strong relative cause or effect but still is influenced by, or influences other, affinities. It is

Table 6.16	
	Tentative SID Assignments
6	Primary Driver
2	Secondary Driver
5	Circulator / Pivot
3	Secondary Outcome
4	Secondary Outcome
1	Primary Outcome

appropriate in this situation to label these affinities as *primary*. Affinity 1 in Table 6.16 is an example of an affinity with no zeros in the *Out* column. Because it has the highest negative delta, it is labeled *Primary Outcome*.

When identifying tentative SID assignments, examine the *In* and *Out* columns first. The delta sort represents the difference between *Outs* and *Ins*. The final version of the sorted IRD will be in descending order of delta, subject to the *Zero Outs* and *Zero Ins* rules:

❖ Affinities with zero *Ins* will always be at the top of the list, regardless of their delta value.

❖ Affinities with zero *Outs* will likewise be at the bottom, regardless of their delta value. In the IRD in Table 6.17, observe the zero *Outs* in the seventh row, as well as the zero *Ins* in the first, third, and fourth rows. These affinities will migrate to the extremes of the system. Consult the Tentative SID Assignment chart (Table 6.18) to see how the affinities are to be organized.

One should not get too caught up in the naming of the affinities as *primary* or *secondary, driver* or *outcome;* rather, pay attention to the identifying of zero *Ins* and zero *Outs,* the ordering of the affinities based on delta, and the two *Zero* rules. Based on this order, affinities will later be laid out in a specific pattern that will aid in the drawing of the system.

Focus Group System Influence Diagram

The SID is a visual representation of an entire system of influences and outcomes and is created by representing the information present in the IRD as a system of affinities and relationships among them. The graphic

Table 6.17

Tabular IRD—Sorted in Descending Order of Δ													
	1	2	3	4	5	6	7	8	9	10	11	Out	In	Δ
7	↑	↑	↑	↑	↑	↑			↑	↑		8	0	8
5		↑	↑	↑		↑	←	←	↑	↑		6	2	4
11						↑			↑	↑		3	0	3
8			↑		↑							2	0	2
9		↑	↑	↑	←	↑	←			↑	←	5	3	2
10		↑	↑	↑	←	↑	←		←		←	4	4	0
1		←					←					0	2	−2
6		↑	↑	↑	←		←		←	←	←	3	5	−2
3		↑		↑	←	←	←	←	←	←		2	6	−4
4		↑	←		←	←	←		←	←		1	6	−5
2	↑		←	←	←	←	←		←	←		1	7	−6

Table 6.18

Tentative SID Assignments	
7	Primary Driver
11	Primary Driver
8	Primary Driver
5	Secondary Driver
9	Secondary Driver
10	Circulator / Pivot / ?
6	Secondary Outcome
3	Secondary Outcome
4	Secondary Outcome
2	Secondary Outcome
1	Primary Outcome

representation of relationships allows one to see vividly how the system maintains its dynamics and where a system might be influenced to change its outcomes. It highlights relationships among affinities that might be responsible for a system's dynamics, and it invites analysis (and even intervention) to improve or influence the system.

Recursions or feedback loops are especially worthy of analysis. Feedback requires at least three affinities and has no beginning and no end. Previous affinities (those placed toward the *driver* zones) influence successive ones (those place toward the *outcome* zones), which in turn influence previous affinities. Although there is nothing in systems theory (or in the IQA application of systems theory) that demands that every system must recurse, the IQA protocols allow for the identification of recursion, unlike more traditional or quantitative path analytic approaches. As a visual representation of the mindmap developed from the data, the SID may be considered as a *set of qualitative structural equations* or as a *path diagram;* however, it is distinguished from traditional path diagrams in that recursion or feedback loops are allowed.

In developing the SID, all of the affinities are arranged according to the Tentative SID Assignment chart; this chart is efficiently created with a flow chart or outlining or "mindmapping" software program, such as Inspiration.[9] Begin by placing the affinities on the screen in rough order of topological zones: Primary Drivers to the left of the screen, and the Primary Outcomes to the right. Secondary Drivers and Secondary Outcomes should then be placed between the primaries. Each affinity number or name is placed in a shape (an oval, circle, or square). With arrows, draw connections between each affinity in the direction of the relationship as represented in the IRD.

Cluttered SIDs. The first version of the SID contains each link present in the IRD and is referred to as *Cluttered.* The system is *saturated* with links, a term appropriated from organic chemistry. Just as saturated hydrocarbons are composed of carbon atoms linked to as many hydrogen atoms as their structure will allow, the cluttered SID contains all of the links identified by participants in the protocol leading to the IRD.

The Problem With Saturation: Uncluttered SIDs. The problem with saturation is that a cluttered SID, while being comprehensive and rich, can be very difficult to interpret, even for a modest number of affinities that are highly interlocked or embedded within the system. In other words, many systems have so many links that the explanatory power of the system becomes bogged down in the details of the relationships. Comprehensiveness and richness are certainly objectives of the SID; on the other hand, so is parsimony. A way to reconcile the richness–parsimony dialectic is to produce a supplementary or secondary SID called the *Uncluttered* SID, one that has redundant links removed. Figure 6.4 demonstrates the concept of a redundant link in its simplest manifestation.

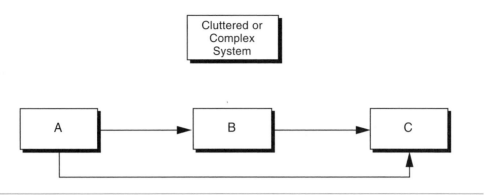

Figure 6.4

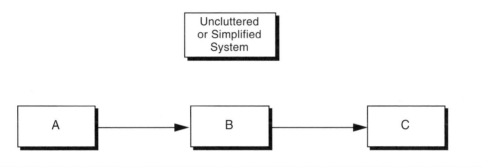

Figure 6.5

The system in Figure 6.4 represents the perception of an individual or a group as follows: A influences B; B influences C; and A influences C. We can both simplify the model and provide one answer (not necessarily *the* answer) to the question, *How does A influence C?* by eliminating the redundant link, as shown in Figure 6.5.

The link from A to C has been removed because it is redundant; not in the sense that A does not influence C in some meaningful, and possibly even direct, manner (it might), but in the sense that one way in which A influences C is through the mediation of B. In other words, one way to explain how A influences C is by pointing to B. It may be true in some absolute universe that A directly influences C; even so, without B, how do we explain the influence? Thus, by eliminating links that skip over mediating affinities, we achieve a simpler, more interpretable mental model—one that has optimum explanatory power.

This is not to say that cluttered mental models are not useful; nor is it to say that either the cluttered or the uncluttered version is right while the other is wrong. We make it a practice to use both (as well as a third version, the *Clean* system described later), but we rely most heavily on the uncluttered version for interpretation, analysis, and forecasting. Often the only statement one can make of some highly saturated or cluttered SIDs is that everything is linked to everything else in the participants' minds. This statement, while no doubt true, is of limited utility for many theoretical and practical applications of IQA.

Redundant links are eliminated after the system is first rationalized. If there is an intervening variable, it remains, and the direct link that skips over the mediator or intervener is removed as redundant.

Protocol for Drawing the SID and Removing Redundant Links

In creating the SID, the affinities are laid out horizontally in rough topological zones in their tentative SID order (Table 6.19). In zones that contain more than one affinity, the affinities are placed vertically in descending order of delta (as represented by affinities 3 and 4 in Figure 6.6).

Table 6.19	
Tentative SID Assignments	
6	Primary Driver
2	Secondary Driver
5	Circulator / Pivot
3	Secondary Outcome
4	Secondary Outcome
1	Primary Outcome

Arrows are drawn according to the Affinity Relationship Table to represent the relationships between the affinities. A SID with all links drawn is known as the *Cluttered SID* (Figure 6.7).

Too often relationships are difficult to identify when the SID is laid out flat in topological zones. By spreading the SID into a circle, relationships can be easily identified. Arranging the arrows so that they have a common output or input point also makes the SID easier to read. When systems grow to have 10 or more affinities, the necessity for this step is ever more apparent. The Cluttered SID is complete at this point (see Figure 6.8).

The Cluttered SID is developed and spread out in a circular fashion in order to make it easier to identify and remove redundant links. Redundant links are those between two affinities in which, even if removed, a path from the driver to the outcome can be achieved through an intermediary affinity. Redundant links can be thought of as the "paths of least resistance."

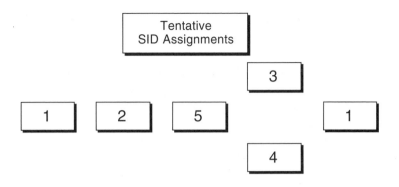

Figure 6.6

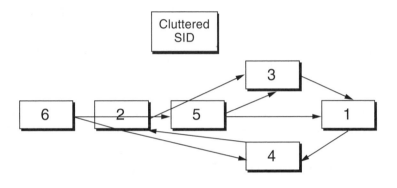

Figure 6.7

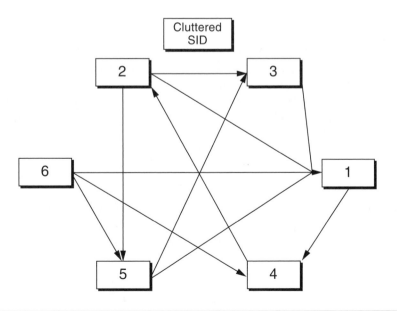

Figure 6.8

Redundant links are removed according to their delta and SID assignments, which is to say the analysis begins by comparing affinities at the extreme left and the extreme right, then working back to the left. The relationship between the highest positive delta and the highest negative delta is examined. If there is any path between the two deltas other than the direct link, that link can be removed. Next, the relationship between the highest positive delta and the next-highest negative delta is examined. If there is any path between the two deltas other than the direct link, that link can be removed. For the six-affinity table below, examine the relationships in Table 6.20.

As an example, the focus group indicated that affinity 6 influences affinities 1, 4, and 5. Examination of the Uncluttered SID reveals that 6 *does indeed* influence 1 (mediated by 5 and 3); 6 influences 4 through the mediation of 5, 3, and 1; and 6 influences 5 directly. Each of the relationships in the IRD is represented in the Uncluttered SID in the sense that each of the arrows in the IRD is a route from a point of origin (cause) to a destination (effect).

Here, then, is the central theorem of IQA representation: *Given any set of affinities and a set of binary unidirectional relationships among these, there exists one, and only one, Uncluttered SID.* The following are some implications of this theory.

❖ Every system has a unique, simplest representation, topologically speaking. Two different analysts working from the same protocol on the same IRD will produce the same Uncluttered SID (although they may have a different appearance, they will be topologically identical).

❖ The process of constructing the system (rationalizing the system via IRD and SID) is not dependent on the "meaning content" of the affinities. The focus group's or the analyst's understanding of, or opinions about, or emotional involvement with, the affinities (what each affinity stands for) has nothing to do with the way in which the Uncluttered SID is constructed. As far as the process of rationalization is concerned, the affinities and the relationships among them are simply abstract symbols that are assembled into a structure according to a set of rules.

Because the same topology may have infinitely many representations, affinities may be arranged so that the SID best communicates the structure of the system (as long as no links are broken). We read from left to right, so arranging the affinities in order of delta from left to right is a good general rule of thumb for representing the system.

A Third Representation: The Clean SID. The final version of SID, the Clean SID, shows the Uncluttered SID (the mindmap containing only the minimum number of links required to completely represent the underlying logic of the IRD) in bold, with the redundant links in a diminished color.

Table 6.20

1. 6–1	9. 2–5
2. 6–4	10. 5–1
3. 6–3	11. 5–4
4. 6–5	12. 5–3
5. 6–2	13. 3–1
6. 2–1	14. 3–4
7. 2–4	15. 4–1
8. 2–3	

Tentative SID Assignments	
6	Primary Driver
2	Secondary Driver
5	Circulator / Pivot
3	Secondary Outcome
4	Secondary Outcome
1	Primary Outcome

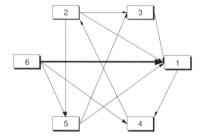

1. There is a path from 6–5–1 or 6–3–1. Therefore 6–1 can be removed.

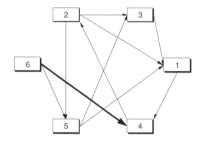

2. There is no intermediate way to get from 6 to 4. Therefore the link remains.

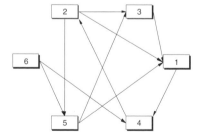

3. Because the only other link coming from 6 is 6 to 5 and there is no intermediary, all redundant links from 6 have been removed.

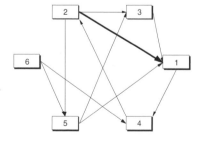

4. There is a path from 2–3–1 or 2–5–3–1. Therefore 2–1 can be removed.

(Continued)

Table 6.20 (Continued)

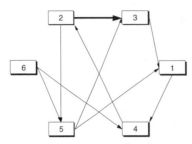

5. There is a path from 2–5–3. Therefore 2–3 can be removed.

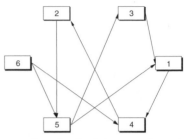

6. Because the only other link coming from 2 is 2 to 5 and there is no intermediary, all redundant links from 2 have been removed.

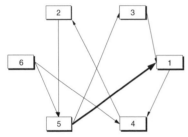

7. There is a path from 5–3–1. Therefore 5–1 can be removed.

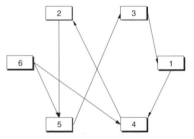

8. Because the only other link coming from 5 is 5 to 3 and there is no intermediary, all redundant links from 5 have been removed.

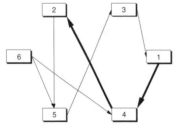

9. The 4–2 and 1–4 links point backward in order of delta. They are recursive links and are not removed.

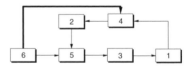

10. Rearranging the affinities roughly in order of delta may show redundant links caused by recursions that were not immediately apparent. There is a path from 6–5–3–1–4. Therefore 6–4 can be removed.

11. The Uncluttered SID now has all redundant links removed. The Uncluttered SID is the simplest possible representation consistent with all the relationships contained in the IRD (see Table 6.15). The IRD from which the Uncluttered SID above was derived (a word chosen deliberately, since it is the product of a set of deductive procedures that are independent of the nature of the affinities) is reproduced below to make it more convenient to verify this claim.

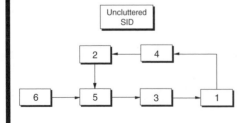

Interpretation of the final SID depends primarily upon the Uncluttered SID (because it is the simplest, yet paradoxically has the most explanatory power), but reinsertion of the redundant links produces a representation that captures the mindmap of the participant in both its original (or unrationalized) form and its rationalized form. As an example, note that in the mindmap shown in Figure 6.9, the participant reported a link between affinities 6 and 4. This link was not part of the uncluttered path, but that does not mean there is no "direct" link in the participant's mind; there very well may be. The important question, however, is, "What could explain the perception that affinity 6 influences affinity 4?" One can look at the uncluttered path on the final SID and see immediately that the logic is as follows: 6 influences 5, which influences 3, which in turn influences 1, which finally influences 4. In other words, the Clean SID elaborates the simple 6–4 relationship as 6–5–3–1–4. In order to describe how 6 and 4 are related in the perception of the participant, the researcher can point to the chain of influences among these affinities.

The important question is not whether 6 influences 4 directly, on the one hand, or indirectly, on the other. This is a false dilemma that results from a misunderstanding of the dialectical nature of reality and language; after all, it surely is correct to say that a slamming door makes a noise. It is also correct to say that the collision of the door with the doorjamb creates a disturbance in the air at the point of contact that travels in a waveform outward from the door. When this wave strikes the eardrum of the listener, mechanical energy is transformed to electrical impulses that travel to the brain, which interprets the signals as a loud noise. Both explanations are correct, although the first explanation describes the relationship between the door slamming and the noise as a "direct" one, while the second describes a series of "intervening" affinities. The issue is not the correctness of one description over the other, but is one of the desired detail of representation.

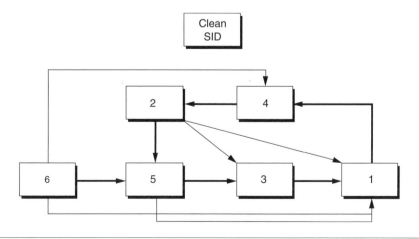

Figure 6.9

Conclusion

This chapter has examined both the theoretical rationale and the operational aspects of using focus groups to articulate relationships among elements of a system. Variations of this activity, called *theoretical coding*, were presented and implications for each variation were examined. Finally, an introduction to diagrammatic representation of the focus group theoretical codes was presented, including a description and analysis of three kinds of system diagrams called SIDs (System Influence Diagrams). Detailed examples of these topics are included in the case material that follows.

CASE EXAMPLE

Before continuing with this part of the case example, the reader may wish to go back to Chapter 5 and review the names and meanings of the affinities developed by the focus groups.

The focus group SID is useful in sharpening and clarifying the meaning of the affinities. The SID is used to identify vaguely defined affinities or irregularities. There is a better chance of avoiding such issues by examining the SID before going into the interviews. Because this case study was designed to use the full IQA process (interviews), the SID developed with the focus group was used only to develop the interview protocol.

With the affinities described, it was time to see if relationships existed between each pair of affinities. Once again, the focus group helped with this step. Each focus group member was given a blank Affinity Relationship Table with the appropriate number of affinities. The affinities were arranged in alphabetical order so as not to give any one affinity undue weight because of its number. The participants recorded the affinity names in the blanks provided in the ART. They were asked to go down the list one by one and determine if they thought there might be a relationship. If there was a relationship, they were to draw an arrow indicating the direction of the relationship. To aid in the identification of causal relationships, they were asked to construct a hypothesis in the form of "If ... [cause; independent variable], then ... [effect; dependent variable]," drawing an arrow from the cause to the effect. If there was no relationship, they were to do nothing.

When each focus group member had finished determining relationships, they were asked about their results. A master ART was used by the facilitator to record relationships. Each affinity pair was read out to the group. For example, the facilitator stated, "How many of you think that the relationship is from 1 to 2?" Hands were raised and counted. The facilitator then asked, "How many of you think that the relationship is from 2 to 1?" Again, the hands were raised and counted. Lastly, the facilitator asked for a show of hands from those who saw no relationship between the two variables. A majority hand vote determined the direction of the relationship and it was recorded as a directional arrow in the ART. The process was repeated with both the Tuesday traditional class and the Wednesday technology-integrated class. Table 6.21 shows the ART for the Tuesday focus groups.

After the focus group had finished voting on the relationships, they were dismissed with appreciation for their efforts. The focus group and researcher had worked for about three hours to get to this point. The focus group's work was completed.

The next step in the process was to rationalize the system. Relationships recorded in the ART were moved into the Interrelationship Diagram (IRD), where each relationship was recorded twice: once with an up arrow, and once with a left arrow. The completed IRD is symmetrical along the diagonal line of gray-shaded cells. The arrows were counted and the totals placed in the appropriate cell. Arrows facing upward were counted and placed in the *Out* cells of the table. Arrows facing to the left were counted and placed in the *In* cells. (Note that the sum of all of the numbers in the *Out* column should be equal to the sum of all of the numbers in the *In* column. This number is also the number of affinity pair relationships with an arrow in the ART.) Delta (Δ) was tabulated by subtracting the *Ins* from the *Outs*. Deltas with positive numbers were noted as *Drivers*—those affinities that were causing the phenomenon—and those with negative numbers were noted as *Outcomes*—those affinities that were the result of the cause-effect relationships.

The resulting Tabular IRD (see Table 6.22) serves as a topical skeleton of the next phase of the IQA process. This is a tool to check one's work. It is important to check and recheck the data and calculations in the IRD at this point. Any mistakes made here will affect the data throughout the study.

Once the IRD is filled in, it is sorted in descending order of delta (see Table 6.23, on page 188). Sorting is done in preparation for the placement of affinities in the SID. The SID is drawn with all *Drivers* on the left and all *Outcomes* on the right. Delta value alone does not necessarily indicate a primary driver or a primary outcome. The *Out* and *In* columns are first examined for affinities with a zero value. A zero value is always a primary driver. In this case, affinities 1 and 4 have a higher delta value than affinities 7 and 10, yet affinities 7 and 10 have zero *Ins,* which gives them primary status. They are moved up above 1 and 4 in the Tentative SID Assignments chart (Table 6.24, on page 188).

Table 6.21

<table>
<tr><td colspan="2">Affinity Name</td></tr>
<tr><td colspan="2">

1. Collaboration
2. Communication
3. Comprehension
   - ❖ Understanding
   - ❖ Difficulties
4. Course Structure
   - ❖ Design
   - ❖ Pace
   - ❖ Scope
5. Emotional Environment
6. Instructor
7. IQA as a Method
   - ❖ Applicability
   - ❖ Process
8. Learning Resources
9. Peer Relationships
10. Physical Environment
</td></tr>
</table>

Possible Relationships
A → B
A ← B
A <> B (No relationship)

Tuesday Focus Group Affinity Relationship Table								
Affinity Pair Relationship			*Affinity Pair Relationship*			*Affinity Pair Relationship*		
1	→	2	2	←	9	5	←	6
1	→	3	2	<>	10	5	←	7
1	→	4	3	→	5	5	←	8
1	→	5	3	←	6	5	←	9
1	←	6	3	←	7	5	←	10
1	<>	7	3	←	8	6	<>	7
1	<>	8	3	←	9	6	→	8
1	→	9	3	→	5	6	<>	9
1	<>	10	3	←	10	6	<>	10
2	→	3	4	→	5	7	<>	8
2	←	4	4	←	6	7	<>	9
2	→	5	4	<>	7	7	<>	10
2	←	6	4	→	8	8	<>	9
2	<>	7	4	→	9	8	<>	10
2	←	8	4	<>	10	9	<>	10

Table 6.22

	1	2	3	4	5	6	7	8	9	10	Out	In	Δ
					Tuesday Focus Group Tabular IRD								
1		↑	↑	↑	↑	←			↑		5	1	4
2	←		↑	←	↑	←		←	←		2	5	−3
3	←	←		←	↑	←	←	←	←	←	1	8	−7
4	←	↑	↑		↑	←		↑	↑		5	2	3
5	←	←	←	←		←	←	←	←	←	0	9	−9
6	↑	↑	↑	↑	↑			↑			6	0	6
7			↑		↑						2	0	2
8		↑	↑	←	↑	←					3	2	1
9	←	↑	↑	←	↑						3	2	1
10			↑		↑						2	0	2

The Tentative SID Assignments chart is used to identify the placement of affinities in the SID. The SID is a visual of every relationship pair identified earlier in the process. The three drivers identified in this study are placed on the left, as shown in the Cluttered SID in Figure 6.10. The outcome is placed on the right. The other affinities are filled in based upon their Tentative SID Assignments chart order. Note the circular pattern of the affinity placement. Reading from left to right and top to bottom, the affinities are placed in order according to the Tentative SID Assignments chart.

An Uncluttered SID, shown in Figure 6.11, is developed by using the protocol for removing redundant links. The affinities are then arranged to illustrate the system with the most powerful power of visual representation.

These procedures were used for creating an IRD and SID for the Tuesday traditional class. The same procedures were used for the technology-integrated Wednesday class with the following results, shown in Tables 6.10 through 6.28 (page 191 to 193) and Figures 6.12 (page 193) and 6.13 (page 194).

Table 6.23

	1	2	3	4	5	6	7	8	9	10	Out	In	Δ
6	↑	↑	↑	↑	↑			↑			6	0	6
1		↑	↑	↑	↑	←			↑		5	1	4
4	←	↑	↑		↑	←		↑	↑		5	2	3
7			↑		↑						2	0	2
10			↑		↑						2	0	2
8		↑	↑	←	↑	←					3	2	1
9	←	↑	↑	←	↑						3	2	1
2	←		↑	←	↑	←		←	←		2	5	−3
3	←	←		←	↑	←	←	←	←	←	1	8	−7
5	←	←	←	←		←	←	←	←	←	0	9	−9

Tuesday Focus Group
Tabular IRD: Sorted in Descending Order of Δ

Table 6.24

	Tentative SID Assignments
6	Primary Driver
7	Primary Driver
10	Primary Driver
1	Secondary Driver
4	Secondary Driver
8	Secondary Driver
9	Secondary Driver
2	Secondary Outcome
3	Secondary Outcome
5	Primary Outcome

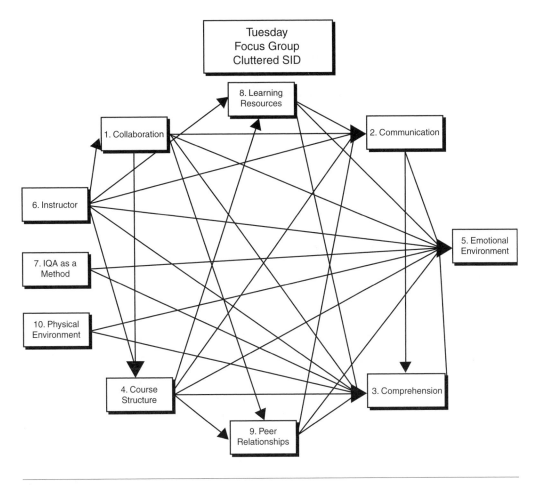

Figure 6.10

Collective and individual SIDs (mindmaps) are produced to visually illustrate that phenomenon representative of the constituencies' experiences and the relationships among those experiences. IQA methodology is reflective of the assumption that constituencies play a vital role in the research design and the mindmap comparison phases of the process.

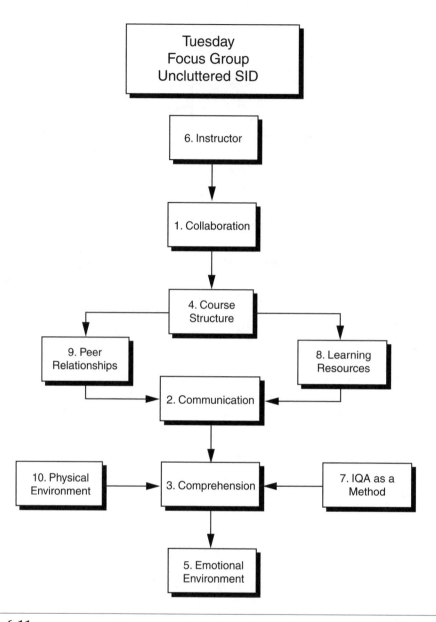

Figure 6.11

Table 6.25

Affinity Name
1. Application Toward Dissertation
2. Classroom Climate
3. Cognitive Reaction (Dialectic)
❖ Confusion
❖ Clarity
❖ Growth
4. Collaboration
5. Course Structure
6. IQA Process
7. Physical Environment
8. Teacher Style
9. Technology

Possible Relationships
A → B
A ← B
A <> B (No Relationship)

Wednesday Focus Group Affinity Relationship Table		
Affinity Pair Relationship	Affinity Pair Relationship	Affinity Pair Relationship
1 ← 2	3 ← 4	6 <> 7
1 ← 3	3 ← 5	6 ← 8
1 <> 4	3 ← 6	6 → 9
1 ← 5	3 ← 7	7 <> 8
1 ← 6	3 ← 8	7 <> 9
1 <> 7	3 ← 9	8 → 9
1 ← 8	4 ← 5	
1 ← 9	4 ← 6	
2 → 3	4 <> 7	
2 ← 4	4 ← 8	
2 ← 5	4 ← 9	
2 ← 6	5 ← 6	
2 ← 7	5 <> 7	
2 ← 8	5 ← 8	
2 ← 9	5 ← 9	

Table 6.26

										Out	In	Δ

Wednesday
Focus Group Tabular IRD

	1	2	3	4	5	6	7	8	9	Out	In	Δ
1		←	←		←	←		←	←	0	6	−6
2	↑		↑	←	←	←	←	←	←	2	6	−4
3	↑	←		←	←	←	←	←	←	1	7	−6
4		↑	↑		←	←			←	2	3	−1
5	↑	↑	↑	↑		←		←	←	4	3	1
6	↑	↑	↑	↑	↑			←	↑	6	1	5
7		↑	↑							2	0	2
8	↑	↑	↑	↑	↑	↑			↑	7	0	7
9	↑	↑	↑	↑	↑	←		←		5	2	3

Table 6.27

Wednesday Focus Group
Tabular IRD—Sorted in Descending Order of Δ

	1	2	3	4	5	6	7	8	9	Out	In	Δ
8	↑	↑	↑	↑	↑	↑			↑	7	0	7
6	↑	↑	↑	↑	↑			←	↑	6	1	5
9	↑	↑	↑	↑	↑	←		←		5	2	3
7		↑	↑							2	0	2
5		↑	↑	↑		←		←	←	4	3	1
4		↑	↑		←	←			←	2	3	−1
2	↑		↑	←	←	←	←	←	←	2	6	−4
1		←	←		←	←		←	←	0	6	−6
3	↑	←		←	←	←	←	←	←	1	7	−6

Table 6.28	
	Tentative SID Assignments
8	Primary Driver
7	Primary Driver
6	Secondary Driver
9	Secondary Driver
5	Secondary Driver
4	Secondary Outcome
2	Secondary Outcome
3	Secondary Outcome
1	Primary Outcome

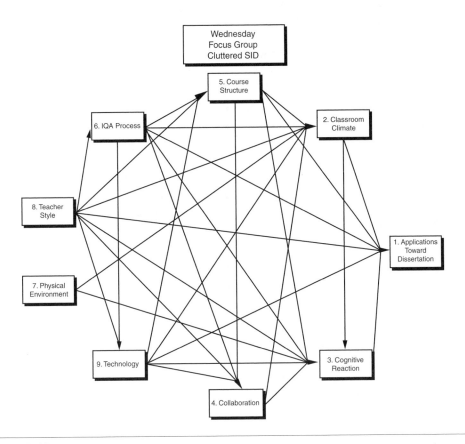

Figure 6.12

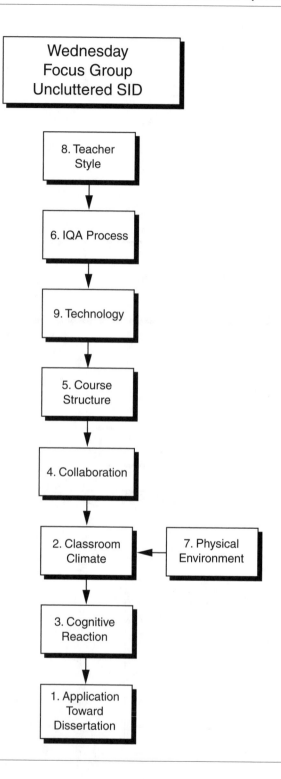

Figure 6.13

Notes

1. Although Karl Popper, that fierce critic of induction, disagreed, and by some accounts threatened Wittgenstein with a red-hot fireplace poker during an argument at Oxford University over the relationship of language to reality.

2. See *www.princeton.edu/%7Epsych/PsychSite/fac_phil.html* for an entertaining glimpse into the interests of Johnson-Laird and associates.

3. See Ruth Byrne's excellent treatment at *www.tcd.ie/Psychology/Ruth_Byrne/mental_models/*.

4. For example, see Staggers, N., & Norcio, A. (1993). Mental Models: Concepts for human-computer interaction research. *International Journal of Man-Machine Studies* 38: 587–605.

5. For a more recent picture of her thinking, see Carley's 1997 chapter, Network Text Analysis: The Network Position of Concepts. In C. W. Roberts (Ed.), *Text Analysis for the Social Sciences* (pp 79–100). Mahwah, NJ, Lawrence Erlbaum.

6. We equate Carley's and Palmquists's use of *network of concepts* to our use of the word *system*.

7. Ergo the emphasis in IQA on group processes, as well as on contrast and comparison among, and between, individual and group mindmaps.

8. Because we do not yet know the order of the relationships (e.g., $1 \rightarrow 2$ is just as possible as $2 \rightarrow 1$), there are 30 possibilities to be examined rather than 15.

9. The authors' personal favorite. See *www.inspiration.com/home.cfm* for details.

Individual Reality 7

The IQA Interview

Interviews are a critical component to most qualitative studies, and there is hardly a dearth of methodology sources. For example, a search on the Web site for Sage Publications[1] (a major publisher of qualitative research methods and scholarly works) reveals, as of October 2003, 24 books on interviewing, each of which focuses on different aspects—such as structure of the interview (highly structured to almost no structure at all); interviews conducted for specific purposes or within localized contexts (e.g., employment interview methodology); interviews with more generalized objectives (e.g., narrative or life story interviews); therapeutic interviews; telephone interviews; and individual versus focus group interviews. In reviewing the material on interview methodology, two questions seem often to be unanswered or at least given little attention:

- ❖ How will the focus or content of the interview be determined?
- ❖ How will the interview data be analyzed?

Interactive Qualitative Analysis (IQA) is a systems approach to qualitative research, which is to say the primary purpose is to represent the meaning of a phenomenon in terms of elements (affinities) and the relationships among them. Therefore, the content of the interview is determined by the affinities developed from the focus group. To put the matter simply, the researcher shares the focus group's definition of each affinity with the participant and then engages in a dialogue by saying, "Tell me what this means to you." This first phase of the IQA interview is relatively open-ended, with the purpose being to encourage the participant to reflect on the personal meaning and experiences relevant to each affinity.

It is useful at this point to contrast the IQA interview process to more traditional ones. A researcher who is interested in describing the meaning of participating in a doctoral program at a major state university might very well begin with observation or interviews, which immediately raises the question of what to look for or what to ask. The methodological literature seems to direct the researcher in opposing directions at this juncture, as illustrated here:

❖ *Researcher 1.* Lacking—or deliberately avoiding—any predetermined lens through which to view this phenomenon, the researcher begins an interview with a doctoral program participant by taking a life history approach and asking the participant to share his or her experiences to date with the program, beginning from the time a decision was made to enter the program. After conducting several similar interviews, the researcher typically begins to look for patterns within the data. The experiences of the students might be summarized and arranged chronologically (application, entry, candidacy, dissertation); or in terms of roles (student work, faculty interactions, dealing with the bureaucracy); or from a critical perspective (gender and power in the doctoral program); or from any number of other perspectives. Regardless of the perspective, at some point (with the possible exception of extreme phenomenologists who resist abstraction) the investigator summarizes the interview data, typically into a finite number of themes or categories, which then may or may not be related to each other as part of a higher level of abstraction.

❖ *Researcher 2.* Taking the admonition to do an "exhaustive literature review" seriously, the researcher searches for other studies of the doctoral experience as well as writings, both empirical and theoretical, that seem to be relevant to the topic. From this material, the researcher begins to form a schema or a way of looking at the phenomenon, leading (one hopes) to at least a broad outline for the focus of the interview. The interview protocol for Researcher 2 is likely to be more highly structured than that of Interviewer 1, because the latter researcher has already developed a preliminary "theoretical sensitivity," in the phrase used by grounded theorists. After the interviews are completed, however, the task of Researcher 2 is much the same as Researcher 1: to summarize the interview into a coherent narrative. The major difference between the two is the amount of initial conceptual structure embedded within the interview, naturally influencing the way in which the researchers analyze the interview data.

The Power of the Gods

The two different approaches just described are used frequently in a variety of disciplines, and both have been put to good use, but both raise the same question when we come to the task of making sense of the data. Why, one wonders, must sense making occur *ex post facto*, and why must the researcher carry the hermeneutical load alone? Zeus designated his son Hermes to carry the gods' messages to humanity,[2] but by what authority does the researcher make an exclusive claim to the role of messenger? Are "member checking" and a high sensitivity to the problem of reflexivity the only methodological tools available to help us deal with the problem? On the other hand, should we limit our research to the straightforward objective, as some theorists seem to tell us, to just "telling the story" of someone? If so, then it seems that there is already a well-developed discipline from which we should draw our basic assumptions and procedures to do our research, and that is journalism.

Data, Analysis, and IQA

The problem stems from an often implicit and unrecognized (and, in our view, artificial) distinction between data and analysis and, consequently, in the implicit methodological implication that data are generated by the participants in order to be analyzed by the researcher. The "I" and the "A" in IQA stand for interactive and analysis, respectively, which is meant to communicate the systemic relationship of data to analysis, as well as the intimate and systemic relationships between the researcher as facilitator and analyst, and the participant as both a source of data and an analyst. Rather than asking the researcher to shoulder the burden of identifying categories of meaning (qualitative researchers often call this *open* or *emergent coding*), the IQA process exploits the participants' own definitions of meaning by using those very categories as the outline for the interviews. Furthermore, the structure of the interview corresponds exactly to the manner in which the data will be analyzed (recall that the overriding purpose of an IQA study is twofold: to identify elements of meaning and to describe the perceived cause-and-effect relationships among them, thereby creating a system called a *mindmap*). The intimate connection among the content of the interview, its structure, and the way the interview data are analyzed is taken into account by a systems approach that integrates these three. After having explored the personal meaning, relevance, and life history examples of each affinity with the participant, the last phase of the IQA interview is more highly structured. The purpose of the second phase is to explore the perceived relationships among the affinities and to record them in a way that facilitates efficient analysis and summary. The product of an IQA interview, then, is twofold:

- ❖ A rich, detailed, and exemplified description of each affinity from the participant's point of view
- ❖ A mindmap of the phenomenon for the participant

The following sections provide details on the construction, conduct, and recording of both phases of an IQA interview.

Structure and Purpose of the IQA Interview

The affinities produced by the focus group are used to create an interview protocol. The purpose of the interview protocol is to use the affinities identified through focus group data collection and analysis to inform and shape questions for the second round of data gathering: the interview. The focus group serves as the resource for the interview and also serves as a pilot study to guide further research by providing a tentative (albeit limited) snapshot of the group mindmap.

Structuring the interviews with the same questions around affinities that are discussed in a prescribed order (although follow-up questions or probes in the first phase will naturally vary) allows the researcher to ensure that each affinity is explored thoroughly and consistently. Following this carefully prepared protocol then frees the researcher to focus attention on eliciting and responding to each interviewee's distinct responses. This process enables the researcher to achieve several critical purposes with the IQA interviews:

❖ To provide data representing the respondent's personal mindmap

❖ To help the researcher code the impact and influences of these affinities in order to create a System Influence Diagram (SID)

❖ To provide data representing the group's collective SID (mindmap)

This careful, procedural preparation supports the interviewer's art in engaging and eliciting each person's experience.

Procedure for Creating an Interview Protocol

The creation of an IQA interview protocol is straightforward. The interview protocol consists of two parts: (1) the open-ended *axial interview* designed to provide rich description of affinities by the respondents; and (2) the structured *theoretical interview* designed to identify relationships between affinities. The axial interview section is derived from the affinity write-up, while the theoretical interview is presented through an Affinity Relationship Table.

The affinity write-up (see Chapter 5) is the basis of the open-ended questions of the axial interview. The interviewer need only address the affinity names themselves. The write-up provides the interviewer with a quick reference as to the agreed-upon meaning of the affinity defined by the focus

Table 7.1   Sample Interview Protocol Affinity Relationship Table

Affinity Name		Possible Relationships
1.		$A \rightarrow B$
2.		
3.		$A \leftarrow B$
4.		
5.		$A <> B$ (No relationship)
6.		
7.		
8.		

Interview Affinity Relationship Table

Affinity Pair		Relationship	Affinity Pair		Relationship
1	2		3	6	
1	3		3	7	
1	4		3	8	
1	5		4	5	
1	6		4	6	
1	7		4	7	
1	8		4	8	
2	3		5	6	
2	4		5	7	
2	5		5	8	
2	6		6	7	
2	7		6	8	
2	8		7	8	
3	4				
3	5				

group. As stated previously, the interviewer seeks to address, "What does the affinity mean to you? Tell me about your experience with the affinity."

The Affinity Relationship Table (ART; see Chapter 6) is the basis for the theoretical interview. The table provides a quick reference of all of the possible relationships between affinities. Presented with a copy of the table, the respondents are asked if they believe there is a relationship between each affinity and to explain why they believe so. They are probed to provide their experiences with the relationship. (See Table 7.1 for a sample ART.)

Preparing for the Interview

The interviewer will prepare for the interview by paying attention to two areas: content familiarity and logistics set-up.

Content Familiarity. Critical to the success of the interview is a thorough understanding of the interview protocol and each affinity within it. Although the interview will begin with the questions agreed to in the interview protocol, the interviewer must be able to respond to and move with the flow of conversation created by the interviewee's answers.

For example, if the interviewee responds to the first affinity question by referring to the fifth affinity as a cause or result of the first one, the interviewer should be familiar enough with that affinity to explore the topic when the interviewee first mentions it. Exploring the topic at the prompt of the interviewee will increase authenticity of the individual's personal report on the topic, uninfluenced even by the interviewer's specific questions.

Total familiarity with the affinities to be addressed also allows the interviewer to devote all attention to listen to and respond to the interviewer, rather than having concerns about skipping or repeating an affinity question. Although some minimal record keeping or marking off of topics will not seriously detract from the interview, the less attention required to ensuring all questions are asked leaves more attention for noticing and probing items of interest prompted by the subject.

Logistical Set-Up. Similarly, careful set-up of logistics helps the interviewer reserve attention for focusing on the interviewee. The logistics set-up includes performing an equipment and sound check for tape-recording the interview, securing a new tape and batteries to eliminate potential problems, and having printouts of the ART with a quick reference list of affinities. The objective is to prepare effectively so as to preserve all attention in the interview for observing and responding to the interviewee.

After suitable introduction and orientation, the first phase of the interview consists of a series of iterations of the following steps. The first three steps comprise the relatively unstructured portion of the interview and are designed to explore the range of meaning of each affinity with the respondent, which provides the researcher with a narrative of how the respondent perceives the elements of the phenomenon. The fourth step is designed to provide the researcher with data concerning the relationships of the phenomenological system, which are the perceived cause-and-effect connections among the elements. The four steps are detailed below:

1. Hand the respondent a list of the names and descriptions of each affinity (the affinity write-ups). Introduce the affinity to the respondent, relying on the write-up of the affinity and any supporting materials or examples produced by the focus group.

2. Ask the respondent to reflect on his or her personal experience vis-à-vis the affinity by saying, "Tell me about your experience with this."

3. Ask follow-up questions and use probes to elicit examples of the affinity in the respondent's experience and to elucidate the meaning of the affinity to the respondent.

4. After the respondent has covered all the affinities, conduct the second part of the interview, in which the respondent uses an Affinity Relationship Table to examine how he or she perceives the connections between all possible pairs of affinities.

Following are some methodological suggestions for conducting an IQA interview:

❖ *Probes.* Experiences, opinion, values, and feelings are the objectives of probes. Although some writers caution against the use of "why" questions (Patton, 2001), we have had good results with them and tend not to worry much about the distinction between "what" and "why"; after all, the whole purpose of the second phase of an IQA interview is, in one sense, one great "why" question. On the other hand, much of the standard advice about conducting open-ended interviews, such as avoiding binary or yes/no questions, is relevant to the IQA interview.

❖ *Progression and Order.* Because the researcher, having analyzed the theoretical codes from the focus group, has a tentative sense of the systemic order of the affinities (from Primary Drivers to Primary Outcomes; see Chapter 6, the section on "Determining Drivers and Outcomes," for more information), the first inclination might be to address the affinities in this same order. Our experience suggests that this is a good strategy, subject to the following considerations:

❖ Some affinities are more conceptually complex than others. Start with the simpler ones.

❖ Some affinities are more emotionally charged than others. Start with the less emotional ones.

❖ Quite often, a respondent will mention or make a reference to Affinity B while responding to a line of questions about Affinity A. Do not hesitate to take this cue from the respondent and move to Affinity B with an appropriate segue such as, "You mentioned . . . just a few minutes ago. That seems to relate to Affinity B. Let's take a look at this topic." In other words, the researcher should have an affinity sequence planned for the interview, but should allow the respondent's discourse to modify the order.

❖ *Subaffinities.* It is important not to forget subaffinities during the interview. If a subaffinity is not mentioned, segue into it, where appropriate, and probe into its meaning for the respondent.

Logistical and Operational Details

The purpose of interviewing is to find out what is on someone else's mind. The task of the interviewer is to make it possible for the respondent to "bring the interviewer into his or her world" (Patton, 2001, p. 280). IQA uses a standardized open-ended interview that feels natural and conversational to the participant, a characteristic that results primarily from the flexibility allowed by the protocol in sequencing the questions and topics to be covered. The following is an overview, in checklist format, that highlights the most important logistical issues to consider in an IQA interview. The list is presented in the general order of occurrence during an interview.

IQA INTERVIEW TO-DO'S

❖ Establish a relaxed atmosphere that encourages the interviewee to respond to each question sincerely. A casual flow should transpire so that the questions and answers feel more like a conversation than an interview.

❖ Memorize, or become completely familiar with, the interview protocol. Memorize the affinity names, their descriptions, and the general order in which they should be covered in the interview. Familiarity with the content is not as difficult as first appears, because the IQA interview does not involve a long list of predetermined questions. Mastery of the content, combined with active listening that guides the progress of the interview, allows the interviewer to ask questions naturally as topics come up. In addition, the interviewer will be able to maintain more eye contact and genuine interest while the interviewee is responding.

❖ Test the equipment set-up. Make sure the power source for the tape recorder is working properly. Test volume levels and clarity.

❖ Introduce yourself and provide basic information regarding the project.

❖ Explain the confidentiality of the interviewee's responses. Get permission to tape the interview.

❖ Get to know something about the respondent by gathering some general information. Do not fail to gather any demographic or other information that may be used in later breakouts of the interview data. Present the issue statement.

❖ Start with the Primary Driver on the protocol unless, as often happens during introductions, the interviewee mentions a "burning topic" that provides a natural lead-in to one of the affinities.

❖ Because the interview protocol has been created, in a very real sense, by a group to which the current participant is representative, you should not be surprised to hear the respondent reflecting without prompting on many of the affinities contained in the protocol. You should use these apparently ad lib utterances to guide the sequence of the interview, which gives the interview its conversational and natural feel.

❖ Make a prefatory statement for each affinity to give the respondent a few seconds to gather thoughts. The attention-getting preface should identify the affinity and review briefly the meaning of the affinity. It is very likely that the respondent will have already alluded to the affinity, which allows the interviewer to reprise that discussion as a segue to detailed examination of the affinity.

❖ Always wait for the interviewee to finish speaking before you probe or move on to the next question.

❖ Probe for deeper meaning or extended examples, which can be accomplished by a simple "What do you mean by that?" or "You said that. . . . Can you give me an example?"

❖ Remember that although the IQA interview is divided into an axial phase and a theoretical phase, these are the interviewer's/analyst's categories, not the respondent's. Respondents will quite naturally define affinities in terms of their relationships to others in the axial phase of the interview. An interviewer/analyst may be annoyed by such untidy discourse, since it would seem to blur what is in the analyst's mind as a clear demarcation between the nature of affinities on the one hand and the relations between the affinities on the other. You should instead regard these incidents as opportunities that can greatly improve the quality of analysis for both phases of the interview, and you should listen carefully to such responses and make mental notes (or even written ones, if the task does not distract) regarding relationships that emerge between the data and reprise in the theoretical phase of the interview.

❖ Provide examples if the interviewee does not respond or is unclear.

❖ Summarize when making a transition to next topic. Tell the respondent what will be asked next (direct announcement format).

❖ Be especially attentive to metaphorical language. Probe each instance with the purpose of encouraging the respondent to examine the logic and structure of the metaphor.

❖ Remember to include the subaffinities. If the interviewee does not mention them voluntarily, bring them up by way of example to determine the respondent's views on them.

❖ Thank the interviewee for his or her assistance.

IQA INTERVIEW NOT-TO-DO'S

- ❖ Talking too much, thereby monopolizing the interview

- ❖ Asking "Yes"/"No" questions that provide too little information

- ❖ Asking questions that may divert the focus of the interview

- ❖ Failing to ask for examples, especially in the theoretical section of the interview

- ❖ Failing to be attentive to interview fatigue. Although an IQA interview is not necessarily very long (our modal completion time across a wide variety of systems constructed of 8–12 affinities is 45–55 minutes), respondents may show fatigue, especially during the theoretical section, which requires a high level of deductive thinking on the part of the respondent. If fatigue is a problem, take a short break to get refreshments or just chat.

Improvisation Within Structure

The effective IQA interview is choreographed much like a *pas de deux,* but with jazz influences. The interviewer begins the dance by leading, but at any moment he or she may surrender the lead to the respondent, especially during the axial phase of the interview. The effective IQA interviewer possesses a willingness to be moved and influenced by the responses of the interviewee. The dance is not totally improvisational, however; both partners understand that when the music ends, they will have delved into the meaning of each affinity, as well as explored all possible connections between the affinities. An effective interview will leave the respondent feeling listened to through what appears to be an interesting conversation about her or his experience. Behind that impression is a carefully orchestrated exploration of specifically identified affinities and the beginning of an intricate map of how they influence each other.

Having presented an overview of the IQA interview procedure in checklist form, we now elaborate on specific portions of the interview in the following sections.

Some More Tips for Interviewing

OPENING THE INTERVIEW

The interviewer opens the interview by establishing rapport, expectations, and agreements, making special note to initiate the following:

❖ A friendly greeting, self-introduction, description of the research study, and the respondent's role

❖ Discussions of confidentiality, anonymity for the interviewee, and use of a tape recorder to record the discussion, as well as a description of how interview results will and will not be used to establish expectations and agreements between interviewer and subject

ASKING AXIAL QUESTIONS AND PROBING

Once the interviewee agrees to the conditions, and the interviewer establishes for the record, and on tape, the gender of the interviewee, the questions begin.

The interviewer begins with the first question: "Tell me about your experience with affinity [the driver]." While listening to ensure that the interviewee responds to the question asked, the interviewer also begins to listen for the interviewee to describe what might have caused the affinity or what might have resulted from the affinity. If the interviewee offers these explanations clearly, even if this means referring to an affinity addressed later in the interview protocol, the interviewer moves to the topic prompted by the subject.

The interviewer might also make clarifying or confirming statements to ensure understanding of the interviewee's assertions. An example of a clarifying question is, "So why is that important for you?" An example of a confirming statement or question is, "So what was it in the situation that caused you difficulty?" The objective is to record a clear statement from the interviewee about her or his experience with that affinity and some information that will contribute to theoretical coding of its cause or its result.

Continue the axial phase of the interview until all the affinities have been covered.

ASKING THEORETICAL QUESTIONS AND PROBING

Responding to theoretical questions can feel awkward to a respondent in the early part of this stage of the interview. The following are some suggestions for facilitating the theoretical section of the interview:

❖ Give the respondent his or her own copy of the ART (prepared in advance) to guide the second phase of the interview, which is the respondent's examination of perceived relationships between all possible pairs of affinities under the guidance of the interviewer.

❖ Begin the theoretical coding phase with an introduction such as:

Now that we have talked about each of these topics, I would like to explore the connections you see between them. For example, in our earlier discussion, you mentioned a connection between [reprises a connection made by the respondent between two affinities in the first phase of the interview, say, Affinity A and B]. This suggests that you see A influencing B [if that, indeed, is what the respondent said]. So, I would like you to work through these pairs with me and to tell me what you see as the connections.

❖ Proceed through the ART, asking whether or not the respondent perceives a relationship between the elements of each pair. If a relationship is identified, ask for examples, and then translate the respondent's statement into a clarifying statement so that the direction of the relationship may be accurately coded (and the example may be accurately indexed to the code on the interview transcript). For example, a dialogue concerning the affinities *Faculty Impact* and *Emotional Response* between Interviewer I and the Respondent R might look like this:

I: Our next pair is *Faculty Impact* and *Emotional Response.* Do you see a connection between these?

R: Oh yes, definitely.

I: Would you give me an example?

R: Well, it's like I said earlier. When a prof talks down to me, it makes me feel like a dummy and I'm not about to open my mouth again in his class.

I: So, if I'm hearing you correctly, you're telling me that *Faculty Impact* influences your *Emotional Response?*

R: Right.

❖ The ART can be completed in real time by the researcher, or preferably by an assistant, as the interview progresses. When the transcript is ready, the examples are indexed to the entries in the ART.

WRAP UP THE INTERVIEW

At the end of the interview, ask the interviewee for any final thoughts, thank him or her, and reiterate confidentiality guidelines.

DEBRIEFING

When possible, conducting a debriefing session with the respondent is highly recommended. After the respondent's mindmap is prepared from the data in the ART, the system is shown to the respondent in a debriefing session. (It is possible, with efficient use of the techniques described in Chapter 8, to show the respondent his or her mindmap within 15 minutes of the conclusion of the interview.) The researcher walks the respondent through the system, asking for comments and reflections in order to validate the representation and to gain a deeper understanding of the meaning of the system.

One of the ways in which mindmaps are interpreted is to examine them for subsystems or components that seem to have a functionality of their own and to give them names. This is an interpretive task for which the respondent is naturally well qualified once he or she is familiar with the system structure. For example, one respondent, on being introduced to the components of a feedback loop within her personal mindmap of the doctoral experience, immediately recognized and named it as her "spiritual belief system," leading to a whole new discussion of how her interpretation of spirituality was embedded within and linked to her understanding of the doctoral experience. Another respondent, after being asked to talk about her group's mindmap of the experience in the doctoral program, noticed that the system seemed to be composed of three distinct, but interrelated, tracks or paths. Being an auto racing fan, she suggested a metaphorical name for each track: The Hard Road, The Happy Trail, and The Pit Stop, which were indeed rich metaphors for subsystems that identified the academic and bureaucratic obstacles to be overcome—the psychological, intellectual, and career benefits of the doctoral program, and the reinvigorating effects of a network of friends and associates.

From the researcher's point of view, debriefing the respondent on the mindmap is highly desirable in order to gain more insight into the systemic interactions, and to increase the researcher's interpretive vocabulary by using descriptors and metaphors that come directly from the respondents.

DOCUMENTING THE INTERVIEW

Adhering to some general formatting procedures in preparing the transcript of the interview allows for quick and easy coding of data. Interviews should be transcribed word for word. Redacting interjections, such as "uh" and "oh," that often occur in conversation is encouraged, but is not necessary, to make reading easier. The transcript should be titled to reflect the alias of the respondent to protect confidentiality. A filing system must be developed for efficient retrieval.

A heading should be placed in the transcript to reflect the section of the interview (the axial phase or the theoretical phase). A heading of *Axial Interview* and *Theoretical Interview* will help to quickly locate information, as shown by the following excerpt of an interview with Mr. X:

MR. X INTERVIEW

Axial Interview

Q: June 21st. We are interviewing Mr. X about his experiences in the doctoral program at the University of Texas. We're going to do two things in this interview. First of all, I'm going to name some themes or affinities that previous doctoral students at UT have brought up time and again. I'm going to name each one and give you a little summary of what the students have said that means to them. What I would like for you to do is after I name each one and talk about it a little, what I'm going to ask you to do is tell me what this, if anything, means to you, how this played out in your experiences.

X: Okay . . .

Theoretical Interview

Q: Now, I just handed you a piece of paper and if you will notice up there we went through eight different topics. I will review them briefly. Career advancement, right? Intellectual and personal growth—very important to you. Connections, right? Sources of stress, playing the game, you talked to me about that, pride and fun and managing money, which turned out to be not that big a deal to you.

X: Right . . .

The bolding of key words in the transcript will quickly draw the researcher's eye to important codes. The first time the interviewer mentions the affinity, it should be **bolded**. This will help mark the beginning of the section for possible coding of axial quotes. For example:

Q: As a person who's almost finished with the whole program, the second thing I'd like for you to think about as we go through the list and it's not long, the second thing that we are interested in is I want, I need help from you in thinking about how these themes connect to each other, how they influence each other.

X: Okay.

Q: So I want you to be thinking about those two things as we go through this. Does that make sense?

X: Got it.

Q: All right. The first one has been called career advancement. **Tell me about career advancement.**

X: That really wasn't an issue for me, in terms of that, where I was in the school district that I was at when I started the program didn't require that. The doctoral for me was not one of career advancement but more of a personal goal.

The same method should be used in the theoretical interview section, in which all possible affinity pairs are systematically examined. Note that if the interviewer uses both the affinity name and numbers in the question during the interview, the code can be quickly and easily identified.

Q: Look at the first one, **one** and **two.** Here's the question that I want you to ask yourself. Okay, look at **career advancement** and **intellectual and personal growth**, as you think about what we've said about that, do you see a direct hit between those two and some sort of influence between those two?

X: Not really on that one.

Once the transcript has been formatted for quick reference, the transcript should have line numbers added. Line numbers will allow the researcher to refer back to any particular quote from any interview transcript with ease and accuracy, as shown in Table 7.2.

Table 7.2		
22	Q:	As a person who's almost finished with the whole program. Also, the
23		second thing I'd like for you to think about as we go through the list
24		and it's not long, the second thing that we are interested in is I want, I
25		need help from you in thinking about how these themes connect to
26		each other, how they influence each other.
27	X:	Okay.
28	Q:	So I want you to be thinking about those two things as we go through
29		this. Does that make sense?
30	X:	Got it.
31	Q:	All right. The first one has been called career advancement. Tell me
32		about *career advancement.*
33	X:	That really wasn't an issue for me, in terms of that, where I was in the
34		school district that I was at when I started the program didn't require
35		that. The doctoral for me was not one of career advancement but more
36		of a personal goal.
37		

Conclusion

Documentation of the interview concludes this stage of an IQA study, and prepares us for the next chapter dealing with analysis of interview results. The following sections demonstrate, with our case example, involving doctoral students' experiences with IQA, how an interview protocol is developed. The case is further developed by presenting one full interview.

CASE EXAMPLE

The case study continues, picking up where we left it in Chapter 6.

Reconciling Affinities

The purpose of the focus group session is to generate categories of meaning or affinities to be used later in an interview protocol. Through a series of interviews, respondents are asked to discuss what each affinity means to them. Later, in a more comprehensive write-up, the affinities are described based on the interviews.

Also developed from the focus group is a group mindmap or SID. The researcher uses the group SID to address any ambiguities that may have occurred in the affinities. Such ambiguities might include two affinities, which are dialectic. They may represent a pendulum swing of the same category of meaning and would be better represented under one affinity.

Figures 7.1 and 7.2 show the Uncluttered SIDS that emerged from the two focus groups.

When the SIDs are compared side by side, at a basic level they resemble each other. Both classes have the instructor and the physical environment identified as drivers. Comprehension and an emotional aspect are the result of the model. The other affinities that lie in between may be in a different order yet resemble each other. The model reflects drivers that are external forces, middle affinities that reflect student class interaction, and outcomes that are internal to the student. Because the models themselves are so similar, it is reasonable to reconcile the affinity names with each other. Cards generated by the focus group and reflected in the affinity write-up indicate that even though affinities may be named similarly, a difference may exist as to how the experience with any particular affinity may be perceived. The result may be a positive or a negative experience to the affinity, but it is still the same category of meaning.

Obviously, a separate interview protocol for each group could have been developed, but doing so ignores the equally obvious similarities between the two systems and leads to difficulties in comparing the two groups, which is one of the important objectives of the study. The optimum solution to this

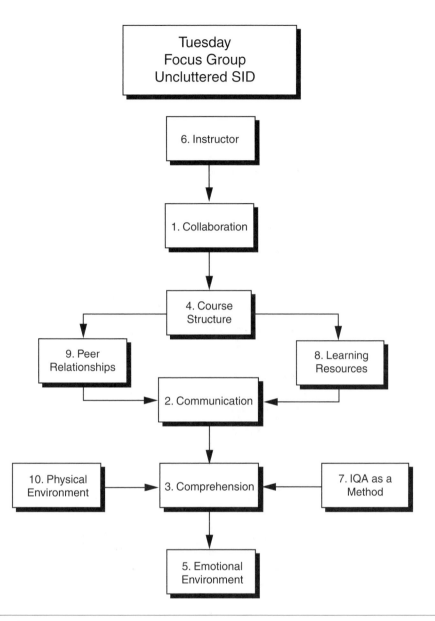

Figure 7.1

situation is to prepare a single reconciled protocol that incorporates the commonalities between the two, while maintaining the integrity of each of the original systems. Reconciled protocols are recommended for ease of comparison and are justified by the evidence that disparate constituencies vary primarily in the way they perceive the affinities to be related, rather than in the affinities themselves. Although different constituencies will often give different names to the same affinities, there is always a common core of affinities (meaning) across constituencies. It follows that a common protocol should contain these common meanings,

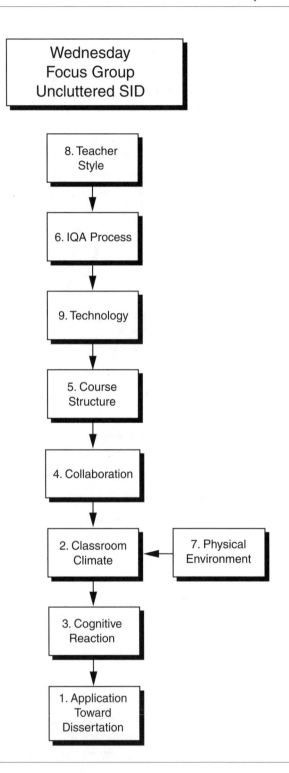

Figure 7.2

plus any other affinities that are unique to any constituency. The following is a discussion of how a reconciled protocol was developed.

A Common Protocol

In this case, the researcher noticed that both groups generated nearly the same affinities. Naming may have been different, but affinities could be paired off as having the same meaning. On several occasions, one group identified an affinity, whereas the other group identified a category of meaning that they believed to be a subaffinity, or the dialectic, of a larger category of meaning. The researcher noticed that whether it was an affinity or subaffinity, the two groups had produced similar categories. The researcher resolved the issue by compiling a new affinity list that took into account both focus group responses, with the results shown in Table 7.3.

Table 7.3

Tuesday Affinities	*Wednesday Affinities*	*Combined Affinities*
Collaboration	Collaboration	Collaboration
Communication		Communication
Comprehension • Understanding • Difficulties	Cognitive Reaction (Dialectic) • Confusion • Clarity • Growth	Cognitive Reaction (Dialectic) / Comprehension • Confusion • Clarity • Growth
Course Structure • Design • Pace • Scope	Course Structure	Course Structure • Design • Pace • Scope
Emotional Environment	Classroom Climate	Emotional Environment / Classroom Climate
Instructor	Teacher Style	Instructor Style
IQA as a Method • Applicability • Process	IQA Process	IQA Process as a Method of Research
Learning Resources	Technology	Learning Resources / Technology
Peer Relationships		Peer Relationships
Physical Environment	Physical Environment	Physical Environment
	Application Toward Dissertation	Application Toward Dissertation

216   INTERACTIVE QUALITATIVE ANALYSIS

Although many of the affinities had the exact same name between both groups, on first appearance a few seem to be unique to one group. In order to check to see if an affinity was unique to just one group, the researcher had to go back to the cards to see if there were any references to that affinity in the other group. The Tuesday class identified *Communication* as an affinity, but the Wednesday class did not. Does this mean that communication was not a factor for the Wednesday class? The Tuesday class had many cards that referred to email as a mode of communication between the student and professor. The Wednesday class placed cards about email in the *Technology* affinity. It is easy to see how one could classify email as technology, but when looking at the cards from the *Learning Resources* and *Technology* affinities, those affinities seemed to deal more with actual physical resources made available to the student, such as books or the CD. It seems reasonable to err on the side of the Tuesday class and accept *Communication* as an affinity experienced by both classes. By examining the Tuesday SID, one can see that *Learning Resources* effects, or brings about, *Communication*. This same reasoning was hidden in the Wednesday cards as reflected in the card *Good communication (email)*.

Peer Relationships was another affinity not directly named by the Wednesday class, but instead friends were mentioned in the *Classroom Climate* affinity. References to *friendly people* and *supportive classmates* indicate a relationship where friends make one feel good. Therefore, *Peer Relationships* was identified as an affinity for both classes.

The Wednesday class identified *Application Toward Dissertation* as an affinity. The Tuesday class had a subaffinity, *Applicability,* under *IQA as a Method*. With *IQA as a Method* being a driver in both classes and *Application Toward Dissertation* being an outcome, it seems *Applicability* may have been misplaced and was indeed an affinity.

Eight affinities were clearly similar in meaning. Three others could be resolved by examining the model and the cards. The result was a single affinity list that appears to be a complete list of elements of a system. Although the tone of the experiences may be different, the categories are similar. The result is a list of affinities to be used in the interview protocol.

1. Application Toward Dissertation

2. Cognitive Reaction (Dialectic) / Comprehension

    ❖ Confusion

    ❖ Clarity

    ❖ Growth

3. Collaboration

4. Communication

5. Course Structure

 ❖ Design

 ❖ Pace

 ❖ Scope

6. Emotional Environment / Classroom Climate

7. Instructor Style

8. IQA Process as a Method of Research

9. Learning Resources / Technology

10. Peer Relationships

11. Physical Environment

Interview Protocol

The following protocol is derived from the reconciled affinity list. A brief definition is used to describe the affinity so as not to influence the responses given during the interview. A copy of the protocol is handed to each person being interviewed as a point of reference. The protocol is divided into two interview sections: (1) axial and (2) theoretical. Providing respondents with the Interview ART allows them to follow along when asked about each relationship. Theoretical interviews can get tedious when there are many affinities, and the table helps to keep focus.

Because both classes identified *Instructor Style* and *Physical Environment* as drivers, that is the place to start the axial interview. *Instructor Style* is probably the better of the two because the cards were overwhelmingly in support of the instructor. It appears as if most participants had a positive experience with the instructor. This should get the interview off on a good foot. The *Physical Environment,* on the other hand, seemed to be a bit of a problem for students and is not the best place to start. Avoid starting with outcomes such as *Emotional Environment / Classroom Climate* or *Application Toward Dissertation.* People tend to speak in terms of relationships, and the conversation will naturally turn toward the outcomes.

Experience With the IQA Course: Interview Protocol

AXIAL CODING

The IQA class has identified several common themes or affinities that described their experiences in the classrooms. Let's look at each of these themes one at a time while you tell me about your experiences to each.

1. Application Toward Dissertation

The focus group described this affinity as an outcome of the class, whether IQA or some other method will play a role in their dissertation. Tell me about application toward dissertation.

2. Cognitive Reaction (Dialectic) / Comprehension

This affinity describes the reactions of students confronted with a large amount of information and new learning. It describes students' assessments of their understanding/mastery of the IQA research method from one extreme to the other on a comprehension spectrum.

The components of cognitive reaction are:

❖ Confusion

❖ Clarity

❖ Growth

Tell me about your experiences with each of these components.

3. Collaboration

This affinity consists of ways collaboration was used in the class. Tell me about collaboration.

4. Communication

This affinity reflects the students' experience in communication primarily with the instructor. Tell me about communication.

5. Course Structure

Students identified course structure as an affinity to describe the aspects of design, pace, and scope of the course.

The components of course structure are:

❖ Design
❖ Pace
❖ Scope

Tell me about your experiences with each of these components.

6. Emotional Environment / Classroom Climate

This affinity represents how the group felt about the classroom as a learning environment. Tell me about the emotional environment of the classroom.

7. Instructor Style

The group explained this affinity as how the teacher interacted with the class. Tell me about the instructor style.

8. IQA Process as a Method of Research

IQA as a Method is the affinity the focus group used to describe the actual material or method of qualitative research that was being studied in the course. Tell me about IQA as a method.

9. Learning Resources / Technology

This affinity represents all the possible tools used to reinforce the learning of the IQA method and other information in the course. Tell me about learning resources.

10. Peer Relationships

This affinity describes the relationship of the students in the class. Tell me about peer relationships.

11. Physical Environment

This affinity had to do with the classroom and the time the class was being taught. Tell me about the physical environment.

THEORETICAL CODING

Many of the themes or affinities identified have some kind of relationship; one effects or causes the other. Let's look at each theme and decide if, or how, it relates to another theme. Tell me about your experiences with such relationships. Please give specific examples of how the relationships have affected your experience.

Table 7.4

Affinity Name
1. Application Toward Dissertation
2. Cognitive Reaction (Dialectic)/ Comprehension
3. Collaboration
4. Communication
5. Course Structure
6. Emotional Environment/ Classroom Climate
7. Instructor Style
8. IQA Process as a Method of Research
9. Learning Resources/Technology
10. Peer Relationships
11. Physical Environment

Possible Relationships
A → B
A ← B
A <> B (No Relationship)

Interview Affinity Relationship Table							
Affinity Pair	Relationship	Affinity Pair	Relationship	Affinity Pair	Relationship	Affinity Pair	Relationship
1	2	2	8	4	8	7	8
1	3	2	9	4	9	7	9
1	4	2	10	4	10	7	10
1	5	2	11	4	11	7	11
1	6	3	4	5	6	8	9
1	7	3	5	5	7	8	10
1	8	3	6	5	8	8	11
1	9	3	7	5	9	9	10
1	10	3	8	5	10	9	11
1	11	3	9	5	11	10	11
2	3	3	10	6	7		
2	4	3	11	6	8		
2	5	4	5	6	9		
2	6	4	6	6	10		
2	7	4	7	6	11		

INTERVIEW TRANSCRIPT

The following transcript is a typical IQA interview. The transcript has been formatted so that specific sections can be quickly identified. The interview took place between two students in the Wednesday class (students assumed the roles of both respondents and interviewers for training purposes). The responses are taken directly from the original transcript of the respondent. Some interviewer text has been modified for demonstration purposes with no effect on the interview content.

INTERVIEW RESPONDENT 11

Axial Interview

Q: Thank you for agreeing to do this interview. With your permission, I will just let you know that this is going to be taped and everything in the interview will be confidential. The interview will be transcribed and no reference to your identity will ever be linked to the interview. Do you agree to be interviewed?

R: Yes, thank you.

Q: Could you start out by introducing yourself and giving some background on yourself?

R: Sure. I am a third-year doctoral student in educational administration and, this is, I'm kind of coming to the tail end of my course work here. I'm 30 and a female.

Q: Thank you. This study is designed to examine student experiences in the IQA class. This interview will take place in two parts. In the first part, the IQA class has identified several common themes or affinities that describe their experiences in the classrooms. We will look at each of the themes one at a time and you are going tell me about your experiences with these. In the second part, we will look at how each of these affinities relates to each other. The group identified instructor style as a big part of the class. The group explained this affinity as how the teacher interacted with the class. Tell me about the **instructor style**.

R: Sure. I actually think we have a lot of uniqueness in that regard and when we're speaking about the professor. I don't feel as though he pulls any punches. He's a very real person in the sense that what you see is what you get. I really admire that in an instructor because I feel as though sometimes instructors are put on a pedestal or they remain in this ivory tower. That, as being a woman, and being a relatively young woman in the scope of being in this program I feel as though it's easy for us to be in the shadow of that greatness and feel as though we'll never achieve this degree, you know. Sometimes there's this overarching kind of, I don't know if I'll say it right but kind of the put-you-down element. And he does not have that. I think he says this is what you need to do to get through it. And I'm going to help you get through it. And so he has a big supportive style to his instruction and I, I see that and feel that on a very regular basis.

Q: Application toward dissertation, the focus group described this affinity as an outcome of the class, whether IQA or some other method will play a role in their dissertation. Tell me about **application toward dissertation.**

R: Okay, I do think I'm going to end up working with qualitative study. I'm going to do something in fund-raising and I'm either going to look at the motivations of alumni giving or maybe look at presidential leadership in regard to fund-raising, so I'm going to be utilizing the qualitative method. As what I've seen in this class, the IQA process is a very practical subject to see the dissertation through, so I imagine that I'm going to tap into the subject several times over when I am doing my research. So I think it's going to be highly utilized.

Q: You mentioned the IQA process is a very practical subject. IQA as a method is the affinity the focus group used to describe the actual material or method of qualitative research that was being studied in the course. **Tell me about IQA.**

R: Yeah, I think from what I can get, remember from our group coming up with, affinities we talked about the IQA process both as a subject but then as an application aspect. So as a subject, we're learning about the qualitative research method and that is coming, actually believe it or not, relatively easily. I think because qualitative research has such a big element of relationships with individuals and speaking with someone one-on-one about their participation whatever that group you're studying, that resonates with me. I want to know about individual people and so the subject of qualitative research seems to work well for me. In regard to the IQA process from a more practical sense or an application sense, again it just seems to resonate with me. The way that Inspiration is, it's, it's easy to utilize that as a resource as a tool to do your work. The CD-ROM made sense to me. The reading made sense to me, so I really think from a practical standpoint, and of course doing this as we are right now, being interviewed and then turning around and interviewing someone else, I feel as though that the practicalness of the IQA process seems to work for me.

Q: Great. You talked about, you mentioned twice, things resonating with you from the course so if we could talk about the actual comprehension that's taken place. **Cognitive reaction/comprehension** describes the reactions of students confronted with a large amount of information and new learning. It describes students' assessments of their understanding/mastery of the IQA research method from one extreme to the other on a comprehension spectrum. The components of cognitive reaction are **confusion, clarity,** and **growth.** Tell me about your experiences with each of these components.

R: Sure, not a problem. In terms of the **clarity,** I think I've had what I've kind of dubbed as several "Aha" moments, like "Oh, I get it," and a lot of that was facilitated through the technology we were given and utilized throughout the course. The CD has been such a good way for me to take what I've read in the chapters that we were given and then actually see it come to fruition, to actually say "Oh well by moving the boxes around" like we had to do on that CD. I actually was getting it instead of just having this kind of philosophical discussion about it when we would read the chapter. So I felt as though there were a lot of points of clarity for me. I would say there are probably a few points of **confusion** for me, although I think the clarity outweighed the confusion. But, there was confusion mainly in regard to the mindmaps. I think that was the thing that I had the most hurdles on. But again because I had the CD as a tool and because we spent time in the Mac lab and even when he had that extra session, I attended that, it gave me a better familiarity with it and so I felt more comfortable with it, so confusion was quickly replaced with clarity. In terms of **growth**, I think my learning curve was very steep. I've never done anything with qualitative research before. I think what knowledge I do have about research has tended to be quantitative in nature, even taking statistics in my master's class, master's coursework was talking about the quantitative elements of research. It was just statistically based and it really didn't talk about focus groups and interviews and things of that nature. So this is really the first time I've had the opportunity with this and my growth has been just triplefold, I mean more than even that. Just tons of growth so I think that that relationship between confusion-clarity, confusion and clarity and the unknown to the known has really led to growth.

Q: Great. And in that growth and some of the previous questions I've asked you I noticed that you mentioned some of the tools through the process including the CD. Learning Resources/Technology represents all the possible tools used to reinforce the learning of the IQA method and other information in the course. Tell me about **learning resources.**

R: Yeah, I think that technology has been the biggest learning tool for me. I mean just things that I think I've kind of taken for granted but through this interview I'm tapping into. Just even from an example of, we acquired our reading though an attachment of an email and so I think given the stage we are in our lives with technology I do think that we even take things like that for granted so the technology is even beyond I think what we comprehend, we just take it for granted. The emailing of attachments, the way that they created the template for us to put our material into, to them taking that CD-ROM and bringing it to class and going through it in class, technology has been probably THE class. So I view it very positively. I think it's fortunate we used Macintosh computers, although I do have experience in both. I think my Macintosh experience has now outweighed my IBM experience so I was able to hit the ground running on many aspects of the technology that I think some people did struggle with. But from my experience, I was able to manipulate the programs relatively easy easily to get to my, get to the point where I was learning and actually fulfilling the assignment or doing the requirement. So technology was huge for me. And even to a certain extent this interview, we're utilizing technology. And even in the transcription so again, I think it's just beyond what we even conceive, you know if we really start to think of it, it's much deeper.

Q: Okay. And talking about, you know you said that the technology component basically it was THE class. Tell me about the **course structure** and how you assess the design of the course and please talk about the **pace** and the **scope**.

R: Okay, I can do that. The **design** of the course I think was well thought out and it, again, it spoke to me in the sense that it made sense. We needed to begin our experiences with learning the material and so we were given the chapters of the book as well as the CD-ROM as a supplement to the, to the reading. And that was a good way to begin the course because we needed to have that knowledge base in order to see, to be able to utilize it in the sense that we are right now. So, we kind of in a sense paid our dues the first six or seven weeks of class. Then we started to actually hold and put our hands on the utilizing it. We were actually making a mindmap. We're now, we're actually subjects of a research study. So, the design of the class made sense to me. I do believe that the **pace** is a little bit heavier weighted on this end, which I'm not sure how to reconcile that, but I do feel as though we're doing and because maybe it has to do with the Thanksgiving holiday, we're doing what I feel like is half the class in less than half the class's time. And again, I'm not sure there's a way to reconcile that because again you have to pay your dues on gaining that knowledge in order to then turn around and apply it. So I'm okay with it but I do and that could be also because I take other courses and I'm pressured in other ways and pressured at work that the pace, I feel a little jittery about it. In terms of the **scope** of the class and in terms of the course structure. It's kind of a unique experience I think and I'm very glad for the IQA process because there is such a heavy practical aspect to this class and the other qualitative-based classes that I think we will all take as students in ed. admin. Focusing on higher education is more and I know this isn't the exact right term, but a philosophical book in qualitative research and that is good as the backdrop but frankly for me I need to touch it, I need to hold it, I need to practice it, and this class is actually giving me that. So, I actually think if I were to take Advanced Qualitative it would go back to more the philosophy and so the scope of this class actually exceeds my expectation because I'm actually getting to do the things I need to know how to do later.

Q: Okay, thank you. We were talking about the technological component you mentioned that they would email and we would receive attachments.

R: Right.

Q: And things like that, can you talk a little bit more about the **communication** from the professor or from the assistant and what your experience was in terms of communication?

R: Sure, I can definitely talk about that. There was so much more communication with the professor than I have experienced in any of my other classes and again I think that has to do with the practicality of the, of the course utilizing and doing the subject. Because there's a lot of checks and balances, "Okay, can I understand this?" "Okay, yes I can understand it. Now do this." "Okay, but I need you to rework it because you didn't quite get it." And there's more of an element of execution in this class so the communication is upped as a result of that. I've asked the professor a couple of times if I kind of quote-unquote got it right and he emailed me back and said yeah you got it, actually these elements were yours and so you get it. So, because of that kind of checks and balances the communication is great. I do feel like we communicated 90% of the time in regard to my specific growth outside of the classroom, which was great, and I felt there was a heavy availability there, but there was a high level of communication within the class because of the collaborative nature of the class. It wasn't a lecture format where we spent three hours just listening and taking notes. So I think the communication was actually probably greater between us and among the class members and the professor than the average class.

R: Did that answer your question?

Q: It does answer.

R: Okay.

Q: Thank you.

Q: Okay. Let's move on to, we talked a little bit just a minute ago about your relationship with the instructor and the students' relationships with the instructor. Can you talk to me about the **peer relationships?**

R: I actually think there's a ton of peer relationships in the class. I guess we have fun a lot. There's a lot of humor. There is, you know we're sometimes sidetracked by the joke making so the peer relationships exist because I don't think people would be comfortable cutting up as much if they didn't know that they were going to be kind of accepted by their peers in doing so. But I would say that I don't know a lot of people in the class, so from my limited experience I don't have a great amount of peer relationships. I have just a few, a handful, maybe four or five. But I would say the peer relationships I do have with those four or five people are very rich relationships. And I can count on them and I can get feedback from them and I can say, "What do you think about this?" But I think the peer relationships in the class are very apparent due to the, to the humor and also because of the collaborative nature of the course, which I know I made mention of that earlier. Because we work in tables where five people are sitting at the table, you're obviously going to have peer relationships with them.

Q: Can you tell me more about **collaboration?**

R: Oh yeah. I think innumerable, a number of times the peer relationships and when I say that I guess I mean more the collaboration element of it. I think because the professor did not lecture and was really constantly checking on us whether we get it, that facilitated the collaborative nature at the table. If I was looking over at one of my peers and they kind of had the scrunched eyebrows then I knew to ask, "Do you get it?" And then we had the collaborative discussion whether or not they did and maybe I was the one with the scrunched eyebrows. So, I think that that occurred very often and I think again it was facilitated by the professor's instructor style. Also there's times when frankly you just don't get it but you don't always want to ask the professor because there are those people that frankly ask the professor too many questions. So you, you found that relationship in the peer. You would ask them, "Am I just the only one here that's not getting this?" and then get further information about whatever that question might be. But there is a huge collaborative element and I think also just again doing this project we have to be collaborative to get our work done. We're going to pull together a mindmap of what we've done and then we're going to pull all those together to create the assistant's research. So we're in, we're in the same boat. And I feel like we're in the Wednesday night boat as compared to the Tuesday night boat. We're, we're not in the same ship. We're probably in the same ocean but we're not in the same ship.

Q: Okay, well thanks. That gives me some insight as to the collaborative environment. Can you switch gears just a little bit and tell me about the **emotional environment** of the classroom and how you feel about the classroom as a learning environment?

R: Sure. I think because there's such a collaborative environment and because the instructor style facilitated collaboration, the environment for learning was really high, I guess. We had fun. And I think when you have fun you're more open to learn. So I think that the classroom climate from the emotional aspect facilitated my ability to learn. You know, we laughed a lot, we even had a birthday celebration. We just, there isn't, there has not been a class that has gone by where I haven't laughed several times, and that really opens to the learning environment.

Q: Our last one is the physical environment; tell me about the **physical environment** of the class.

R: I think the physical environment was challenging at times. I do, I felt as though we had probably close to thirty people in that classroom and given the structure of the tables we, I think, at times felt relatively cramped. There's no way to avoid the collaboration, which actually is probably a good point. But again I think because of the emotional environment in the classroom climate and because of the instructor's style, I probably did not have as negative opinion of the physical environment because you felt like you were in it with other people who actually cared about both the subject and then you're acquiring the knowledge of the subject as well as people who just frankly care about you. You know because of the relationships that I have with that handful of people they would ask me how was your day, and that helps a lot to overcome if you have to sit for three hours in a row, for example. Or the chairs are hard or you don't have enough workspace because there's too many people sitting at the table; you know you can overcome that physical environment because of the structure of the class and because of the instructor style and because of the collaborative nature and because of the peer relationships. I think all of that kind of helps to overcome that.

Q: Well, that concludes this first half of the interview. Do you have anything else that was not covered in some of these questions about the class that you would like to add?

R: I can't think of anything.

Q: Well, thank you so much for your time. Let's take a break.

R: Sure.

Theoretical Interview

Q: Okay, we're going to start the second portion and go through the affinities. Many of the themes or affinities identified have some kind of relationship; one effects or causes the other. Lets look at each theme and decide if or how it relates to each other theme. For example, let's look at emotions and peer relationships. You might say the peer relationships effect emotions because you made friends in class and those friendships make you happy. Tell me about your experiences with such relationships. Please give specific examples of how the relationships have affected your experience.

R: Sure.

Q: Let's look at **application toward dissertation** and then the second affinity the **cognitive reaction or comprehension**.

R: Okay, I definitely think that 2 leads to 1. The comprehension leads to the application toward dissertation. Because if you don't get the IQA model, you're going to have a hard time writing the dissertation.

Q: Okay, what about the **application toward dissertation** and **collaboration**?

R: I actually think that the, if I remember correctly, collaboration is more with the peers, I actually think the collaborative nature of our class is going to lead to the application toward dissertation because if I have any questions about this process I'm going to go to my peers because of the collaborative nature that we established and apply it toward the dissertation.

Q: Okay. What about **the application toward dissertation** and the **communication**, and that communication again is primarily from the instructor?

R: I actually think that the communication from the instructor is definitely going to lead toward the dissertation. So, 4 leads to 1.

Q: What about **application toward dissertation** and **course structure**?

R: Again, I believe the course structure leads toward the application toward dissertation. So 5 to 1 on that. Because, remember how I had spent that time saying that we had to pay our dues? If we didn't pay our dues and gain the knowledge and then apply it by doing this interview by coding it by doing everything in a practical sense, then I'm not going to know how to do the dissertation.

Q: What about the relationship between the **application toward dissertation** and the **emotional environment** or the classroom climate?

R: I do believe that 6 is going to lead to 1 on this because the classroom climate that we've created is friendly and so I'm going to kind of draw a couple of links here. The classroom climate is friendly and we have these peer relationships that are good, and again when I start to write my dissertation or have trouble and need assistance I'm going to springboard that idea off my colleagues. So I think because if I had a negative experience in this class, for example, I couldn't go to these people when I'm writing my dissertation. It just would not happen.

Q: What about the **application toward dissertation** and the **instructor style**?

R: The instructor style is definitely going to lead toward the application toward dissertation. If he was very disorganized, it's not going to help me so his style, his, you know, our ability to ask questions and to feel as though he's a resource, is going to help us when we write our dissertation.

Q: And how about the **application toward dissertation** and the **IQA process** as a method of research?

R: Absolutely 8 to 1. Because, I'm going to use qualitative and I'm going to use big elements of the IQA process for my dissertation that's a connection.

Q: **Application toward dissertation** and **learning resources or technology**?

R: 9 leads to 1 on this one for me because the, I'm going to actually use Inspiration and that was why we got that thirty-day trial so I'm going to utilize that for the dissertation and use these tables and code things the way we've learned so obviously I'm going to use the technology in writing the dissertation.

Q: What about the **application toward dissertation** and **peer relationships**?

R: For me the peer relationships lead to applications toward dissertations because again we built relationships in this class that has fostered a kind of, we're kind of all in the same boat and I think it's going to help me write my dissertation. If I'm stuck or need to collaborate with someone, the relationships we've built in this class will help me to do that.

Q: And **application toward dissertation** and **physical environment**?

R: No relationship.

Q: Cognitive reaction or **comprehension** and **collaboration** among peers.

R: Let me think about this one for a second. The collaboration led to the comprehension because when I had that scrunched eyebrow I could ask the student sitting beside me to walk through that, why I wasn't getting that, and if it were not a collaborative environment then I would never get that comprehension, so I think that the collaboration led to comprehension.

Q: How about the **comprehension** and the **communication**?

R: Definitely 4 leads to 2. By the way that he communicated with us in his instructor style, which I know is a little bit different but I linked them so closely. It led to my comprehension.

Q: What about **comprehension** and **the course structure**?

R: Definitely the course structure leads to comprehension. If he had said all right at first we do an interview . . . go. I would say okay, Q drop, no not really, but I would have been a little bit more apprehensive about doing it and it definitely would have led to my comprehension.

Q: What about **comprehension** and the **emotional environment**?

R: I mentioned this before when we talked a few minutes ago, that 6 leads to 2. And that's because sometimes when you're fatigued or it's late at night or you're sitting close to someone you like that person and you've giggled with them or established this relationship, you're going to be more open to comprehend things.

Q: And how about **comprehension** and the **instructor style**?

R: Okay, 7 leads to 2 and I kind of already talked about this a little bit. His style, not lecture style, not being Socratic method or anything crazy like that allowed me to comprehend the material.

Q: And how about **comprehension** and the **IQA process** as a method of research?

R: Okay, let me see here, I think for me this is kind of a funky one. I'm going to say comprehension, 2 leads to 8 and I'm going to walk you through it. Because if I look at comprehension, in little bits and pieces like understanding how to write an issue statement and then understanding how to interview or conduct a focus group, that comprehension leads to the IQA process, which I think of more as a global subject.

Q: What about **comprehension** and the **learning resources** or technology?

R: Okay, I'm going to say technology led to comprehension. Because remember how I was saying earlier I read the articles and then I used the CD? You know reading the articles alone I think I grasped it but it was really nailed when I did the CD.

Q: And **comprehension** and **peer relationships**?

R: I talked a lot about that earlier, that the peer relationships lead to comprehension because of the collaborativeness and because of the instructor style and all those things helped us to have a higher level of comprehension in my opinion.

Q: What about **comprehension** and **physical environment**?

R: I think that the physical environment leads to comprehension. For example, we were doing something with the technology and the lights were out, I might get a little more tired and so my comprehension might be lowered.

Q: What about **collaboration** and **communication**?

R: Okay, let me think here. I think the communication by the instructor leads to collaboration because of the way he didn't do a lecture style allowed us to be collaborative. If he had come in and been very dictatorship oriented, then we wouldn't have collaborated. So, his communication style really led to collaborativeness.

Q: And, **collaboration** and **course structure**?

R: The course structure led to collaboration for kind of the same reasons the communication did. He set it up where we had a collaborative environment.

Q: **Collaboration** and the **emotional environment** or the classroom climate?

R: Let me think here. Okay, I'm going to say, this is 6, right? 6 leads to 3 because if the students weren't humorous or happy or open or willing to engage other class members, then we would have no collaboration.

Q: Okay. **Collaboration** and **instructor style**?

R: 7 leads to 3 on that. And again for some of the same reasons. Collaborative, the course structure, instructor style all led toward a collaboration. He dictated whether that was going to happen or not.

Q: Okay. **Collaboration** and the **IQA process** as a method of research?

R: Okay. Let me think here because I'm going to say 3 leads to 8 on this one. Which at first it kind of looks funny but my reasoning is because if you don't have collaboration, for example, with this interview, it's not happening. So, and that's a part of the IQA process as a method of research. So you need to have the collaborative element at least how this class was structured in order for us to have the IQA process as a research method.

Q: **Collaboration** and the **learning resources** or technology?

R: I'm going to say that technology leads toward collaboration. Because the assistant, the way that he would instruct us would be is particularly in the Mac lab we would have this element of we're going to do it up on the screen and then we're going to do it together as a group. And so to me that was more collaborative and again the instructor's style facilitated that collaboration.

Q: **Collaboration** and **peer relationships**.

R: Peer relationships lead to collaboration because again if they're closed down to the opportunity of doing it. If everyone's so fatigued that if they're not opening up we're not going to collaborate. And that kind of leads to 11. I know you're going to ask me that.

Q: Yes, **collaboration** and the **physical environment**?

R: Yeah, if everybody's fatigued, if the lights are off the entire time, we're not going to have a collaborative environment.

Q: So, the physical environment leads to collaboration?

R: Yeah, 11 to 3 on that one for me.

Q: What about **communication** and **course structure**?

R: Okay, the communication by the instructor and the course structure. Communication by the instructor leads to course structure. So, 4 to 5. He's the one who is ultimately creating the course structure so it's his communication that's doing that.

Q: Okay. **Communication** and the **emotional environment** or classroom climate?

R: 4, okay, communication, 4 leads to 6. Because if he is saying dictatorship, then there's going to be no classroom climate.

Q: Okay **communication** and the **instructor style**?

R: Oh jeez, this is so hard laid out. Probably instructor style leads to communication. Because how he teaches is going to determine how he communicates with us.

Q: Okay. **Communication** and the **IQA process** as a method of research?

R: Okay. I think 4 leads to 8 because he's teaching us about that method of research.

Q: **Communication** and the **learning resources** or technology?

R: Okay. You know what, I'm not sure there's a relationship there.

Q: No relationship?

R: Okay, communication by instructor and technology. Well, I guess he did use that technology. Yeah, it's 4 to 9.

Q: And that's because?

R: I think it's because his choice to use email, for example, and attachments led to technology for us as our experience.

Q: Okay, **communication** and **peer relationships**?

R: Probably 4 to 10 because if he did not communicate with us. . . . Okay, I don't think our peer relationships would be the same in the class and because we're talking about our experience in the class versus our experience out of the class, he is a major affector of that. If he's saying "shut up, don't talk." We're not going to have peer relationships. We will outside of the class only because we facilitated them like if you're my buddy, you're going to be my buddy outside of class, but fostering that within it.

Q: **Communication** and the **physical environment**?

R: You know what, I think kind of bizarrely but I do think physical environment can affect the communication of the instructor.

Q: So, 11 to 4?

R: Yeah, because if we are all fatigued and if we are all cramped and hating our chairs we're sitting in, it may affect how he talks to us and he may be more frustrated. And, that's happened and I think he's extremely patient but I think we've tried him on a couple of occasions.

Q: Okay.

R: And it may be because we're just poopy tired.

Q: Okay. **Course structure** and **emotional environment** or classroom environment?

R: The course structure leads, 5 to 6, to the classroom climate because again if he's not setting it up that way, we're not having that emotive experience.

Q: Okay. **Course structure** and **instructor style**?

R: Instructor style leads to the course structure. He's saying you know if he has a way that he's doing this he is himself every semester. How he is affects that individual course and that may change from qualitative to quantitative to the courses that he teaches.

Q: Okay, **course structure** and the **IQA process** as a method of research?

R: Okay, the course structure leads to the IQA process as a method of research, so 5 to 8. Because how he sets up the course makes us understand the IQA process.

Q: Okay, **course structure** and the **learning resources** or technology?

R: Course structure leads to technology because he can decide whether or not he wants to use it. Perfect example is Tuesday night's class. You know I don't know very much about it but I do know that they're not, they didn't have the CD. And the way that he structured the class determined that.

Q: What about the **course structure** and **peer relationships**?

R: Again I think course structure leads to peer relationships if you have a very, you know, aggressive teacher that lectures the entire time again we're not going to have those relationships.

Q: And, **course structure** and the **physical environment**?

R: No relationship.

Q: What about the **emotional environment** or classroom climate and the **instructor style**?

R: So 6 and 7, is that what we're looking at?

Q: Yes.

R: The instructor style leads to classroom climate so 7 to 6. And, that's just again I've said it probably about sixteen times now, he, if he doesn't allow for that opportunity to be fostered in our environment, we're not going to have those relationships. We're not going to have the happiness, we're not going to celebrate a birthday, for God's sakes.

Q: Right.

R: That's just not going to happen.

Q: And, **emotional environment** or classroom climate and the **IQA process** as a method of research?

R: So we're looking at 6 and 8?

Q: 6 and 8.

R: No relationship.

Q: **Emotional environment** and the **learning resources** or technology?

R: Technology leads to the classroom climate. Because people were having sometimes a negative experience, that could affect the emotion in the class. And then when we're getting it, we're happy and we're humorous.

Q: Okay, the **emotional environment** or classroom climate and **peer relationships?**

R: Let me think about this one. Peer relationships lead to classroom climate. 6, 6, 10 to 6. Because we built this relationship, we've opened up to one another. And that's going to affect our humor and how we enjoy things.

Q: **Emotional environment** and the **physical environment?**

R: The physical environment is going to affect the emotional environment. If we're all tired and we're not talking, then we're not going to have those emotive relationships.

Q: **Instructor style** and the **IQA process** as a method of research?

R: I think the instructor style leads to the IQA process because he's the one teaching us and then if we use that, 7 to 8, then we're going to, you know, if he allows us to understand and if he fosters the environment of learning, we're going to get it and we're going to use it.

Q: **Instructor style** and the **learning resources** and technology?

R: The instructor style leads to technology and again my example there is his style, he made the choice to split the class between a technical section, our class, and the nontechnical section. So his, his decision and his style to do that created whether or not technology was used. So I think 7 to 9.

Q: Okay, **instructor style** and **peer relationships?**

R: 7 leads to 10. Because again if he's walking in and saying, "be quiet, be quiet," we're not going to have those relationships.

Q: Okay, **instructor style** and the **physical environment?**

R: I don't think there's a relationship between that. I'm trying to think. Actually 11 probably leads to 7. Sorry about that.

Q: That's okay. And, why do you think that?

R: I think because the physical environment if we're all cramped and we're edgy, that may affect how his style changes.

Q: Okay, the **IQA process** as a method of research and the **learning resources** or technology?

R: Technology leads toward the IQA process. 9 to 8 because you know Inspiration is the example I kind of used before. That's a big component of the IQA process.

Q: The **IQA process** as a method of research and **peer relationships?**

R: No relationship.

Q: The **IQA process** as a method of research and the **physical environment**?

R: No hit.

Q: The **learning resources** or technology and **peer relationships**?

R: I actually think the technology fostered peer relationships because we collaborated so much.

Q: Okay.

R: You know if I didn't get the technology, I was, you better bet I was asking my neighbor.

Q: Okay. The **learning resources** or technology and the **physical environment**?

R: You know, I could kind of look at this two ways. But, I think the technology affected the physical environment because if we're in the Mac lab, we're in the Mac lab, we had to go to the computers, we're in a different environment.

Q: What about and this is the last one, the **peer relationships** and the **physical environment**?

R: Physical environment led to peer relationships. Because the tables were set up and we had to sit in a circle that fosters a relationship so I would say that 11 leads to 10.

Q: Okay, well, thank you for that. Is there anything you wanted to add about any of the relationships or any of the affinities?

R: No, I don't think so.

Q: Okay, well, thank you very much.

R: You're welcome.

Notes

1. *www.sagepub.com/*. Accessed October 16, 2003.

2. An act that clearly reveals the gender bias of the gods; witness the fate of one of Zeus's many daughters, poor Persephone, who was sentenced to spend one-third of each year in Hades for the seemingly innocent act of eating a single pomegranate seed while being held prisoner there.

Individual Reality 8

System Relationships

Let's quickly review. The second section of this book described how to represent *group reality* in terms of a system composed of affinities (Chapter 5) and relationships among affinities (Chapter 6). Because Interactive Qualitative Analysis (IQA) methodology uses a consistent integrated set of protocols for observation and analysis regardless of whether the reality to be represented is from the point of view of a group or from an individual, the third section (Chapters 7 and 8) is the individual analogue to the one that preceded it.

1. *Chapter 7 is the individual analogue to Chapter 5.* Chapter 7 examined the development of an IQA protocol for interviewing individuals informed by the reality represented by the focus group. The chapter then outlined a set of procedures for examining the range of meaning within a group concerning each affinity (axial coding) and the perceived cause-and-effect relationships among these same affinities (theoretical coding).

2. *Chapter 8 is the individual analogue to Chapter 6.* Chapter 8 examines how interviews are documented and coded to reveal the range of meaning among individuals concerning each affinity and the perceived cause-and-effect relationships among these affinities.

In both settings (group and individual), the purpose is identical—to represent a particular reality in terms of a mindmap. Consequently, the analytical tools are identical: Axial coding produces examples of the range of meaning of the affinities, and theoretical coding produces the relationships among them. The only significant difference between the two sets of protocols is the context in which the observations are made.

237

Because of the conceptual equivalence of the individual and group analytics, many of the interview analytics are essentially identical to those discussed in Chapter 6 for the focus group, so they should be familiar. This chapter will address the organization of interview data to produce an individual and a composite group System Influence Diagram (SID). Whereas previous chapters were separated into theoretical and applied sections in which the case study material was kept physically separate from the theoretical, this chapter includes case material throughout. Because most of the necessary theoretical concepts have been developed in previous chapters, Chapter 8 is the most "applied" chapter of all.

The Goal of IQA Interview Analysis. For the reasons just described, most of the analytical concepts deployed in this chapter have already been introduced in the context of the focus group. What is necessary now is to demonstrate how these concepts are applied when the unit of analysis is changed from the group to the individual. Similar to the focus group data, individual interview data are coded first axially, to produce a richer and deeper description of the ways in which the affinities acquire a personal meaning to different individuals. Each interview is also theoretically coded so that the perceived relationships among the affinities are articulated for each individual. Just as in the focus group, theoretical codes are documented in an Affinity Relationship Table (ART) and then tabulated into an Interrelationship Diagram (IRD) for each individual, which makes it possible to produce an individual mindmap of the phenomenon for each person interviewed.

Theoretical Sidebar: In Deep Water. While a focus group produces a single IRD and SID through consensual procedures (although it is possible, in some focus group protocols, to produce individual mindmaps—see Chapter 6), individual interviews present a different analytical problem as well as a different set of possibilities. In the focus group setting, individual differences are subordinated to the group reality, a situation that is both predictable and appropriate. Predictable, because the focus group presumes that the members all share some common construction of the reality presented in the issue statement, and the primary purpose of an IQA study at this point is to represent that shared or social construction. Subordinating individual differences to the group is also appropriate, because the focus group is followed by the individual interview stage, which creates two opportunities for analysis and interpretation:

1. Individual differences in meaning vis-à-vis the issue can be explored systematically in the interview phase of the study. Because the interviews for a given number of representatives of a constituency produce exactly as many descriptions of each affinity, and exactly as many mindmaps, these descriptions and mindmaps may be contrasted and compared in terms of their systemic components, that is, elements (affinities) and relationships among them. The value of being able to describe individual differences is

obvious and has a parallel to descriptive research in the quantitative arena. If one knows only the average depth of a lake—three feet—then one may very well find oneself in over his head.

2. The interview mindmaps, or, more precisely, the composite of the interview mindmaps, serve to partially "triangulate" the focus group results. "Triangulation" in this sense is formally stated in the following proposition:

> If the person being interviewed is representative of the constituency(ies) from which the group SID was derived, then the composite of all such interviews should be similar to the focus group SID.

This proposition clearly indicates that the triangulation is neither *de novo* nor exhaustive. Because the content of the interview, or at least the major topics, is determined by the focus group affinities, there is little chance in the IQA interview for new categories of meaning to arise. The triangulation lies largely in the expectation that the composite mindmap of the interviews will have a similar structure to that of the focus group.

The Difference Between the Two Analytics. The primary difference between the analytics for the focus group and the interview, then, is the protocol for creating a composite mindmap from the individual interviews. The composite is produced via a straightforward adaptation of a statistical procedure called the Pareto Protocol combined with Power Analysis using the MinMax criterion (procedures that were first introduced in Chapter 6), all of which are intimidating names for uncomplicated procedures requiring only basic arithmetic and sorting. Each of these is described in this chapter. The following sections begin with the first step in interview analysis, documenting the axial codes in an Axial Code Table (ACT). This section is followed by a discussion of the TCT, or Theoretical Code Table, which is then summarized in an ART, or Affinity Relationship Table. The ART is tabulated into the now-familiar IRD, and the accompanying Cluttered and Uncluttered mindmaps are shown for this IRD. All examples are taken from a single individual's responses in the case example.

Tributaries: Documents Flowing Into the Larger Stream. As a final stage of this quick review, we present once more a system representing the flow of a typical IQA study (see Figure 8.1).

Recall that a typical IQA study is "front-loaded," which is to say it begins with a focus group, one major purpose of which is to provide the protocol for follow-up interviews that provide deeper and wider information. Focus group data are coded both axially and theoretically by group members themselves, and a focus group SID is produced by the researcher based on the rules for rationalizing systems. Subsequently (or, depending on local conditions, in parallel), interview data are coded in an identical manner—again, by the respondents themselves—and the researcher follows a protocol

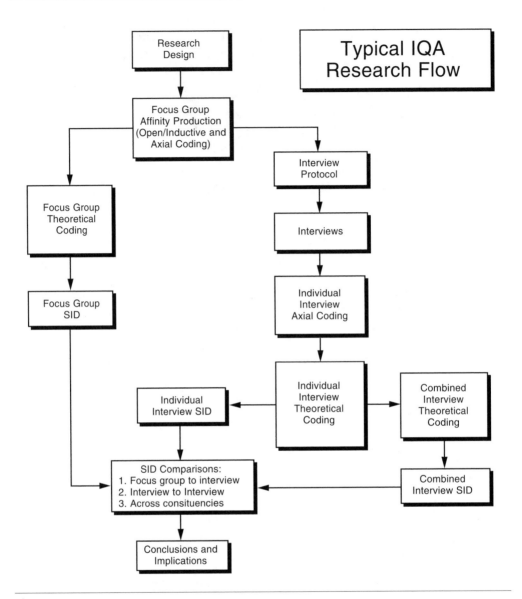

Figure 8.1

essentially identical to that used to produce the focus group mindmap, resulting in at least a composite interview mindmap. *Note that each of the elements in the IQA research flow is represented by a protocol, and each protocol is supported by a document or set of documents,* resulting in a public data collection and analysis audit trail for the entire study. In other words, issues of credibility and trustworthiness are addressed at least in part not only by a standard analytical protocol that is dependent neither on the subject matter (the nature of the affinities) nor on the inclinations of the researcher but by the standardization and documentation of each step in the research process. Compare the system shown in Figure 8.2, which summarizes the IQA document flow, to the research flow system just presented.

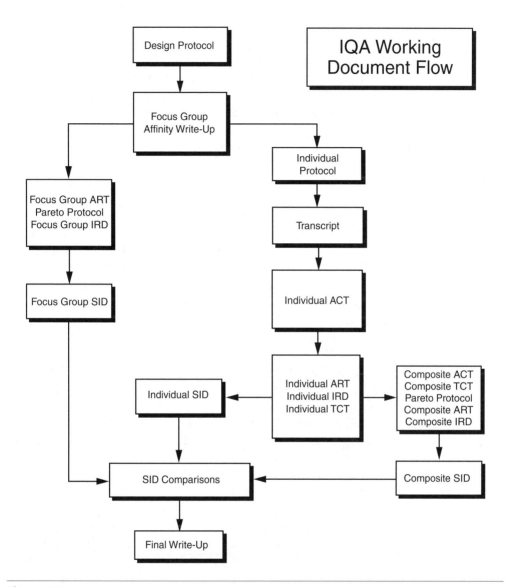

Figure 8.2

Note that for each element in the research flow, which represents a particular protocol in the first system diagram, there is a supporting document or a set of documents that serves two purposes: First, an audit trail of both data gathering or generation and analysis is created that is open to public inspection; and second, information and analytical results from each step feed to the next.

The last portion of this chapter examines combined interview coding. A partial example of a combined ACT shows by way of illustration how the totals are recorded in a combined Interview Theoretical Code Frequency table. An example of the use of the Pareto Protocol in conjunction with Power Analysis is given for the Wednesday class.

Individual Interview Coding

Axial Coding. Coding an interview is the first step toward creating a mindmap. Once the transcript has been prepared, the researcher analyzes the text for *axial codes,* which are *specific examples of discourse that illustrate or allude to an affinity.* The structure of the interview was designed to make this step very easy. The meaning of each affinity is explored with each respondent according to a standard (but flexible) protocol, and their descriptions are transcribed line by line. The researcher reviews each line of the interview transcript and looks for phrases or statements that define and provide examples of a specific affinity. These examples may be symbolic or metaphorical statements concerning the affinity, clearly stated descriptions of how the affinity becomes manifest in the experience of the respondent, or proximate descriptions of other affinities in the context of the one being addressed.[1] Respondents will often describe how one affinity relates to another in the process of discussing the nature of one affinity. Do not discourage such descriptions, even though relationships will be formally coded in the second phase of the interview.

The researcher identifies axial codes by noting key words or phrases that describe or illustrate an affinity. He or she then documents the reference for retrieval by recording the affinity number on the line of transcript that refers to the affinity, and by documenting the line numbers and affinity numbers in the Individual Interview ACT. Quotes relating to a specific affinity can be cut and pasted into the third column of the ACT, along with the line(s) of the transcript that were the source of the axial quote. There will usually be multiple axial quotes for any given affinity, each quote represented by another row in the ACT.

A Note About the Tables in This Chapter. In the interests of brevity, many of the tables containing quotes (axial and theoretical codes) are partial, rather than complete; for example, a complete axial code table contains all the quotes describing all affinities, which requires dozens of pages of text. Wherever appropriate, only the portion of a table necessary to explain its function appears in this and succeeding chapters. The complete tables are provided on the CD. Material in Table 8.1 shows those portions of the interview that were selected as axial codes. The axial codes may differ somewhat from the interview transcript because the codes have been cleaned up to eliminate the stumbles and hesitations that are a normal part of an interview.

(Text continues on page 251)

Table 8.1

| | | *Respondent 11 (Wednesday)*
Interview Axial Code Table | | |
Affinity	*Transcript Line*	*Axial Quotation*	*Researcher Notes*
1. Application Toward Dissertation	15	Okay, I do think I'm going to end up working with qualitative study. The IQA process is a very practical subject to see the dissertation through. I imagine that I am going to tap into the subject several times over when I am doing my research. I think it is going to be highly utilized.	
2. Cognitive Reaction (Dialectic) / Comprehension	50	In terms of the clarity, I think I have had several "aha" moments, like, "Oh, I get it." Most of that was facilitated through the technology we were given and utilized throughout the course. The CD has been such a good way for me to take what I have read in the chapters that we were given and then actually see it come to fruition, to actually say, "Oh well, by moving the boxes around" like we had to do on that CD. I was getting it instead of just having this kind of philosophical discussion about it when we would read the chapter. I felt as though there were many points of clarity for me. I would say there are probably a few points of confusion for me, although I think the clarity outweighed the confusion. There was confusion, mainly with the mindmaps. I think that was where I had the most hurdles. Because I had the CD as a tool, we spent time in the Mac lab and he had that extra session; it gave me a better familiarity with it. I felt more comfortable with it. Confusion was quickly replaced with clarity.	The CD helped build the basic skills.

(Continued)

Table 8.1 (Continued)

		Respondent 11 (Wednesday) Interview Axial Code Table	
Affinity	Transcript Line	Axial Quotation	Researcher Notes
	58	In terms of growth, I think my learning curve was very steep. I have never done anything with qualitative research before. I think what knowledge I do have about research has tended to be quantitative in nature. Taking statistics in my master's class, master's coursework was talking about the quantitative elements of research. It was just statistically based and it really did not talk about focus groups, interviews, and things of that nature. This is really the first time I have had the opportunity with this and my growth has been just triplefold, just tons of growth. I think that that relationship between confusion-clarity, confusion and clarity and the unknown to the known has really led to growth.	Large amount of growth for person who has never been exposed to research.
3. Collaboration	195	I think because the professor did not lecture and was constantly checking on whether we get it that facilitated the collaborative nature at the table. If I was looking over at one of my peers and they had the scrunched eyebrows, then I knew to ask, "Do you get it?" and then we had the collaborative discussion whether or not they did. Maybe I was the one with the scrunched eyebrows. I think that that occurred very often. I think again that it was facilitated by the professor's instructor style.	Most collaboration takes place at the table more than as a class as a whole.
	198	There were times when frankly, you just do not get it but you do not always want to ask the	

		Respondent 11 (Wednesday) Interview Axial Code Table	
Affinity	Transcript Line	Axial Quotation	Researcher Notes
		professor. There are those people that frankly ask the professor too many questions so you found that relationship in the peer. You would ask them, "Am I just the only one here that is not getting this?" and then get further information about whatever that question might be. There is a huge collaborative element. I think doing this project we have to be collaborative to get our work done. We are going to pull together a mindmap of what we have done and then we are going to pull all those together to create the assistant's research. We are in the same boat. I feel like we are in the Wednesday night boat as compared to the Tuesday night boat. We are not in the same ship.	
4. Communication	140	There was so much more communication with the professor than I have experienced in any of my other classes. I think that has to do with the practicality of the course utilizing and doing the subject. Because there are a lot of checks and balances, "Okay, can you understand this?" "Okay, yes, you can understand it, now do this." "Okay, but I need you to rework it because you did not quite get it." There is more of an element of execution in this class so the	Students do not get this much attention from professors in other classes. A lecture is not communication. The conversation is one-way.

(Continued)

Table 8.1 (Continued)

		Respondent 11 (Wednesday) Interview Axial Code Table	
Affinity	*Transcript Line*	*Axial Quotation*	*Researcher Notes*
		communication is upped because of that. I have asked the professor a couple of times if I "got it right" and he emailed me back and said yeah you got it, actually these elements were your strengths and so you get it. Because of that kind of checks and balances, the communication is great. I do feel like we communicated 90% of the time in regards to my specific growth outside of the classroom, which was great. I felt there was a heavy availability there but there was a high level of communication within the class because of the collaborative nature of the class. It was not a lecture format where we spent three hours just listening and taking notes. I think the communication was actually probably greater between us and among the class members and the professor than the average class.	
5. Course Structure	105	The **design** of the course I think was well thought out. It again it spoke to me in the sense that it made sense. We needed to begin our experiences with learning the material and so we were given the chapters of the book as well as the CD-ROM as a supplement to the, to the reading. That was a good way to begin the course. We needed to have that knowledge base to be able to utilize it in the sense that we are right now. We paid our dues the first six or seven weeks of class. Then we started to actually hold and put our hands on utilizing it.	"We paid our dues the first six or seven weeks of class." They recognize the skill building as a precursor to higher applications.

		Respondent 11 (Wednesday) Interview Axial Code Table	
Affinity	Transcript Line	Axial Quotation	Researcher Notes
		We were actually making a mindmap. We're now, we are actually subjects of a research study. The design of the class made sense to me.	
	110	I do believe that the **pace** is a little bit heavier weighted on this end, which I am not sure to how to reconcile. Because maybe it has to do with the Thanksgiving holiday. We are doing what I feel like is half the class in less than half the class time. I am not sure there is a way to reconcile that. You have to pay your dues on gaining that knowledge in order to then turn around and apply it. I am OK with that. I do, and that could be also because I take other courses, I'm pressured in other ways and pressured at work that the pace, I feel a little jittery about it. In terms of the **scope** of the class and in terms of the course structure. It is a unique experience. I think and I am very glad for the IQA process because there is such a heavy practical aspect to this class. The other qualitative-based classes that I think we will all take as students in ed. admin., focusing on higher education, is more a theoretical book in qualitative research. That is good as the backdrop but frankly I need to touch it, I need to hold it, I need to practice it and this class is actually giving me that. I actually think if I were to take Advanced Qualitative it would go back to more the philosophy and so the scope of this class actually exceeds my expectation because I am actually getting to do the things I need to know how to do later.	The holiday did interfere with one class session, which divided up the content for that class before and after the holiday. The Tuesday class met for their class that week but Wednesday was canceled.

(Continued)

Table 8.1 (Continued)

| | | Respondent 11 (Wednesday) | |
| | | Interview Axial Code Table | |

Affinity	Transcript Line	Axial Quotation	Researcher Notes
6. Emotional Environment / Classroom Climate	220	I think because there is such a collaborative environment and because the instructor style facilitated collaboration, the environment for learning was high. We had fun. I think when you have fun you are more open to learn. I think that the classroom climate from the emotional aspect facilitated my ability to learn. You know, we laughed a lot, we even had a birthday celebration. There has not been a class where I have not laughed several times, and that really opens to the learning environment.	
7. Instructor Style	164	I do not feel as though he pulls any punches. He is a very real person in the sense that what you see is what you get. I really admire that in an instructor. I feel as though sometimes instructors are put on a pedestal or they remain in this ivory tower. Being a relatively young woman in the scope of being in this program I feel as though it is easy for us to be in the shadow of that greatness and feel as though we will never achieve this degree. Sometimes there is this overarching kind of, I don't know if I'll say it right but, put-you-down element. And he does not have that. I think he says, "This is what you need to do to get through it. I am going to help you get through it." He has a big supportive style to his instruction and I see that and feel that on a very regular basis.	
8. IQA Process as a Method of Research	27–32	We talked about the IQA process both as a subject but then as an application aspect. So as a subject we're learning	

		Respondent 11 (Wednesday) Interview Axial Code Table	
Affinity	Transcript Line	Axial Quotation	Researcher Notes
		about the qualitative research method and that is coming, actually believe it or not, relatively easily. I think because qualitative research has such a big element of relationships with individuals and speaking with someone one-on-one about their participation whatever that group your studying, that resonates with me.	
9. Learning Resources / Technology	35	Inspiration is easy to utilize as a resource, as a tool to do your work. The CD-ROM made sense to me. The reading made sense to me.	
	81	I think that technology has been the biggest learning tool for me. Things that I have taken for granted, through this interview, I am tapping into. An example, we acquired our reading though an attachment of an email. Given the stage we are in our lives with technology, I think that we take things like that for granted. The technology is even beyond what we comprehend. We just take it for granted. The emailing of attachments, the way that they created the template for us to put our material into, to them taking that CD-ROM and bringing it to class and going through it in class, technology has been probably THE class. I view it very positively. I think it is fortunate we used Macintosh computers, although I do have experience in both. I think my Macintosh experience has now outweighed my IBM experience. I was able to hit the ground running on many aspects of the technology that some people did struggle with. From my experience, I was able to manipulate the programs relatively easily to	

(Continued)

Table 8.1 (Continued)

	Respondent 11 (Wednesday) Interview Axial Code Table		
Affinity	Transcript Line	Axial Quotation	Researcher Notes
		get to the point where I was learning and actually fulfilling the assignment or doing the requirement. Technology was huge for me. Even to a certain extent this interview, we are utilizing technology. Even in the transcription so again. I think it is just beyond what we even conceive, you know if we really start to think of it, it is much deeper.	
10. Peer Relationships	180	I guess we have fun a lot. There is a lot of humor. We were sometimes sidetracked by the joke making. The peer relationships exist because I do not think people would be comfortable cutting up as much if they did not know that they were going to be accepted by their peers in doing so. I would say that I do not know a lot of people in the class, so from my limited experience, I do not have a great amount of peer relationships. I have just a few, maybe four or five. I would say the peer relationships I do have with those four or five people are very rich relationships. I can count on them, I can get feedback from them, and I can say, "What do you think about this?" I think the peer relationships in the class are very apparent due to the humor and because of the collaborative nature of the course. Because we work in tables where five people are sitting at the table, you are obviously going to have peer relationships with them.	
11. Physical Environment	230	I think the physical environment was challenging at times. I felt as though	Other ways students

Respondent 11 (Wednesday) Interview Axial Code Table			
Affinity	Transcript Line	Axial Quotation	Researcher Notes
		we had probably close to thirty people in that classroom and given the structure of the tables we, I think, at times felt relatively cramped. There is no way to avoid the collaboration, which actually is probably a good point. I think because of the emotional environment in the classroom climate and because of the instructor's style I probably did not have as negative opinion of the physical environment. You felt like you were in it with other people who actually cared about both the subject and then you're acquiring the knowledge of the subject as well as people who just frankly care about you. You know because of the relationships that I have with that handful of people they would ask me how was your day, and that helps a lot to overcome if you have to sit for three hours in a row, for example. The chairs are hard or you do not have enough workspace because there are too many people sitting at the table. You know you can overcome that physical environment because of the structure of the class, the instructor style, the collaborative nature, and because of the peer relationships.	overcome the environment

Theoretical Coding. The researcher also identifies, through a formal line of questioning in the second phase of the IQA interview, theoretical codes that *illustrate a relationship between two or more affinities.* Preparation of the transcript should quickly point the researcher to the code. The relationship is recorded by placing the appropriate arrow in the Individual Interview Theoretical Code ACT (Table 8.2). Each line of the interview transcript should be reviewed, looking for phases or statements that

(Text continues on page 261)

Table 8.2

		Wednesday Respondent 11 *Interview Theoretical Code* *Affinity Relationship Table*	
Affinity Pair *Relationship*	*Line Number*	*Theoretical Quotation*	*Researcher* *Notes**
1 ← 2	258–260	The comprehension leads to the application toward dissertation. Because if you don't get the IQA model, you're going to have a hard time writing the dissertation.	
1 ← 3	263–266	I actually think the collaborative nature of our class is going to lead to the application toward dissertation because if I have any questions about this process, I'm going to go to my peers because of the collaborative nature that we established and apply it toward the dissertation.	
1 ← 4	269–270	I actually think that the communication from the instructor is definitely going to lead toward the dissertation.	
1 ← 5	272–277	I believe the course structure leads toward the application toward dissertation. So 5 to 1 on that. Because, remember how I had spent that time saying that we had to pay our dues? If we didn't pay our dues and gain the knowledge and then apply it by doing this interview by coding it by doing everything in a practical sense, then I'm not going to know how to do the dissertation.	
1 ← 6	280–286	I do believe that 6 is going to lead to 1 on this because the classroom climate that we've created is friendly and so I'm going to kind of draw a couple of links here. The classroom climate is friendly and we have these peer relationships that are good, and again when I start to write my dissertation or have trouble and need assistance, I'm going to	

		Wednesday Respondent 11 Interview Theoretical Code Affinity Relationship Table		
Affinity Pair Relationship	Line Number	Theoretical Quotation	Researcher Notes*
		springboard that idea off my colleagues. So I think because if I had a negative experience in this class, for example, I couldn't go to these people when I'm writing my dissertation. It just would not happen.	
1 ← 7	289–291	The instructor style is definitely going to lead toward the application toward dissertation. If he was very disorganized, it's not going to help me so his style, his, you know, our ability to ask questions and to feel as though he's a resource, is going to help us when we write our dissertation.	
1 ← 8	294–295	Absolutely 8 to 1. Because, I'm going to use qualitative and I'm going to use big elements of the IQA process for my dissertation that's a connection.	
1 ← 9	297–300	9 leads to 1 on this one for me because the, I'm going to actually use Inspiration and that was why we got that thirty-day trial so I'm going to utilize that for the dissertation and use these tables and code things the way we've learned so obviously I'm going to use the technology in writing the dissertation.	
1 ← 10	302–306	For me the peer relationships leads to applications toward dissertations because again we built relationships in this class that has fostered a kind of, we're kind of all in the same boat and I think it's going to help me write my dissertation.	
1 <> 11	308	No relationship.	

(Continued)

Table 8.2 (Continued)

		Wednesday Respondent 11 Interview Theoretical Code Affinity Relationship Table	
Affinity Pair Relationship	Line Number	Theoretical Quotation	Researcher Notes*
2 ← 3	310–314	The collaboration led to the comprehension because when I had that scrunched eyebrow I could ask the student sitting beside me to walk through that, why I wasn't getting that, and if it were not a collaborative environment then I would never get that comprehension so I think that the collaboration led to comprehension.	
2 ← 4	316–318	Definitely 4 leads to 2. By the way that he communicated with us in his instructor style, which I know is a little bit different but I linked them so closely. It led to my comprehension.	
2 ← 5	320–323	Definitely the course structure leads to comprehension. If he had said all right at first we do an interview . . . go. I would say okay, Q drop, no not really, but I would have been a little bit more apprehensive about doing it and it definitely would have led to my comprehension.	
2 ← 6	325–328	6 leads to 2. And that's because sometimes when you're fatigued or it's late at night or you're sitting close to someone you like that person and you've giggled with them or established this relationship you're going to be more open to comprehend things.	
2 ← 7	330–332	Okay, 7 leads to 2 and I kind of already talked about this a little bit. His style not lecture style, not being Socratic method or anything crazy like that allowed me to comprehend the material.	

	Wednesday Respondent 11 Interview Theoretical Code Affinity Relationship Table		
Affinity Pair Relationship	Line Number	Theoretical Quotation	Researcher Notes*
2 → 8	335–338	2 leads to 8 and I'm going to walk you through it. Because if I look at comprehension, in little bits and pieces like understanding how to write an issue statement and then understanding how to interview or conduct a focus group, that comprehension leads to the IQA process, which I think of more as a global subject.	
2 ← 9	340–342	Technology led to comprehension. Because remember how I was saying earlier I read the articles and then I used the CD? You know reading the articles alone I think I grasped it but it was really nailed when I did the CD.	
2 ← 10	344–346	The peer relationships lead to comprehension because of the collaborativeness and because of the instructor style and all those things helped us to have a higher level of comprehension in my opinion.	
2 ← 11	348–350	I think that the physical environment leads to comprehension. For example, we were doing something with the technology and the lights were out, I might get a little more tired and so my comprehension might be lowered.	
3 ← 4	352–356	I think the communication by the instructor leads to collaboration because of the way he didn't do a lecture style allowed us to be collaborative. If he had come in and been very dictatorship oriented, then we wouldn't have collaborated. So, his communication style really led to collaborativeness.	

(Continued)

Table 8.2 (Continued)

	Wednesday Respondent 11 Interview Theoretical Code Affinity Relationship Table		
Affinity Pair Relationship	Line Number	Theoretical Quotation	Researcher Notes*
3 ← 5	358–359	The course structure led to collaboration for kind of the same reasons the communication did. He set it up where we had a collaborative environment.	
3 ← 6	361–363	6 leads to 3 because if the students weren't humorous or happy or open or willing to engage other class members, then we would have no collaboration.	
3 ← 7	365–367	7 leads to 3 on that. And again for some of the same reasons. Collaborative, the course structure, instructor style all led toward a collaboration. He dictated whether that was going to happen or not.	
3 → 8	369–374	3 leads to 8 on this one. Which at first it kind of looks funny but my reasoning is because if you don't have collaboration, for example, with this interview, it's not happening. So, and that's a part of the IQA process as a method of research. So you need to have the collaborative element at least how this class was structured in order for us to have the IQA process as a research method.	
3 ← 9	376–380	Technology leads toward collaboration. Because the assistant, the way that he would instruct us would be is particularly in the Mac lab we would have this element of we're going to do it up on the screen and then we're going to do it together as a group. And so to me that was more collaborative and again the instructor's style facilitated that collaboration.	

		Wednesday Respondent 11 Interview Theoretical Code Affinity Relationship Table		
Affinity Pair Relationship	Line Number	Theoretical Quotation	Researcher Notes*
3 ← 10	382–384	Peer relationships lead to collaboration because again if they're closed down to the opportunity of doing it. If everyone's so fatigued that if they're not opening up we're not going to collaborate. And that kind of leads to 11.	
3 ← 11	387–388	Yeah if everybody's fatigued, if the lights are off the entire time, we're not going to have a collaborative environment.	
4 → 5	393–395	4 to 5. He's the one who is ultimately creating the course structure so it's his communication that's doing that.	
4 → 6	398–399	4 leads to 6. Because if he is saying dictatorship, then there's going to be no classroom climate.	
4 ← 7	401–402	Probably instructor style leads to communication. Because how he teaches is going to determine how he communicates with us.	
4 → 8	405	I think 4 leads to 8 because he's teaching us about that method of research.	
4 → 9	412–413	I think it's because his choice to use email, for example, and attachments led to technology for us as our experience.	
4 → 10	415–418	Probably 4 to 10 because if he did not communicate with us. . . . Okay, I don't think our peer relationships would be the same in the class and because we're talking about our experience in the class versus our experience out of the class, he is a major affector of that.	
4 ← 11	426–429	Because if we are all fatigued and if we are all cramped and hating our chairs	

(Continued)

Table 8.2 (Continued)

		Wednesday Respondent 11 Interview Theoretical Code Affinity Relationship Table	
Affinity Pair Relationship	Line Number	Theoretical Quotation	Researcher Notes*
		we're sitting in, it may affect how he talks to us and he may be more frustrated. And, that's happened and I think he's extremely patient but I think we've tried him on a couple of occasions.	
5 → 6	433–434	The course structure leads, 5 to 6, to the classroom climate because again if he's not setting it up that way, we're not having that emotive experience.	
5 ← 7	436–439	Instructor style leads to the course structure. He's saying, you know, if he has a way that he's doing this he is himself every semester. How he is affects that individual course and that may change from qualitative to quantitative to the courses that he teaches.	
5 → 8	441–442	The course structure leads to the IQA process as a method of research, so 5 to 8. Because how he sets up the course makes us understand the IQA process.	
5 → 9	444–446	Course structure leads to technology because he can decide whether or not he wants to use it. Perfect example is Tuesday night's class. You know I don't know very much about it, but I do know that they're not, they didn't have the CD. And the way that he structured the class determined that.	
5 → 10	449–451	Course structure leads to peer relationships if you have a very, you know, aggressive teacher that lectures the entire time again, we're not going to have those relationships.	

	Wednesday Respondent 11 Interview Theoretical Code Affinity Relationship Table		
Affinity Pair Relationship	Line Number	Theoretical Quotation	Researcher Notes*
5 <> 11	453	No relationship.	
6 ← 7	458–460	The instructor style leads to classroom climate so 7 to 6. And, that's just again I've said it probably about sixteen times now, he, if he doesn't allow for that opportunity to be fostered in our environment, we're not going to have those relationships.	
6 <> 8	469	No relationship.	
6 ← 9	471–473	Technology leads to the classroom climate. Because people were having sometimes a negative experience, that could affect the emotion in the class. And then when we're getting it, we're happy and we're humorous.	
6 ← 10	476–477	Because we built this relationship, we've opened up to one another. And that's going to affect our humor and how we enjoy things.	
6 ← 11	479–481	The physical environment is going to affect the emotional environment. If we're all tired and we're not talking, then we're not going to have those emotive relationships.	
7 → 8	483–486	I think the instructor style leads to the IQA process because he's the one teaching us, and then if we use that, 7 to 8, then we're going to, you know, if he allows us to understand and if he fosters the environment of learning, we're going to get it and we're going to use it.	
7 → 9	488–490	The instructor style leads to technology and again my example there is his style, he made the choice to split the class	

(Continued)

Table 8.2 (Continued)

		Wednesday Respondent 11 Interview Theoretical Code Affinity Relationship Table	
Affinity Pair Relationship	Line Number	Theoretical Quotation	Researcher Notes*
		between a technical section, our class, and the nontechnical section.	
7 → 10	493–494	7 leads to 10. Because again if he's walking in and saying, "Be quiet, be quiet," we're not going to have those relationships.	
7 ← 11	499–500	I think because the physical environment if we're all cramped and we're edgy, that may affect how his style changes.	
8 ← 9	503–504	Technology leads toward the IQA process. 9 to 8 because you know Inspiration is the example I kind of used before. That's a big component of the IQA process.	
8 <> 10	506	No relationship.	
8 <> 11	508	No relationship.	
9 → 10	510–511	I actually think the technology fostered peer relationships because we collaborated so much.	
9 → 11	516–518	The technology affected the physical environment because if we're in the Mac lab, we're in the Mac lab, we had to go to the computers, we're in a different environment.	
10 ← 11	521–522	Physical environment led to peer relationships. Because the tables were set up and we had to sit in a circle that fosters a relationship so I would say that 11 leads to 10.	

NOTE: * The Researcher Notes column is intended only as a demonstration and was not completed in this example. Research notes are typically much more thorough.

illustrate a link between affinities. The quotation is also placed in the table. Additional relational quotations (offered without prompting) may be found in the axial interview and should be placed in the table. The transcript line should be recorded in the table.

Interview Mindmap. After completing the theoretical coding for the interview, an IRD and SID for that individual are created. A SID for an individual is called a *mindmap,* which *reflects the individual's experience with the phenomenon.* For each interview, the following should be developed: a transcript, an axial code table, a theoretical code table, an IRD, and a SID. Together these documents produce a system that reflects the individual's thoughts, as well as providing rich detail in the respondent's own words. Table 8.3 shows the ART summarizing the respondent's analysis of all possible pairwise relationships among the eleven affinities; Table 8.4 is the corresponding IRD for this respondent.

The data in the preliminary IRD (Table 8.4) are presented in order of affinity number. Because our goal is to get a sense of the order in which the affinities fit into a system, the next step is to sort the data in Table 8.4 in descending order of delta so that they will be arranged in a rough order of causation, as shown in Table 8.5.

Sorting the affinities in descending order of delta—that is, from drivers to outcomes—allows us to group the affinities into approximate topological zones, as shown in Table 8.6. Now the IRD is complete.

As always, the next step after creating the IRD is the Cluttered SID, which contains all the relationships contained in the IRD. Because the details for creating the various kinds of SIDs have already been discussed (see Chapter 6), comments on this procedure will be kept to a minimum in this chapter. Also, interpretations will be minimized here because this is a topic for a later chapter (see Chapter 11).

Using the tentative SID assignments in Table 8.6, the affinities are arranged in the standard circular pattern of drivers to outcomes—left to right and top to bottom. All the relationships in the IRD are then copied to this circular diagram to create the Cluttered SID shown in Figure 8.3.

Although rich in complexity and detail, the Cluttered SID deserves its name—it is very difficult to interpret because of its very complexity. Removing the redundant links produces an Uncluttered SID for Respondent 11 that is much more straightforward, yet is entirely consistent with all the theoretical codes in Respondent 11's IRD.

We will reserve describing and interpreting this SID for Chapters 9 and 10, but it is worth noticing for the time being that although Respondent 11's mindmap exhibits approximately the same drivers (Instructor Style, Communication, Course Structure, Physical Environment) as does the composite for the entire class, the SID is unusual in that it begins with a

(Text continues on page 265)

Table 8.3

Affinity Name
1. Application Toward Dissertation
2. Cognitive Reaction (Dialectic) / Comprehension
3. Collaboration
4. Communication
5. Course Structure
6. Emotional Environment / Classroom Climate
7. Instructor Style
8. IQA Process as a Method of Research
9. Learning Resources / Technology
10. Peer Relationships
11. Physical Environment

Possible Relationships
A → B
A ← B
A <> B (No Relationship)

Wednesday Respondent 11
Interview Affinity Relationship Table

Affinity Pair Relationship	Affinity Pair Relationship	Affinity Pair Relationship	Affinity Pair Relationship
1 ← 2	2 → 8	4 → 8	7 → 8
1 → 3	2 ← 9	4 → 9	7 → 9
1 → 4	2 ← 10	4 → 10	7 → 10
1 → 5	2 ← 11	4 ← 11	7 ← 11
1 → 6	3 ← 4	5 → 6	8 ← 9
1 → 7	3 ← 5	5 ← 7	8 <> 10
1 → 8	3 ← 6	5 → 8	8 <> 11
1 → 9	3 ← 7	5 → 9	9 → 10
1 → 10	3 → 8	5 → 10	9 → 11
1 <> 11	3 ← 9	5 <> 11	10 ← 11
2 ← 3	3 ← 10	6 ← 7	
2 ← 4	3 ← 11	6 <> 8	
2 ← 5	4 → 5	6 ← 9	
2 ← 6	4 → 6	6 ← 10	
2 ← 7	4 ← 7	6 ← 11	

Table 8.4

		1	2	3	4	5	6	7	8	9	10	11	Out	In	Δ
Wednesday Respondent 11 Tabular IRD															
1			←	←	←	←	←	←	←	←	←		0	9	−9
2		↑		←	←	←	←	←	↑	←	←	←	2	8	−6
3		↑	↑		←	←	←	←	↑	←	←	←	3	7	−2
4		↑	↑	↑		↑	↑	←	↑	↑	↑	←	8	2	6
5		↑	↑	↑	←		↑	←	↑	↑	↑		7	2	5
6		↑	↑	↑	←	←		←		←	←	←	3	6	−3
7		↑	↑	↑	↑	↑	↑		↑	↑	↑	←	9	1	8
8		↑	←	←	←	←		←		←			1	6	−5
9		↑	↑	↑	←	←	↑	←	↑		↑	↑	7	3	4
10		↑	↑	↑	←	←	↑	←		←		←	4	5	−1
11			↑	↑	↑		↑	↑		←	↑		6	1	5

Table 8.5

		1	2	3	4	5	6	7	8	9	10	11	Out	In	Δ
Wednesday Respondent 11 Tabular IRD—Sorted in Descending Order of Δ															
7		↑	↑	↑	↑	↑	↑		↑	↑	↑	←	9	1	8
4		↑	↑	↑		↑	↑	←	↑	↑	↑	←	8	2	6
5		↑	↑	↑	←		↑	←	↑	↑	↑		7	2	5
11			↑	↑	↑		↑	↑		←	↑		6	1	5
9		↑	↑	↑	←	←	↑	←	↑		↑	↑	7	3	4
10		↑	↑	↑	←	←	↑	←		←		←	4	5	−1
6		↑	↑	↑	←	←		←		←	←	←	3	6	−3
3		↑	↑		←	←	←	←	↑	←	←	←	3	7	−4
8		↑	←	←	←	←		←		←			1	6	−5
2		↑		←	←	←	←	←	↑	←	←	←	2	8	−6
1			←	←	←	←	←	←	←	←	←		0	9	−9

Table 8.6

	Tentative SID Assignments
7	Primary Driver
4	Secondary Driver
5	Secondary Driver
11	Secondary Driver
9	Secondary Driver
10	Secondary Outcome
6	Secondary Outcome
3	Secondary Outcome
8	Secondary Outcome
2	Secondary Outcome
1	Primary Outcome

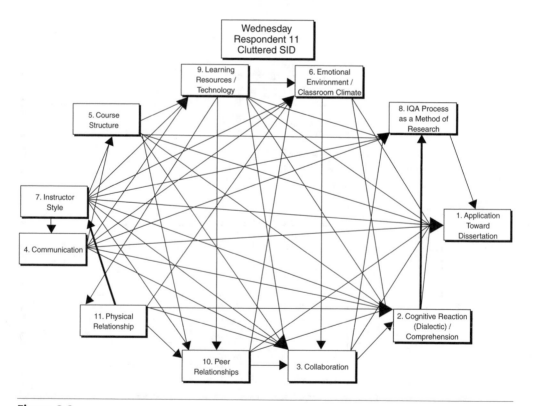

Figure 8.3

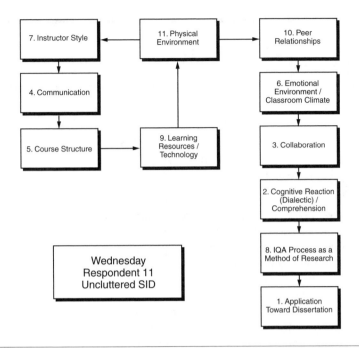

Figure 8.4

feedback loop involving all the components one usually associates with the class environment itself. Each of the other members of the class has his or her own unique mindmap (only one of which is presented here). The next step is to produce a composite SID based on combining the interview theoretical codes.

Combined Interview Coding

Aggregating Axial Codes. Once all interviews have been coded, the data from the interviews are summarized to create a combined SID that represents a composite of the individuals' experience with the phenomenon. Axial data are transferred from each Individual Interview ACT to a Combined Interview ACT. By combining all interviews into one table, the researcher creates a database for the entire set of respondents containing all axial codes for all affinities, with each code containing a link or a reference to the transcript and line numbers that produced the code. This table is very similar to the one used to record axial codes for an individual interview except that it also contains a link to the transcript that produced the code. (See, for example, Table 8.7.)

(Text continues on page 271)

Table 8.7

	Communication	
	Wednesday Combined Interview Axial Code Table	
Transcript Line	*Axial Quotation*	*Researcher Notes**
1/64	I never felt left out, lost, or as if I did not know what his expectations were. I felt that he was clear about things.	
2/52	There was the email that he would send us that I checked several times a day. He used the technology as a communications device to help clarify. That was a good use of that technology because it was immediate. If you needed to clarify yourself, and there were certain times where I had to communicate with them individually, he would send it right back. The accessibility was improved by the email.	Immediate feedback.
2/61	I think he could maybe at times be a bit daunting for some people who are not comfortable with the give-and-take, but I have never felt that. He knows when to joke; yet, he knows when to be serious about it too. He knows how to give concrete information, give good, hard-core information, and then break it up with a little levity or something to where we can kind of step back and breathe. That as a professor, instructor, as an individual, he can be very direct and yet be respectful at the same time.	Communication in the classroom not just electronically.
2/69	I have only tried to call him once, and that was not very successful. That is where the technology really has advantages. I know that he checks his email. I know he checks his technology and that is his preferred mode of communicating. He does it very well and he is responsive.	
4/22	Email was used very well although some emails were sent out the same afternoon	Students need to check email more often and the

	Communication Wednesday Combined Interview Axial Code Table	
Transcript Line	**Axial Quotation**	**Researcher Notes***
	that we had that class, I could see how people ran into difficulties that only checked their email once every other day.	Instructor cannot send last minute messages of importance.
5/135	There were a couple of incidents that I have had with the professor where I thought that he was sort of short with me but I got over that. Overall, I found him to be helpful and to engage your questions but at the same time, he would cut you off so there were times when I would ask a question and I would feel like I was shorted.	Only complaint but this person had several issues.
11/140	There was so much more communication with the professor than I have experienced in any of my other classes. I think that has to do with the practicality of the course utilizing and doing the subject. Because there is a lot of checks and balances, "Okay, can you understand this?" "Okay, yes, you can understand it, now do this." "Okay, but I need you to rework it because you did not quite get it." There is more of an element of execution in this class so the communication is upped because of that. I have asked the professor a couple of times if I "got it right" and he emailed me back and said yeah you got it, actually these elements were your strengths and so you get it. Because of that kind of checks and balances, the communication is great. I do feel like we communicated 90% of the time in regards to my specific growth outside of the classroom, which was great. I felt there was a heavy availability there but there was a high level of communication within the class because of the	Students do not get this much attention from professors in other classes. A lecture is not communication. The conversation is one-way.

(Continued)

Table 8.7 (Continued)

	Communication *Wednesday Combined Interview Axial Code Table*	
Transcript Line	*Axial Quotation*	*Researcher Notes**
	collaborative nature of the class. It was not a lecture format where we spent three hours just listening and taking notes. I think the communication was actually probably greater between us and among the class members and the professors than the average class.	
12/174	The professor had a TA that assisted me, clarified questions. That facilitated the process to where we could ask the teacher's assistant some questions that maybe we were not able to ask the professor but we could ask him. I felt that I could always ask him a question and he would always give me an answer.	Additional resources such as a TA aid communication when the teacher is not available.
12/46	The professor was always sending us emails about upcoming assignments or for follow-up emails with assignments that we had covered in class the previous class and then he would elaborate on it a little bit more. Communication in the class was excellent.	Communication lets the student have a preview of what is to come. "Tell them what you are going to tell them."
12/76	I always felt that if I did not get a question answered during class time, I could always email it to him and he would respond right away. It was also neat, it was the first class that I have taken where you can turn in assignments online rather than turning in a hard copy; just cut and paste.	Asynchronous learning. Time-saving.
16/112	Something that I appreciate is when you email a professor an assignment, or you hand in an assignment, and you receive feedback on it. That was helpful. Even for him just to email back "I got it, I got your assignment." I like that because that makes me aware that he has received it,	Any feedback is good.

Communication Wednesday Combined Interview Axial Code Table		
Transcript Line	Axial Quotation	Researcher Notes*
	it is acceptable. If something needs to be improved on the assignment, you get feedback on it.	
16/76	We got many emails, and it was hard sometimes to say, to pick out which ones are the most important. My school email is my work email and I get so much email during the day. I just felt like it was too much because I get them throughout the day and I cannot focus on my schoolwork six or seven times throughout the day.	Some students have lives outside of school and only work on schoolwork during set-aside blocks of time. They may not receive full benefit from the added communication.
23/68	I have emailed him and he emails me back immediately. I have received all the emails that we're supposed to. Communication in the classroom itself is very, very open. He just leaves himself open, he takes any kind of question and he will stay after class and answers questions. He gives us his home phone number, his cell phone number. If you want to talk to the man, you can talk to the man. Communication is definitely one of the strengths of the class.	
30/160	I have never seen some instructors outside the classroom. When he gives you his home phone, his cell phone, and his office phone that is available.	
39/167	I always feel like when I ask the professor, or even the assistant, a question, I am going to get the best answer they can give, given to me in a way that I can understand. They are not just going to, as some professors will, just spout everything they know and hope you will get something out of it. They are going to pinpoint, they are very good at pinpointing what the point of your	Communication is talking *with* them, not *at* them.

(Continued)

Table 8.7 (Continued)

	Communication Wednesday Combined Interview Axial Code Table	
Transcript Line	Axial Quotation	Researcher Notes*
	question is, whether you can state it well or not, they can pinpoint the idea of what you were asking.	
40/108	You can raise your hand and the professor will call on you. He is good about explaining and then checking back to make sure that he answered the question that you really asked. I feel like he is a very good listener when you are asking questions. He tries very hard to answer what you have asked.	Listening on the part of the instructor is a part of communication.
46/103	The professor and the assistant are serious about communicating with students. They work hard at maintaining the attention of everyone in the classroom. I think a researcher would be impressed with the time students spend on task. I have appreciated the willingness of instructors to correspond with me as a student. Communication is not limited to interactions in the class. We frequently get assignments and feedback by email.	
46/37	The instructor has used technology as a primary communication vehicle. He communicates regularly by email with students.	
52/104	I never felt like I was not being paid attention to.	
52/82	This is the only professor that I have been in this much contact with since I have been here. I knew what was going to be happening every week because of communication. For instance, the emails that would come from the professor which said, "Next week we	

Communication Wednesday Combined Interview Axial Code Table		
Transcript Line	*Axial Quotation*	*Researcher Notes**
	will be doing this" and seeing how that all fit into this entire IQA process.	
55/83	I talked to him on the phone a couple of times about a possible dissertation topic, and he pretty much walked me through it and tried to give me another direction, to see it from another point of view. He would not tear your point of view down.	

NOTE: * The Researcher Notes column is intended only as a demonstration. Research notes are typically much more thorough.

Theoretical Coding. The procedure just outlined is also used for combining theoretical data, with the exception that a count of each theoretical code is entered into the Combined Interview Theoretical Code ART. Because individual respondents may have defined relationships differently, and may in fact disagree about the direction of a relationship, this table lists both directions for relationships. (See Table 8.8 for an example.) *Count the number of respondents who identified the relationship in the same direction and place the tally in the frequency. Do the same for all respondents who identified the relationship in the opposite direction and tally those totals in the frequency column.*

(Text continues on page 279)

Table 8.8

Wednesday Interview Theoretical Code Affinity Relationship Table			
Affinity Relationship	*Transcript and Line #*	*Theoretical Quotation*	*Researcher Notes**
1 → 2			
1 ← 2	4/112	Whenever I felt like I got a grasp about something, I immediately tried to apply it toward my dissertation.	
	29/194	As soon as we started putting things together in reading the information and seeing the relationships before, I am not	

(Continued)

Table 8.8 (Continued)

Affinity Relationship	Transcript and Line #	Theoretical Quotation	Researcher Notes*
		Wednesday Interview Theoretical Code Affinity Relationship Table	
		sure how many weeks ago that was, but when we started doing the pictorial diagrams where you can see the relationships, I think that is where I saw it as an option.	
	30/234	Obviously, I have learned a lot since I knew nothing about this to start with and I feel like I am now at a point were I am somewhat capable of utilizing this information in the dissertation.	
	11/258	If you do not get the IQA model, you are going to have a hard time writing the dissertation.	
	31/106	I definitely think the cognitive reaction impacts the application toward dissertation because every time I learned a new piece, I was looking for how to apply it to the dissertation.	
	51/180	The more I understand the IQA process, I have worked through the components of confusion, clarity, and growth, the more likely I am to use the IQA process for my dissertation.	
1 → 3			
1 ← 3	11/263	I actually think the collaborative nature of our class is going to lead to the application toward dissertation because if I have any questions about this process, I am going to go to my peers because of the collaborative nature that we established and apply it toward the dissertation.	
	31/111	People who sat at the tables where I sat . . . we talked about the applications to dissertation . . . almost every class.	

Wednesday Interview Theoretical Code Affinity Relationship Table			
Affinity Relationship	Transcript and Line #	Theoretical Quotation	Researcher Notes*
	51/186	The more I can collaborate with a colleague, a peer in class, to understand how it works, that facilitates greater comprehension.	
1 → 4			
1 ← 4	4/122	Not only in the class, but outside the class when we met, this definitely . . . the communication with the professor definitely affected what ideas and concepts I could take toward my dissertation.	
	16/351	If there is open communication, then I feel like I will be better able to ask questions and have that apply to my dissertation.	
	23/156	The more I communicate, the more I talk it out either in my own head or with my peers, it is going to make it clear, so therefore, it will influence whether I will use it in my dissertation.	
	31/116	I do I think the communication with the professor, particularly through questions, helped with understanding the application of IQA to the dissertation.	
	40/196	I think that the fact that the instructor is a good communicator is another reason why I would apply this to my dissertation.	
	48/305	I feel like my communication with him (the instructor) and his communication with me, I trust him and I feel like that can be applied in my dissertation because he will help me.	
	54/434	Communication was via email. It helped people to get questions answered. Also, the information was well explained and	

(Continued)

Table 8.8 (Continued)

		Wednesday Interview Theoretical Code Affinity Relationship Table	
Affinity Relationship	Transcript and Line #	Theoretical Quotation	Researcher Notes*
		application of the process was well communicated by the instructor; this was done by giving out handouts and putting the handouts on computer.	
1 → 5			
1 ← 5	7/159	We actually applied the IQA method in terms of the research questions, so that would definitely affect my decision to use it in the dissertation.	
	11/272	If we did not pay our dues and gain the knowledge and then apply it by doing this interview by coding it by doing everything in a practical sense, then I am not going to know how to do the dissertation.	
	16/357	Having gone through and experience . . . ourselves, it will be much easier for me to apply it toward my dissertation.	
	18/234	I can say that the way the course structure was, the use of technology and all of that, made me learn, or made it more understandable, made the IQA research more understandable, then I could say that 5 influences 1.	
	23/160	I think that if this course had not been designed well and I had not been happy with IQA for reasons other than the IQA either because I did not understand it or they did not teach it well, then I would be less likely to use it toward my dissertation. I think because the course structure it has become understandable to me and therefore I will be likely to use it.	
	31/120	I think course structure impacts application of dissertation because of the sequence that it was set up in because I could see the early parts of how it would apply to the dissertation and as it got more complex, I could see that application.	

		Wednesday Interview Theoretical Code Affinity Relationship Table	
Affinity Relationship	Transcript and Line #	Theoretical Quotation	Researcher Notes*
	35/182	If I did not feel, if the course had been differently paced, and more hectic, and so on, I think that I would have been discouraged about saying, well, I am going to apply to this.	
	45/178	The course structure has led us to the methodology. The use of email, the CD-ROM, and continual reinforcing feedback has led me to appreciate what IQA has to offer. That structure drives whether I will use this on the dissertation.	
	51/198	I think that the course structure is critical simply because if this were just thrown around, you could really screw something up here. If you did not have good design, adequate pacing, and a comprehensive scope, a person may not feel comfortable enough to be able to apply it.	
1 → 6			
1 ← 6	11/280	The classroom climate that we have created is friendly and so I am going to kind of draw a couple of links here. The classroom climate is friendly and we have these peer relationships that are good and again when I start to write my dissertation or have trouble and need assistance, I am going to springboard that idea off my colleagues. So, I think because if I had a negative experience in this class, for example, I could not go to these people when I am writing my dissertation. It just would not happen.	
	16/363	Having experienced what the emotional environment is, I think we will be better able to sort of assess how the people that we are interviewing for our actual dissertation will be, and some other components of that, so I think that also affects the application.	

(Continued)

Table 8.8 (Continued)

		Wednesday Interview Theoretical Code Affinity Relationship Table		
Affinity Relationship	*Transcript and Line #*	*Theoretical Quotation*	*Researcher Notes**
	23/166	I am very much a person who if the climate is good, if I like the professor, then I am going to be more interested in it. If I do not like the professor, If I, you know, hate the classroom, then I am going to be, like, "screw it up."	
	51/205	If there is a good classroom climate, a good emotional environment, that is going to enhance my experience, which is going to make me more receptive to applying the IQA.	
1 → 7			
1 → 7	2/187	The way he taught it helped me understand how to better apply it.	
	11/289	If he was very disorganized, it is not going to help me so his style, his, you know, our ability to ask questions and to feel as though he is a resource, is going to help us when we write our dissertation.	
	12/247	If the instructor's style is appealing to me, perhaps I might want to use IQA in my dissertation, so I would say 7 to 1.	
	16/369	I think that the professor set a good tone for us and a good model for us, so that when we are out in the field conducting interviews and things like that, we will know how to conduct ourselves.	
	31/131	I think the instructors have something that all great teachers have to have, and that is high expectations. His expectations are that we are going to earn our doctorates and we are going to successfully defend dissertations and almost every class he told us about that expectation in subtle ways too.	
	35/193	I think that the more versatile and flexible, supportive the instructor is, I think the	

		Wednesday Interview Theoretical Code Affinity Relationship Table	
Affinity Relationship	Transcript and Line #	Theoretical Quotation	Researcher Notes*
		more students are . . . well, the way I felt, that I can go to him anytime in pursuing more information.	
	45/192	No question that the instructor's style influences just about everything in this course. Certainly, the way the instructor has led us into the psychology or this-is-a-way-of-viewing-life approach would drive the application toward dissertation. His assurances that we can do this lead the class along when they are in doubt.	
	46/178	The professor's message that, "Gang, it's not that hard," made it easy to believe that I could use IQA in my dissertation.	
	48/321	I am going to do this for my dissertation because he is so cool and I know that he will help me at any point during the process.	
1 → 8			
1 ← 8	11/294	I am going to use qualitative and I am going to use big elements of the IQA process for my dissertation that is a connection.	
	39/268	If I do use IQA toward a dissertation, it would simply be because the process is an effective methodology for research. As long as it is an effective methodology and fits my research question on my dissertation, I am going to use it.	
	45/201	IQA method is new to all of us. While the topic of qualitative has been around for a while, this is a clear-cut approach. By the time we finish, we should have a complete manual, done by ourselves, on how to do this. Then many of us may choose this method.	

(Continued)

Table 8.8 (Continued)

		Wednesday Interview Theoretical Code Affinity Relationship Table	
Affinity Relationship	Transcript and Line #	Theoretical Quotation	Researcher Notes*
	48/330	It fits with my personality; how it fits with my experience; how it fits with my understanding this process makes so much sense it was that a-ha moment of how this process all fit that it was, like, just everything fell into place.	
	51/214	The IQA process, just the process itself, is cool. And the more I think that, the more I am going to apply that toward my dissertation.	
1 → 9			
1 ← 9	2/194	That CD-ROM and the Inspiration helped me imagine how I could best apply it to the dissertation.	
	11/297	I am going to actually use Inspiration and that was why we got that thirty-day trial so I am going to utilize that for the dissertation and use these tables and code things the way we have learned, so obviously I am going to use the technology in writing the dissertation.	
	20/444	The learning resources and technology are important because in order to apply myself with those resources, using those resources would certainly help to determine whether I would be able to use it, apply it toward my dissertation.	
	41/175	The use of, especially the use of technology, the CD, reinforcement, the Inspiration, the visual part of it helped solidify the content of the whole process for me and because of that, I can see how it could be used for a dissertation.	

Wednesday Interview Theoretical Code Affinity Relationship Table			
Affinity Relationship	*Transcript and Line #*	*Theoretical Quotation*	*Researcher Notes**
	45/211	Technology/learning resources would drive application toward dissertation. The ease of using IQA with the provided tables and Inspiration program would have a lot to do with my choice of this method for a dissertation. This is the most technology-driven course I have had. The updates from the assistant and the professor are so numerous as to put other instructors to shame. The CD-ROM clearly reflected hours or work; and it too has been updated through emails during the course.	

NOTE: * The Researcher Notes column is intended only as a demonstration and was not completed in this example. Research notes are typically much more thorough.

Theoretical Code Frequency Table. Up to this point, the tables have all been produced in Microsoft Word. Now that we have numerical data (frequencies of relationships), a spreadsheet program such as Microsoft Excel is a handy tool for completing the last two steps of the analysis—Pareto Protocol and Power Analysis. Tasks such as sorting frequencies in descending order, calculating cumulative frequencies and percents, and using these data to calculate power are easily accomplished in Excel. Tables 8.9 through 8.12 were all produced in Excel, the templates for which are provided on the CD.

A modal approach is used to prepare an IRD for the combined interview group. The Combined Interview Theoretical Code Frequency Table is analogous to an ART used for focus groups. Much like the vote that occurs when the focus group is asked to identify relationships, the frequency of relationships determines the direction. To use the chart, examine each Individual Interview Theoretical Code Table and tally the frequency of each relationship in a table, such as the one in Table 8.9. Examine each affinity pair to determine the direction of the relationship. An overwhelming majority (Pareto Principle rule of thumb is 80%) determines the direction of the relationship. Examine codes for conflicts (e.g., $1 \rightarrow 4$ and $4 \leftarrow 1$) where the frequencies are close in number. Flag the affinity pair as "?" for consideration as a recursion. Once the tally of all interviews is complete, the Pareto Protocol can be completed.

The relationships (the number of permutations of 11 things taken 2 at a time, or 110) are sorted in descending order of frequency. Cumulative frequencies are expressed both as a percentage of total relationships (110) and as a percentage of the total number of nominations (945, a measure of the total system variation). Power is computed as the difference between these two percents, and a cut point is chosen based on the MinMax criterion. Table 8.10 contains the information necessary for a power analysis.

(*Text continues on page 288*)

Table 8.9

Wednesday Combined Interview *Theoretical Code* *Frequency Table*				
Affinity Pair Relationship	*Frequency*		*Affinity Pair Relationship*	*Frequency*
1 → 2	6		4 → 6	14
1 ← 2	19		4 ← 6	9
1 → 3	3		4 → 7	2
1 ← 3	7		4 ← 7	21
1 → 4	3		4 → 8	5
1 ← 4	15		4 ← 8	7
1 → 5	2		4 → 9	8
1 ← 5	15		4 ← 9	13
1 → 6	4		4 → 10	7
1 ← 6	5		4 ← 10	8
1 → 7	2		4 → 11	1
1 ← 7	13		4 ← 11	5
1 → 8	3		5 → 6	22
1 ← 8	21		5 ← 6	1
1 → 9	2		5 → 7	2
1 ← 9	15		5 ← 7	19
1 → 10	2		5 → 8	5
1 ← 10	3		5 ← 8	14
1 → 11	2		5 → 9	15
1 ← 11	1		5 ← 9	2
2 → 3	1		5 → 10	16
2 ← 3	24		5 ← 10	1
2 → 4	2		5 → 11	6
2 ← 4	22		5 ← 11	2
2 → 5	1		6 → 7	0
2 ← 5	22		6 ← 7	23

Wednesday Combined Interview Theoretical Code Frequency Table			
Affinity Pair Relationship	Frequency	Affinity Pair Relationship	Frequency
2 → 6	3	6 → 8	3
2 ← 6	19	6 ← 8	8
2 → 7	0	6 → 9	6
2 ← 7	22	6 ← 9	11
2 → 8	7	6 → 10	7
2 ← 8	10	6 ← 10	17
2 → 9	2	6 → 11	2
2 ← 9	23	6 ← 11	15
2 → 10	2	7 → 8	14
2 ← 10	23	7 ← 8	2
2 → 11	1	7 → 9	18
2 ← 11	17	7 ← 9	4
3 → 4	9	7 → 10	17
3 ← 4	8	7 ← 10	1
3 → 5	2	7 → 11	8
3 ← 5	21	7 ← 11	2
3 → 6	15	8 → 9	13
3 ← 6	8	8 ← 9	7
3 → 7	2	8 → 10	5
3 ← 7	20	8 ← 10	3
3 → 8	4	8 → 11	3
3 ← 8	11	8 ← 11	2
3 → 9	5	9 → 10	6
3 ← 9	9	9 ← 10	7
3 → 10	13	9 → 11	3
3 ← 10	9	9 ← 11	1
3 → 11	4	10 → 11	4
3 ← 11	13	10 ← 11	9
4 → 5	0		
4 ← 5	22		

Table 8.10

A	B	C	D	E	F
		Affinities in Descending Order of Frequency With Pareto and Power Analysis			
Affinity Pair Relationship	Frequency Sorted (Descending)	Cumulative Frequency	Cumulative Percent (Relation)	Cumulative Percent (Frequency)	Power
1. 2 ← 3	24	24	0.9	2.5	1.6
2. 2 ← 9	23	47	1.8	5.0	3.2
3. 2 ← 10	23	70	2.7	7.4	4.7
4. 6 ← 7	23	93	3.6	9.8	6.2
5. 2 ← 7	22	115	4.5	12.2	7.6
6. 4 ← 5	22	137	5.5	14.5	9.0
7. 2 ← 5	22	159	6.4	16.8	10.5
8. 5 → 6	22	181	7.3	19.2	11.9
9. 2 ← 4	22	203	8.2	21.5	13.3
10. 4 ← 7	21	224	9.1	23.7	14.6
11. 1 ← 8	21	245	10.0	25.9	15.9
12. 3 ← 5	21	266	10.9	28.1	17.2
13. 3 ← 7	20	286	11.8	30.3	18.4
14. 5 ← 7	19	305	12.7	32.3	19.5
15. 1 ← 2	19	324	13.6	34.3	20.6
16. 2 ← 6	19	343	14.5	36.3	21.8
17. 7 → 9	18	361	15.5	38.2	22.7
18. 2 ← 11	17	378	16.4	40.0	23.6
19. 7 → 10	17	395	17.3	41.8	24.5
20. 6 ← 10	17	412	18.2	43.6	25.4
21. 5 → 10	16	428	19.1	45.3	26.2
22. 1 ← 4	15	443	20.0	46.9	26.9
23. 1 ← 9	15	458	20.9	48.5	27.6
24. 5 → 9	15	473	21.8	50.1	28.2
25. 1 ← 5	15	488	22.7	51.6	28.9
26. 3 → 6	15	503	23.6	53.2	29.6
27. 6 ← 11	15	518	24.5	54.8	30.3

A	B	C	D	E	F
		Affinities in Descending Order of Frequency			
		With Pareto and Power Analysis			
Affinity Pair Relationship	*Frequency Sorted (Descending)*	*Cumulative Frequency*	*Cumulative Percent (Relation)*	*Cumulative Percent (Frequency)*	*Power*
28. 7 → 8	14	532	25.5	56.3	30.8
29. 4 → 6	14	546	26.4	57.8	31.4
30. 5 ← 8	14	560	27.3	59.3	32.0
31. 1 ← 7	13	573	28.2	60.6	32.5
32. 3 → 10	13	586	29.1	62.0	32.9
33. 8 → 9	13	599	30.0	63.4	33.4
34. 3 ← 11	13	612	30.9	64.8	33.9
35. 4 ← 9	13	625	31.8	66.1	34.3
36. 3 ← 8	11	636	32.7	67.3	34.6
37. 6 ← 9	11	647	33.6	68.5	34.8
38. 2 ← 8	10	657	34.5	69.5	35.0
39. 3 → 4	9	666	35.5	70.5	35.0
40. 3 ← 9	9	675	36.4	71.4	35.1
41. 3 ← 10	9	684	37.3	72.4	35.1
42. 4 ← 6	9	693	38.2	73.3	35.2
43. 10 ← 11	9	702	39.1	74.3	35.2
44. 4 ← 10	8	710	40.0	75.1	35.1
45. 3 ← 4	8	718	40.9	76.0	35.1
46. 3 ← 6	8	726	41.8	76.8	35.0
47. 4 → 9	8	734	42.7	77.7	34.9
48. 6 ← 8	8	742	43.6	78.5	34.9
49. 7 → 11	8	750	44.5	79.4	34.8
50. 1 ← 3	7	757	45.5	80.1	34.7
51. 2 → 8	7	764	46.4	80.8	34.5
52. 4 ← 8	7	771	47.3	81.6	34.3
53. 4 → 10	7	778	48.2	82.3	34.1
54. 6 → 10	7	785	49.1	83.1	34.0
55. 8 ← 9	7	792	50.0	83.8	33.8
56. 9 ← 10	7	799	50.9	84.6	33.6

(Continued)

Table 8.10 (Continued)

A	B	C	D	E	F
		Affinities in Descending Order of Frequency With Pareto and Power Analysis			
Affinity Pair Relationship	Frequency Sorted (Descending)	Cumulative Frequency	Cumulative Percent (Relation)	Cumulative Percent (Frequency)	Power
57. 1 → 2	6	805	51.8	85.2	33.4
58. 5 → 11	6	811	52.7	85.8	33.1
59. 6 → 9	6	817	53.6	86.5	32.8
60. 9 → 10	6	823	54.5	87.1	32.5
61. 1 ← 6	5	828	55.5	87.6	32.2
62. 3 → 9	5	833	56.4	88.1	31.8
63. 4 → 8	5	838	57.3	88.7	31.4
64. 4 → 11	5	843	58.2	89.2	31.0
65. 5 ← 8	5	848	59.1	89.7	30.6
66. 8 → 10	5	853	60.0	90.3	30.3
67. 1 → 6	4	857	60.9	90.7	29.8
68. 3 → 11	4	861	61.8	91.1	29.3
69. 7 ← 9	4	865	62.7	91.5	28.8
70. 10 → 11	4	869	63.6	92.0	28.3
71. 3 → 8	4	873	64.5	92.4	27.8
72. 1 → 3	3	876	65.5	92.7	27.2
73. 1 → 4	3	879	66.4	93.0	26.7
74. 1 → 8	3	882	67.3	93.3	26.1
75. 1 ← 10	3	885	68.2	93.7	25.5
76. 2 → 6	3	888	69.1	94.0	24.9
77. 6 → 8	3	891	70.0	94.3	24.3
78. 8 ← 10	3	894	70.9	94.6	23.7
79. 8 → 11	3	897	71.8	94.9	23.1
80. 9 → 11	3	900	72.7	95.2	22.5
81. 1 → 5	2	902	73.6	95.4	21.8
82. 1 → 7	2	904	74.5	95.7	21.1
83. 1 → 9	2	906	75.5	95.9	20.4
84. 1 → 10	2	908	76.4	96.1	19.7
85. 1 → 11	2	910	77.3	96.3	19.0

A	B	C	D	E	F
Affinity Pair Relationship	Frequency Sorted (Descending)	Cumulative Frequency	Cumulative Percent (Relation)	Cumulative Percent (Frequency)	Power
86. 2 → 4	2	912	78.2	96.5	18.3
87. 2 → 9	2	914	79.1	96.7	17.6
88. 2 → 10	2	916	80.0	96.9	16.9
89. 3 → 5	2	918	80.9	97.1	16.2
90. 3 → 7	2	920	81.8	97.4	15.5
91. 4 → 7	2	922	82.7	97.6	14.8
92. 5 → 7	2	924	83.6	97.8	14.1
93. 5 ← 9	2	926	84.5	98.0	13.4
94. 5 ← 11	2	928	85.5	98.2	12.7
95. 6 → 11	2	930	86.4	98.4	12.0
96. 7 ← 11	2	932	87.3	98.6	11.4
97. 8 ← 11	2	934	88.2	98.8	10.7
98. 7 ← 8	2	936	89.1	99.0	10.0
99. 1 ← 11	1	937	90.0	99.2	9.2
100. 2 → 3	1	938	90.9	99.3	8.4
101. 2 → 5	1	939	91.8	99.4	7.5
102. 2 → 11	1	940	92.7	99.5	6.7
103. 4 → 11	1	941	93.6	99.6	5.9
104. 5 ← 6	1	942	94.5	99.7	5.1
105. 5 ← 10	1	943	95.5	99.8	4.3
106. 7 ← 10	1	944	96.4	99.9	3.5
107. 9 ← 11	1	945	97.3	100.0	2.7
108. 2 → 7	0	945	98.2	100.0	1.8
109. 4 → 5	0	945	99.1	100.0	0.9
110. 6 → 7	0	945	100.0	100.0	0.0
Total Frequency	945				

Affinities in Descending Order of Frequency
With Pareto and Power Analysis

Table 8.11

A	B	C	D	E	F
		80% Cumulative Frequency Conflict Identification Table			
Affinity Pair Relationship	Frequency	Conflict?			
1 ← 2	19		**Instructions:** Paste the two columns (A & B) from the Frequency Ordered sheet (Table 8.10) in the first two columns. Select columns A & B and sort by ascending order.		
1 ← 3	7				
1 ← 4	15				
1 ← 5	15				
1 ← 7	13				
1 ← 8	21				
1 ← 9	15		Examine the affinity pair relationships for conflict. If both affinity pairs (ex. 1 ← 2 and 1 → 2) are present, place a question mark in the conflict box.		
10 ← 11	9				
2 ← 10	23				
2 ← 11	17				
2 ← 3	24				
2 ← 4	22				
2 ← 5	22		Use all nonconflicting relationships to create your IRD. For conflicting relationships, use the highest frequency. Note the affinity pair and reconcile conflicting relationships in the SID.		
2 ← 6	19				
2 ← 7	22				
2 ← 8	10	?			
2 ← 9	23				
2 ← 8	7	?			
3 ← 10	9	?			
3 ← 11	13				
3 ← 4	8	?			
3 ← 5	21				
3 ← 6	8	?			
3 ← 7	20				
3 ← 8	11				
3 ← 9	9				
3 ← 10	13	?			

A	B	C	D	E	F
		80% Cumulative Frequency Conflict Identification Table			
Affinity Pair Relationship	Frequency	Conflict?			
3 ← 4	9	?			
3 ← 6	15	?			
4 ← 10	8	?			
4 ← 5	22				
4 ← 6	9	?			
4 ← 7	21				
4 ← 8	7				
4 ← 9	13	?			
4 ← 10	7	?			
4 ← 6	14	?			
4 ← 9	8	?			
5 ← 7	19				
5 ← 8	14				
5 ← 10	16				
5 ← 6	22				
5 ← 9	15				
6 ← 10	17	?			
6 ← 11	15				
6 ← 7	23				
6 ← 8	8				
6 ← 9	11				
6 ← 10	7	?			
7 ← 10	17				
7 ← 11	8				
7 ← 8	14				
7 ← 9	18				
8 ← 9	7	?			
8 ← 9	13	?			
9 ← 10	7				

Table 8.12

	Mischievous Topologies: Relationship Conflict Summary	
Affinity Pair Relationship	Frequency	Use (Indicated affinities to be used in the IRD)
2 ← 8	10	Use
2 → 8	7	
3 ← 10	9	
3 → 10	13	Use
4 ← 6	9	
4 → 6	14	Use
4 ← 10	8	Use
4 → 10	7	
6 ← 10	17	Use
6 → 10	7	
8 ← 9	7	
8 → 9	13	Use

Power Analysis Graphs. Graphs of the cumulative frequency distribution and the resulting power analysis are shown in Figures 8.5 and 8.6.

The power curve peaks at a value of 34.7, which is associated with 80.1% of the total variance in the Wednesday interview system; that is, the MinMax criterion suggests that a system with about 50 relationships is the optimum in that it accounts for the greatest amount of system variance with the fewest relationships. Relationship number 50 has a frequency of 7, which is followed by six more relationships (numbers 51 through 56), which have identical frequencies. Because we have no empirical or logical reason for selecting one of these over another, we set the cut point at 7 and accept all relationships that have a frequency of 7 or more. This produces a final optimal (or very nearly optimal) system of 56 variables (51% of the total) accounting for 84.6% of the total system variation.

Flagging Apparent Conflicts. So far, we have reduced the complexity of the original system by almost half while retaining more than four-fifths of its explanatory power. The next step is to sort out the "survivors" or "finalists" in such a way as to easily identify conflicts, namely, relationships that

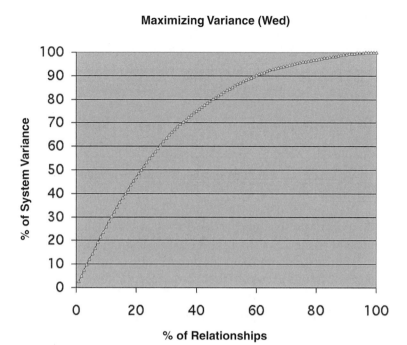

Figure 8.5

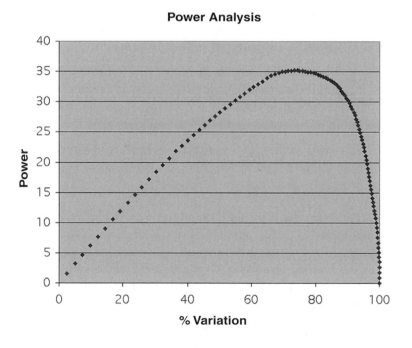

Figure 8.6

have ambiguous directionality. Table 8.11 shows the 56 finalists sorted back in ascending order of relationships. (Note that the directions for constructing the table are contained in the table itself.) Identifying conflicts is easy because these pairs will sort out next to or close to each other. Conflicting relationships are flagged with a question mark.

Troublesome Relationships. Here we have a common example of the "mischievous topology" issue discussed in Chapter 6. The Conflict Identification Table (CIT) identifies exactly six ambiguous pairs, the data for which are extracted from the CIT and presented in Table 8.12 for easy identification.

Because the IRD allows for only one of two possibilities with respect to these relationships (e.g., either 2 ← 8 or 2 → 8, but not both), a choice must be made for each of the six pairs shown in Table 8.12. The most logical choice is the modal, or most frequently occurring pair. In case of a tie, more observations (interviews) are needed to resolve the tie.

Theoretical Sidebar: $Power_1$, $Power_2$, and $Power_3$. Readers familiar with statistical concepts may recognize the problem of ties as a power issue, where "power" in this case refers specifically to statistical power, or the ability of a procedure to detect a relationship. "Power" in this work is used in three different contexts:

1. Power in the social organizational sense of having influence or control over another; for example, one of the two elements in the definition of a constituency is power over the phenomenon.

2. Power in the context of optimizing a phenomenological system; for example, the power of the system used as an illustration in this chapter is maximal in a system containing about 50 of the potential 110 affinities.

3. Power in the classic statistical sense of sensitivity or the likelihood of avoiding a Type II error; for example, one way to increase the sensitivity of our model is to conduct more interviews.

Although there are good theoretical reasons for ties (see "mischievous topologies"), a large number of ties is clearly a situation to be avoided. Experience and basic arithmetic, or, more accurately, a sensitivity analysis of the frequencies produced by different numbers of interviews, suggest that fewer than about 15 interviews will very likely result in an undesirable number of ties, depending on the number of affinities in the system. Defining the requisite number of interviews in the absence of any context is very difficult, because the number of interviews depends on three factors: the number of affinities in the system, the degree of interrelatedness of the affinities, and the degree of agreement among respondents concerning the relationships. Nevertheless, experience suggests that fewer than 15 interviews will likely result in poor power characteristics, and that 25 interviews is a much safer number. If there is a very small population available, a composite SID may not be possible in the absence of consensus, and the researcher may have to make do with examining individual mindmaps. This subject will be revisited later in a discussion on reinterviewing.

Returning to Familiar Territory: Preparing the ART. In our example, there are no ties, although one relationship (4 to 10) is very close. Examination of Table 8.11 reveals that affinity 10 in particular is involved in many of these ambiguous relationships. IQA systems theory about mischievous topologies leads us to predict that affinity 10 in particular is probably an important element in a feedback loop. If this turns out to be true when we examine the Uncluttered SID, then we have more confidence in our resolution of the ties; after all, if several elements are part of a feedback loop, then it is meaningful to say that each influences the other (through the mediating influence of other affinities), and therefore the question of which "comes first" is largely irrelevant. The feedback loop suggests that any discussion of how any one element of the feedback loop behaves must always be conducted in the context of the other elements of the loop.[2] In a manner identical to the focus group, an ART is constructed after the resolution of ties in preparation for the IRD. (See Table 8.13.)

Turning the Crank: The Composite IRD. At this point, the analytical train simply follows the track to its destination. An IRD is created, and *Ins, Outs,* and *Delta* are calculated. (See Table 8.14.)

The IRD is sorted out in descending order of delta in preparation for assignment of affinities to approximate topological zones. (See Tables 8.15 and 8.16.) Next, a Cluttered SID is produced, which is shown in Figure 8.7. (page 294).

While the Cluttered SID is extremely rich in descriptive capability, it serves better as an *objet d'art* (depending on one's sense of aesthetics) than as an interpretive device. Using the protocol for rationalizing a system described in Chapter 6, an uncluttered version of the SID, one that contains only those links consistent with the interview data as represented in the IRD, is drawn in Figure 8.8.

Theoretical Sidebar: From Analysis to Interpretation. The nature of the interaction between researcher and phenomenon continues to be the subject of great concern in qualitative research. IQA's response to this issue is

Table 8.13

Wednesday Composite Interview Affinity Relationship Table			
Affinity Pair Relationship	Affinity Pair Relationship	Affinity Pair Relationship	Affinity Pair Relationship
1 ← 2	2 ← 8	4 ← 8	7 → 8
1 ← 3	2 ← 9	4 ← 9	7 → 9
1 ← 4	2 ← 10	4 ← 10	7 → 10
1 ← 5	2 ← 11	4 <> 11	7 → 11
1 <> 6	3 → 4	5 → 6	8 → 9
1 ← 7	3 ← 5	5 ← 7	8 <> 10
1 ← 8	3 → 6	5 ← 8	8 <> 11
1 ← 9	3 ← 7	5 → 9	9 ← 10
1 <> 10	3 ← 8	5 → 10	9 <> 11
1 <> 11	3 ← 9	5 <> 11	10 ← 11
2 ← 3	3 → 10	6 ← 7	
2 ← 4	3 ← 11	6 ← 8	
2 ← 5	4 ← 5	6 ← 9	
2 ← 6	4 → 6	6 ← 10	
2 ← 7	4 ← 7	6 ← 11	

to break down the research process into stages and then vary the nature and extent of researcher engagement by stage. Consider the diagram shown in Table 8.17.

IQA is composed of the subsystems of research design, data collection (or construction), analysis, and interpretation, with each subsystem having clear links to successive ones. The researcher's engagement is highest at the beginning (design), decreases during data collection, is at a relative minimum during analysis (which is largely protocol or rule driven), and increases during the interpretive stage.

Consistent with these stages, the researcher uses mainly induction during the design stage (seeing patterns and organizing a mass of ideas into coherent topics); both induction and deduction in the collection phase (facilitating inductive and axial coding on the part of participants); deduction during the analysis (following the analysis protocols); and finally induction and deduction in the interpretation stage (following the

Table 8.14

	1	2	3	4	5	6	7	8	9	10	11	Out	In	Δ
						Wednesday Composite Interview Tabular IRD								
1		←	←	←	←		←	←	←			0	7	−7
2	↑		←	←	←	←	←	←	←	←	←	1	9	−8
3	↑	↑		↑	←	↑	←	←	←	↑	←	5	5	0
4	↑	↑	←		←	↑	←	←	←	↑		4	5	−1
5	↑	↑	↑	↑		↑	←	←	↑	↑		7	2	5
6		↑	←	←	←		←	←	←	←	←	1	8	−7
7	↑	↑	↑	↑	↑	↑		↑	↑	↑	↑	10	0	10
8	↑	↑	←	↑	↑	↑	←		↑			7	1	6
9	↑	↑	↑	↑	←	↑	←	←		←		5	4	1
10		↑	←	←	←	↑	←		↑		←	3	5	−2
11		↑	↑			↑	←			↑		4	1	3

Table 8.15

	1	2	3	4	5	6	7	8	9	10	11	Out	In	Δ
			Wednesday Composite Interview Tabular IRD—Sorted in Descending Order of Δ											
7	↑	↑	↑	↑	↑	↑		↑	↑	↑	↑	10	0	10
8	↑	↑	↑	↑	↑	↑	←		↑			7	1	6
5	↑	↑	↑	↑		↑	←	←	↑	↑		7	2	5
11		↑	↑			↑	←			↑		4	1	3
9	↑	↑	↑	↑	←	↑	←	←		←		5	4	1
3	↑	↑		↑	←	↑	←	←	←	↑	←	5	5	0
4	↑	↑	←		←	↑	←	←	←	↑		4	5	−1
10		↑	←	←	←	↑	←		↑		←	3	5	−2
6		↑	←	←	←		←	←	←	←	←	1	8	−7
2	↑		←	←	←	←	←	←	←	←	←	1	9	−8
1			←	←	←		←	←	←			0	7	−7

Table 8.16

	Tentative SID Assignments
7	Primary Driver
8	Secondary Driver
5	Secondary Driver
11	Secondary Driver
9	Secondary Driver
3	Secondary Outcome
4	Secondary Outcome
10	Secondary Outcome
6	Secondary Outcome
2	Secondary Outcome
1	Primary Outcome

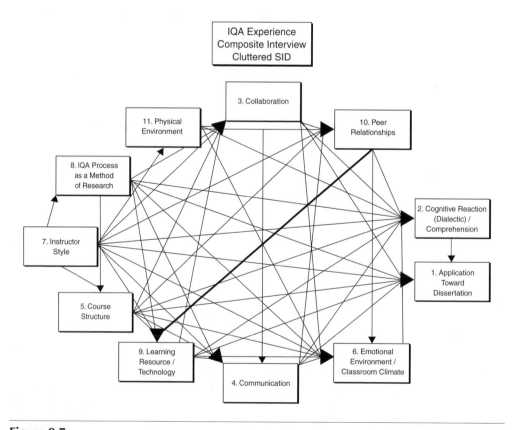

Figure 8.7

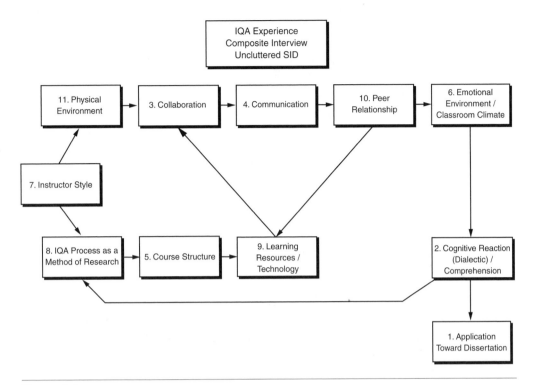

Figure 8.8

Project Stage	Level of Engagement	Researcher's Primary Logical Operation
Design	Very high	Induction
Collect/Construct	High	Induction and Deduction
Analyze	Lowest	Deduction
Interpret	High	Induction and Deduction

Table 8.17

rules for comparison and seeing connections to larger patterns). IQA protocols at each stage are designed to facilitate exactly these different modes of thinking at the appropriate stages.

The ultimate output of IQA analysis is a mindmap or more frequently a collection of mindmaps. These mindmaps (SIDs), together with the participants' axial codes (descriptions of the affinities), are the foundation for interpretation, the last stage of the study.

Looking Back and Looking Forward. This chapter began with a review of IQA analysis, including a discussion of the parallels between focus group and interviews, and between the logical or systemic flow of IQA research design, the protocols for each step, and the documents designed to support each step. Examples were given of the method for producing individual mindmaps; the use of the Pareto Protocol, with its associated concepts of power as a trade-off between complexity and parsimony, was also presented by way of example. Chapter 9 develops a theory of interpretation based on intra- and intersystemic comparisons and gives examples of applications of this theory developed from the case example introduced in earlier chapters.

Notes

1. One indication of a sound interview protocol is that respondents will mention or refer to, without cueing, one of the affinities other than the one that is the current focus of discussion. The interviewer should use this text to segue to the next affinity, producing an interview that has the look and feel of a normal conversation. Once an affinity is selected to begin the interview, it is not unusual for the respondent to give the interviewer an entré for each successive affinity. For this reason, the order of affinities is not predetermined in the IQA interview. IQA interviewers are trained not only to listen "in the moment" but also to be attentive to references to other affinities and to use these as transitions to succeeding topics in the axial portion of the interview.

2. A situation that presents ideological difficulties for those of us who are part of a culture that insists on rankings as the *sine qua non* of interpretation: David Letterman satirizes Americans' love for rankings with his Top Ten List. The mob yelling, "We're number one!" with equal gusto whether the occasion be a touchdown at a football game or the news of a successful Allied attack in the mountains of Tora Bora in Afghanistan, and the evil human resources director Catbert's list of priorities for determining who gets laid off in the *Dilbert* cartoon are all popular manifestations of this tendency.

Description 9

IQA Theory and Presentation Format

Although there are several choices of formats for a study of Interactive Qualitative Analysis (IQA), the dissertation format is most frequently used. Dissertations usually follow a five-chapter format, but this organization can vary, depending on methodological approach and paradigmatic assumptions underlying a study. The following discussion briefly summarizes the organization of a typical IQA study using the five-chapter format:

Chapter 1: Introduction and Problem Statement. The first chapter is an introduction to the nature of the phenomenon of interest, followed by a more specific description of the focus of the study. In this chapter, the writer usually shapes the problem as a set of research questions, preparing the reader for what is to come. The research question as a form of discourse is particularly suitable for IQA studies for two reasons: IQA studies describe systems, and there are only a finite number of ways to query systems:

1. What are the elements of the system (What are the affinities)?

2. How are the elements configured in a system of perceived influence?

3. How do different systems compare?

Chapter 2: Literature Review. The next chapter summarizes the literature that informed the investigator's thinking as the study evolved from vague ideas and concerns to a more focused and refined design. Effective use of the literature establishes a dialogue between the researcher and others who have something to say about the problem, and a good "lit review" invites the reader to join in this dialogue. IQA encourages the investigator to engage with the literature at two major points in the study: in the design (the "traditional" lit review) or proposal stage, and again in the interpretation stage. More will be said about the function of the lit review later.

Chapter 3: Methodology. The methodology chapter describes all the salient aspects of the data collection and analysis procedures employed to address the research questions. The IQA emphasis on credibility via methodological transparency leads to a systematic and well-documented set of protocols that offer the investigator significant support in writing this chapter.

Chapter 4: Results. "Results" on the one hand and "implications" on the other are arguably a distinction without a difference. These terms have a strong positivist flavor, and indeed the ontological barrier between our findings and the meaning we give them is much more permeable than the names imply. Nevertheless, the distinction can be useful for presentational purposes, and IQA makes a distinction that is consistent with the one just described. "Results," in IQA terminology, refers to *describing systems.* "Implications" refers to comparing systems and setting these comparisons into the two larger contexts of theory (conceptual implications) and application (pragmatic implications). The short name for comparing systems and placing these comparisons in context is *interpretation.*

Chapter 5: Implications. As just described, the last chapter compares systems and sets these comparisons within the contexts of theory and application. In the theoretical section of chapter 5, the investigator reengages with the literature to accomplish two goals: first, to reinterpret the literature reviewed in chapter 2 in light of what has been learned; and second, to identify other areas of literature that now have relevance in light of what has been learned. The applications section of this chapter is the investigator's response to the question of pragmatic utility: What is the study good for?

The following is a generic outline, which should not be taken as dogma but rather as a conceptual schematic.[1]

The IQA Cookbook: A Detailed Outline for the "Typical IQA" Study

I. *Introduction.* The introduction should pull readers in and make them want to read the paper. Often in a qualitative study, telling a story can help create interest. Once readers are interested, it is time to briefly introduce the study. Let readers know what questions the study will answer and give them a little look into how the paper is laid out. The introduction should be the very last thing the researcher writes. It should include the following items:

❖ Catchy Introduction

❖ The Problem

- ❖ Purpose
- ❖ Research Questions
- ❖ Brief Overview of Paper

II. *Literature Review.* The literature review introduces readers to the major players and writing on the subject of the study. It provides background on the subject. Because IQA is a theory-generation study, an additional literature review should be conducted after the study has been completed.

III. *Methodology.* The methodology section should introduce the reader to the method used. Describe the IQA process and introduce the reader to the tools used in IQA (i.e., ART, IRD, SID, etc.). A generic overview of procedures is needed to explain how the researcher analyzed the actual data in later chapters. This chapter does not contain actual data. Some of the questions addressed in this chapter include the following:

- ❖ What is IQA? Provide an overview of IQA, focusing on the philosophy of IQA as a qualitative data-gathering and analysis process that depends heavily on group process to capture a socially constructed view of the respondents' reality. Briefly, introduce readers to the use of focus groups, brainstorming (silent nominal), and interviews.
- ❖ Overview of the IQA Research Flow
- ❖ IQA Research Design
- ❖ Group Realities: IQA Focus Groups
  - o Identifying Factors
    - − Silent nominal brainstorming phase
    - − Clarification of meaning phase
    - − Affinity grouping (inductive coding)
    - − Affinity naming and revision
  - o Identifying Relationships Among Factors
    - − Construct the group Interrelationship Diagram (IRD).
    - − Construct the System Influence Diagram (SID).
- ❖ Individual Realities: IQA Interviews
  - o Constructing an Interview Protocol
    - − Use the affinities as the topical skeleton of the interview.
    - − Describe the two sections of an IQA interview.
- ❖ Axial
- ❖ Theoretical
  - o Conducting Interviews
    - − Typical interview setting
    - − Typical interview procedure
- ❖ Group Realities: IQA Combined Interviews

- ❖ Data Analysis
  - ○ Interview Analysis
    - – Axial coding
    - – Theoretical coding
    - – Summarize and tabulate the theoretical codes.
    - – Construct a SID from the interview data for a single interview.
    - – Construct a SID from the composite interview data (Pareto Protocol).
- ❖ IQA Results and Interpretation

IV. *Results.* The Results chapter provides to readers the facts to be used in later discussion. This chapter should be as free from researcher interpretation and opinion as possible. By presenting only the facts, the researcher adds credibility to the data. This also provides an audit trail for later arguments. Providing just the data allows readers to draw their own conclusions, free from researcher bias.

- ❖ Group Reality: System Elements
  - ○ Problem Statement
  - ○ Identifying Constituencies
  - ○ Research Questions
  - ○ The Participants (Demographic Data)
  - ○ Identifying Affinities
  - ○ Interview Protocol Part 1 (Axial)
  - ○ Composite Affinity Descriptions (Affinity Write-Up)
    - – Describe each affinity from the point of view of the group as a whole (use your write-up of the focus group results).

- ❖ Group Reality: System Relationships
  - ○ Interview Protocol Part 2 (Theoretical)
  - ○ Theoretical Code Frequency Table
  - ○ Pareto Protocol
  - ○ The Affinity Relationship Table (ART)
  - ○ The IRD
  - ○ The SID
  - ○ Composite Theoretical Descriptions (Theoretical Write-Up)
    - – Draw the Cluttered SID one affinity at a time while describing the relationships.
  - ○ System Influence Diagram (SID)
    - – Present the Uncluttered SID.
    - – Brief tour through the system.
- ❖ Describe overall placement of the affinities in the systems. Describe links, building the model from left to right. Give examples (you can put theoretical quotes directly onto your SID) of each link.
    - – Identify feedback loops.

❖ Group Reality: System Statistics
    o Provide any statistical data gathered.

V. *Implications.* The Implications chapter provides a forum for the researcher to analyze and interpret the data as well as draw conclusions based on the data. How one chooses to make comparisons is a matter of choice. We have chosen to analyze the composite system first. Next, we chose to identify opposing individual experiences and to compare them. Finally, we chose to treat the system as a theoretical model that can be applied to other situations and make predictions based on the model.

❖ Composite System
    o Describe overall placement of the affinities in the systems.
    o Describe the overall timbre (hot to cold, positive to negative, lots of variation, little variation) of the affinity.
    o Highlight and name any feedback loops. Give an example of how each loop works; in particular, how it can "implode" or go negative. Describe way(s) to "escape" from a negative feedback loop.
    o Zoom out by substituting the feedback loop names for the affinities comprising the loops, working from right (outcomes) to left (drivers).
    o "Exercise the model" by presuming some given states or conditions of the drivers, then examining what the expected results would be (prospective scenario). Then, do the reverse (retrospective scenario) by assuming some states or conditions of the outcomes, and then examine the model to see what conditions or states of the drivers could have produced these outcomes.

❖ Individual System
    o Describe the overall timbre (hot to cold, positive to negative, bad to good, pleasant to unpleasant, lots of variation, little variation) of the affinity.
    o Describe overall placement of the affinities in the systems.
    o Describe links, building the model from left to right. Give examples (you can put theoretical quotes directly onto your SID) of each link.
    o Highlight and name any feedback loops. Give an example of how each loop works; in particular, how it can "implode" or go negative. Describe way(s) to "escape" from a negative feedback loop.
    o In the individual SID, identify the affinity, which, if its timbre becomes "negative" enough, will likely lead to a decision to abandon the doctoral program. (This step is particular to our case study.)
    o Zoom out by substituting the feedback loop names for the affinities comprising the loops, working from right (outcomes) to left (drivers).
    o "Exercise the model" by describing the individuals path through the system.

❖ Comparison
  ○ Contrast drivers to outcomes and the overall placement of the affinities in the systems.
  ○ Compare the timbre of the individual's affinities to that of the composite.
❖ Predictions and Interventions
❖ Describe how the system can be used outside the context of the study.

VI. *Theoretical Implications.* A theoretical implications chapter is one the researcher may be tempted to overlook, but a return to the literature is a good idea. In the Theoretical Implications chapter, the researcher returns to the literature, this time looking for theories and other streams of research, scholarship, or thought that may inform the findings. In this section, the researcher should think beyond the narrow conceptual scope of the data to examine wider possibilities: For example, a case study of the way an organization conducts environmental scanning and planning may well lead to more fundamental questions about dissemination of information, and, even more fundamentally, about the relationship between action and information as it is mediated by organizational and leadership influences.

Affinities and Researcher Engagement

One of the first tasks the researcher does after a focus group has concluded is to facilitate the writing of descriptions of the affinities. These write-ups or descriptions tend to be brief and not developed in great detail because the focus group protocol does not lend itself to "thick description." This apparent superficiality presents no great difficulties, however, because the main purpose of the descriptions at this point in an IQA study is to provide an outline for the protocol of the interviews that follow. Once interview axial coding is completed, the investigator has an opportunity to develop much deeper and more comprehensive descriptions of the affinities; in doing so, the researcher confronts issues of level of engagement, voice of the author, and reflexivity once again.

Once all interviews have been organized and coded, and systems have been built, all that is left to do is present the material in a manner that is informative, organized, and fun to read. Because we are all prolific writers, this step is easy and needs no further explanation. But for that rare researcher who looks at a blank piece of paper and has no idea where to start, IQA once again takes a systematic approach to writing up the study. The transparent nature of the IQA process allows the researcher to present the results in an open forum, and it allows readers to examine the data along with the researcher and to draw their own conclusions about the study. Most researchers work so hard and become so involved in the study that they cannot resist drawing conclusions and making predictions, as is proper. But all too often researchers blur the line between presenting the data and making interpretations. A systematic approach can help to avoid the pitfalls by drawing distinct lines between describing the results and interpreting the results.

Turning the Write-Up Crank

The system shown in Figure 9.1 represents the data and process flow of an IQA write-up. Following the advice of a sage when asked how to eat

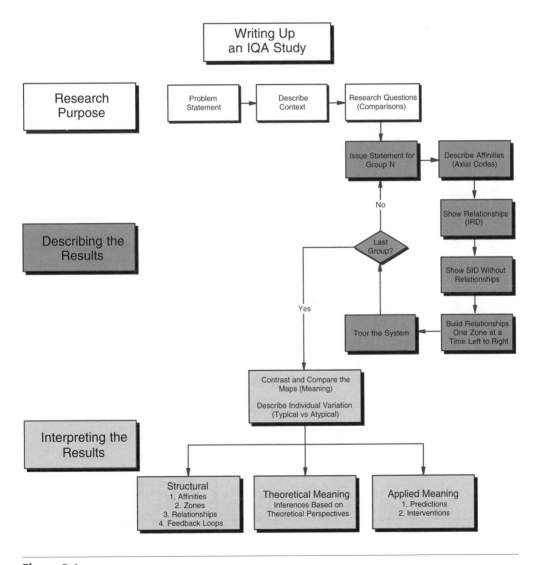

Figure 9.1

an elephant,[2] the IQA writing process breaks down description and interpretation into functional chunks according to the definitions contained in the analysis of the dissertation format presented previously. What appears to be a massive indigestible mass, especially to the novice investigator, becomes much more palatable when the bites are smaller and have a functional relationship to each other.

CASE EXAMPLE: RESEARCH PURPOSE

We now turn to the IQA class study to provide examples of the write-up. The research-purpose section of the write-up is derived from material generated during the research-design phase of IQA. In IQA terms, the research purpose chapter documents the problem statement, context of the study, the constituencies, and the research questions, as shown in Figure 9.2.

Some of the following material has been presented previously, beginning with Chapter 4; it is reproduced in this chapter in order to illustrate the continuity among the pieces and to show how the different segments fit into the write-up protocol illustrated in Figure 9.1.

Problem Statement. The concept of IQA has matured to the point that a text containing theoretical and applied material, and an integrated set of interactive instructional materials on CD-ROM, are ready for more extensive field testing. Before this time, IQA concepts were presented using traditional techniques, such as lectures, demonstrations, small-group work, and case studies. Little or no use had been made of communications technology such as email; nor was the course organized to exploit the capabilities of current technologies, such as office productivity applications (Microsoft Word and Excel with associated graphics capabilities),

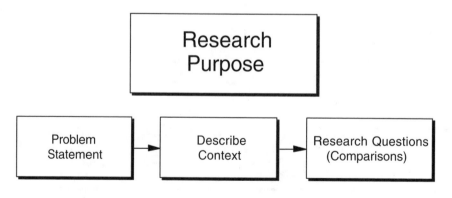

Figure 9.2

specialized concept-mapping software (Inspiration), statistical software (SPSS), or interactive computer-driven instructional software. In other words, as is often the case, the course had evolved rather than developed.

An IQA course offered to doctoral students as a research methods course in the College of Education at the University of Texas at Austin (UT) was designed and constructed on systematic principles of instructional design. Briefly, the features of the new version of the course were as follows:

1. Goals and student performance objectives were written first, along with ways to measure performance and to give students feedback regarding progress.

2. Activities and evaluation materials were developed next. The nature of a particular activity determined whether it would be included in the text itself or would be presented as an interactive computer-mediated exercise on CD-ROM.

3. Material for the textbook was subsequently written to coordinate with the performance objectives and the activities. The text contained both theoretical or conceptual sections, as well as "how-to" chapters that were primarily expository or demonstrative in nature. Applications of the IQA theory or procedures requiring step-by-step development and feedback to the student were assigned to the interactive CD-ROM system.

4. All materials in prototype form were available the first day of the IQA class including a detailed instructor manual with lesson plans for each of the 15 sessions, multimedia presentations, classroom activities, and testing exercises. Students were provided with a draft of the text and an interactive CD-ROM.

Several constituents would have something to say about this course: administrators, instructional designers, students, and teachers. If provided with all of the necessary resources, including unlimited time, each constituency could be analyzed and compared to all the others. Because neither time nor resources were unlimited, the first question to be addressed was, "If I could talk to only one group, to whom would I talk?" Because the problem statement implied a comparison, it was clear that a two-constituency design was required at a minimum. Students in a traditional classroom, and those in an instructionally designed course, are closest to the phenomenon and would probably have the most insight into the phenomenon. Administrators, though they would have something to say about the matter, are far removed from the classroom and might not be the best option to address the problem.

Research Questions. Because it appears that a two-student constituency design is the best compromise, the first research question seemed clear:

What are the differences between how students perceive their experiences in the traditional class and in the instructionally designed course?

Other questions could have been addressed had it been possible to include other constituencies in the design. Research question possibilities included:

❖ How do instructional designers and teachers differ in their approach to developing courses?

❖ How do teachers perceive support from administrators and how do the administrators categorize their support?

❖ Do teachers who teach with one method have different experiences than those who teach with the other?

A study involving two student constituencies, one participating in a technology-integrated IQA curriculum and the other in a more traditional approach to teaching IQA, yielded four research questions, as follows:

1. What factors comprise students' perceptions of, and reactions to, the IQA course?

2. How do these factors relate to each other in a perceived system of influence or cause and effect?

3. How does the individual's experience compare to that of the group as a whole?

4. How do the two groups' experiences compare to each other?

The goal was not just to outline a research method, but also to develop a curriculum with the students' needs in mind, one that contained both theoretical and applied material. Those interested in theory could delve into the more esoteric sections, but those not so theoretically inclined could still benefit from the chapters that are more oriented to the "nuts and bolts" of research. Students completing the text, CD, and classroom exercises should have a thorough understanding of the mechanics of IQA, as well as a foundation in the concepts of research. Students should feel comfortable with the method and should see utility in IQA and relevance to their academic and professional careers. Therefore, a usability study was designed to evaluate the effectiveness of the course and the course materials. All of these considerations, enlightened by the original version of the purpose and the "generic" systemic research questions, led to a final set of research questions:

1. Can IQA be applied to instructional systems evaluation, and what would be the nature and conclusions drawn from such an evaluation? In other words, if IQA were as robust a concept as claimed, could IQA itself be used to evaluate a course whose subject is IQA?

2. Would students exposed to two different approaches to teaching IQA have different experiences in learning how to do IQA research, and what are the implications of any such differences for the instructional design of the course?

3. No matter the method of instruction, what do students think of IQA as a research methodology?

To test this, two sections of the IQA course were offered; one was taught the usual way by the instructor (except that the draft text materials comprised the text for the course); the other (taught by the same instructor) used the integrated system just described. IQA itself would be used as the evaluation process to examine differential experiences between the two classes; that is, IQA (as a research process) would be used to evaluate IQA (as an instructional offering).

The purpose of such a study, as reflected in the threefold problem description just given, was:

1. To develop a systematic description from the students' point of view of participation in two different modes of presentation in a graduate qualitative research methods class (IQA)

2. To determine the feasibility and utility of using the IQA approach as a method of evaluating instructional design

The Participants. Fifty-one doctoral students (24 in the Tuesday traditional class and 27 in the Wednesday multimedia integrated class) from a variety of departments at UT participated in the study. Students were assigned more or less randomly, subject to the necessity to accommodate individual schedules and program requirements, to one of two sections of the IQA class. The major exception to random assignment to the two classes was represented by seven Community College Leadership Program students who participated in a cohort or "block" program that prevented their taking the course on one of the two nights the course was offered. (These seven were all assigned to the Wednesday class.) By random choice, the Tuesday night class was selected for the traditional approach and the Wednesday class was selected for the technology-supplemented integrated approach.

Literature Review

Using the Literature to Interpret. The review of the literature is a necessary component of any research study, but the increasing popularity of less deductive and more exploratory qualitative approaches to research has created not a small amount of discussion and controversy about the role of the "lit review" in qualitative research. The following is a discussion on the role of the lit review within IQA studies, after which some case examples will be presented.

Theoretical Sidebar: The Literature Review, Function, and Form. Under the positivist regime, the lit review's place is secure and predictable. Because research is understood to be primarily deductive (to test hypotheses generated by theory), a lit review consists of the research and theory forming the conceptual basis of the study. A good literature review is presented in such a way that the reader can clearly understand how the hypotheses[3] of the study are a logical and indeed practically inevitable extension of the current state of theory.

With the increasing acceptance of alternative ways of conceptualizing and doing research, the lit review has been the ground over which not a few academic battles have been fought. The heated debate among the founders of grounded theory and their early disciples serves as an instructive microcosm of the issue. As we read in Titscher and colleagues (2000, pp. 81–82), Strauss and Corbin (1997) insist on approaching the study with "open" questions, while Glaser (1978, 1992) is leery of stating either research problems or questions.[4] As a result of this fundamental disagreement over the basic design of a study, it is not surprising to find that Glaser demands that a field of study be addressed with no prior contact with the scientific literature, fearing that the direction and results of the study might be contaminated, as it were. Strauss and Corbin, on the other hand, permit and even encourage a study of the relevant literature before fieldwork begins.

Theoretical Sidebar: Mistaking Form for Function. The point is not to settle this debate, because both sides have good reasons for their arguments, but to observe that the nature of the lit review is, or should be, consistent with the nature and purpose of the study, which is to say the form of the lit review should follow its function. Too often, students (and, sad to say, professors) take stern admonitions such as "You must not bias your thinking with previous research!" or "You must read and report on everything that has ever been written on yours and all related topics!" at face value without understanding the relationship of lit review to the conceptual foundation of the study and of its relationship to the primary logic (inductive or deductive) of the study.

The purpose of IQA is to draw mindmaps (SIDs) of how people understand or construct a phenomenon, and to draw inferences based on a comparison of these. Creating mindmaps is largely inductive (although the way in which they are represented is largely deductive), and this part of an IQA study resembles many qualitative studies that are characterized as "exploratory." Indeed, a mindmap meets the standard requirements for a theory (a set of relationships from which hypotheses can be deduced). In its focus on creating mindmaps, IQA is similar to and is inspired by the great body of work by Glaser, Strauss, and Corbin, which implies an "open" or "emergent" approach to the literature in which the literature serves more as a conceptual lens through which to view the findings of a study.

Comparing mindmaps, on the other hand, demands something else of the review of the literature, and that is to provide a fresh set of eyes or a different lens through which to view the mindmaps and the comparisons among them. It is at this stage that IQA researchers are encouraged to "revisit the literature," which means not only to use the mindmaps (which are themselves theories) to critique the literature thought to be relevant when the study was in the design stage but also to search for other literature that may not have even occurred to the investigator during the design stage. Consider the example offered by the IQA class case study.

CASE EXAMPLE: LITERATURE REVIEW

The original conception of the IQA class case study was to examine two ways of teaching a research methodology: The "traditional" class was an informal, more or less seat-of-the-pants approach characterized by a flexible curriculum sequence, an evolving structure, little reliance on technology, improvisational classroom activities, and the ad hoc creation of instructional materials. The "designed" class covered exactly the same concepts (had an identical scope), but was constructed as an integrated instructional "package" according to the guidelines of a specific design protocol. Accordingly, this class was much more formal with a predetermined structure and sequence, relatively little opportunity for improvisation on the part of the instructor,[5] and a significant reliance on communications technology.

The initial engagement with the literature, reflecting the understanding just described as essentially one of curriculum design, focused naturally on issues of curriculum design and philosophy. As documented in his research proposal at the time, McCoy (1992) identifies three strands of inquiry influencing curriculum design: progressivism, perennialism, and the standards-based movement, presenting the arguments for each as represented by the most influential writers. The historical influence of progressivism is traced through an examination of the theories of developmental psychologists such as Granville Stanley Hall, Jean Piaget, and Lev Vygotsky. Perennialism and its influence on curriculum are similarly analyzed by comparing the ideas of Franklin Bobbitt, Jerome Bruner, and William Bennett. Next, McCoy (1992) reviews the contributions of Gagne and others to the theory of instructional design, then finishes his lit review by identifying his own stance on the issues and presenting an instructional design system whose genealogy is quite clearly articulated.

Many students of research (and texts, for that matter) do not understand the recursive relationship between literature review and interpretation. To illustrate this relationship, let us look at the case example to see how our understanding of the findings (our interpretation), which was formed by the literature review, gives us a different lens through which to view the lit review—which in turn leads to a more sophisticated understanding of our findings. We fast-forward now to the Interpretation stage of the study. Here is one interpretation of some of the findings radiating from just one affinity, Instructor Style:

❖ Students' evaluation of the curriculum is inextricable from their reaction to the instructor; to some extent, the medium is indeed the message.

❖ Instructor enthusiasm and passion are communicable to the students, and so is instructor anxiety.

❖ The classroom is a system in which, broadly speaking, there are two paths of communication: Instructor–Student and Student–Student. Furthermore, the paths may be constructed as either uni- or bidirectional.

❖ Despite the driving influence of Instructor Style, the classroom emotional environment is mediated in significant ways by the communication structure created by the instructor.

❖ Systems that employ primarily a unidirectional Instructor–Student path tend to foster an environment characterized by student isolation, alienation, competition, and a lower perceived quality of learning.

❖ Systems employing primarily bidirectional paths of both kinds, or collaborative systems, tend to reduce student isolation and alienation while promoting group cohesion, individual morale, cooperation, and a higher perceived quality of learning.

❖ Electronic communications technology presents opportunities for creating the necessary communications pathways that are not possible otherwise; however . . .
  o Students must master the technical skills of electronic communication early on in the sequence of the course, else they will become frustrated by their inability to communicate and will look for someone to blame, typically the instructor; and . . .
  o The instructor must "walk the talk" with respect to both his or her personal command of technology and a deep commitment to and valuing of collaboration. A lack of technical competence will very likely make the instructor anxious, and this anxiety will infect the classroom environment as rapidly as the typhoid bacillus will

infect a community served by tainted well water. Similarly, students will quickly recognize, even though all the formal structures and technological bells and whistles are in place, that collaboration is nevertheless not a core value of an instructor, and will react accordingly.

Theoretical Sidebar: Different Lenses, Different Lit. Because we now have a very different understanding of the phenomenon than at the beginning of the study,[6] we can view the literature through a different lens, and this view can lead us to new and sometimes even surprising venues:

- ❖ The literature on leadership, especially as it is practiced in the classroom
- ❖ Classroom communications systems theory
- ❖ Studies focusing especially on affective aspects of communications technology
- ❖ Certain theories of therapy (family systems therapy is one, group therapy is another)
- ❖ Theories on the physical and mathematical properties of communication (information theory)
- ❖ Philosophical literature relevant to concepts of alienation and isolation (e.g., Durkheim's concept of *anomie*)

Theoretical Sidebar: Back to Glaser. Areas of literature not mentioned in the preceding list may very well occur to the reader, which suggests that although Glaser's desire to avoid giving premature focus and direction to the research is laudable, it is impossible from a practical standpoint and also perhaps suggests a different function of the lit review. The practical impossibility stems from the fundamental condition of reflexivity: We bring ourselves, the most relevant aspect of which is our knowledge of the literature, to the study in the beginning, and it seems naïve to pretend otherwise. Second, a recursive rather than a linear understanding of the function of the lit review seems to provide at least a partial response to Glaser's very reasonable concerns. Using the literature recursively in a study suggests the following protocol:

1. Use your understanding of the literature to inform the research design process (see Chapter 4) and document both thoroughly. This step corresponds closely to the classical function and form of the lit review, and is represented in the first two chapters of most studies or dissertations (Purpose and Lit Review).

2. After interpretation is complete (affinity and SID comparisons have been conducted), conduct another search of the literature, of which

the list above is an example. Look for literature that now is relevant in the light of your understanding of the phenomenon.

3. Reinterpret your findings in the light of the new literature and document both the interpretation and the sources thoroughly.

4. Go back to Step 2.

Interpretation, like design, is a recursive system, as illustrated in Figure 9.3. The functional relationship of the lit review to interpretation is made even clearer if the interpretive loop is shown in its relationship to the entire scope of the research project. This view is shown in Figure 9.4.

Theoretical Sidebar: Quagmires and Clarity. A systems view of the research process suggests why and at what points inexperienced researchers get bogged down. IQA systems theory suggests that feedback loops are, in this case, intellectual quagmires into which clarity and organization may potentially sink out of sight. The research process is linear overall (as is usually presented by the textbooks), but it begins and ends with recursions. The first recursion is the design phase, and the last is the interpretation phase. Are these two phases not the two greatest sources of difficulty for beginning researchers? In the main, students are taught to conceive of research as a linear sequence, and certainly if one zooms out far enough, the system is linear and nonbranching. Zooming in, however, reveals the recursive nature of both design and interpretation, and a lack of understanding of the dynamics of these two loops creates unfortunate conditions for both novice and experienced researchers:

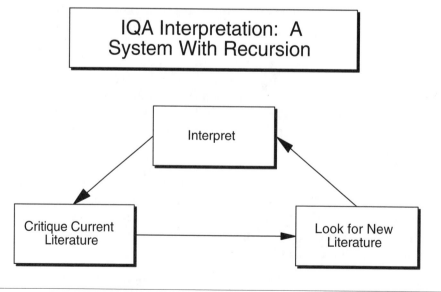

Figure 9.3

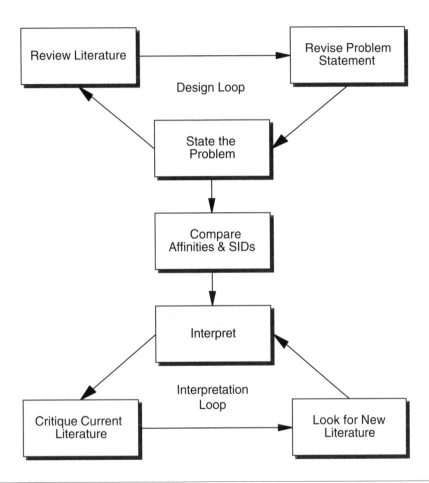

Figure 9.4

- ❖ Novices caught in the design loop tend to disappear off the graduate school radar after a while because they can never get to the proposal stage.

- ❖ Novices caught in the interpretive loop often are consigned to an intellectual purgatory in which they never can quite produce a defensible finished document.

- ❖ Debates by experienced researchers over issues such as researcher engagement with the literature and with the phenomenon are (mis)informed by a confusion of form with function.

Theoretical Sidebar: Recursion Versus Iteration. Feedback loops can be insidious because they are difficult to both break into and get out of. A general rule of thumb for breaking into either of the two loops above is to enter wherever you like; once inside, however, make sure that you are recursing rather than simply iterating, which means you're doing the same thing again and again without progress. The rule of thumb for breaking out is to ask, after each recursion, a series of questions such as these:

- ❖ Do I think it is good enough?

- ❖ How much time and energy do I have left?

- ❖ Do trusted colleagues think it is good enough?

The relative weighting of these questions is a result of a calculus that cannot be found in this text, and the personal calculus used in determining the content and length of this section demands that we move on.

Methodology Documentation

The detail at which methodology should be described depends on how much the reader is assumed to know about the method. Widely accepted practices need relatively less detail (after all, no one has felt compelled for several decades to include in their research write-up the equations defining, for example, the *F* ratio). Perhaps someday IQA will become part of the research lexicon; until that day arrives, however, an adequate methodology section describes at least the major features of the entire IQA process as well as the protocols employed.

Describing the Results

In the Describing the Results chapter, the researcher addresses the first two research questions, *What are the affinities?* and *How are they related?* Affinities and relationships are described in the respondents' words. The analytical process represented in Figure 9.5 is employed for each constituency.

Describing Affinities. Affinities are described with the words of the group. Because IQA is designed to describe the perceptions of the phenomenon or the lived reality of the group, it makes sense to describe the affinity

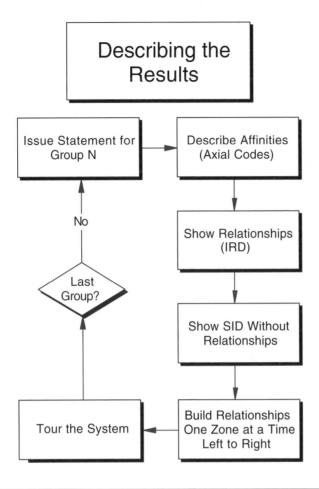

Figure 9.5

purely in the words of the group. Here IQA takes an unusual path in the way it handles the words of the group.

After all interviews have been transcribed word for word, the researcher analyzes the text for *axial codes,* which are *specific examples of discourse that illustrate or allude to an affinity.* The researcher documents the reference for retrieval by recording the affinity number on the line of transcript that refers to the affinity, and by documenting the line numbers and affinity numbers in the Individual Interview Axial Code Table (ACT). Quotes relating to a specific affinity are cut and pasted into the third column of the ACT, along with the line(s) of the transcript that were the source of the axial quote. Once all interviews are coded, the data from the interviews are summarized to create a composite of the individuals' experience with the phenomenon. Axial data are transferred from each Individual Interview Axial Code Table to a Combined Interview Axial Code Table. By combining all interviews into one table, the researcher creates a database for the entire set of respondents containing all axial codes for all affinities, with each code containing a link or a reference to the transcript and line numbers that produced the code.

Theoretical Sidebar: Rules of Evidence and Juicy Quotes: An Example of Affinity Interpretation. The IQA approach to these issues is best explained by way of example. The two IQA classes in the case study jointly identified 11 affinities, the focus group descriptions of which were presented in Chapter 5. For the sake of brevity, we will focus on only one affinity, Instructor Style.[7] What follows is the investigator's write-up of this same affinity based on the interview axial codes from all students. The write-up itself is presented in a different font. At appropriate points in the write-up, comments on level of engagement and voice of the author are in standard font.

With all the quotes for a particular affinity contained in one table, the meaning of the affinity can begin to take shape. Because the group is the best source of describing their experience, why not describe it purely in their own words? Much like an affinity analysis is performed, quotes can be organized into common themes. By cutting the ACT into strips of paper containing a single quote, the research can in effect create cards for an affinity analysis.

The quotes for a particular affinity can be organized into subgroups. These subgroups contain quotes that address a common theme describing that affinity. Multiple quotes can then be woven together to develop a composite quote. The following is a composite description of affinities based on quotes obtained from all the interviews. Note how little commentary the researcher uses in describing the affinity.

CASE EXAMPLE: DESCRIBING THE RESULTS

Opening Statement

The instructor is the key force in the classroom, influencing all aspects of the student experience by means of personality, professionalism, and reputation. Instructor Style is a major component (driver) in a system that, largely, is seen as an innovative and unique experience. Clear communication of goals, a sense of humor, and frequent coordinated interaction between the two instructors in the classroom (team teaching) are also critical components of instructor style that contribute to a relaxed low-pressure classroom atmosphere.

The investigator begins by making an *opening statement,* much in the same manner as that of an attorney in a courtroom. The opening statement takes the reader (the jury) on a tour of the investigator's understanding of Instructor Style, highlighting what he or she judges to be the most important features of the affinity. The investigator also makes certain claims, the evidence for which will be presented later.

The investigator presents the evidence for the claims made in the opening statement. The evidence is organized and presented according to a specific protocol (*Rules of Evidence*) that will be described as the illustration continues.

He doesn't have to prove how much he knows. For many, the IQA *instructor's style* was a unique experience. "The instructor style is so different from other classes I have taken. I guess he is very open-minded, very friendly and also supportive, so I will not be intimidated by him. I always felt that he always treated us very much on his level, which I really appreciate. I have had professors in this program that are quite condescending and I did not get that feeling from him at all. I definitely got the feeling that he is genuinely concerned about students grasping the subject matter. Whenever an instructor does not have a lot of ego that is extraordinarily competent, I mean it is obvious that the professor is really a cut above most professors with whom I have had learning experiences. He does not have to prove how much he knows; he just knows it. He is very unassuming and those character qualities facilitate good communication between him and his students. Many instructors tend to just throw out the material and it is up to you to learn it. I felt like this instructor was genuinely concerned about giving us a hands-on experience so that we were able to learn his method. I do not feel as though he pulls any punches. He is a very real person in the sense that what you see is what you get. I really admire that in an instructor. I feel as though sometimes instructors are put up on a pedestal or they remain in this ivory tower. I feel as though it is easy for us to be in the shadow of that greatness and feel as though we will never achieve this degree. Sometimes there is this overarching put-you-down element. The professor does not have that. I think he says, 'This is what you need to do to get through it. I am going to help you get through it.' He has a big supportive style to his instruction and I see that and feel that on a very regular basis."

Examine the punctuation of this first paragraph. The important features are as follows:

❖ The paragraph begins with a sentence in **bold.**

❖ The second sentence contains a noun or phrase used as a noun that is *italicized.*

❖ The remainder of the paragraph is enclosed in quotes.

Presentation of evidence continues according to the preceding *Punctuation Rules.*

Sometimes they interrupt each other, but that's OK. Students were also receptive to the *team teaching approach.* "I think they are a good team. I know just in providing us information, both have played a role in that. I feel as though I can approach both of them for feedback and perhaps one might be able to add a little bit more than the other or perhaps clarify it a little bit differently so that I have two styles of clarification that will help me to comprehend the information. The assistant has added to the course and they work well together. Sometimes they interrupt each other but that is okay because in the mix they are adding something to our knowledge."

I was hoping that the same magic would happen here. Many students took the course because they had *previous experience with the instructor* or knew the instructor by *reputation.* "I would say the main reason I am even in the course is because I have experienced the instructor's style before. Not only do I enjoy it, but I learned as well. I took the quantitative research class. I was hoping that the same magic would happen here, and I think it has. I like his very genuine nature. I enjoy having fun. I enjoy the verbal give-and-take. That is something that he likes to do too. It is something that prompted me to even try to get into his class."

Others take a professor because of reputation. "This is my first experience with the professor and I have heard many good things about him. He carries a highly regarded reputation at the university. I was very happy and pleased to get into his class. I must admit that it has lived up to every bit of the hype. From day one, he makes people feel like they are part of the class and their opinion will be respected and that it is encouraged. He wants people to learn. He wants you to push your boundaries, you do so, and it makes it a safe environment. His instruction style is very open. He throws in humor to keep you at ease. He is one of the better instructors I have ever had."

They emanate some type of excitement. Students quickly respond to the instructor's *passion for the subject.* "He seems to have a passion for what he does. Not only does he have the passion but his assistant also does. They both seem to have that. They love what they are doing, and you can see it, they emanate some type of excitement. It makes me want to learn about what is going on and how to do the process or what is taking place in class. He is very knowledgeable about his subject area, and he seems to have the desire to make sure that his students actually learn the material that is covered. He does not have any problem going back over something if you have a question about it. He also has the ability to just go in a different direction. We had two gentlemen in charge of the class and both of them were equally important. They both had good stature, and they know what they are talking about. You had two good role models up there as instructors. You were very one with the key person. The supporting individual was just knowledgeable, but spoke very quickly and I had to become keenly aware of his vernacular, how he pronounced words and get used to his personality. It was a little fast, a new pace for me. They are both very comfortable with technology. They have shared several powerful ways in which technology can be used to support IQA research."

By now, the reader may have inferred some other rules of evidence in addition to the punctuation rules. The following are the *Voice Rules:*

- ❖ The first sentence (bolded sentence) is in the voice of a participant.
- ❖ The second sentence is in the voice of the author.
- ❖ The remainder of the argument (contained in quotes) is in the voice of participants.

Presentation of evidence continues according to the preceding punctuation and voice rules:

Alternative techniques that are not the norm. Students appreciate *innovation* in an instructor. "I think his style helps the students learn both in traditional methods, both from the instructor's position as a lecturer or as a conveyer of knowledge, but also there are innovative ways that he uses technology. He uses input from the students, a teaching assistant, and so on. It is just different alternative techniques that are not the norm for the traditional classroom. I would describe the instructor's style as very dedicated and very innovative. I think the professor has shown an ability to connect with students. I felt that he was from the very beginning very open, helpful, focused, accessible, patient, and very energetic. I think considering the high-tech learning delivery system as this one was planned to be, that that requires high touch in terms of social interaction. I would hate that to be lost as this is replicated. I believe he has also used some very innovative techniques to engage students to allow them to express their thoughts and their concerns about the course and about its content. What I really like about him is that he emulates the whole adult education theory that we have learned about in my master's program and this program here. There is no pressure. You learn what you want to learn, you can go at your own pace if you want, he is not focused on grades, he is funny, he knows everything about everything, he is not afraid to be silly, he is not afraid to tease, and he is completely himself. The instructor's style is probably one of the best I have ever seen in adult education. I felt like he knows exactly how to work with adults and is willing to share his learning experiences when they were both positive and negative with the class. The professor is a very well-organized, structured, and excellent professor. He has a certain plan that he sticks to and makes good use of that in terms of instructional design we call modeling, scaffolding, and providing consistent feedback. It would be interesting to have taken this topic from a different professor to see if I was as interested in it with a different professor as I am with him. He really injects his personality into IQA. The professor is almost like a third equation."

No wrong answers. An instructor can set a *relaxed atmosphere* where students are free to ask questions. "The style of the instructor, in my perception, is very relaxed and yet very explicit. I was able to talk freely and speak to him freely about my thoughts and to answer the questions because he made me feel as if there were no wrong answers and you could say what was on your mind. He was very tolerant, very patient, very understanding. He was very willing to listen to you even though he was very talkative and very informative. He had a lot to say and needed to say because it is a lot of material to cover. He seemed willing and made you feel very comfortable. If you interrupted him, it did not destroy him. I had some experiences where people did not want to be interrupted. You could actually interrupt him and you could disagree with him. He never made you feel that you were insecure or less intelligent because of your response. He promotes the atmosphere where you feel free to ask questions that you might feel silly about asking in some other class. He gives you freedom to be able to try to learn by asking questions, instead of feeling that if you do not know, you are stupid. I think that he was very communicative in ways that relaxed you. He would make a statement that would cause you to smile. He had a way of relating to other concepts and different theories that would relate to the question and it certainly made it very interesting. He had a way also of encouraging you to relax, to answer questions that you felt were important from your perspective, and I never felt that he was trying to wreck my thinking or trying to placate me or make me feel uncomfortable in any way. The instructor had a very laid-back style, in my opinion. He seemed very concerned about developing a good rapport with the class, which I find very important. He communicated very well. He tries to keep the group alive and awake that late at night. It is relaxed and friendly. You do not feel threatened. For most of us, this is like our first research class, and the whole process is a little bit intimidating. It is nice to feel that comfort level."

The following are the *Structural Rules* that the investigator follows as he or she continues presenting the evidence:

- ❖ The lead sentence interprets the paragraph in the voice of a participant (notice that the lead is repeated later in the paragraph).
- ❖ The second sentence interprets the paragraph in the voice of the investigator.
- ❖ The remaining material (in quotes) consists of examples selected by the investigator.

Presentation of evidence continues, guided by still more rules yet to come.

They do not leave anybody behind. A good instructor *makes the goal clear,* then shows everyone, not just the brightest ones, how to get there. "You know where you stand, you know what you need to do, and you just go about the business of making sure that you do it. I mean, and one of the things that I really appreciate about the instructor and the assistant as well, is that they do make an effort to make sure that everybody has it before they keep moving on. They do not leave anybody behind. I just, I enjoy having him as an instructor. I think he made every effort and went beyond his duties as a teacher to get the method across to us and have us understand it. He is very straightforward. He communicates well. I have no problems with his communication methods in teaching the course. He is so good to recognize when people do not get it. He brings them up to speed and he makes sure that everybody understands. He really senses that nonverbal communication. He is really good to sense when people got it and when they did not and maybe ask a different question or go in depth a little bit more so that people would get it."

One student expressed some concerns. "Sometimes, though, I think the information gets confusing, and there is a little bit too much at one time. He, especially the assistant, they do not do a great job of breaking things down and taking their time and explaining things. I do not think, and more so the assistant, that they are patient enough and take the time to explain the concepts so that it really sinks in. I think they give a superficial surface concept idea, but they do not go deeper than that. I think they think they know it so well, and it is very easy to them to understand, whereas they do not understand why we cannot just grasp it instantly."

Unlike the preceding sections, this section contains a *demurral* (to continue the courtroom metaphor). This section illustrates the use of the *Selection Rule.* In contrast to the courtroom, where each side is obligated only to present evidence favorable to one side, the investigator is bound by a different principle: Select all the relevant evidence, not just some of it. The presentation continues with one final set of rules in force.

I am just always waiting for the next joke. A *sense of humor* can be comforting to a class. "I think that there were just lots of elements of good instruction, based on the instructor's personality and style. The fact that he was with it, understanding what people needed at different times, the fact that he interjected humor, and kept us from becoming too completely anxiety-ridden with the whole deal of doing research, I thought was great. I am just always waiting for the next joke that the professor is going to launch because he is so funny, you just never know when he is going to throw something out there and make you just laugh and laugh and laugh. He has a good sense of timing and he knows when to loosen things up. He was also very humorous, both of them, when they were talking or when there was an error or something. They used humor very well to keep the class even and upbeat. Sometimes he allowed the class to become more relaxed so that their humor may be disruptive to where he is going but he always keeps it on task. The joking and all of that, that makes me feel more comfortable and makes me more open to learning. I do not have interference as a result. Interference meaning noise or confusion or anxiety about, 'Will I look stupid if I ask a question?'"

Focus on learning, rather than on grades. Students will perform when *pressures are removed.* "I think the thing I appreciated most was our professor's knack of taking away pressure from the learning process. He really allowed us to focus on learning, rather than on grades, deadlines, and all that other stuff. It motivated me to want to learn the material. I think that he is very much interested in learning, not so much about assignments. More just comprehending and applying the material that we learned. I think he is interested in their ability, not just to score well on tests or turn in the correct assignments, but more importantly to learn the material. He is concerned with his students' performance and whether they are getting it right or not. He is open to questions and very attentive during the class putting his best into it. I like his style and I think this is one of those few classes where we did not worry too much about the grades because of his emphasis on learning and doing. I give him all the credit for making this class one of the best so far."

The last set, the *Editorial Rules,* involves effectiveness of communication:

- ❖ Get the attention of the jury with a "juicy quote" (the lead sentence) that is in the voice of the participants and captures the essence of the topic.
- ❖ Interpret the juicy quote for the jury.
- ❖ Redact the individual quotes (the supporting material) minimally but order them in a way that makes them sound as if they are of one voice (subject to the requirements of the Selection Rule).

Trial Preparation

Knowing the rules of evidence is one thing, but how did the attorney prepare before the trial began? The investigator follows this protocol:

1. Assemble the axial quotes for each affinity.

2. Conduct an affinity analysis on the quotes within each affinity, which yields the interpretive subaffinities that comprise its structure; after all, if affinity analysis is appropriate for participants in the data collection stage of the study, is it not appropriate for the researcher during the interpretive stage?

3. Present the subaffinities in an order that communicates best.

Describing Relationships

Just as the groups' words were used to describe the affinities, they can be used to describe the relationships. Quotes from the Combined Interview Theoretical Code Table are used to describe the relationships. The Cluttered SID, or, more accurately, portions of the cluttered SID, can be used to provide graphic reinforcement to descriptions of relationships.

CASE EXAMPLE: DESCRIBING RELATIONSHIPS

The following is an example how just one affinity (Instructor Style, chosen because it is the primary driver) links directly to other affinities in the system. Students' theoretical codes describing the link between Instructor Style and all of the other 10 affinities are interpreted here.

Instructor Style Influences

The instructor style is an overwhelming driver of the students' experience. The instructor has a direct influence on all aspects of the classroom experience, as illustrated by Figure 9.6 (that portion of the Cluttered SID containing only Instructor Style links).

Notice that this subset of the Cluttered SID shows the affinities in the delta order (which determines the order of presentation of the descriptions of relationships), so that the reader gets a sense of the relative placement of the affinities in the final SID. Each of the links emanating from Instructor Style is documented here with theoretical quotes drawn from interview transcripts.

IQA Process as a Method of Research. Students' evaluations of the methodology *were hardly independent of their reaction to the personal qualities* of the instructor. "I think the instructor's style impacts how accepting the IQA process as a research method is going to be because I think there are a lot of characteristics in this method of qualitative research. It would have to be reflected in the professor or the consultant who is delivering. I think that his style came across in the process and it is logical, he was very familiar with the process and that came across. Here is an instructor who has been driven to develop a method of research to reflect his views on the validity of qualitative research. He is a true believer and has crafted this to the point that, as he said one evening, 'this is a way of looking at life.' Now that is style!"

324

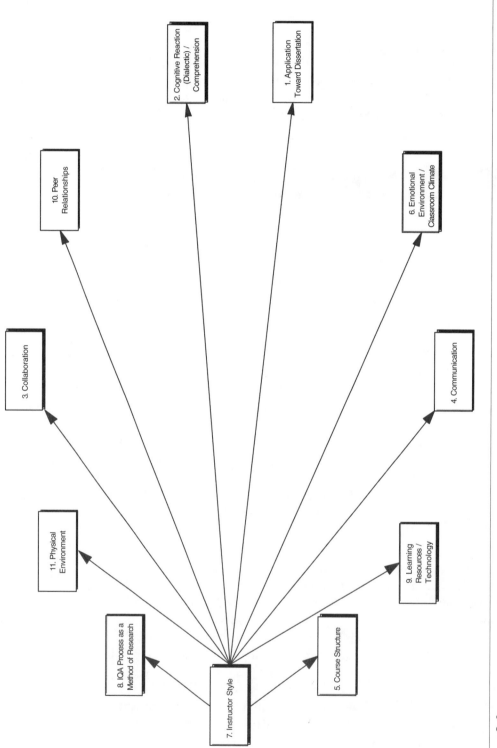

Figure 9.6

Course Structure. Largely, students understood that *the structure of the course was a mirror of the instructor's mind.* "I think the instructor's style impacts course structure. He designed it. It is the nature of his teaching attitude that creates this high level of support in something that cognitively rigorous. The instructor style was an omniscient presence in this course. He is not only a qualitative teacher, he also teaches quantitative. So he is structured, his thinking is structured. Because of his thinking and his style he has created a course that is structured, everything leads to something and you are not wasting your time."

Physical Environment. *The instructor can overcome physical constraints.* "I do believe the instructor's style has negated the disadvantages of the physical environment. His humor and focus on the challenge of the course as opposed to the challenges of the classroom negate the classroom challenges. He tried to make it as comfortable for us as possible in spite of the physical environment. I like the fact that we received a break and able to be dismissed from class a little early. He did change the pace of the class by working in the computer lab during some class sessions. Because he wants it structured in a certain way, he will change the environment. He also picked the time of the class. The classroom was the only one that I had some negative feelings about because the seats in the classroom are hard and not very comfortable. Sometimes it is hard to get comfortable at the end of the day and the class is offered late into the evening. Many times, I am tired at the end of the day, but I do want to say that the professor kept things going well enough. I never got really, really tired because he keeps things moving."

Learning Resources / Technology. *If ease with technology is part of the instructor's style, students are much more likely to be receptive to using technology in the classroom.* "The instructor uses technology in his delivery of the material. It was effective in allowing us to use it and to see it being applied with IQA. He made the resources accessible quickly by emailing important information to us. He seizes any opportunity he can to make the work easier and more understandable. If the instructor's style was to use technology or to promote technology, then therefore we were going to use technology and that is what happened in the classroom. Both of them are comfortable with the computer technology. Because they use these resources with ease, we are asked to use them. He has allowed us to use technology and helped us to understand the software program that we did not know before. We would not have had the technology we did if not for the innovative style of the instructor. The book was just so above my level. But once I went to class and heard what they had to say, I could go back and make sense of the reading real easily. So the book was good in that way because we have to learn to read scholarly material and write scholarly material.

Collaboration. Collaborative instructors lead to collaborative students (and, by inference, a noncollaborative instructor has little chance of creating successful collaborative structures or of convincing students of its worth). "The instructor's style is one that lends itself very freely to collaboration. He fosters that and promotes it. He encouraged group discussion and group work and a lot of hands-on. He is also very open to questions so we have a lot of discussion in the classroom. This kind of personal style actually really influenced the collaboration. The professor, unlike many instructors, really understands how to use the technique of collaboration. I have done a lot of collaborative learning, studied it quite a bit, run workshops in it, when I used to teach. Most instructors do not understand how to use collaborative learning effectively or correctly. They have a style that reinforces the idea of working together. They make it so that working together is not seen as a shortcut, but it is something that is just natural. The instructor's style made it very comfortable in class so everybody was at ease, which helped collaboration. I believe the instructor feels that collaboration is a strong way to teach. He teaches based on collaboration with someone else. He is interested in your learning. I think if you get another person to collaborate with, you will be able to see another way of approaching a situation or research. The instructor style has drawn me to collaborate. The instructor has mentioned on more than one occasion that collaboration is necessary for us to understand the process. They have reinforced this with trips to the computer lab as well as having us interview one another."

Communication. Similar to the effect on collaboration, the communication style of the instructor must be seen by students as consistent with the communication style he or she demands of students. "The instructor style was a driving force in facilitating communication. The instructor does more communicating in more ways than any other professor does. We continue to get feedback on our efforts through email. This is like having a tutor with us every time we study. No doubt, it is their comfort level with technology that allows them to do this so easily. I think the instructor's style influences to what degree he or she communicates with students and vice versa. The better, the looser the style, the more interactive he is, the more interested he is, the funnier he is, that just facilitates communication in a positive way. The instructor was humorous and friendly, but cares for the students and that they learn the material. The class was loose, which made the communication very free. The professor is very open. He is willing to allow us to talk during class, and he is willing to allow us to approach him after class too if you need to. How he teaches is going to determine how he communicates with us. His style is one where all aspects of communication are considered and he is a great communicator."

Peer Relationships. An instructor who treats students more as peers than subordinates tends to foster effective relationships among the students themselves. "He is so good at knowing the people in the class he makes people know other people more. He knows somebody and he will say something about them and then you know them a little bit. I think that a thing that is neat about him is that he gets to know the people and therefore facilitates people kind of getting to know each other. The professor believes in the use of collaborative teaching strategies. His encouragement of collaboration between students has helped foster peer relationships. He was not just a sit-behind-the-desk type of professor. He was out and about. He promoted dialogue and questions and so that just opened up discussions around the table and promoted peer relationships. If your professor is open enough to be able to let you talk it out and better understand the material by talking with other people, it really affected how well you got along with others in the class."

Emotional Environment/Classroom Climate. Instructor enthusiasm and passion infect the classroom emotional environment, and so does anxiety. "The instructor's style definitely led to classroom climate. He is a great guy. I mean, he is fun, he is enthusiastic, and he is truly excited about the material and the course. That enthusiasm easily bled over to everyone in the class and set the particular climate for it. He did not sit behind a desk. I have class right now, where the professor sits behind the desk with his notes. He does not get up. He has a tie on. He has a jacket on. He has been in the business for 30 years and he just sits there and talks for three hours. His style is what he is known for and that he is why the students flock to his courses. Because of that style, the classroom was fun, easy, and open. I never felt intimidated in the classroom and I actually look forward to going every week. What he created in the classroom was a very open, relaxed environment for a class to learn IQA method. There was no pressure as far as you got a hundred pages to read, you need to read them tomorrow. He was very relaxed about the reading. He treated you as an adult and said that is what you have to do, you got next week to do it, and that was it. The class was relaxing because the instructor is relaxing. He made me feel comfortable and the information is interesting. The class was also fun and interesting, friendly, and engaging. I felt nervous about what to expect, but when I entered the class, I was much more comfortable because of the teacher's style. I am thinking about the very beginning of the course when people were asking questions that maybe some folks might perceive as dumb questions and just that the way that the instructor responded and did not mind going over some things that they had gone over previously. I think that really helped to create the atmosphere where people knew that it was safe to ask anything. The fact that he is very open for questions, he is very lighthearted and very loving and that made the class more enjoyable. The instructor style determined the classroom climate. The class responds to the instructor style and that has improved the classroom climate. A comparison with almost any other class would make this point. This is a class that people look forward to attending. As they used to say when Dandy Don and Howard were hosting Monday Night Football, thank goodness it is Wednesday."

Cognitive Reaction/Comprehension. Modeling is critical, especially when students understand they are learning novel concepts and techniques. "My comprehension was definitely enhanced due to the modeling by the instructors and then them putting us into the situation where we had to interact with it. The only way to do that successfully is if you do understand, so it is a sense of checking on us. I felt that they were very good about providing support. His style helps me learn because I do not feel intimidated. I do not feel any of my questions will go unanswered. So that gives me the support I need to learn what I need to learn, and I am not shy about asking my questions. He does not have any problem going back over something if you have a question about it. He also has the ability to just go in a different direction. Like, if you cannot get it this way, he can approach it in another way to make sure you know what is going on. Because of everything he does, how he structured the class, how he communicates with us, email, it makes it enjoyable. He did not put pressure on us for a grade. He just said, hey, you guys are adults; you will learn it or you will not. I said I have to learn it. If I have an instructor who's style is more laid back, more learning by doing, I feel more comfortable with that, and I am going to be able to comprehend what he is trying to teach me. Whereas, if he has a lecture-driven dictatorial style, I am going to be turned off by that and it is definitely going to affect my learning. Again, the instructor style drove the comprehension, and that is the primary reason I took the class. You know the way that a person is, how a person holds himself, how they talk, the jokes they say make it easier for me to focus on the material and want to learn it. His style was that of enthusiasm. He loved the material itself and enthusiasm is contagious, especially with me. His style, not lecture style, not the Socratic method or anything crazy like that, allowed me to comprehend the material. I think that the approach that the instructor used in terms of being open and on top of stuff, smart, collaborative himself, all of that contributes to clarity. It is when the instructor is closed off and noninteractive that we do not get that kind of high level of learning. He is so nonintimidating and he makes learning look and be easy. Because of his style, I know that I have learned more in the classroom and certainly, I had a good time doing it. If the instructor were not so actively involved in getting to know the class, this would not be the case. I do not know when I have seen an instructor so active as to refine the syllabus, email the entire class, and write the textbook as we go."

Application Toward Dissertation. Perceived utility is one part practicality and one part inspiration. "If the instructor cannot show me that this method is useful, then I would not consider applying it to my dissertation. With some professors, my type of learning may not correlate with his type of teaching, and there may be a disconnect there to where I would not be able to learn the method, which in turn would not allow me to use the method for my dissertation. The way he taught it helped me understand how to better apply it. If he was very disorganized, it is not going to help me. Our ability to ask questions and to feel as though he is a resource is going to help us when we write our dissertation. If the instructor's style is appealing to me, perhaps I might want to use IQA in my dissertation. I think that the professor set a good tone and a good model for us, so that when we are out in the field conducting interviews and things like that, we will know how to conduct ourselves. I think the instructors have something that all great teachers have to have, and that is high expectations. His expectations are that we are going to earn our doctorates and we are going to successfully defend dissertations and almost every class he told us about that expectation in subtle ways too. I think that the more versatile, flexible, and supportive the instructor is, the more students are . . . well, the way I felt, that I can go to him anytime in pursuing more information. There is no question that the instructor's style influences just about everything in this course. Certainly, the way the instructor has led us into the psychology or this-is-a-way-of-viewing-life approach would drive the application toward dissertation. His assurances that we can do this lead the class along when they are in doubt. His message that, 'gang, it's not that hard,' made it easy to believe that I could use IQA in my dissertation. I am going to do this for my dissertation because he is so cool and I know that he will help me at any point during the process. The professor, being who he is and his style, might actually inspire to use this toward your dissertation."

Uncluttered SID

Once the cluttered system has been built and described in the groups' words, the Uncluttered SID can be presented. Any Pareto reconciliations are described. Finally, the reader is given a tour through the system, which summarizes how the students feel about the journey.

The Composite Interview Uncluttered SID

The Cluttered SID contains all of the relationships described by the group. It is saturated with relationship. The problem with saturation is that a Cluttered SID, while being comprehensive and rich, can be very difficult to interpret, even for a modest number of affinities that are highly interlocked or embedded within the system. In other words, many systems have so many links that the explanatory power of the system becomes bogged down in the details of the relationships. Comprehensiveness and richness are certainly objectives of the SID; on the other hand, so is parsimony. A way to reconcile the richness–parsimony dialectic is to produce a supplementary or secondary SID called the *Uncluttered* SID, one that has redundant links removed. Figure 9.7 shows the Uncluttered Composite SID.

330

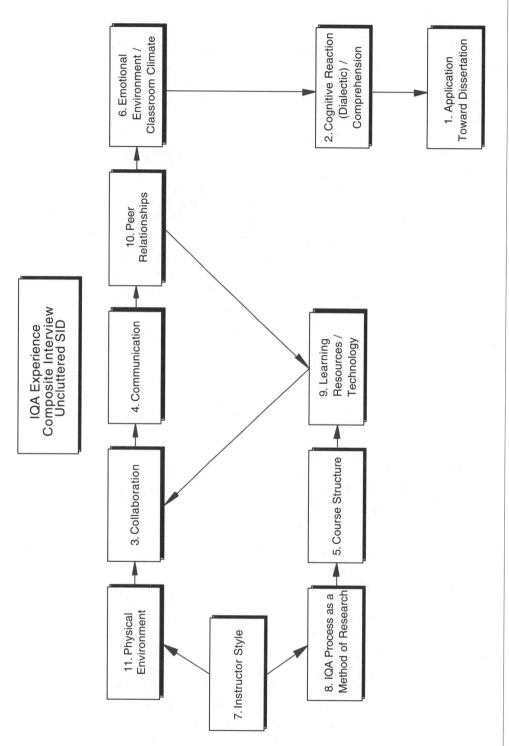

IQA Experience
Composite Interview
Uncluttered SID

6. Emotional Environment / Classroom Climate

10. Peer Relationships

4. Communication

3. Collaboration

11. Physical Environment

7. Instructor Style

8. IQA Process as a Method of Research

5. Course Structure

9. Learning Resources / Technology

2. Cognitive Reaction (Dialectic) / Comprehension

1. Application Toward Dissertation

Figure 9.7

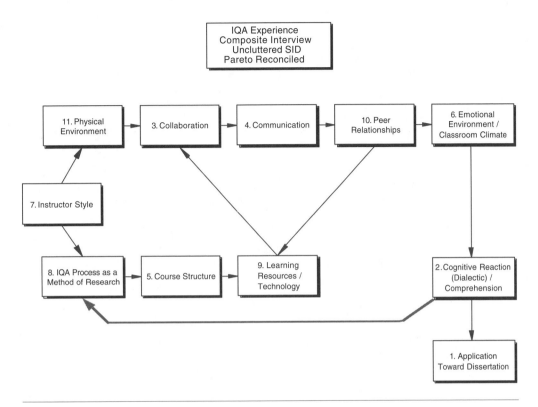

Figure 9.8

Pareto Reconciled SID. Because a SID must be consistent with its associated IRD, a link not directly described in the composite theoretical descriptions was added to the SID. Once the researcher had removed all redundant links, the Pareto Protocol was examined for conflicting relationships, which occur when the same affinity pair has relationships occurring with a significant frequency in both directions. The lesser frequency was temporarily ignored in the IRD but is reconciled in the uncluttered SID. To account for the relationships, the system was examined to see if the conflicting relationship was indicated in the system, possibly as part of a feedback loop. If such was the case, nothing needed to be done. As seen in Figure 9.8, an arrow was placed from Comprehension to IQA as a Process to reconcile one of these conflicts.

Figure 9.9 shows the Composite Interview Uncluttered SID that will be used throughout the study.

A Tour Through the System

The student perception of the IQA class can be described as a journey, which begins with the instructor and ends with utility for what they

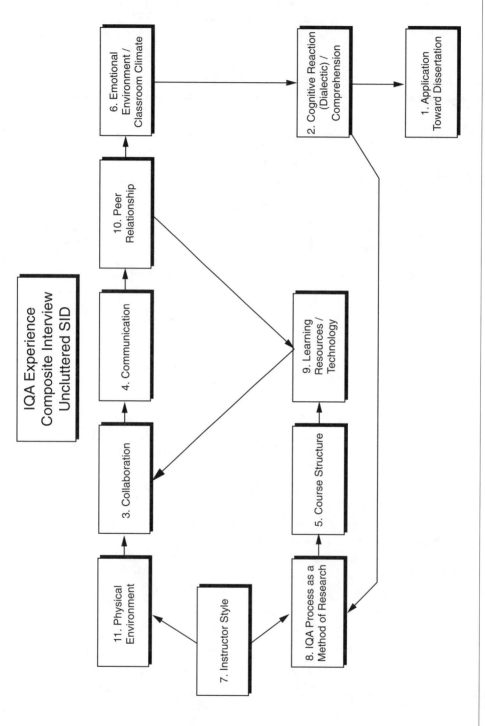

IQA Experience
Composite Interview
Uncluttered SID

6. Emotional Environment / Classroom Climate

2. Cognitive Reaction (Dialectic) / Comprehension

1. Application Toward Dissertation

10. Peer Relationship

4. Communication

9. Learning Resources / Technology

3. Collaboration

5. Course Structure

11. Physical Environment

7. Instructor Style

8. IQA Process as a Method of Research

332

Figure 9.9

learned in the classroom. The system can be traced as a path where each element influences the next. How the affinity is perceived, either positively or negatively, can influence the experience of the next affinity.

The journey begins with the instructor. The instructor drives the classroom experience. Although not always the case in many institutions but perceived by the students, the instructor chooses the time and place of the class. The instructor also chooses what is to be taught in the class. The curriculum being taught dictates how the course is organized and taught. Once the course sequence is laid out, the resources to be used and ways to use technology can be chosen. The use of technology such as email can foster collaboration. Arranging tables can also effect how much collaboration occurs in a class. Tables set up to encourage small-group discussions can foster collaboration better than tables in rows. The encouragement to collaborate requires that students spend time working together, increasing communication levels. Communication with fellow students can lead to friendships. Close peer relationships become a resource for information and help. Additionally, peers can effect how students feel in the classroom. Close relationships can have positive effects, while some students do not mesh well and a negative emotional environment can occur. A classroom environment that is comfortable and non-threatening can positively affect a student's learning. As students begin to comprehend and learn, the utility of the course becomes more apparent and the student can see how IQA could be used for their dissertations. If students comprehend the material, they begin to see the subject in a positive light. If students are not learning the material, they begin to see the curriculum in a more negative light and the methodology itself is perceived to be less credible.

Facilitating the Tour. A verbal tour through the system should be supplemented with a visual one. Superimposing representative theoretical codes onto each link in the uncluttered SID accomplishes this task, producing a Theoretical Summary SID. The Theoretical Summary SID for the case example is shown in Figure 9.10.

Different Views of Reality. The next step in interpretation after producing and describing the SID for a particular constituency is to look for opportunities to produce different views of the system. Zooming in and out allows the investigator to develop different views of a system ranging from a view taken through a close-up lens (the one created by the participants) to one taken through a telephoto lens (as if viewed by an observer from a distance). Zooming and its relationship to feedback loops are reviewed briefly in the following section before continuing with a case example.

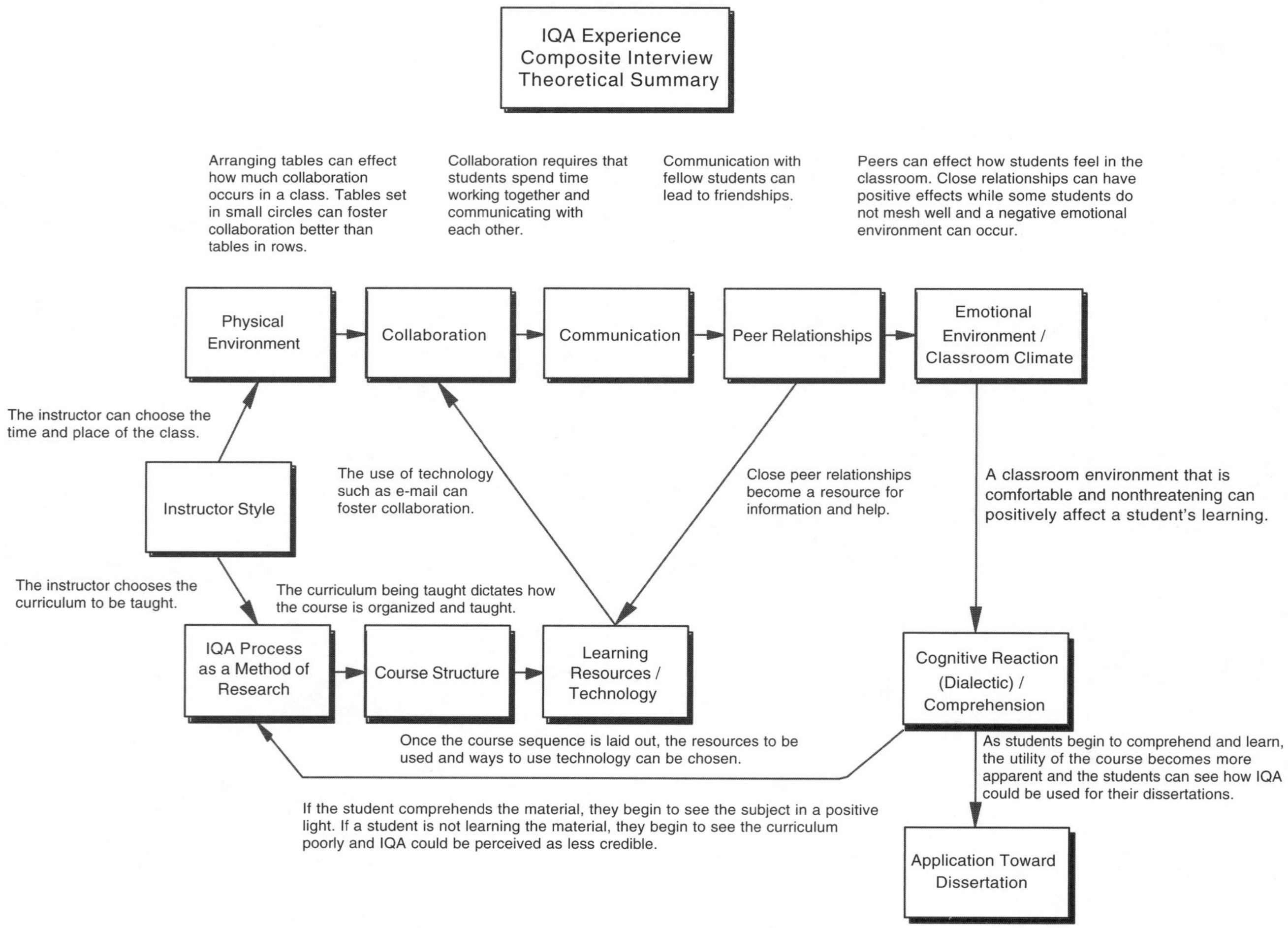

IQA Experience
Composite Interview
Theoretical Summary

Physical Environment

Arranging tables can effect how much collaboration occurs in a class. Tables set in small circles can foster collaboration better than tables in rows.

Instructor Style

The instructor can choose the time and place of the class.

The instructor chooses the curriculum to be taught.

IQA Process as a Method of Research

Collaboration

The use of technology such as e-mail can foster collaboration.

Collaboration requires that students spend time working together and communicating with each other.

Communication

Communication with fellow students can lead to friendships.

Peer Relationships

Peers can effect how students feel in the classroom. Close relationships can have positive effects while some students do not mesh well and a negative emotional environment can occur.

Emotional Environment / Classroom Climate

A classroom environment that is comfortable and nonthreatening can positively affect a student's learning.

Close peer relationships become a resource for information and help.

The curriculum being taught dictates how the course is organized and taught.

Course Structure

Once the course sequence is laid out, the resources to be used and ways to use technology can be chosen.

Learning Resources / Technology

If the student comprehends the material, they begin to see the subject in a positive light. If a student is not learning the material, they begin to see the curriculum poorly and IQA could be perceived as less credible.

Cognitive Reaction (Dialectic) / Comprehension

As students begin to comprehend and learn, the utility of the course becomes more apparent and the students can see how IQA could be used for their dissertations.

Application Toward Dissertation

Figure 9.10

334

Feedback Loops, Zooming, and Naming

Feedback loops consist of a system of least three affinities, each influencing the other either directly or indirectly. For example, the system (A → B, B → C, C → A) comprises a feedback loop in which each of the three affinities A, B, and C influence each other.

Although one purpose of a SID is to sort out the affinities from relative "causes" (drivers) to relative "effects" (outcomes), it is important to recognize that within a feedback loop, the distinction between drivers and outcomes is blurred. In the previous example, A might be a driver, B a secondary driver or outcome, and C a primary outcome in the larger system of which A, B, and C exist. But relative to each other, these distinctions are largely irrelevant because they all influence each other. A, B, and C have meanings not only independent of each other (as implied by the individual names A, B, and C), but because of their interconnectedness, they also have meaning as a dynamic set of affinities.

"Zooming" is naming feedback loops and substituting this name for the names of their individual components. By zooming out, progressively simpler (less branching, fewer feedback loops, and fewer affinities) views are constructed, but each view has progressively less detail. Zooming is an important interpretive tool for the investigator, much in the same way different levels of schematic plans are useful to the architect or engineer.[8]

CASE EXAMPLE: FEEDBACK LOOPS, ZOOMING, AND NAMING

Inspection of the system quickly reveals a feedback loop consisting of Collaboration, Communication, Peer Relationships, and Learning Resources / Technology (affinities 3, 4, 10, and 9). Because the SID suggests these four affinities operate together and interact with each other, there may indeed be a name for such an interaction. A review of the axial codes and descriptions, together with the placement of the loop in the overall system, suggests that we have defined the components of a subsystem called Communication Dynamics. Therefore, this new "superaffinity" can replace the feedback loop 3–4–10–9–3 via simple substitution in a new view that is zoomed out—as if viewed from farther away—one level, as seen in Figure 9.11.

Note that this new system is identical to the first except that the four affinities composed of the feedback loop 3–4–10–9–3 have been collapsed or zoomed out into a more general term, Communication Dynamics. The Intermediate View produces a "higher-level" perspective of the phenomenon than the original.

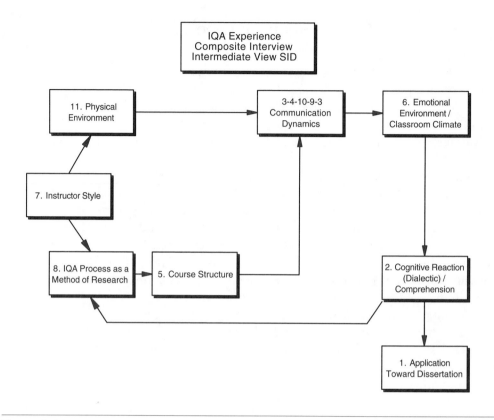

Figure 9.11

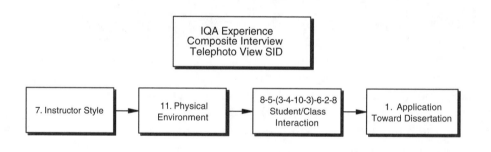

Figure 9.12

Zooming out can continue as long as there are feedback loops or sequences of affinities and relationships that have some underlying semantic dimension. In this example, Communication Dynamics resides inside yet another loop: 8–5–[Communications Dynamics]–6–2–8. Examination of this loop suggests the name Student / Class Interaction. Again, we make a simple algebraic substitution of Student / Class Interaction for the loop 8–5–(3–4–10–9–3)–6–2–8 and obtain the Telephoto View shown in Figure 9.12.

This last system cannot be zoomed any further because of its properties: It is a simple linear system with no branching—unless one can find a useful term for the sequential interaction of Instructor Style, Physical Environment, and Student Class Interaction, in which case the resultant would have only two elements, the bare minimum for a system.

Using Zoomed Views. SIDs representing different levels of zooming are nevertheless SIDS and can be presented exactly according to the protocols already described. The investigator has a choice as to the order in which zoomed SIDs should be presented. The order in which the views are developed is necessarily from close-up to telephoto, but the authors have found that the opposite order, from telephoto to close-up, is quite effective for communications purposes.

Turn the Crank Again

The descriptive process outlined throughout this chapter is repeated for each constituency. Affinity descriptions are produced for each affinity and constituency (because affinities often have the same meaning across constituencies, this step is not so onerous as it appears) using the interview axial codes. Theoretical codes provide the database for analogous descriptions of the relationships, proceeding from left to right in delta order. Finally, an Uncluttered SID, the final representation of the phenomenon, is produced for each constituency. Now the investigator is prepared for the last step, interpretation.

Notes

1. If you get an idea, put it in your write-up chapters, never mind whether it is according to the recipe or not. There are master chefs, sous chefs, petit chefs, and frycooks. They all use cookbooks, but the first on the list has mastered the craft so that he or she can go beyond the recipe and often create works of art, while the last is simply a minimum-wage worker working in a hot room with spatula and dirty apron. If you canonize the recipe, you will always be a frycook.

2. One bite at a time.

3. With time, the regime loosened up enough to allow research questions, an indulgence later regretted by some. In present times, the Choleric wing of the Old Guard, ensconced in comfortable, overstuffed chairs in faculty lounges while nursing glasses of port, gouty knees, and bruised paradigms, point to this development as the day the walls of the positivist fortress began to crumble under the assault of the postmodern barbarians. With no apparent irony, Cholerics equate the historical significance of research questions as a form of discourse to the

Catholic Church's allowing Thomas Aquinas to argue that reason was a legitimate tool of theology. "Thin end of the wedge," "nose of the camel," and "slippery slope" are phrases often heard in these discussions.

4. Although Glaser would probably not appreciate the comparison, that rock-ribbed behaviorist, B. F. Skinner, shared Glaser's distaste for hypotheses and research questions. Perhaps quantitative and qualitative researchers are, after all, members of the same species.

5. Much to his discomfort; now and again he chafed under the discipline required by this regimen.

6. Under certain conditions, experienced researchers and professors are almost as susceptible to learning as students.

7. The reader may want to return to Chapter 5 and reread the focus group cards for the Instructor Style affinity, as well as the write-up.

8. Zooming is actually just another form of affinity analysis conducted by the investigator for interpretive purposes.

Interpretation 10

Representation and Interpretation

The last phase of an Interactive Qualitative Analysis (IQA) or any study is that of interpretation, which in the case of an IQA study proceeds not only from the descriptions of the affinities produced by the respondents but from two other sources as well: (1) the respondents' judgments of the cause-and-effect relationships among the affinities and the system these judgments create; and (2) comparison of mindmaps, both at an aggregate level (focus group composite System Influence Diagrams, or SIDs, from interviews for different constituencies) and at an individual level (examining individual mindmaps or the variability within a constituency). Before presenting the details of the protocol for IQA interpretation, let us first examine the ontological foundation for the protocol. In Chapter 2, we presented several metaphors for theories of truth. Now, we extend and formalize that discussion and describe how interpretation, knowingly or otherwise, is always informed by one's theory of truth.

Interpretation: Questions or Answers? Many qualitative methods books (and quantitative ones, for that matter) have a chapter or section called "Writing Up Your Results," or words to that effect. The section may be written at a high conceptual level in which matters such as rhetorical structure and authorial representation are discussed; or it may be written at a more pragmatic and journeyman level in which the points of interest are matters of document organization, proper documentation of sources and quotes, and other issues of tradecraft.

Useful and as well written as many are, these chapters often miss the point. The first task of interpretation is deciding how to interrogate the data, or, to put it another way, deciding what questions to ask. Only after the method of interrogation is clear do issues of how to document the answers to the questions matter. Accordingly, this chapter emphasizes the questions to be asked rather than the form in which the answers are presented or even the answers themselves.

Theoretical Sidebar: Truth, Theory, and the IQA Way. Many qualitative researchers, especially those with postmodern inclinations, are reluctant to make truth claims. Any claim to truth automatically privileges some epistemological position; because no position ought to be exalted over another ("hegemony" is the pejorative of choice), it follows that all claims on truth are, in some sense, false.

There is a lot of truth in the postmodern wariness of truth, but, as always, a good idea taken too far becomes a bad idea. IQA methodology attempts to reveal "truth" as constructed by a particular person or constituency by incorporating concepts from the three most important understandings of the meaning of truth, or theories of truth: Correspondence, Coherence, and Constructive.

The Correspondence Theory of Truth (CTT). CTT understands truth to be a correspondence with facts, or, more generally, with reality as determined by experience. CTT is therefore empirical in nature, demanding that truth be consistent with an external reality as it is observed or experienced. CTT is obviously closely related to an ontology that is often called "naïve realism," and it is the theory that informs many of our day-to-day activities. Indeed, we could hardly function without CTT—who is the more naïve, the person who, having apprehended a brick wall via sight and touch, walks around it unscathed, or the one who, not trusting the reality of apprehension, slams into the wall and is left with a bloody nose?

CTT has its limitations, however. First, there seem to be true statements that have no corresponding facts, what Kant called "noumena." Mathematicians beginning with Euclid have accepted as true the statement that there is no greatest prime number, yet there is no corresponding "fact" for this truth. Mathematics in particular is chock-full of truths that are not verified empirically but rather by reasoning, either inductive or deductive.

In the second place, there are many nonempirical statements that are, at the very least, conditionally true. Statements about morality (You ought to keep your promises) and values (Integrity is an important aspect of character) should not be discounted simply because they have no associated empirical facts.

The Coherence Theory of Truth (CoTT). CoTT understands truth not as a correspondence between a statement and an external reality but as the agreement of an experience with the system of rules by which we constitute our experience and our logic under normal conditions (the categories). In this understanding, a statement is true to the extent that it coheres, or is consistent with, other true statements.

Qualitative research is, in the main, highly informed by the CoTT, especially in its focus on narratives. Applied to a narrative, CoTT suggests three sets of criteria:

1. *Structural coherence.* The story has parts (IQA calls these parts "elements" and "relationships") that form a meaningful structure, and, as de Saussure suggested (1907/1965), the human mind uses language to create this structure.

2. *Referential coherence.* The story fits into a larger system with other stories.

3. *Dramatic or characterological coherence.* The "characters" are believable; they resonate with our own experience and are recognizable.

Like CTT, we do and must use CoTT in our daily lives, because we live not only in the empirical world but also in the world of values, beliefs, and suppositions. The concept of a "belief system" implies the substance of CoTT: Our beliefs (what we hold to be true) are held together in a web of coherence rather than by observable facts or, as is often the case, even by logic.

The objection to CoTT is straightforward. Kant held that human beings apprehend the world in the same way, but surely there are important individual differences in the meaning not only in beliefs and values but even of observable "facts"? In other words, if beliefs and values are different, which one is "right"? And is not CoTT particularly vulnerable to the criticism that there is another name for many sets of coherent beliefs, and that is prejudice?

The Constructivist Theory of Truth (CsTT). "Constructive" is used here in the sense of "useful" or "pragmatic." Pragmatists such as Dewey and James argued that discussions of reality and truth devoid of a recognition of the problem-solving nature of humanity are simply sterile academic debates. Although certainly not discounting either of the first two theories of truth, the pragmatist suggests that the "real" truth, the truth that matters, of a proposition lies in its potential for solving a problem.

CsTT is obviously vulnerable to at least two major criticisms: First, pragmatists tend to confuse ends with means or, even worse, deny the importance of means altogether. Second, wrong beliefs can lead to solutions and right beliefs may not produce solutions. Nevertheless, CsTT adds the important dimension of value to the qualitative researcher's quest for truth, and it demands that we constantly ask ourselves of our research, "What is it good for?"

IQA deliberately incorporates elements of all three theories into its methodology. The purpose of IQA is to represent the structure of a phenomenon grounded in the reality of a constituency (CTT) that is internally consistent (CoTT) and can be used to make useful descriptions and to draw out implications to solve problems or at least to generate interesting questions (CsTT). More specifically, IQA mindmaps (SIDs) are constructed by rules designed to meet the following criteria:

1. The elements of the mindmap (affinities and relationships) represent categories and links of perceived influence that belong to the constituency, rather than being inferred or superimposed.

2. There is no link (relationship) in the mindmap not present in the IRD.

3. All the links in the IRD, which by definition are direct links, are represented in the SID either directly or indirectly; that is, if A → X exists in the IRD, the corresponding SID will contain a path from A to X. The SID, subject to the limitations imposed by our desire for parsimony, (1) is entirely consistent with the data as represented by the IRD and (2) contains nothing that is not in the data.

People construct theories, however intuitive or inarticulate, in order to understand the multitude of phenomena around them, and these theories are no different in fundamental structure from those emanating from the ivory towers of academia. Campbell and Stanley (1963), in their seminal work on research design in education, gave us a concise and elegant definition of "theory": a set of relationships from which hypotheses can be deduced. Although this famous definition chafes and feels a bit constraining almost 50 years later,[1] nevertheless it is consistent with the structure of mindmaps. A mindmap is a coherent set of relationships, a systematic internally consistent picture of the theory in action that informs and guides a group's or an individual's understanding of the meaning of a particular phenomenon.

Interpreting the Results

In the Interpreting the Results section, the researcher begins to make comparisons and draw conclusions based on the data. Composite systems for each constituency are compared to each other. Individual respondent systems are compared to show typical or atypical variation from that of the group. Inferences based on theoretical perspective are drawn. Finally, the researcher can make predictions based on the model or suggest interventions one may attempt to change the outcome of the system.

The examples of interpretation in this chapter all follow a general protocol based on the IQA theory of description and interpretation described in Chapter 9. The diagram in Figure 10.1 summarizes this protocol.

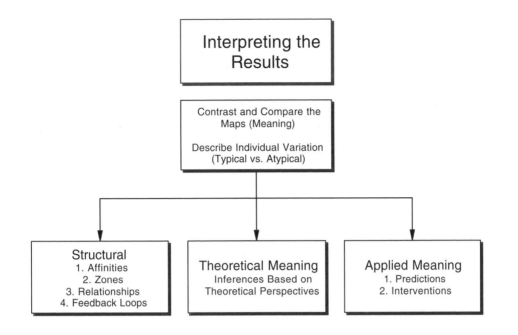

Figure 10.1

This protocol suggests that contrasts and comparisons, on both the individual and system level, can be conducted from three different frames of reference:

1. Structural, in which systems or SIDS are compared and contrasted in terms of their systemic properties

2. Theoretical, in which systems are examined vis-à-vis existing theoretical perspectives or to critique existing perspectives

3. Inferential, in which systems are "exercised" by casting one or more of the following scenarios:
   a. If the drivers of a system are in certain conditions, what will be the likely conditions of the outcomes (*prospective or forward scenario*)?
   b. If the outcomes of a system are in certain conditions, what were the likely conditions of the drivers (*retrospective or backward scenario*)?
   c. What are the likely effects or implications of extrasystemic influences?

Another view of this protocol results when we zoom in on some of the elements in Figure 10.1, as seen in Figure 10.2.

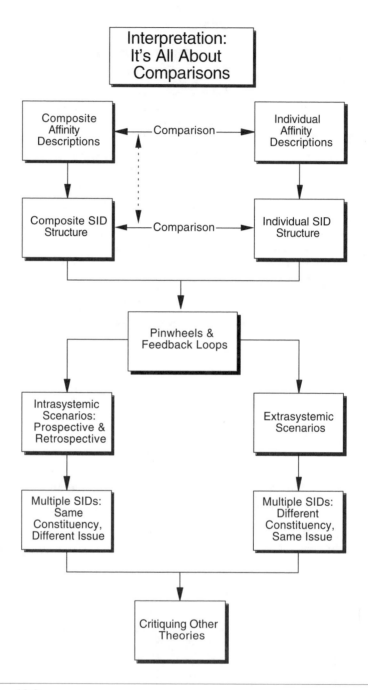

Figure 10.2

How Systems Are Different. Mindmaps or SIDS may be different in only a finite number of ways:

1. The elements (affinities) of two systems have either the same or different meanings.

2. An affinity, while representing a specific category of meaning,[2] is by no means fixed or static in the sense that it is experienced in the same way by all members of a constituency. Elements that have the same meaning may have a different timbre or "feel" between constituencies, between an individual and a constituency, and therefore between individuals. "Timbre" is to "affinity" roughly as "value" is to "variable" in the quantitative research world. Just as temperature (variable) may range from hot to cold, timbre is a characteristic of an affinity that has a range. In general, there are three kinds of affinities: Structural, scalar, and dialectic.

    a. Some affinities are described by participants in terms of functional or *structural features*.[3] For example, "IQA Process as a Method of Research" was the name given to the curriculum by the students in both classes, and its meaning is elaborated by the different topics covered in the class. It would be a mistake, however, to assume that structural affinities do not differ in timbre. As Lakoff (1991) has observed, people form categories (and subcategories, our current topic) by means of imaginative processes such as metonymy and metaphor that are not "transcendental," which is to say the processes are more products of the mind than of an external reality. Although students in both classes agreed on the functional or structural features of the affinity, they attached different values to the features and to the affinity as a whole. The features or subaffinities of an affinity are more than just an unordered list. All comments that describe the affinity have some value placed on them, and it is this difference in value that creates the timbre of an affinity. In the case of the affinity describing IQA as a Research Process, some students in both classes thought IQA was a good thing, but others were wary of it because it was new and untested.

    b. Other affinities attend more to the value component than to the structural. Descriptions of scalar affinities are usually short and do not require a long list of subaffinities: For example, "Affective Reaction is how the course makes me feel." The range of expression for *scalar*[4] affinities varies from one extreme to another, the extremes of which can be represented as a simple polarity. Participants might describe such affinities as having a range from pleasant to unpleasant (e.g., "Affective Reaction"); low to high (e.g., "Communication"), or negative to positive (e.g., "Faculty Impact").

    c. Those familiar with the theory of levels of measurement will recognize the first two affinity types as comprising the entire range of the levels from nominal to ratio. Traditional level of measurement concepts, however, fail to adequately describe the third type of affinity, the *dialectic*. Dialectical affinities, which quite often are the most interesting elements of a system, contain polarities, but are different from continuous affinities in that each polarity or opposition is required for the existence of the other; that is, the affinity is a *process* or a *dynamic,* the reality of which is best understood as the dynamic interaction of opposites. For example, "Cognitive Reaction" was identified by the participants of the IQA class case study as a dialectic consisting of these subaffinities: confusion, clarity, and growth. These three subaffinities are more than just a nominal list, and they certainly are more than a simple list ordered from confusion to growth. Rather, the participants were describing an interactive process in which "learning" (their shorthand for Cognitive Reaction) is a dynamic resultant of the continuous interplay of confusion and clarity resulting in growth. The implications of this dialectical meaning of the affinity are that both subaffinities are essential components of the phenomenon (learning or Cognitive Reaction), even though they are in a very real sense opposites. A further implication of this dialectical meaning is that if one of the opposites ceases to be, then the phenomenon vanishes. In this case, the participants were saying that if one remains in a state of confusion or clarity, learning vanishes.

3. Systems may differ or be the same in how the affinities connect to each other. More detail will be presented in a later section on comparing systems.

Comparing Affinities

The building blocks of IQA systems are affinities, so interpretation begins with a grounded description[5] of these affinities. The interpretive interrogation of affinities consists of these questions:

1. What kinds of affinities comprise the systems (categorical, continuous, dialectic), and what are the implications of the "mix" in the system?

2. How do the affinities themselves compare across constituencies, or to what extent are the elements of the systems the same? When asked to build a wall, a mason may understand the elements to be bricks, while a carpenter may understand the elements to be pieces of framing lumber and drywall. Constituencies, when presented with the same issue statement, will construct either the same set of affinities or different sets. What are the implications of similar versus different sets of affinities for the same phenomenon?

Same Sets Example. In the case study presented in this book, the two different sections produced essentially the same set of 11 affinities to describe the experience of participating in an IQA methods class. Even though there were differences in naming and in level of description between them, the two sets were so similar that both classes were easily able to agree on a common set of affinities and a common description for each, suggesting that the difference in the way the two classes experienced the course was not to be found in the elements of the system (affinities), but either in the timbre of the elements or the way in which the elements were connected.

Different Sets Example. In a study conducted in the authors' class, men and women were organized into two separate focus groups to consider the material described below, contained in the opening section of a guided imagery issue statement:

> I would like you to think for a while about being powerful—about the ability to get things done in your organization or your world.

> You have known about individuals who seem to be able to accomplish just about anything they set out to do. Maybe at times you have experienced this yourself.

> You have seen examples of powerful people. You have heard stories of powerful people. You might have felt what it is like to know you are or have acted powerfully.

> In a few minutes, I am going to ask you to tell me what you have noticed about how you (*or other men/women*) have been powerful.

The only difference between the two issue statements was that men were asked to think about powerful men, and women about powerful women (italicized here). Yet the two sets of affinities could hardly have been more different. Although there were similarities (both constituencies identified Personal Qualities), the differences were far more dramatic. It will be left as an exercise for the reader to speculate on which constituency identified Perseverance, Vision, Personal Comfort and Health, Double Standard, and Collaboration, and which constituency identified Planning, Money, Prestige, and Respect.[6]

How do interesting individual meanings compare to the composite and to each other? "Interesting" has different meanings depending on the context of a specific study, but in general, the idea is to explore individual variation along a dimension salient to the purposes of the study within a constituency. Here are some examples of possibilities for examining individual variation in a study of the meaning of graduate school:

How does the meaning (timbre, for example) of affinities differ for a student who . . .

- ❖ Is self-supporting versus one who is not?
- ❖ Is about to drop out of graduate school versus one who is thoroughly enjoying herself?
- ❖ Is a natural collaborator versus one who is a lone wolf?

As another example, consider the case study in this book. Within either class (instructional designed technology-heavy versus traditional), we could ask, How does the meaning of affinities differ for a student who . . .

- ❖ Is struggling with the curriculum material versus one who is not?
- ❖ Is a commuter student versus a local?
- ❖ Is more quantitatively oriented than another who is qualitatively oriented?

Prospecting and Retrospecting. In a later section, we will introduce the idea of casting prospective and retrospective scenarios in the context of interpreting entire SIDs, but the same interpretive device has application to interpreting affinities. The examples just given are "prospective" affinity comparisons. Contrast them to the following:

> In examining the individual interview axial codes, two students are selected because of radically different reactions to the physical environment (one loves it, the other hates it). What might account for the different reactions?

The first set of questions are *prospective,* in that we select individuals based on external characteristics, and then ask, Is there an associated difference in meaning? The second question is *retrospective,* in that we select individuals based on a difference in meaning, and then ask, What could explain the difference in meaning?

Theoretical Sidebar: Significant Differences in Qualitative Studies? Although some may recoil in horror at the idea of using statistical hypothesis testing in an otherwise qualitative study,[7] we see no reason not to use any tool of logic or analysis that seems consistent with our purposes. Each section (affinity) of each interview was rated by the investigators on a simple Likert scale of value, as described below, and a contingency table analysis was conducted to obtain a more "quantitative" assessment of the affinity-by-affinity difference in value or timbre between the two instructional settings. The SID that follows exhibits not only the overall structure of the mindmap for the two classes, but it also displays a quantitative measure of the timbre of each affinity, highlighting the affinities that produced statistically significant differences.

CASE EXAMPLE: COMPARING AFFINITIES

Comparing timbre of similar affinities is a powerful way to highlight differences in experience. Each affinity was closely examined to identify the valuative experience of each respondent with respect to the affinity. Based on suggestive comments, tone, or direct comments indicating a valuation, a simple Likert-scale code was recorded for that affinity. A negative perception of an affinity received a 1, a neutral experience received a 2, and a positive experience received a 3. The overall experience was also coded. In order to establish greater consistency from respondent to respondent, respondents were not directly asked to quantify their experience.

The data for all interviews were compiled, and a statistical analysis was run. A chi square analysis was performed to identify if there was a significant difference between affinities for each class. The same analysis was done for the overall perceptions of each class as a group. A significance level of less than .05 indicates a significant difference in the experiences of the classes. Six affinities were significantly different, Application Toward Dissertation, Course Structure, Emotional Environment / Classroom Climate, IQA Process as a Method of Research, Peer Relationships, and Physical Environment. Additionally, the overall experience was significantly different. (See Table 10.1 for the statistical analyses for the two classes.)

Table 10.1

1. Application Toward Dissertation
2. Cognitive Reaction (Dialectic) / Comprehension
3. Collaboration
4. Communication
5. Course Structure
6. Emotional Environment / Classroom Climate
7. Instructor Style
8. IQA Process as a Method of Research
9. Learning Resources / Technology
10. Peer Relationships
11. Physical Environment

(Continued)

Table 10.1 (Continued)

Individual Interview Perceptions Tuesday											
Interview Number	A1*	A2	A3	A4	A5	A6	A7	A8	A9	A10	A11	Overall
3	2	3	3	3	3	3	3	3	3	3	2	3
8	3	3	3	3	3	3	3	2	3	3	2	3
10	2	3	3	3	3	3	3	3	3	3	2	3
13	2	3	3	3	1	3	3	3	3	3	1	3
15	3	3	3	3	3	3	3	3	3	3	2	3
21	3	3	3	3	3	3	3	3	3	3	2	3
22	3	3	3	3	3	3	3	3	3	2	3	3
24	3	3	3	3	3	3	3	3	3	3	3	3
26	3	3	3	3	3	3	3	3	3	3	2	3
32	1	3	3	3	2	3	3	3	3	3	2	3
33	2	2	3	3	3	3	3	3	3	3	2	3
37	3	3	3	3	3	3	3	3	3	3	2	3
38	3	3	3	3	3	3	3	3	3	3	3	3
44	3	3	3	3	3	3	3	3	3	3	3	3
47	3	3	3	3	3	3	3	3	3	3	3	3
49	3	3	3	3	1	2	3	3	3	3	1	3
50	3	3	3	3	3	3	3	3	3	3	2	3
14	2	3	3	3	2	3	3	2	3	3	2	2
25	3	3	3	3	2	2	3	3	3	3	2	2
6	1	1	3	3	1	2	2	3	3	3	1	1
9	3	2	2	2	1	1	2	2	1	1	1	1
19	3	1	1	2	2	1	3	3	1	1	3	1
27	2	3	1	2	1	1	2	1	2	1	1	1
34	1	2	3	3	1	2	3	3	3	3	1	1
	1 Negative				2 Neutral			3 Positive			

Individual Interview Perceptions Wednesday											
Interview Number	A1*	A2	A3	A4	A5	A6	A7	A8	A9	A10	A11	Overall
1	3	3	3	3	2	3	3	3	3	3	1	3
2	3	3	3	3	3	3	3	3	3	3	2	3
4	3	3	3	3	3	3	3	3	3	3	3	3
7	3	3	3	3	3	3	3	3	3	3	2	3
11	3	3	3	3	3	3	3	3	3	3	3	3
12	3	3	3	3	3	3	3	3	3	3	2	3
16	3	3	3	3	3	3	3	3	3	3	2	3
18	3	3	3	3	3	3	3	3	3	3	2	3
20	3	3	3	3	3	3	3	3	3	3	3	3
23	3	3	3	3	3	3	3	3	3	3	2	3
29	3	3	3	3	3	3	3	3	3	3	3	3
30	3	3	3	3	3	3	3	3	3	3	3	3
31	3	3	3	3	3	3	3	3	3	3	2	3
35	3	3	3	3	3	3	3	3	3	3	2	3
39	3	3	3	3	3	3	3	3	3	3	3	3
40	3	3	3	3	3	3	3	3	3	3	3	3
41	3	3	3	3	3	3	3	3	3	3	3	3
42	3	3	3	3	3	3	3	3	3	3	3	3
45	3	3	3	3	3	3	3	3	3	3	3	3
46	3	3	3	3	3	3	3	3	3	3	2	3
48	3	3	3	3	3	3	3	3	3	3	3	3
51	3	3	3	3	3	3	3	3	3	3	3	3
52	3	3	3	3	3	3	3	3	3	3	3	3
54	3	3	3	3	3	3	3	3	3	3	2	3
55	3	3	3	3	3	3	3	3	3	3	2	3
5	3	1	3	2	2	3	3	3	2	3	2	2
	1 Negative				2 Neutral				3 Positive			

NOTE: * A stands for "Affinity."

For each affinity, a statistical analysis was completed. Table 10.2 and Figure 10.3 show an example of the Instructor Style affinity.

Table 10.2

	Instructor Style Perceptions		
	Tuesday	Wednesday	Total
Negative or Neutral	12.50%		6.00%
Positive	87.50%	100.00%	94.00%
	100.00%	100.00%	100.00%
Chi Square		Significance Level	
3.5		0.063	

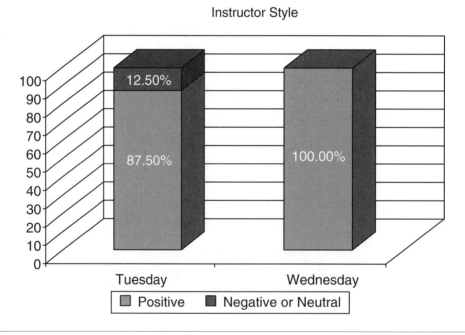

Instructor Style

Figure 10.3

Overall, the two classes experienced the courses differently. (See Figure 10.4 for a composite of both classes' interviews and reactions.) The Wednesday class had an overwhelmingly positive reaction, while a significant number of students in the Tuesday class indicated some negative reaction. Interviews were examined for direct indication of experience or tone. A scale of 1 to 3 was used to record the experience (1 = negative,

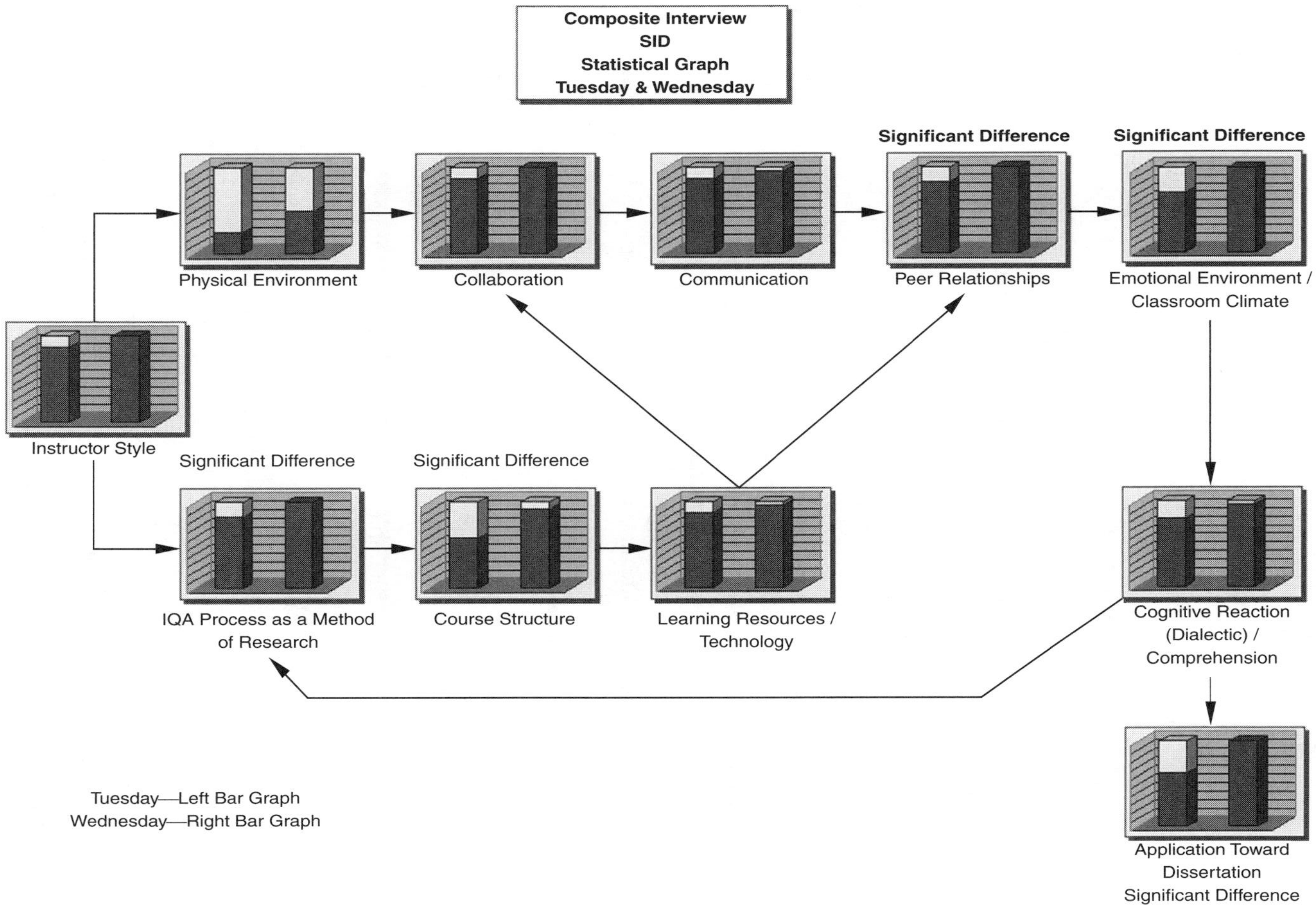

Figure 10.4

Composite Interview
SID
Statistical Graph
Tuesday & Wednesday

Significant Difference

Emotional Environment /
Classroom Climate

Cognitive Reaction
(Dialectic) /
Comprehension

Application Toward
Dissertation
Significant Difference

Significant Difference

Peer Relationships

Communication

Collaboration

Learning Resources /
Technology

Physical Environment

Significant Difference

Course Structure

Instructor Style

Significant Difference

IQA Process as a Method
of Research

Tuesday—Left Bar Graph
Wednesday—Right Bar Graph

353

2 = neutral, 3 = positive), and a contingency analysis was performed to identify significant differences in experience. Five affinities (IQA Process as a Method of Research, Course Structure, Peer Relationships, Emotional Environment, and Application Toward Dissertation) as well as the students' own assessment of their overall experience were identified as significantly different between the two instructional settings. For the Tuesday class, 5 out of the 24 students had an overall negative experience, indicating negative experience with many of the affinities. Additionally, two other students indicated a neutral experience due to some negative or neutral experience with a few affinities. Only 1 out of the 27 students in the Wednesday class indicated a neutral experience, while the rest evaluated the course overall as positive. This section will examine how the affinities are similar or different. Reasons for the differences will be examined later.

Instructor Style. Both classes perceived the instructor positively. A rough-and-ready content analysis of the terms used by students to describe the instructor suggested that students evaluated his style in two dimensions, the personal (those traits of the instructor that were seen as largely independent of the classroom environment) and the interpersonal (the nature of the interactions between the instructor and student). Table 10.3 summarizes the results of this content analysis; it is presented not to make the point that a good instructor must be a living saint or sage, but to observe that most of the interpersonal attributes relate to building and maintaining a supportive, safe, and anxiety-reducing classroom environment.

Table 10.3

Personal Skills	Interpersonal Skills	
Authentic	Accessible	Highly regarded reputation
Dedicated	Approachable	Informative
Energetic	Breaks things down	Nonthreatening
Explicit	Calming	Not condescending
Flexible	Can disagree with him	Not egotistic
Focused	Comfortable with technology	Open
Humorous	Communicative	Outgoing
Innovative	Demystifies	Sense of timing
Knowledgeable	Desire to make sure students learn	Senses nonverbal communication
Organized	Does not put others down	Student oriented
Passionate		Takes time
Patient		

Personal Skills	Interpersonal Skills	
Relaxed	Empathy	Tolerant
Wise	Facilitates interactions	Treats students on his level
	Fair	Understanding
	Friendly	Vulnerable
	Fun	Willing to listen
	Genuine concern	

All students in the Wednesday class perceived the instructor as positive, while 3 of 24 in the Tuesday class had neutral impressions.

Physical Environment. The majority of both classes reacted negatively to the physical environment. Half of the Wednesday class and three-quarters of the Tuesday class indicated a negative or neutral perception of the classroom. Students complained about the late hours of the class, which often was accompanied by hunger and sleepiness. The seats in the room were uncomfortable, and the lighting and acoustics of the room were distracting. While not significantly different from a statistical standpoint, the Tuesday class possessed a higher percentage of dissatisfied students, even though both classes were taught in the same classroom and at the same hour.

IQA Process as a Method of Research. There was a difference in how the classes perceived IQA. The Wednesday class all reacted very positively to IQA, while several students in the Tuesday class indicated a desire to be introduced to a different method, to be "taught something else." Those who reacted positively to IQA saw it as a balance between qualitative and quantitative research; they were impressed with the method's novelty and even ingenuity, noting that the method was "organized and easy." Those who had a negative perception of IQA cited a lack of credibility and reliability, evaluating the novelty of the approach as a liability. These students indicated that they felt the curriculum of the class was too restricting, seeing no connection between IQA and other research perspectives.

Course Structure. Course structure involves the design, the pace, and the scope of the course. Because the two courses were designed differently, the two classes experienced the courses differently. More than 40% of the Tuesday class indicated a negative or neutral (more negative than neutral) reaction to at least a major component of the design, although a majority evaluated the syllabus and the progressive nature of the course favorably. Like Goldilocks, reactions of the Tuesday class members were all over the spectrum: Some thought the class was too fast, other thought it was too slow, while still others thought the pace was just right. Some disagreed with the scope, citing a need for addition methodology.

The Wednesday class overwhelmingly saw the course structure positively, with only two students indicating a neutral reaction. Most Wednesday students described the course as having a "snowball" effect in which each small chunk built upon previous pieces. Wednesday students evaluated the course as well organized and logical. The Wednesday class indicated that the pace was acceptable, but several suggested that the pace was a bit slow in the beginning. On the other hand, no Wednesday students ever felt the pace was too fast. With the exception of one student, the class indicated an exceptionally favorable reaction to the scope of the course. For many Wednesday students, the scope went beyond expectations in that it provided practical hands-on experience rather than theory.

Learning Resources / Technology. Although the learning resources and technology component were different between the two, both classes evaluated the resources positively. Several students in the Tuesday class indicated a frustration using technology of various kinds, admitting they lacked some skills. Both classes indicated a positive reaction to the book (with some exceptions to be noted later), while recognizing that it was in draft form. The classes enjoyed the use of technology, including email, Microsoft PowerPoint, and Inspiration.[8] All students in the Wednesday class, the only one to receive the interactive tutorials on CD, had a positive response to this form of instruction.

Collaboration. Everyone in the Wednesday class enjoyed the collaborative aspect of the class, as did all but two students in the Tuesday class. Those who had a negative experience characterized themselves as "loners" who preferred to learn independently of other students. In both classes, the instructor encouraged small-group discussion by both physical and interpersonal means. The students in both classes were clearly aware of this goal, indicating that the professor "drove" collaboration, for example, by arranging tables to facilitate small-group discussion so that students were forced to sit in small groups. Regardless of their reaction, most students in both classes indicated that collaboration was a singular experience compared to other classes.

Communication. Students in both classes had an overwhelming positive reaction to communication. Students expressed amazement to the access they had to the professor and assistant. They expressed great surprise at the quick response to email inquiries. They perceived the instructor as very approachable and felt comfortable asking questions. They also indicated a positive response to communication among their classmates.

Peer Relationships. All of the Wednesday class expressed a positive experience with peer relationships. Some students entered class as part of a cohort and already had a positive relationship with many of their class-mates, while others entered the course as strangers but quickly made friends, particularly with those who sat at the same table. Some indicated that peers were a source of support. The loners in the Tuesday class who indicated a negative experience in collaboration also indicated a negative peer relationship. They felt more comfortable working in isolation and made little effort to encourage relationships. In the Tuesday class, some students expressed irritation at the behavior of others.

Emotional Environment / Classroom Climate. Emotional environment was significantly different in the two classes. All of the Wednesday class indi-cated they were happy in the class, while almost a third of the Tuesday class indicated some anxiety or negative reaction to the class. Those who believed the experience was positive described the class as "comfortable" and "laid back." Many Wednesday students expressed excitement and happiness, while those in the Tuesday class who had a negative emotional reaction described feelings of anxiety, fear, confusion, and isolation.

Cognitive Reaction / Comprehension. Nearly one-fifth of the Tuesday class indicated dissatisfaction with their learning, while only one student in the Wednesday class expressed the same feeling (never mind that this differ-ence was not significant by statistical $[p < .05]$ standards). Most in the Wednesday class reported being confused at the beginning, but as the classes progressed, they began to learn and were happy with their level of comprehension. While the majority of the Tuesday class felt that they had learned, several felt they "were just not getting it," reporting feelings of confusion and frustration. Others in the Tuesday class felt that they had learned but were teetering between confusion and comprehension and "did not quite have it yet."

Application Toward Dissertation. With one exception, the Wednesday students saw utility in IQA and could envision using it in their disserta-tions, the exception being a student who saw utility but had already begun a quantitative study. More than a third of the Tuesday class either indicted IQA as being not relevant to their needs, were indifferent, or were unsure about using it.

Comparing Composite Systems

From Affinities to Systems: Interpreting SIDs. Examining and comparing affinities is a useful interpretive exercise, but SIDs provide even more insight into the nature of the phenomenon being investigated. IQA provides for comparing SIDs at both a group (composite of interviews) and individual level. The following sections examine features of SIDS that facilitate interpretation as well as a variety of techniques for their interpretation.

Theoretical Sidebar: Three Perspectives for Interpretation. SIDs are analyzed and compared from three different perspectives as follows:

1. Structural, in which systems are compared and contrasted in terms of their systemic properties

2. Inferential, in which systems are "exercised" by casting one or more of the following scenarios:
   a. If the drivers of a system are in certain conditions, what will be the likely conditions of the outcomes (*prospective or forward scenario*)?
   b. If the outcomes of a system are in certain conditions, what will be the likely conditions of the drivers (*retrospective or backward scenario*)?
   c. What will be the likely effects or implications of extrasystemic influences?

3. Theoretical, in which systems are examined vis-à-vis existing theoretical views or to critique existing perspectives

CASE EXAMPLE: COMPARING COMPOSITE SYSTEMS

Why the Difference?

It can be argued that the desired outcome for a class is a student who has comprehended the material, is satisfied with the learning, and can see utility in what he or she knows. If these are the criteria, then for some students, the Tuesday class was a failure.

The systems represented by the class SIDs give us a basis for understanding why the two classes experienced class differently: If one affinity takes a turn for the worse, the shock can be felt along the rest of the system. If we ask what affinity failed "first" (toward the driver end of the system), we may be able to explain what others may have failed. In examining the system, we see the first affinity that is different is IQA Process as a Method of Research. Because the content and sequence were the same for both classes, it is difficult to explain why the two classes have different opinions of IQA as a method without looking further into the system; that is, if we are unaware of how successive affinities interact (particularly through feedback loops), the question has no answer. We will have to examine the system farther down the line.

When we look at the next affinity that failed, Course Structure, we can begin to draw some conclusions. There was a difference in the two classes from the beginning with regard to how the course was designed.

Cascading Design Failures. The design of the two classes was very different. The Tuesday class was taught in the usual (for this course) loosely structured manner: When the professor entered the class on Tuesday, he had a topic for the night to talk about, but he was generally free to go wherever the night took him. The Wednesday class was developed using instructional design principles and consequently was highly structured. When the instructor entered the class on Wednesday, he had objectives that had to be met and an instructor manual of activities and exercises to follow. In effect, he had to follow a script that allowed but discouraged improvisation. A Tuesday student characterized the structure of the class by saying, "It seems to me like it was just, 'okay, we have class today so let's just get something together and let's have them do it—boom!' Some of the things we do seem like sometimes the instructor has just come up with it right at the beginning of the class. It was not anything that was a progressionary thing—to able to go from one step to the next step to the next step. Many things seemed like they were just thrown in there." The Wednesday class experienced something very different, as illustrated by this comment: "I thought the course was very well designed. It gave us a good theoretical foundation when we first started the course and slowly moved into the application or the software and then got us into applying the concepts individually to our own mindmaps and to how we could interpret them."

The students in the Tuesday class did not agree about the pace of the course. As noted earlier, some believed it was fast, others felt it was slow, and still others said it was fine. This variation was not found in the Wednesday class, who, almost unanimously, thought the pace was very good. The nature of the Tuesday class allowed for the professor to "teach from the hip": He was free to address issues as they arose and had great latitude in the amount of time spent on *ad hoc* issues. In the Wednesday class, the professor's activities were focused on specific objectives for each class session. Lectures as well as Microsoft PowerPoint presentations were prepared in the instructor manual, and the professor reviewed them before class. Because of the strict structure, the professor was forced to stick to a plan. In contrast, in the Tuesday class, it was all too easy for the professor to spend too much time on a topic of momentary interest, leaving not enough time to cover required material. As a result, the pacing of the Tuesday class tended to be erratic, with the professor dwelling on one topic only to rush through another. The pace of the Tuesday class was not unlike the elastic band that tethers the rubber ball to the paddle: Sometimes it was tight, sometimes it was loose, and sometimes it was in the middle. In comparison to the Wednesday course, the Tuesday course was flawed in its design. Students were left feeling lost and confused. Some became bored with the pace, others were anxious because it was too fast, and others wanted to be taught something different. In the Wednesday class, the structure of the design smoothed out the variation in pacing.

Following Failure With Less

The next affinity in the system is Learning Resources. Although there was no significant difference in the perception of the material for the class, the Wednesday class was provided material that the Tuesday class was not. Wednesday students were given an interactive CD-ROM containing practice exercises to reinforce the skills and concepts covered in the reading and in the classroom.

If the instructor skipped some information or the pace was too fast, the Tuesday students' only technological resource was the text, but the Wednesday class had the CD as an additional resource. The impact of this additional CD can be heard in the words of one Wednesday student: "We would do the software [CD], and then we would come back to class and he would explain what we went over. It is well constructed and it gives you a crutch back when you are at home. Having the CD-ROM was like having the answers in the back of the book. The tutorial process gives examples quickly that you can wrap your hands around when things seem fuzzy."

The Tuesday class was satisfied with their resources but were unaware that there were other possibilities. The Wednesday class described how the CD filled in any gaps that the class or book could not. Bauhaus architectural principles to the contrary, sometimes less is simply less.

I Tend to Work in Isolation

The next failure in the system involved peer relationships. Some students choose to work in isolation, as illustrated by this quote: "I got my own software, and I installed my software so I do not even come to the lab. I am very isolated and I guess that is the reason why I did not have that peer relationship thing that you are talking about. I tend to work in isolation." It is possible, of course, that the Wednesday class was filled with team players and the Tuesday class with loners for reasons unrecognized by the investigators, but this seems unlikely. Although the nature of the loner could explain why some would not develop relationships, this probably would not account for significant differences between the two classes. In this case, the course structure may be the culprit again. The design of the Wednesday course called for group work and discussion. Students were not only encouraged to collaborate, but they were required to work in groups; even those in the Wednesday class who, left to their own devices, worked alone reported favorably on the Peer Relationships affinity. The Tuesday class did have some collaborative groups, but there were very few formal collaborative exercises. By providing students an opportunity to interact with each other in class, the Wednesday class students were encouraged to make friends.

The Course Is Disorganized, I Do Not
Have the Resources, and I Have No Friends

No wonder the emotional environment for some in the Tuesday class was bad; these students had three strikes against them. The emotional environment for these students is best described in their own words:

> This class was almost a pilot program, working out the kinks on us for future books to be written and dissertations to be written. That made it a bit less beneficial for me but more beneficial for the professors. However, I think IQA is a good method for some who choose to use it. It has not closed my mind, it has increased my knowledge, but I feel like I could have had much more. As far as how I am feeling, part of it is being seven to ten at night, hungry, tired, having come from nine in the morning to ten at night the day before, working a full day . . . those things all play into the emotional environment. I feel respected, but I do not feel nurtured or special in any way. I am just one in a crowd. Whenever my hand is raised, I may not be noticed because maybe there are others in the class who are more commanding, persistent, loud, and aggressive and get the professor's attention. Because I choose not to behave that way, I may not be answered or have forgotten the question by the time someone gets around to acknowledging my question. Once again, it is just a self-study for me, self-paced, self-motivation that is going to get me through this class.

There Is Something to This That I Am Not Quite Getting

Students who are anxious because the structure of the course is poor, resources are lacking, and there is no one to turn to for help are less likely to learn; consequently, the perceived utility of the course suffers, as indicated by the student who said, "Stuff that I did not understand I am not going to use." Comprehension and the confidence that goes with it are requisites for perceived relevance or utility. A failure of the system in fostering comprehension and confidence results in an attitude characterized by the attitude, "I do not get this stuff, so teach me something else," bringing us back full circle to IQA Process as a Method of Research. There was no difference in terms of objective content in the curriculum of the two classes, but the Tuesday class reacted negatively. It is clear that the class was not predisposed to the negative feelings about IQA because it was new to them. For some students in the Tuesday class, the feedback loop contained in the SID "went negative." Students who were struggling with the concepts found themselves either frustrated or bored and wanting to move on. Because they were frustrated, they were inclined to evaluate IQA negatively and to see little utility in the method; and one logical consequence of this evaluation is that the perceived scope of the class narrows even in the face of arguments from the instructors and from other students that IQA is a robust methodology that can be used in a variety of settings.

Spiral Until Something Breaks

Feedback loops can go either positive (nothing succeeds like success) or negative (failure breeds failure). The previous scenario is an example of how a feedback loop can quickly spiral inward until it implodes. The loop is repeated, with each repetition becoming more negative until something has to give. In this case, the result of the implosion is rejection of the utility of IQA and a demand to be taught something else.

Not That Extreme

Although the previous scenario paints a bleak picture for the Tuesday class, it is nevertheless true that 70% of the class reported a positive learning experience. This large majority of the Tuesday class was satisfied with their learning and saw utility in IQA. Why, then, if the class was so poorly designed, did not all of the members report a negative experience? If course structure is so important, why did 40% of the class complain about structure while 70% of this same class reported a positive overall experience? Somewhere in the system, something must have occurred that helped students overcome the flaws in the course.

Predestination or Redemption? A bad experience by a student with an affinity does not predetermine a bad outcome. Unlike traditional mathematical path analytic structures, SIDs are not Calvinist; there may be opportunities, primarily through the dynamics of feedback loops, for redemption just as there are always dangers of damnation. Good "inputs" do not guarantee success any more than success implies that all the affinities were good. In our example, a positive experience with other regions of the system may provide a mechanism for reversing undesirable effects.

Examine the Intermediate View SID in Figure 10.5, which has been coded to show which affinities exhibited significant differences in timbre between the two classes. A quick glance at the SID suggests that Communication Dynamics may provide the counterbalance needed to explain how poor course structure can, in some circumstances, be overcome. The Communication Dynamics affinity (actually, a superaffinity, but more about this later) is a counterbalance to poor course structure for three reasons:

1. Communication Dynamics is a direct outcome of Course Structure.

2. Communication Dynamics was evaluated positively by both classes.

3. Communication Dynamics and Course Structure are part of a larger feedback loop.

For these reasons, Communication Dynamics deserves a closer look.

The SID shown in Figure 10.5 is an Intermediate View SID that collapses (zooms out) a four-affinity feedback loop into one superaffinity named Communication Dynamics and is therefore a system within a

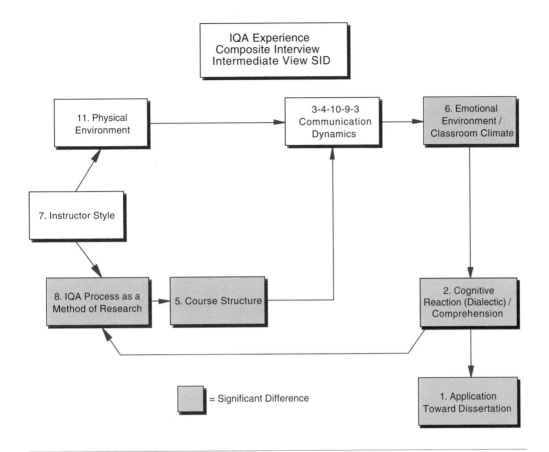

Figure 10.5

system. It is within the Communication Dynamics system where learning takes place: Information is obtained from the learning resources provided, which is then communicated, the outcome of which is learning. This system describes not so much how learning occurs but where or when it occurs in the classroom.

A close examination (zooming in) of the Communication Dynamics system indicates that one affinity, Peer Relationships, is significantly different between the two classes, suggesting that this is the point where the system breaks down for those students who have a poor overall experience in the IQA class. A flawed course structure combined with an erratic pace, uneven coverage of the material, and limited learning resources can easily lead to students who are struggling to get the information they need to learn. The SID suggests that three sources of information are available to the student: the professor (mediated by course structure), the materials themselves, and peers. If the first two are absent or weak, the student must depend on peers. Peer Relationships is the mechanism by which students acquire information, as demonstrated in Figure 10.6.

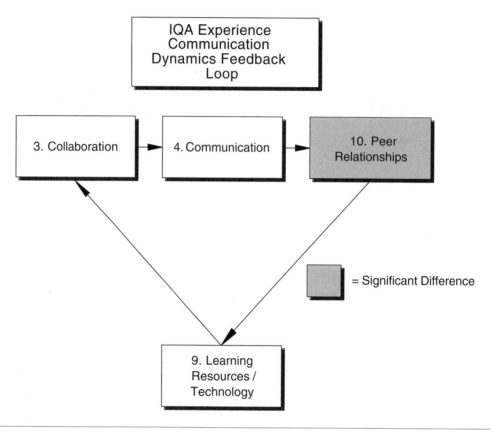

Figure 10.6

Most of those students who reported an overall bad experience and numerous negative affinities had something in common: They felt isolated. Conversely, all of the students who reported a negative peer relationship also reported an overall bad experience. They found themselves working alone and not having peer relationships. Most indicated it was a personal choice: "I feel comfortable working in isolation. I like working with people, only people that I feel comfortable with. I am very self-motivated and so I do not really need others to help me get through classes. I rarely rely on a professor to help me. I almost always rely on myself to help me get through things."

The Downward Spiral. Students who do not rely on peers can quickly find themselves trapped in a downward spiral, especially in a less structured classroom environment. Let us accompany a student caught in a negative feedback loop: A student finds that he is having a problem drawing systems using Inspiration; this is a small technical problem, but a barricade that must be navigated, nevertheless. Lacking the personal attention of the instructor in class or tutorial materials to work on at home, he struggles to use the software, but with only limited success. Because he has no network of peer support, he must figure out how to go around this roadblock on his own. He becomes frustrated, and begins to complain about the class structure and the resources. He tries again and perhaps again, but only becomes more frustrated. Unable to find help either in the materials or from the instructor or peers, he spirals through the system in ever tighter loops, until something breaks. He is not going to attempt it anymore. He concludes that IQA is a terrible method, the class is a terrible experience, and there is no way he will use IQA for his dissertation.

The Upward Spiral. Now let us accompany another student through the same loop, but one that goes positive. The student is struggling with the software. She has noticed that a classmate seated in the next chair at the round table seems to grasp the assignments quickly; besides, the classmate seems friendly enough. She leans over and asks for help, which is quickly forthcoming. In what seems like no time, she realizes what she was doing wrong. Her confidence rises, and the next time she has a problem, she knows she can ask someone at her table and get help. After a while, she even finds herself helping others and becomes excited about learning. She concludes that IQA is a great method, that the class is a wonderful experience, and she cannot wait to use it in a dissertation.

Back to the Differences. These scenarios describe how peer relationships can change a student's outlook but do not explain why the Tuesday class had a different experience with respect to Peer Relationships. The Tuesday class did not in fact have all the loners: Several students in the Wednesday class indicated that they usually work alone. The difference was in how Course Structure drove the Communication Dynamics system. The Wednesday class was designed with collaboration in mind. The Wednesday class contained many built-in exercises requiring students to work together in groups. The Tuesday class all sat at round tables and on occasion worked together informally, but they rarely engaged in formal collaboration. The course structure for the Tuesday class allowed students to isolate themselves if they preferred.

It Is All in the Design. Several factors account for why the Wednesday class served the students much better than Tuesday's, but the root cause was course structure. The poorly planned Tuesday class found themselves lacking in the basic skills needed to perform and understand IQA. When instruction failed, some students naturally relied on their peers to help them overcome the inadequacies. Others chose to isolate themselves and struggled with learning. These students found themselves in a downward spiral resulting in anxiety, dissatisfaction, failed learning, and a poor opinion of IQA. The Wednesday class found themselves with additional resources and an instructor who was forced to stick to a designed plan.

The students were encouraged to collaborate. What resulted was a dramatic difference in the two classes and an overwhelmingly positive response from the Wednesday class.

Describing Individual Variations

Individual variation is another source of comparison for interpretive purposes. Individuals may be compared to each other or to composite descriptions or mindmaps. The individuals themselves may be selected for comparison because either they are typical of some constituency or group or because they vary in some interesting way from other individuals or a group.

Comparing the structure of the composite SIDs of the two IQA case study classes is straightforward because the structure of the composite SIDs is identical for the two classes. The structural equivalence between the two classes suggests that, at a gross level, the two methods of presentation were not different enough to produce radically (radical in the sense of a different order of driver to outcome) different constructions of reality between the two classes. The differences in timbre of the affinities, however, are quite pronounced.

Examining individual differences can add some interpretive meat to the skeleton just described. The rationale for selecting individuals depends on the nature of the study: "Typical"[9] representatives of different constituencies are often compared, or representatives that have been deliberately selected to represent a range on some interesting dimension may be compared. Because both classes produced identical composite SIDs, the latter alternative was used. The next section illustrates comparison at the affinity level for two individuals: The first student evaluated the class as very satisfactory (good), and the second as not satisfactory (bad).

CASE EXAMPLE: DESCRIBING INDIVIDUAL VARIATIONS

Good vs. Bad[10]

Even though the structure of the two SIDs was identical at the composite level for the two classes (traditional and technology intensive), students progress through the system on their own personal journey. For some students, the path may be linear, while others may find themselves recursing through loops. Furthermore, the value attached to different affinities may differ dramatically between two students, even though their construction of the phenomenon is similar at the structural level. What follows is the journey of two students, each typical of his or her class at the structural level. One student from the Wednesday (heavy technology) class had a good overall experience with the course, as reported by the student in an end-of-course evaluation. The other student had a bad experience in the course, which is typical of the Tuesday experience. Quotes have been edited for the sake of brevity and readability.

Instructor Style

Good. "I do not feel as though he pulls any punches. He is a very real person in the sense that what you see is what you get. I really admire that in an instructor because I feel as though sometimes instructors are put on a pedestal or they remain in this ivory tower. Sometimes there is this over-arching, I do not know if I will say it right, but the 'put-you-down' element. This professor does not do that. He has a big supportive style to his instruction and I see that and feel that on a very regular basis."

Bad. "The professor, in particular, is very high-energy. He comes to class enthusiastic about IQA. He is always accessible when you need him. Sometimes I feel like if someone is not understanding something, I feel like there is a resistance [on the student's part, something more akin to 'reluctance'] to ask for clarification because I feel he is so passionate toward IQA that any questioning of it perhaps makes him feel as if his project is not . . . there is some question about the validity of it. But, overall, I think he is very hardworking, extraordinarily knowledgeable about IQA and about qualitative research. It seems like he is very apt at teaching adults. Because this class is a pilot project, maybe things are not as organized exactly to the "T" because he is creating a textbook primarily based on what the students in the class are doing. I would feel like things are more trial and error at this point. The next time he teaches this class with a completed textbook, with the information that we have given him, I think that the procedures are going to go much more smoothly in the future. That is understandable, and it does not bother me that things may not be exactly in sync all of the time because I understand what process he is going through to get to where he wants this class to be."

Interpretive Comparison. Although both students reacted to the instructor quite favorably, even a cursory reading of the two reveals a distinct difference in timbre. The student who had a good experience focuses exclusively on the issue of instructor style, commenting on his supportiveness and accessibility to students. The other student, while observing much the same ("hardworking, accessible, enthusiastic"), reveals, first, a suspicion that the instructor may not be open to criticism because of ownership of the concepts of the class, and second, that what was intended by the instructor to be an open classroom environment that encourages experimentation is presented more as a lack of organization. Underneath these concerns is a subtext ("trial and error") that students are being used as "subjects of an experiment," perhaps even without their completely informed consent.

Physical Environment

Good. "I think the physical environment was challenging at times. I do, I felt as though we had probably close to thirty people in that classroom and given the structure of the tables, we I think at times felt relatively cramped. There is no way to avoid the collaboration, which actually is probably a good point. I think because of the emotional environment in the classroom climate and because of the instructor's style, I probably did not have as negative opinion of the physical environment. You felt like you were in it with other people who actually cared about both the subject and then your acquiring the knowledge of the subject as well as people who just frankly care about you. You can overcome that physical environment because of the structure of the class, because of the instructor style, because of the collaborative nature, and because of the peer relationships. I think all of that helps to overcome that."

Bad. "In order to try to enhance my learning, I try to participate in class discussion when it is open. Because some people do not come with the same philosophy as me, I can comment and some people will not even understand what I have said! Of course, the people in my cohort, the people who are educators, they do understand . . . but others, perhaps, do not understand the basic educational jargon that you learned in undergraduate school. The manner in which ideas are rejected . . . sometimes the unprofessionalism . . . for some people they would find that extraordinarily offensive and they would be on the offensive and verbally lash out. For me, that [lashing out] is just not my style. I just fade into the woodwork, and I think many students in public school do the same thing. But because I do not choose to go to that level as others who are aggressive, loud, and sometimes a bit obnoxious . . . I just choose to regress."

Interpretive Comparison. At first glance, an affinity such as this would be presumed to be a driver; after all, the size of a classroom, the temperature, and the number and configuration of the tables and chairs are all part of an external reality quite apart from our apprehension of them. To the contrary, neither student speaks of these "objective" features of the class in strictly objective terms at all. The first student understands the physical environment as a set of conditions that are strongly related to some of the other affinities (collaboration and peer relationships), and because these have a favorable value for this student, she isn't bothered by the physical environment and even interprets constraints (crowded classroom) as benefits ("no way to avoid collaboration"). In dramatic contrast, the second student, on the surface at least, is not responsive to the question about physical environment but answers almost exclusively in terms of classroom emotional climate and peer relationships, which he found problematic. The instructor's intent was to create an atmosphere in which debate and discussion of the concepts were encouraged, but he failed with this student, whose reaction was to feel misunderstood by other students and to consequently "regress" or withdraw from the discussion.

IQA Process as a Method of Research

Good. "As a subject, we are learning about the qualitative research method and that is coming, actually believe it or not, relatively easily. I think because qualitative research has such a big element of relationships with individuals and speaking one-on-one about their participation, whatever the group, your studying resonates with me. I want to know about individual people and so the subject of qualitative research seems to work well for me. In regard to the IQA process from a more practical sense or an application sense, again it just seems to resonate with me. Inspiration is easy to utilize that as a resource as a tool to do your work. The CD-ROM made sense to me. The reading made sense to me, I really think from a practical standpoint, and of course doing this as we are right now, being interviewed and then turning around and interviewing someone else, I feel as though that the practicality of the IQA process seems to work for me."

Bad. "The professor is a reliable and credible instructor, but I do not believe that IQA is completely credible or reliable. For me, personally, it is based upon theory and I need a little bit more concrete research. Whenever we are making the assumptions, as far as using the affinity charts and so forth and drawing your relationship, that is concrete enough yet it is still qualitative in nature. However, when you are building your axial charts and your theoretical charts, that is when it becomes too theoretical, in my opinion, to be credible, and I have some problem with that. Drivers and outcomes . . . that is credible to me and it is beneficial to me, but when we are eliminating some relationships, I do not feel like that is credible. For me, I would like to have a very well-versed, well-rounded repertoire of research methods. Limiting myself to just one that is very new, that is not well-known and accepted by other researchers outside this university, I feel that is limiting to me. Some things about IQA I like, some things I do not like, some things I feel are credible, and some things not credible and will not be used. I would at least like a list of resources in the form of books, or what have you, that can help me.[11] I do not feel like this alone is going to get me through to my dissertation—it will help me, but I am going to have to research on my own to find more information about other methods."

Interpretive Comparison. The first student is *simpatico* with what she understands is a hallmark of qualitative research, individuals, and their relationships, and further sees IQA as a practical and understandable way of doing qualitative research. The second voices two objections to the concept of IQA: First, he restates a hesitancy to be persuaded by anything so new to the field. Second, he identifies some specific steps in the IQA analytic methodology (recording codes, eliminating redundant links) that are not appealing.[12] He then raises another objection to the course itself, which is that it is too narrowly focused on one kind methodology, rather than a "well-versed, well-rounded repertoire" of methods.

Course Structure

Good. "The design of the course I think was well thought out and it made sense. We were given the chapters of the book as well as the CD-ROM as a supplement to the reading. That was a good way to begin the course because we needed to have that knowledge base. So, we paid our dues the first six or seven weeks of class. Then we started to actually hold and put our hands on utilizing it: We were actually making a mindmap! I do believe that the pace is a little bit more heavy-weighted toward the end because we are doing what I feel like is half the class in less than half the class time. I am not sure there is a way to reconcile that because you have to pay your dues on gaining knowledge in order to then turn around and apply it. I am very glad for the IQA process because there is such a heavy practical aspect to this class compared to the other qualitative-based classes. The other classes are more like reading a philosophical book in qualitative research, and that is good as the backdrop, but frankly, for me I need to touch it, to hold it. I need to practice it and this class is actually giving me that. The scope of this class actually exceeds my expectation because I am actually getting to do the things I need to know how to do later."

Bad. "I feel like, for an introduction to qualitative research, what the class would really need is just an overview of various different methods. Upon that, because of the number of research classes you are required to have, your advanced qualitative research could have been in one particular area. For instance, critical theory—that is something that is very interesting to me; however, I do not understand exactly how to use that method. IQA could be another advanced research method, which you could take after you have a broad knowledge. Because of the lack of exposure, rather than having a broad-based knowledge to begin with, I will not know which method I want to focus in on and once again, that is something I am going to have to go outside of the class and find books, resources, talk to other people about other methods so that I can use them."

Interpretive Comparison. The first student is quite taken with IQA, and casts the course in a favorable light by contrasting the specificity of the various IQA protocols to other classes, which are more like "reading a philosophical book." Although she has some concerns about the pacing, the first respondent uses tactile metaphors to highlight the primary appeal of the course, practicality (or utility). The second student cites the specificity of the course as a source of discomfort, raising again the argument that the course should be a survey course in which students are exposed to a variety of methodologies.

These two understandings could hardly be more different, yet there is a common assumption underlying each: The first student, having assessed IQA methodology in a favorable light, is quite happy to adopt it as her own approach to research without further investigation of other methodologies or philosophies, while the second, with the opposite reaction, is upset that the course has not taught him a different way to do qualitative research and grudgingly observes that "I am going to have to go outside of the class" to find what is needed. Both students presume that most, if not all, of the learning needed to do research should occur within the structure of a course; that is, both have a view of their learning that, largely, does not entertain the possibility that they should learn about research on their own.

Learning Resources/Technology

Good. "Technology was huge for me. I think that technology has been the biggest learning tool for me, even things I took for granted. I was able to manipulate the programs relatively easily to get to the point where I was learning and actually fulfilling the assignment or doing the requirement. For example, we acquired our material though an attachment of an email and I realize now that things we take for granted affect us in ways beyond what we comprehend. Also, the way that the assistant and the professor created the templates for us to put our material in to the CD-ROM to then taking that CD-ROM and bringing it to class and going through it in class technology has been probably THE class. I view it very positively. I was able to hit the ground running on many aspects of the technology that I think some people did struggle with. Even to a certain extent in this interview, we are utilizing technology. And even in the transcription again, I think it is just beyond what we even conceive, you know if we really start to think of it, it is much deeper."

Bad. "Learning resources that we have in this particular class certainly include the Inspiration software. It is also the type of media that are used in the class. Rather than having dry erase boards or chalkboards, our professor uses a computer, which is projected onto a screen so that we can see the actual use of the software. Other resources would include the use of the computer lab and having a group experience of everyone working together . . . once again, that goes back to collaborating and working together in a lab setting. Another resource would be the textbook. Now, we do not get the textbook in one chunk . . . we are only given a chapter at a time . . . and that is because the professor is actually creating the book. The learning resources have been good and I am just happy that I did not have to buy the book! If I had to purchase the book in order to get a complete set, I'd rather take one chapter at a time free."

Interpretive Comparison. The first student's enthusiasm for IQA as a research methodology is exceeded only by her positive reaction to communications and computer technology. The first student seems to have deepened her appreciation for the instructional impact of technology, repeatedly describing how things taken "for granted" are now seen in a new light. In contrast to this rather complex understanding, the second student's response is mostly a listing of the resources and the technological features with few or dispassionate assessments. Returning to the themes of distrust of the process itself as well as dislike of the experimental aspect of the course, the second student offers an oblique criticism of the structure and organization of the course by suggesting that chapters of the text were handed out one at a time as they are written.[13]

Collaboration

Good. "I think because the professor did not lecture and was constantly checking on us to see if we got it—that facilitated the collaborative nature at the table. Also there are times when frankly you just do not get it but you do not always want to ask the professor because there are those people that frankly ask the professor too many questions. You found that relationship in the peer. If I was looking over at one of my peers and they had the scrunched eyebrows [indication of confusion], then I knew to ask them, 'Do you get it?' And then we had this collaborative discussion about whether or not they did and maybe then I was the one with the scrunched eyebrows. You would ask them, 'Am I just the only one here that is not getting this?' We have to be collaborative to get our work done. We are going to pull together a mindmap of what we have done and then we are going to pull all those [individual mindmaps] together to create the assistant's research. We are in the same boat. And I feel like we are in the Wednesday night boat as compared to the Tuesday night boat. We are not in the same ship. We are probably in the same ocean but we are not in the same ship."

Bad. "There is a great deal of collaboration. In the classroom, we are arranged in groups so that much of what we do is done collaboratively working in cooperative learning groups. When someone in our group does not understand something, we are free to talk about it, learn from each other, and learn from our mistakes. This collaboration helps us to understand what is going on. I believe it helps the professors because they are not always there to instruct us and point out all of the details. IQA is so theoretical and so new to so many people that we need that extra time to talk about it and metacognitively learn from each other, but learn as we are explaining. What we do not understand, when we are explaining it to other people, we better clarify those ideas for ourselves."

Interpretive Comparison. The differences in timbre between the two responses are consistent with other affinities. The first student describes collaboration in vivid story form with a liberal use of metaphors (in the same ocean but different ships) including a humorous metonymy (scrunched eyebrows). Although the second student says many good things about the collaborative feature of the course (free to talk, learn from each other, helps us understand), the speaker is much more distanced from the topic in comparison to the first student: The language is more academic (metacognition) than in the first case and less emotionally involved, and again there is a hint of resentment of being used under false pretenses when the respondent creates an us/them separation ("it helps the professors").

Communication

Good. "There was so much more communication with the professor than I have experienced in any of my other classes because a lot of checks and balances are built into the course. 'Okay, can you understand this?' 'Okay, yes I can understand it. Now do this,' or, 'Okay, but I need you to re-work this because you did not quite get it.' And there is more of an element of performance, of actually doing the activities, in this class so the communication is upped as a result of that. I do feel like we communicated 90% of the time outside of the classroom, but there was also a high level of communication within the class because of the collaborative nature of the class. It was not a lecture format where we spent three hours just listening and taking notes. I think the communication was actually probably greater between and among the class members and the professor than the average class."

Bad. "Well, at this point in class, it is hard to get his attention because there are other people who are a bit more demanding. At times like that, I just withdraw because I think it is childish the way some people 'command' the professor's attention as opposed to just being diplomatic about things. My relationship with the professor or the assistant in the classroom, it is very limited because there are more dominant personalities who choose to impose their views and thoughts on others. Outside of class, he emails quite often. We receive several emails a week from him, which is very good. However, if he sends an email the day of class and then I have worked all day, I do not have time to go home and check my email. I feel like I am out of the loop at some points, but I am always able to jump right back in and get back on track. He is always available. If I email him, he emails me back within minutes. I can tell that he is very accessible. I feel like he is making himself very available to his students."

Interpretive Comparison. The first student puts her response in spirited dialogue form to illustrate how she understands the way communication occurs in the class, and she characterizes this interaction with yet another metaphor for feedback (checks and balances). She then expresses satisfaction with communication both among students and between instructor and student. In contrast, we begin to get a picture of the second student as one who does not get the desired attention from the instructor, blaming the aggressive behavior of the more "demanding" and less "diplomatic" students in the class. Although this student characterizes the instructor as accessible outside the classroom (email is the point of contact), the subtext suggests loneliness, a need for more personal interaction with the instructor, and feelings of alienation from some members of the class.[14]

Peer Relationships

Good. "There is a ton of peer relationships in the class. I guess we have fun a lot. There is a lot of humor. Sometimes we get sidetracked by a joke, but jokes tell you that the peer relationships exist because I do not think people would be comfortable cutting up as much if they thought it would hurt their peer relationships. I do not know a lot of people in the class. We work in tables where five people are sitting at the table, you're obviously going to have peer relationships with them. But the relationships I have with the four or five I do know are very rich. I can count on them, I can get feedback from them, and I can say, 'What do you think about this?' But I think the peer relationships in the class are very apparent due to the humor and also because of the collaborative nature of the course."

Bad. "I am very self-motivated and so I do not really need others to help me get through classes. I rarely rely on a professor to help me. I almost always rely on myself to help me get through things. But as far as other students, I would think that my peer relationships with the people in my cohort are very helpful and beneficial. If I do not understand something, I know people outside of my classes and can easily call on them and ask for clarification and between the five of us we will quite often know the answer and help each other by building on our resources. It's amazing to look at other people outside of my cohort—there is in many cases an age difference with totally different lifestyles and viewpoints, As far as our ideas and even being able to use the same jargon in class, at many times— because people are not familiar with educational jargon and maybe the philosophy that I have is very different than the philosophy that they have—I do not choose to work with them or really take in what they are saying because it just does not mesh with my core values."

Interpretive Comparison. The first student views peer relationships as providing a supportive environment for open inquiry ("what do you think about this?") that can be enjoyable ("we have fun a lot"). The second student, although attesting in almost a rote manner to the beneficial aspects of peer relationships, seems to view peers more as a database rather than as points of human contact that can generate interesting questions and humorous insights, never mind whether they seem at the moment to be relevant (as the first student noted, "sometimes we get sidetracked"). Probably the second student would describe himself as independent (self-motivated, does not really need others) rather than lonely, but again themes of separation and anomie ("it's amazing to look at other people . . . the philosophy that I have is very different . . . I do not choose to work with them") emerge, producing a psychological landscape in which both the instructors and other students are seen as the Other.

Emotional Environment/Classroom Climate

Good. "I think because there is such a collaborative environment and because the instructor style facilitated collaboration, we had fun. And I think when you have fun, you are more open to learn. You know we laughed a lot, we even had a birthday celebration. There has not been a class that has gone by where I have not laughed several times and that really opens up the learning environment."

Bad. "This class was almost a pilot program, working out the kinks on us for future books to be written and dissertations to be written. That made it a bit less beneficial for me but more beneficial for the professors. However, I think IQA is a good method for some who choose to use it. It has not closed my mind, it has increased my knowledge, but I feel like I could have had much more. As far as how I am feeling, part of it is being seven to ten at night, hungry, tired, having come from nine in the morning to ten at night the day before, working a full day . . . those things all play into the emotional environment. I feel respected, but I do not feel nurtured or special in any way. I am just one in a crowd. Whenever my hand is raised, I may not be noticed because maybe there are others in the class who are more commanding, persistent, loud, and aggressive and get the professor's attention. Because I choose not to behave that way, I may not be answered or have forgotten the question by the time someone gets around to acknowledging my question. Once again, it is just a self-study for me, self-paced, self-motivation that is going to get me through this class."

Interpretive Comparison. The first student responds directly to the question, and her evaluation of the emotional environment of the classroom is by now no surprise: The first student had fun. The second student returns once again to objections about the developmental nature of the class, expressing a feeling of having been taken advantage of for the benefit of others (other dissertations, other books). Finding no support (or rejecting it, depending on one's point of view) from peers, unrecognized by the instructor (or deliberately avoiding the instructor's attention, again depending on point of view), the second student is just a face in the crowd, and the experience in the IQA class has confirmed the lesson he has learned in other classes ("once again . . .") and probably outside the class as well: It's all up to me.

Cognitive Reaction/Comprehension

Good. "I have had several 'aha' moments, and a lot of that was facilitated through the technology we were given. The CD has been such a good way for me to take what I have read in the chapters that we were given and then actually see it come to fruition. I actually was getting it instead of just having this philosophical discussion about it when we would read the chapter. There was confusion mainly about the mindmaps. I think that was the thing that I had the most hurdles on. But again, because I had the CD as a tool and because we spent time in the Mac lab, confusion was quickly replaced with clarity. In terms of growth, I think my learning curve was very steep. I have never done anything with qualitative research before. I think what knowledge I do have about research has tended to be quantitative in nature, even taking statistics in my master's class. This is really the first time I have had the opportunity with qualitative and my growth has been just triplefold, maybe more than even that. The relationship between confusion and clarity and the unknown to the known has really led to growth."

Bad. "I feel like I comprehend and understand IQA almost to the 'T' but I don't feel like it is a method that I will use 100%. It lends itself to some dissertation topics better than others do. I have had a bit of experience with it and have gone through this procedure before. I feel that it is a great process, I understand the relationships that are made through identifying the affinities, and I have a great comprehension of how to get those relationships. I am very versed in using Total Quality Management tools, and IQA is phenomenally identical to some of the TQM tools. It was not new to me, and it was easy for me to grasp because I have had prior exposure. For instance, the affinity charts that we used in class are tools that are identical to the TQM tools, which can be done with any topic, and even in the classroom, the teacher can use it with different concepts. Also, the graphic organizers that were used with Inspiration software . . . having primary drivers and then outcomes, trying to find those relationships . . . once again that is the same thing. The 80/20 theory, which says that a small percentage of a phenomenon has more impact on something than the other 80% . . . so, anyway, this is the same thing you are finding here with the relationships."

Interpretive Comparison. Pointing out that her previous experience with research had all been quantitative, the first student evaluates the class as contributing to a significant degree of learning, and describes this affinity primarily in terms of personal change ("my learning curve was very steep"), reporting several "aha" moments. The second student reports excellent comprehension (to the "T"), but seems to attribute this high level of understanding not to the class itself but to prior experience with the data gathering and analysis tools of TQM. In the view of the second student, the class added little value to what he already knew, and he buttressed this argument by providing a detailed list of the features of the course that are similar to TQM. Indeed, to this student, IQA is just a few TQM techniques painted up in theoretical makeup and tarted up in academic regalia.

Application Toward Dissertation

Good. "I do think I am going to end up doing a qualitative study. I am going to do something in fund-raising and I am either going to look at the motivations of alumni giving or maybe look at presidential leadership in regard to fund-raising. As what I have seen in this class the IQA process is a very practical way to see the dissertation through, so I imagine that I am going to tap into the subject several times over when I am doing my research. I think it is going to be highly utilized."

Bad. "It is going to help me in writing my dissertation when I use the various parts. I think I know how to do the first four chapters already. I wish I had more information as to how to go about gathering data. That is where I feel like I do not know as much as I need to. Now, IQA is going to help me with chapter 5 because it is going to help me form the relationships, which is a lot of theory, too. It [interpretation] is very subjective, I can see how that part . . . it is a bit more subjective like IQA . . . but I do not think that I will just disregard some aspects just because I find no relationship between them. I would like to include more."

Interpretive Comparison. When the first student talks about "practicality," she refers to the fit between dissertation topic and method, or what another might call *relevance*. The second student seems considerably more ambivalent about the application of IQA toward the dissertation, possibly because this student may not have formed even a vague idea of what the dissertation topic will be (no hint of the topic was given in the interview).

COMPARING INDIVIDUAL SYSTEMS

Drivers and Loops, Sailing Ships and Train Wrecks. The experiences of these students, the first of whom was in the Wednesday (high-tech) class and the second in the more loosely structured Tuesday or traditional class, were vastly different. The student in the Wednesday class (hereafter called Wednesday) indicated she had an experience that affected her view of research profoundly. Consequently, Wednesday was strongly inclined to consider her dissertation in terms of IQA. The Tuesday student (subsequently called Tuesday) was isolated, suspicious of the instructors' motives, dubious about the worth of IQA, and felt overlooked in the crowd. A look at the students' individual systems quickly reveals clues that help explain the differences.[15]

Smooth Sailing: Wednesday's SID[16]

As shown in Figure 10.7, the Wednesday student's system begins with a loop, which exits onto a straight line. The five affinities that make up the loop can be described (zoomed out) as the curriculum and instruction component (C&I loop) of the class, which for the Wednesday student is the single driver of the entire system. The C&I loop is composed of those external elements (with the possible exception of Communication, the overall pattern of which is still controlled by the instructor) over which the student has no control and serves as the source of information about the scope and sequence of the course as well as the method of "transmission" to the student.

Like all loops, C&I is a dynamic interaction of its components (see the "pinwheel" version of Wednesday's SID in Figure 10.8), each one influencing the other, and the resultant of this dynamism influences Peer Relationships for Wednesday.[17] To the first student, the C&I dynamic "makes sense." This student understands (in her own terms) and is comfortable with the relationships among the instructor, the material, the physical environment, and the way the material is presented or communicated to students. In this student's construction of the course experience, the C&I loop encourages positive peer relationships by helping to create an environment where she is comfortable and safe. She feels free, even encouraged, to collaborate with peers, which aids learning and comprehension. Because she is comfortable with the material, she understands the underlying principles of IQA, and therefore can see utility in it and expects to use it in a dissertation.

Wednesday's voyage is in a straightforward journey over smooth waters. Wednesday never finds herself caught up in a loop from which there is no egress. Furthermore, one can imagine drawing a line on this student's SID from Application Toward Dissertation back to the beginning of the system, for this is a loop in which Wednesday frequently found herself. The more relevance Wednesday sees between IQA and the dissertation, the more the curriculum "makes sense"; and the more it makes sense,

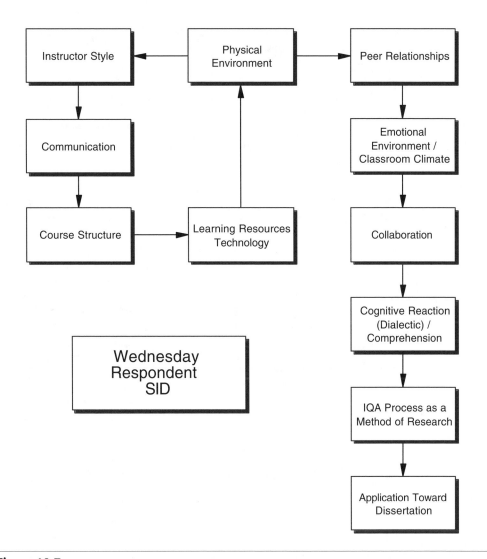

Figure 10.7

the more relevant IQA becomes. Indeed, the first student's mindmap could be seen as one big positive feedback loop, a classic example of success breeding success.

Train Wreck. Tuesday's SID

Unlike the Wednesday student, the Tuesday student's journey is not so simple, as revealed by Figure 10.9 (page 381).

Tuesday is driven by two different elements that converge at a crossroads and lead to two different destinations. Tuesday's system is like a pair of speeding freight trains converging at a crossroads where communication breaks down, resulting in a horrific wreck. Like Wednesday, Tuesday

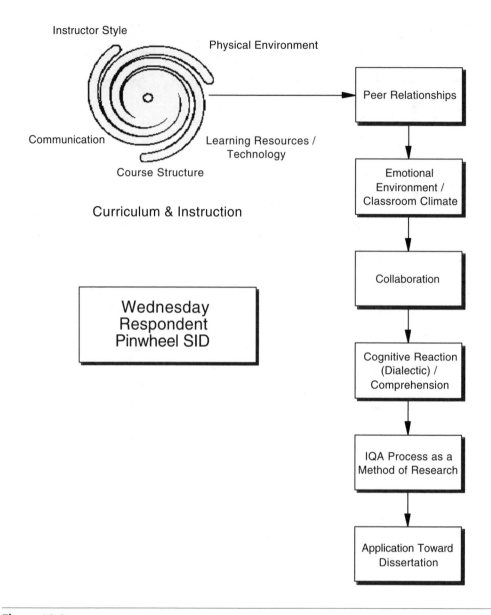

Figure 10.8

student's system is driven by a pinwheel (a loop; see Figure 10.10, page 382) that is very similar to Wednesday's C&I pinwheel. The difference between the two students' loops is that IQA Process as a Method of Research is in the place where Communication resided for the Wednesday student. Still, the drivers of this system are elements the student has little control over. The major difference in the two loops is that for the Tuesday student,

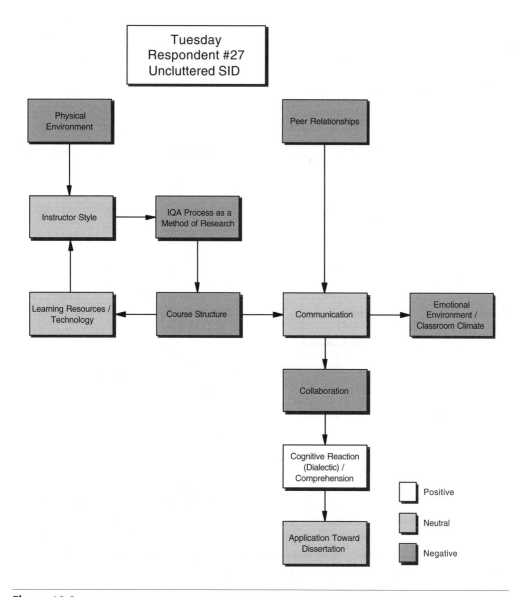

Figure 10.9

the curriculum and instruction system were flawed from the beginning due to an interaction of the student's own qualities and agenda with certain design flaws in the curriculum discussed in the group system; Tuesday finds it difficult to escape from this loop (e.g., Tuesday returned again and again to elements of this loop in the interview, no matter what the question).

Too Many Drivers. The second major difference between the systems of the two students is that the Tuesday student indicated an additional driver, Peer

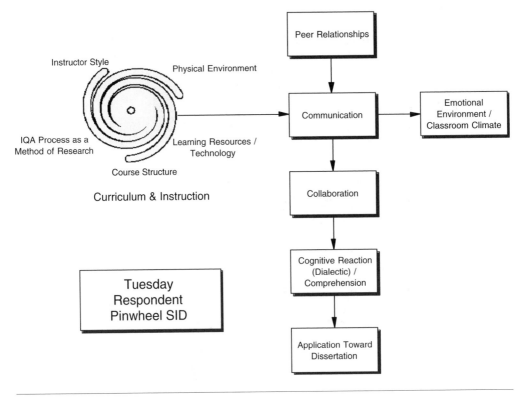

Figure 10.10

Relationships. Peer relationships is an element of the classroom experience the student has some control over, but Tuesday felt isolated and indeed seems to have chosen to remain apart from members of the class. In Tuesday's system, no mechanism existed to develop peer relationships. Tuesday chose not to be deeply engaged in the Peer Relationships affinity, and the structure of the course allowed him to do so. The result is portrayed as we follow Tuesday's SID: Poor peer relationships combined with a negative value of the curriculum lead to poor communication, both with the instructor and with other students, resulting on the one hand in a negative evaluation of the emotional environment and on the other in a very limited amount of collaboration on Tuesday's part. The communications "train wreck" leads to an incomplete or inaccurate understanding of IQA principles, which leads in turn to an ambivalence about IQA as a worthwhile dissertation methodology. Although Tuesday went to great lengths to explain how well he understood the class material, his understanding was processed through a very selective lens. Tuesday felt that because he knew TQM, he therefore knew all that was needed to know about IQA. Yet TQM procedures are only the surface manifestations of IQA theory. Although Tuesday's comments about the Comprehension affinity were rated by the investigators as positive (the only affinity so rated among all of Tuesday's affinities), it could be argued that Tuesday really had no significantly positive experience with any component of the IQA class.

Tuesday's Child. Without question, the instructor and the organizational structure of the IQA class failed in the case of this student; unlike Tuesday's child of the poem, however, the woe is partially Tuesday's own responsibility. Although the mechanism in the Tuesday class for fostering peer relationships was weaker than that of the Wednesday class, our Tuesday student chose to opt out entirely from the peer relationship structure.

Applied Meaning: Forecasts and Interventions

As described in previous sections, the system (SID) produced by the participants in the IQA class study can be used to identify likely points of structural failure. By identifying the place in the system where affinities go negative, one can identify the root causes of failure. The two classes demonstrated the power of the model, for while the structure of the system remains the same for both classes, the values of the path and the outcomes are very different.

At a higher conceptual level, however, *the system can be used to represent a more general theory of classroom structure and interaction.* The system can be used to predict what might happen given a particular scenario. With a few simple name changes, the system developed by the two classes becomes a more universal model[18] to help describe the classroom dynamic. By generalizing beyond the context in which the SID was constructed, we create a general theory of classroom structure and interaction. Specifically, we can make these changes to the model:

❖ Change the context from the IQA Class to The Classroom.

❖ Change the affinity IQA Process as a Method of Research to its more general referent, The Curriculum.

❖ Widen the referent of Application Toward Dissertation to its more general referent, Utility.

This theory is shown in Figure 10.11, page 384.

The Uses of Theory. Theories are used to describe, to understand, and to generate hypotheses. Some examples follow.

The What if? Game
   With this new system, we can predict outcomes based on scenarios of interest. In the *What if?* game, one "disrupts" the system by creating a

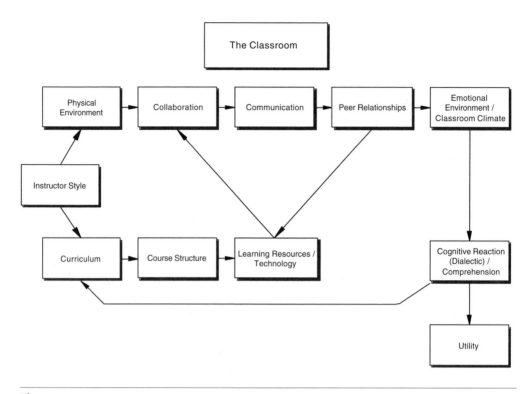

Figure 10.11

scenario in any affinity and seeing how it plays out through the system. In general, three kinds of What if? queries can be made of the theory:

1. If X happens, what might be the outcomes? (Prospective Scenario)

2. If we have a certain outcome or set of outcomes, what are the conditions that could have produced them? (Retrospective Scenario)

3. If a factor outside the system impacts at a given point, how might the system react? (Extrasystemic Scenario)

Some Examples From the Case Study
The IQA class case study provides a ready source of questions for the What if? game:

❖ What if the course is poorly structured? Some students become frustrated, do not learn, and find little use in the curriculum; but others find ways to compensate and even overcome a lack of course structure.

❖ What if students do not make friends? Some students need no resources other than the provided materials and the instructor to answer questions, but others need additional resources. A classroom that encourages development of peer relationships and collaboration increases the probability of success, no matter what the personality of the student.

❖ What if the instructor has poor teaching skills? Conventional wisdom has it that there is no way to "overcome" a less-than-skillful teacher. Certainly there is a great element of truth to this cliché, but the theory outlined here suggests a more nuanced response. The system is not predetermined, such that if a domino were knocked down at the beginning, all must fall down. Rather, the theory describes a system of recursion providing opportunities to reset some of the fallen pieces. As the IQA class study demonstrated, even an outstanding professor cannot completely overcome a poorly designed class. Can a properly designed class help compensate for a poor instructor? This particular case study research cannot answer this question, but the theory suggests that solid instructional design combined with an emphasis on peer relationships and collaboration can certainly compensate for a less-than-charismatic instructor. Regardless, the issue could be illuminated by, as one example, providing such an instructor with a complete instructionally designed package and performing a postcourse IQA analysis.

❖ What if a student is not competent with technology and struggles with the details of computers and email? In today's classrooms, computers are becoming more common. Without going into the pedagogical reasons for why one should use technology and why it works, the benefits of technology are arguably high. Many prerequisite skills are required to function in a classroom that uses technology. Some students lack even basic computer skills yet must work with complex software packages. Once again, the theory offers areas of intervention to help overcome the problem. The first element to come into play is in the curriculum and design of the course. Does the curriculum call for learning new software, or does it assume a requisite knowledge of basic computer skills? For the acquisition of new skills, the design of the class must include instruction and materials for learning the new skills. Even if the course design fails to provide necessary prerequisite skills, peer relationships may be the next line of intervention. If the class fosters relationships and creates a warm environment where students feel comfortable, they can collaborate and aid each other. Students can find themselves in a positive spiral within the communication dynamics loop.

Same Issue, Different Constituencies

The Same Issue, Different Constituencies comparison is one of the most straightforward and useful comparisons, the staple on the menu of system comparisons. In this design, the same issue statement (description of the phenomenon) is given to constituencies who vary on some interesting dimension relating to either distance from or power over the phenomenon. Because the IQA class case study yielded two systems that were identical in elements and structure, we will examine another case as an illustration of this technique: Men, Women, and Power.

In separate focus groups, male and female graduate students were asked to reflect via a guided imagery exercise (described earlier in this chapter) on what power meant to them. The two focus group SIDs are reproduced here. First, the women, as shown in Figure 10.12, and the men, in Figure 10.13.

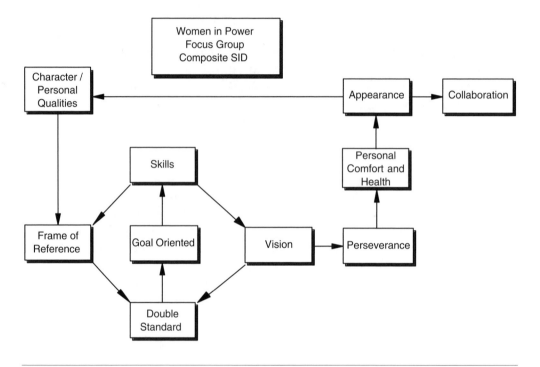

Figure 10.12

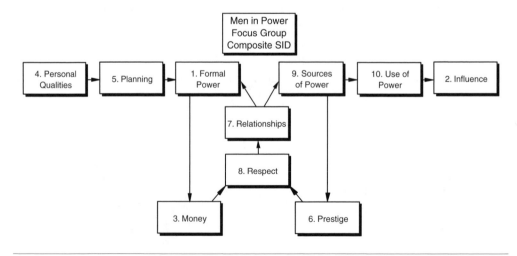

Figure 10.13

Reconnoitering the Systems. Our purpose here is to illustrate a particular kind of comparison rather than to present a complete study; however, it is worthwhile to examine some preliminary results as an illustration of an interpretive device called *reconnaissance.*

When entering unfamiliar territory, the prudent explorer reconnoiters before doing a more detailed survey. Conducting a quick theoretical reconnaissance of the two systems with the assistance of focus groups revealed some interesting features of the landscape:

- ❖ The men's system looks more like the picture of a production line than the women's. Although it contains two interlocking loops in the middle, it can be seen as describing a "process" that begins with Personal Qualities and ends with Influence. The women's system, in contrast, is almost a picture of one big feedback loop, suggesting that, in contrast to the men, power was constructed by the women less as a mechanism (such as the production line model produced by the men) and more as a dynamic unity of interrelated concepts.

- ❖ Although Personal Qualities is a driver in both systems, this affinity is embedded within the two systems quite differently: Personal Qualities is a primary driver in the very strictest sense for the men; this affinity drives the entire system and is "unaffected" by any other affinity within the system. For the women, however, this driver is part of a very large and complicated feedback loop, suggesting that although the axial descriptions of Personal Qualities were similar for both men and women, this affinity nevertheless has a very different meaning between the two groups. The men's system suggests a construction of Personal Qualities that is more like raw material fed into the power process; the women's system suggests a more malleable and dynamic construct that can change as a result of interaction with other elements of the system.

- ❖ The women's system has the individual woman almost exclusively as its referent; the men's system points to both the individual and to institutional or organizational dimensions.

- ❖ The two interlocking feedback loops in the women's system paint a picture of a woman who in order to achieve goals must recognize that she is playing on a field that is not level[19] (Double Standard). Therefore, she must have a high(er) level and great(er) variety of skills; even these aren't enough, however, because the goals and skills must serve some higher purpose (Vision), and the only way to realize the vision is to persevere. The men's system, in contrast to placing the burden of power on themselves, seems to identify a constellation of "tools" (Formal Power, Relationships, and Sources of Power) and associated rewards (Prestige, Money, and Respect) that in turn become instruments of power.

❖ Because the women's system places a very heavy burden on the individual woman to persevere under adverse conditions (in contrast to the "tools" described by the men), the effect of power on the individual is quite different in the two systems. Power enervates in the women's system, requiring periodic R&R (rest and rejuvenation) sessions.[20] No such dynamic is present in the men's system; to be sure, the men's system suggests invigoration rather than enervation. Perhaps power is a reward in itself in the men's system, unlike the women's?

❖ The primary outcome is radically different in the two systems. Influence in the men's system suggests control, authority, and domination. Collaboration in the women's system suggests alliance, alignment of agendas, and teamwork.

Questions, Not Answers. Interpretation is more a matter of searching for questions than answers, of highlighting possibilities rather than closing off avenues of understanding. Comparison between and within systems is a fundamental tool for interpretation, allowing the investigator to raise ever more refined and focused questions with which to interrogate systems.

Same Constituency, Different Issues: Metacomparisons

One Last Comparison. Comparison is the fuel for the interpretive machine, and systems as represented by mindmaps or SIDs provide multiple opportunities for comparison, as summarized here.

POTENTIAL COMPARISONS

At the elementary (affinity) level:

❖ Individual/Individual

❖ Individual/Composite

At the single-system level:

❖ Zooming

❖ Individual/Individual SID

❖ Individual/Composite SID

❖ Prospective Scenario

❖ Retrospective Scenario

❖ Extrasystemic Scenario

At the multiple-system level:

❖ Multiple constituencies, same issue

❖ Same constituency, different (but related) issue (metacomparison)

Examples of all these have been given, save for the last in the list above, which in many ways is the most interesting of all. The last comparison is called a *metacomparison* because it is analogous to a metareview of the literature, in which a variety of different but related studies are compared. The following is the theory and an example of metacomparison.

Metacomparisons: Same Constituency, Different (But Related) Issue. Metacomparisons create the interpretive opportunity to stitch different patches of reality into a larger quilt of meaning. Consider these different IQA studies:

1. A group of graduate students was asked to respond to the issue, "Tell me about your 'life at school' as a graduate student." The SID produced in response to this issue, called The Graduate Experience, is shown in Figure 10.14, page 390.

This system, and the ones to follow, have many fascinating characteristics; however, our purpose is not to drive the reader away in fear and loathing at the prospect of yet another detailed tour through a system, but to highlight just one element of the system: *Relationships.*

2. A group of graduate students was asked to respond to the issue, "Tell me about your 'life at home' [away from the campus] as a graduate student." The response to this is shown in Figure 10.15, page 390.

Note that Relationships is an affinity for the Life Away From School SID.

3. A group of graduate students was asked to respond to the issue, "Tell me about your life in this class" as a graduate student. The SID produced in response to this issue is shown in Figure 10.16, page 391.[21]

Notice again that relationships (Peer Relationships) is an affinity in this SID.

Stitching the Pieces Together. What happens if we assume that the Relationships affinities in the three systems all represent at least approximately the same category of meaning? Making that assumption, while following

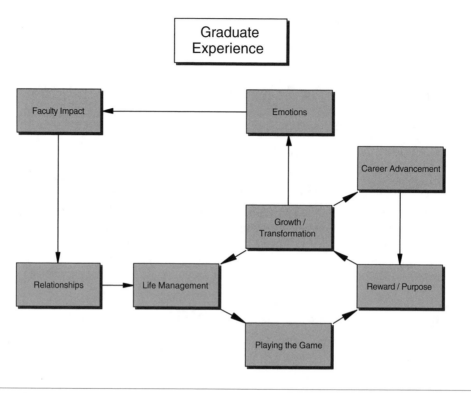

Figure 10.14

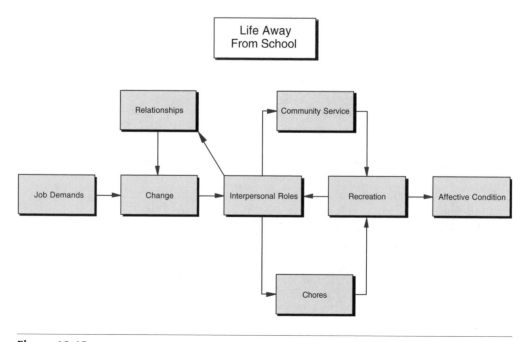

Figure 10.15

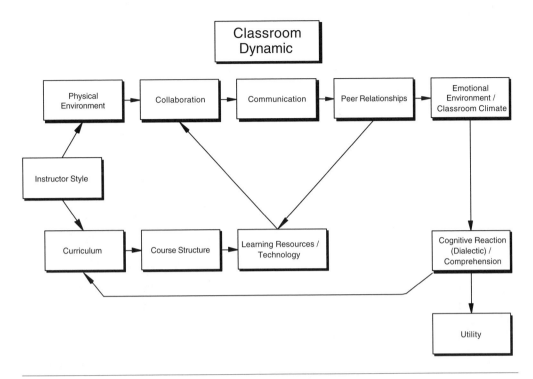

Figure 10.16

the rules for topological representation of systems (i.e., links may be bent but not broken), allows us to stitch the three pieces together as shown in Figure 10.17, page 392.

The resulting MetaSID portrays the interrelationships of three facets of the graduate school experience: on campus, at home or away from campus, and inside a particular classroom. The affinity Relationships is the nexus of all these, and thus is a "pivot" affinity, implying a pivotal or critical function or role.[22]

Beyond Meta. Another affinity arguably represents the same category of meaning across all three systems. This similarity provides yet another opportunity to examine the metasystem that results. Identifying this common affinity and performing the necessary topological transformations will be left as an exercise for the student.

Looking Back and Looking to the End

Form should follow function, suggesting that a study's form of discourse or how it is written up should result from its underlying epistemological

392

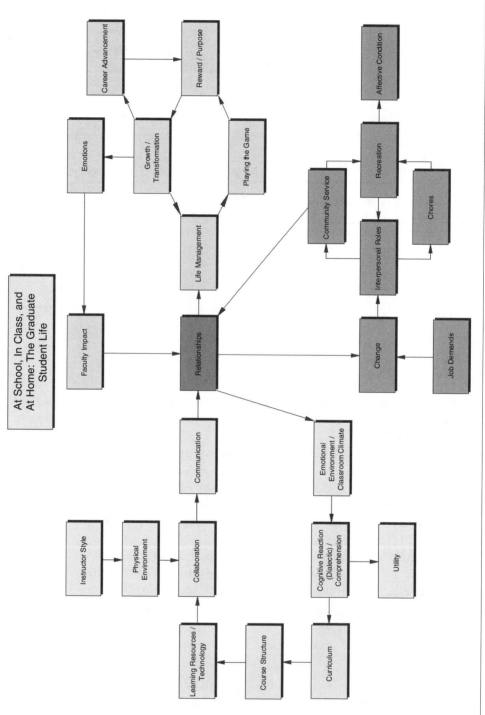

At School, In Class, and At Home: The Graduate Student Life

Figure 10.17

assumptions. Articulating a clear relationship between epistemological goals (description and interpretation) and method allows for a theory of interpretation. This theory, in turn, produces a set of protocols for both description and interpretation. Such a theory and the protocols for interpretation were set forth in this chapter, and the relationship to a common form of discourse in research, the dissertation format, was described.

The last chapter presents the authors' commentary on the interpretational capabilities of IQA, using several studies employing IQA methodology as examples.

Notes

1. In their positivistic emphasis on deduction, Campbell and Stanley took the existence of the elements that are required to make a relationship for granted; we do not. Furthermore, their emphasis on hypothesis testing or deduction as the *sine qua non* of research begs the inductive question, Where do theories come from?

2. Lakoff's (1991) *Women, Fire, and Dangerous Things* is one of the more comprehensive studies of the way in which people create categories; it influenced this analysis of the ways in which affinities are different.

3. In mathematics, such variables are called *nominal variables*, in which each category is simply a name; it is not appropriate to put the categories into any given order. Examples include gender, ethnicity, or color of hair. Affinities, however, always have a value dimension, no matter what their "level of measurement."

4. The name is adapted from Lakoff's (1991) use of the word to denote categories with degrees of membership. Scalar affinities are roughly analogous to continuous mathematical functions, and are represented in the quantitative world by ordinal, interval, or ratio measurements.

5. Grounded in the sense used by grounded theory, which implies descriptions grounded in the participants' reality. Operationally, this implies staying as close as possible to the original language of the participants and the frequent judicious use of both axial and theoretical quotes.

6. By no means are either of these lists complete.

7. After listening with evident increasing frustration to a presentation of the statistical affinity-by-affinity comparison that follows, one faculty member announced, "This just isn't qualitative research!" and made an abrupt exit.

8. The name of the software used in class to draw mindmaps.

9. "Typical" in this context has a very specific meaning: A member of a constituency is typical of that constituency if the mindmap of that member is identical to the composite mindmap for the constituency. Note that typicality (or representativeness, if you prefer the more quantitative term) has to do with structure of the mindmap, not timbre of the affinities.

10. In a previous age, we would have used less-value-laden euphemisms for "good" and "bad" such as "helpful" and "not helpful." By now the reader should understand (if not agree) that we describe the two reactions to the course in such stark terms because these terms are closest to the language of the participants.

11. In the instructor's defense, an annotated bibliography of readings in different traditions of qualitative research was provided to all students at the beginning of the course.

12. Statements like these cry out for a follow-up probe on the part of the interviewer. Unfortunately, a follow-up question was not asked, which is a typical fault of inexperienced interviewers.

13. Which is partially true.

14. This highlights the need for all instructors, but especially this one, to become more familiar with and to operationalize the considerable literature on identifying and establishing contact with reticent or withdrawn students in the classroom.

15. This is an example of casting a *retrospective* scenario with mindmaps; namely, a final condition is stipulated (the student had a good or bad experience) and a question is formulated: What contributed to this overall evaluation?

16. The SIDs that follow contain, in addition to the usual information, the results of a rating assigned by the investigators of the timbre of each affinity on a three-point scale: positive, neutral, or negative. Affinities are coded to reflect this rating. Notice that the Wednesday student's affinities are all rated as favorable, while only one of the Tuesday student's affinities is so rated.

17. The loop has been zoomed out and represented as a pinwheel in the second version of the Wednesday student's SID to communicate the dynamism of loops.

18. The utility of which must be demonstrated with further research in different classroom settings.

19. We apologize in advance for the sports, machine, and military metaphors.

20. The women in the focus group self-mockingly referred to the Personal Comfort and Health affinity as the "Bubble Bath."

21. This third SID is the one produced by the students in the two IQA classes and comes from the study that provides much of the case material in other sections.

22. Which suggests that the Relationships affinity should be zoomed in as the subject of another investigation. Robole (2002; forthcoming) is conducting just such a study.

Comparisons, Interpretations, and Theories

11

Some Examples

In the Prologue, we introduced Interactive Qualitative Analysis (IQA) by presenting one specific case history. This chapter has two objectives: to demonstrate the interpretive potential of IQA methodology and to illustrate the variety of disciplines and topics for which the methodology is appropriate.

IQA has been used in a variety of settings for a number of purposes, such as the following:

- ❖ Examining the lives of social workers in hospital settings
- ❖ Providing user feedback to Web site designers
- ❖ Investigating reactions to English language instruction via public television in a non-English-speaking country
- ❖ Describing the perspective of minorities at predominately white universities
- ❖ Contrasting the views of leadership of women faculty and administrators
- ❖ Describing the meaning of products to consumers
- ❖ Evaluating social programs
- ❖ Analyzing redundancies and inconsistencies in Web networks
- ❖ Clarifying management and personnel issues

In addition to these examples, this chapter presents a collection of IQA studies, with an emphasis on comparisons, interpretation, and the use of IQA for theory building.

CASE I. POWER AND GENDER: TWO DIFFERENT WORLDS

Thinking About Thinking. Members of an IQA class, all mid-career administrative professionals in both education and the private sector, were convened in separate focus groups by gender and asked to reflect on the nature of power in a guided imagery exercise. The protocol for the women's guided imagery is reproduced in Table 11.1.

The men's guided imagery was identical to the women's, with the exception that the words "woman" and "women" were changed to "man" and "men." After the usual nominal group process followed by axial and theoretical coding, the two groups produced the System Influence Diagrams (SIDs) shown in Figures 11.1 and 11.2.

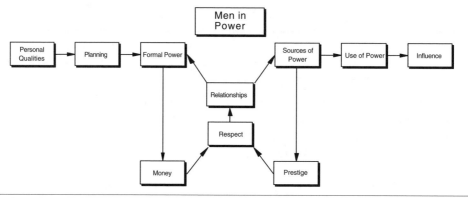

Figure 11.1

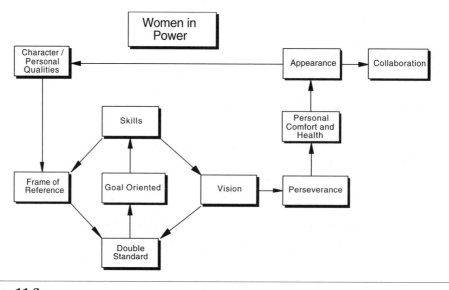

Figure 11.2

Table 11.1   *Women* in Power: Focus Group Warm-Up Exercise

I would like you to think for a while about being powerful—about the ability to get things done in your organization or your world.

You have known about individuals who seem to be able to accomplish just about anything they set out to do. Maybe at times you have experienced this yourself.

You have seen examples of powerful people. You have heard stories of powerful people. You might have felt what it is like to know you are or have acted powerfully.

In a few minutes, I am going to ask you to tell me what you have noticed about how you or other *women* have been powerful.

So let's begin.

- ❖ Please allow yourself to be as comfortable as possible.
- ❖ Put your thoughts from the day aside to allow your attention to focus on this topic.
- ❖ Close your eyes to increase your state of relaxation and your ability to notice what you know about how you and others are powerful in their environment.

You have noticed when some *women* seem more capable to get things done, to get decisions made, to garner support, or to move an agenda forward.

- ❖ Think about a time when you have been successful in accomplishing something important to you. Especially if this was a challenging situation.
- ❖ If no situation for yourself comes to mind, select someone you know or have heard of and ask that person.
- ❖ What were your beliefs about the situation, what were your strategies or decisions, what were the actions you took to accomplish this?

Consider a time when you or another *woman* had to overcome barriers and being powerful meant drawing upon a special set of behaviors or strategies.

- ❖ What were they?
- ❖ How did others participate or not in this scenario?
- ❖ What did this mean to how you experienced power?

Consider a *woman* who has sustained power over time or through challenges.

- ❖ What did this person do that is worth noticing?
- ❖ Look a little closer to detect subtleties of how she did this.

Think of times when you or someone else set out to increase her power.

- ❖ How did you or she do this?

(Continued)

Table 11.1 (Continued)

❖ What are different techniques, strategies, or behaviors that contributed to accomplishing this?

❖ Review all your recollections up to this moment.

❖ As you have thoughts that do not apply, let them float by. Also, notice that they might have suggestions hidden in them that are valuable, as well.

❖ Recall what an experienced *woman* has or might have told you about being powerful.

❖ Think about what you would tell a younger *woman* about being powerful.

❖ Allow all these thoughts to remain calmly in your consciousness and ready to be revealed.

Thank you for allowing these valuable observations and recollections to come forward.

Please allow yourself to gently allow your consciousness back to this time and place, and when you are ready, open your eyes.

Good. Thank you.

And now—with all that you remember—and that is all that you just noticed—please, write down your thoughts on these cards.

Write one thought or experience per card. Feel free to record a word, a phrase, a sentence, or a picture to capture that thought . . . and . . .

. . . Tell me about power.

Although a complete understanding of these and the SIDS to follow requires a complete write-up of each of the affinities, we will omit these write-ups and concentrate on the differences between the two.

The Men's System. Like the women, the men's construction of power begins with personal qualities, but there the similarities end. The men constructed a system that fairly well tracks most classical (masculine, many would say) understandings of power: Power is understood as influence or the ability to move others in a desired direction, and the way to achieve this straightforward goal is first through planning and preparation. These prerequisites feed into what the men called *formal power,* by which term they understood power to be mediated by hierarchy and organizational structure. Power, to the men, has immediate or intermediate (secondary outcomes, in the language of IQA) benefits of money, respect, and prestige, which themselves are part of an interlocking web (feedback loops) of relationships that tend to create additional and informal sources of power, which itself is something to be used.

The Birthright. The construction of power as "something to be used to gain influence" implies the men's construction of power is instrumental—power is a tool with a particular functionality—but it also is self-referential (power = influence), implying that, to the men, power is an end in itself, something that is used to gain even more of that same thing, something that is satisfying and energizing quite apart from the trappings associated with getting and using power. Furthermore, the SID representing this construction looks very much like an industrial process flow model. The raw materials of personal qualities and planning are transformed by the intermediate stages of organizations and relationships into intermediate "products" (money, respect, prestige), which themselves feed back into the machinery (relationships, other sources), and end with use of power leading to influence or more power. Clearly, this is a system created by men for the use of men, suggesting that to many men, power is understood as natural and, given the right mix of character, preparation, and opportunity, almost a birthright.

The Women's System. No such sense of entitlement is communicated by the women's construction of power; neither does this SID resemble a production process. Although both systems begin with the qualities of the individual, the two systems are in stark contrast to each other in the main. In the first place, the women use different language from the men when they construct power; for example, nothing like "frame of reference" appears in the men's system, and neither does "double standard," "perseverance," "personal comfort and health," "appearance," or arguably "collaboration."

Resistance and Support. One woman described "frame of reference" as a supportive environment in which there were "kindred spirits of similar orientation. I can do things with them in order to have power and go with the energy of the group. . . . You only need so much power in a system as there is resistance. If there is not a lot of resistance, you don't need to have a lot of power." Here we find the suggestion of one of the many significant differences between the gender's construction of power. "You only need so much power . . ." implies that, first, power serves a higher purpose rather than being an end in itself; and second, resistance to power in a woman's hands (a masculine metaphor in itself) is assumed as ordinary and natural. The men's SID, in contrast, contains certainly no overt mention or even an implication of resistance.

The Double Standard. Closely associated with frame of reference and its implied foundation of resistance is the double standard. That this affinity is absent from the men's system is hardly surprising, given one woman's pithy explanation of how the double standard operates: "You are always trying to second-guess what the rules are. We are not given the secret handshakes, recipes, and handbooks. The rules change and there are overt rules but also unspoken ones. . . . I worked at [an agency] where I was the only woman director and the rules of that system were that pretty young things should not be directors, and if anything got done, there had to be a man behind it. Therefore, I had to get the right men behind my ideas. My belief is that I actually have more power when others also have power and we can align our agenda."

Turning On the Faucet. The struggle to overcome resistance requires goal orientation (short-term or tactical goals), a variety of skills (communication, organizational, and technical), and a view to the far horizon (vision). These all require (or produce, if the woman is to thrive or even survive, as indicated by the women's system) a high value on perseverance. Again, a woman described why persevering is especially required for members of her gender: "I do not think perseverance is necessary for everybody to have power. People who have the so-called pedigrees or preference do not need it; they just choose to turn it on like a faucet with running water." Her metaphor of power as water is particularly striking. The men's SID suggests that, indeed, all one has to do is turn on the faucet, while the women must construct aqueducts and pumps to overcome both friction and the force of gravity before even reaching the faucet. For the men, taking a drink is relatively effortless and refreshing. For the women, the task requires tactical and strategic intelligence as well as perseverance guided by a long-term vision. As a result, pursuit of power is an enervating process, rather than the refreshing one represented in the men's system.

Enervation Versus Energizing. Fatigue and depletion of personal resources require rest and recreation, so in the women's system, "personal comfort and health" appears, whereas it is absent from the men's; many of the men in the IQA class suppressed snickers and tried to cover up expressions of dismay on their faces when the women presented this portion of their system. A woman highlighted this chasm between the two genders' worlds when the interviewer asked her to help him understand this affinity. She replied coolly, "No, I cannot help you understand it [implying the chasm was far too wide to breach], but I totally get it," and then mischievously fell silent while the male interviewer squirmed in embarrassment as he searched for a follow-up probe.[1] Her point made, she relented and elaborated on the personal comfort and health issue: "What I mean is I don't expect you to get it at all, but I totally do. If a woman doesn't take care of herself in terms of whatever her *real* needs are, whether they be needs for solitude or nourishment of all kinds . . . she will not have the stores of energy to pursue power in this alien environment." In just a few words, the woman quite properly chastened the interviewer for being unaware of his own assumptions about the phenomenon and about her; quickly summarized a complex situation with the metaphor of an alien environment; and revealed that power in itself, by enervating rather than energizing, demanded that she seek nourishment elsewhere.

Appearance and Substance. "Appearance" as an outcome in the women's system also created a chorus of suppressed laughter from the men.[2] The laughing died, however, as the men began to understand what the women meant by this affinity and how it was a quite logical and adaptive result of previous affinities in the women's system. In the words of one woman in the group:

> I really do believe . . . for women to be powerful they have to hit some standard of appearance, but I do not know what that standard is, or who holds it, or if women just have to believe it, or what. It is not the natural attractiveness of a woman, but the important thing is at least if she shows that she is playing by the rules. Anything that a woman does or does not do around her appearance is a statement that will either increase or detract from her power. I saw an interview with a nearby university president last week on the evening news. She looked like she was right out of a gym class and had a not very attractive outfit on and her hair was matted and weird. I got mad at myself for reacting because appearances are supposed to be just appearances. There is something about women: Those that don't perceive themselves to be in the upper 25% of beauty are more powerful because they set up a belief that "I have to do it another way." I think in our culture that appearance is one of a woman's assets and that maximizing it is critical to be taken seriously.

The woman's analysis evokes a scene from the 1988 movie *Working Girl*, in which smart, ambitious, beautiful, but underemployed Tess (Melanie Griffith) tells us she has a "head for business and a body for sin." After realizing her female boss (Sigourney Weaver) does not take her seriously because of her background (too trailer park), her hair (too teased, too bouffant, too candyflossed) and her voice (too, well, just too silly), Tess exploits her boss's absence by impersonating a high-flying dealmaker and financier. Tess changes her hair, her clothes, and her voice in a Cinderella-like transformation. But the triple bind of gender, appearance, and power is highlighted in a scene when Tess, wearing her new personality and a power suit borrowed from her boss's closet, meets with another dealmaker (Harrison Ford as Jack Trainer). Trainer, leering at Tess through a drunken haze, captures Tess's situation perfectly as he says, "You look like a woman dressed like a man trying to look like a woman."

Aligning Agendas. If we have conducted a proper tour of the women's system, it should come as no shock to find that the primary outcome of the women's power system is collaboration (rather than the more unidirectional "influence" of the men's system). Listen once more to the woman:

> I think [collaboration] is the medium of women's power because we do not feel our power is diminished when it is shared with others; if anything, it is increased, which means power through community. Women struggle with a profound interplay of cooperation and boundaries—some women get the cooperation part but not the boundary part.

[*Interviewer:* Tell me a little bit about how women collaborate.]

It goes back to being willing to be satisfied with part of my agenda, getting taken care of in the moment because someone else's agenda gets taken care of too. But [partial success] cannot be seen as the game, but just as part of the game. Collaboration takes a long view, and women collaborate by complementing; they know they do not have to be the whole package. They are willing to assist someone else while advancing their own agenda.

Unlike the men's representation of power, the women's system is considerably more elaborate and in a real sense, much more sophisticated. Overcoming resistance requires perseverance, vision, and both tactical (e.g., appearance) and strategic capabilities. All these factors interact to create a construction of power as collaboration and complementarity, which is elegantly understood by the women as a dialectical interaction between cooperation and boundaries. In this last distinction, one can find the clichéd views of men and women as leaders: If cooperation overwhelms boundaries, the female stereotype emerges, and the male stereotype surfaces when boundaries overwhelm cooperation.

CASE II. BODY IMAGE, EATING DISORDERS, AND MEDIA MESSAGES

Bann (2001) used a combination of causal-comparative design principles and IQA to explore the relationship between body image and media messages. College-age women were convened in two separate focus groups (and subsequent interviews). One focus group consisted of women at risk for eating disorders, as indicated by a self-report measure of symptoms commonly associated with anorexia nervosa and bulimia nervosa. The second group consisted of similar women whose scores indicated no risk for eating disorders. Bann created a large picture board containing photos of models considered as representative of the media ideal of beauty. Laminated magazine photos on a black poster background from five different magazines were employed as the stimulus for a silent nominal process in which focus group members were asked to record their thoughts as they viewed the images. The SIDs representing the interaction of media messages and body images for the at-risk and no-risk groups in Figures 11.3 and 11.4.

Many of the differences between the two groups' constructions of the meaning of the media messages are apparent: The at-risk group identified affinities (invariably negative in timbre) dealing with imperfection, body weight, and dissatisfaction with specific body parts. The no-risk group's system contains no such affinities, suggesting that the latter do not "internalize" the message of perfection.

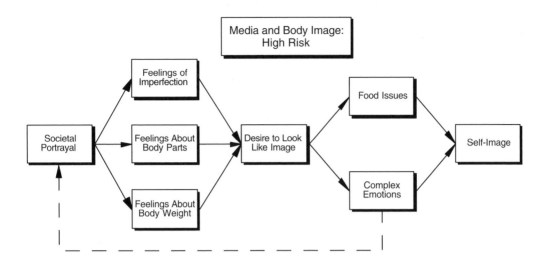

Figure 11.3

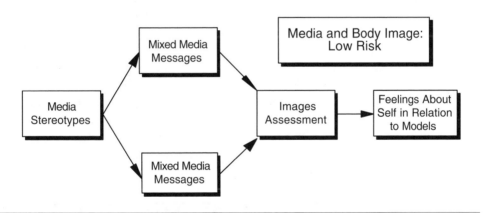

Figure 11.4

Perfection and Implosion. The at-risk group system contains a pivotal affinity, a desire to look like the model, which leads to issues with food and to complex (typically negative) emotions. These feed back to the driver of the at-risk group's system, which they named Societal Portrayal, a term that meant "the group was inclined to view the photos from the picture board as true representation of the ideal in terms of desirability and beauty" (Bann, 2001, p. 145). The net effect of this feedback loop is pernicious: The message of perfection is a very powerful one for the at-risk group, leading to dissatisfaction with one's own body, which in turn facilitates a desire to reach the "perfection" represented in the images. Failure to achieve this perfection feeds back in such a way as to reinforce the strength of the message, which occasions yet another recursion through the loop, a repetitive journey that must, at some point, "implode" in a self-image of worthlessness.

Separating Self From Context. The no-risk group system contains no such dynamic. Rather than internalizing the media message, the no-risk system suggests this group "stood outside" the media message, which is to say that although they were affected by the message, they nevertheless rather coolly assessed the images themselves rather than identify with them. The no-risk group consistently identified the models' appearance as "unrealistic," and showed little tendency to equate the models' appearance with perfection or with the demands that society places on women. Many of the feelings of the no-risk group about themselves in relation to the models were indeed negative, but these negative feelings were accompanied, in the words of the focus group members, by a "reality check." As Bann (2001) points out, "From such comments as, 'I know that this kind of image is supposed to make me think that if I buy the makeup, then I can look like this,' and 'I realize these models are chosen because they look good in these clothes, but they are not really representing someone like me,' it is possible to discern that these subjects could be objective about the media representations without involving their own egos" (p. 169). Bann continues her interpretation of the systems: "The ability to discern the difference between a real woman and an ideal representation of all women was something that Group 2 (no-risk) shared (and that the at-risk group lacked). The phenomena associated with this dichotomy among the groups seem to center around the ability of the subjects to separate self from context" (p. 170). Separating self from context is exactly the phenomenon highlighted clearly by the IQA process.

CASE III. PRINCIPALS' SUPERVISION STYLES IN HIGH- AND LOW-PERFORMING SCHOOLS

Knezek (2001), like Bann, used a causal-comparative design to compare the SIDs constructed by elementary teachers at two kinds of schools: those with low reading achievement student performance and those with high performance. After carefully matching the two kinds of schools on important socioeconomic indicators, Knezek conducted focus groups in which he asked teachers to reflect on the supervisory practices of their principals. The IQA process yielded the following mindmaps for the high- and low-performing schools (see Figures 11.5 and 11.6).

Parents Versus Coaches. The teachers' constructions of how their principals supervised may be characterized as Parent and Disciplinarian in the

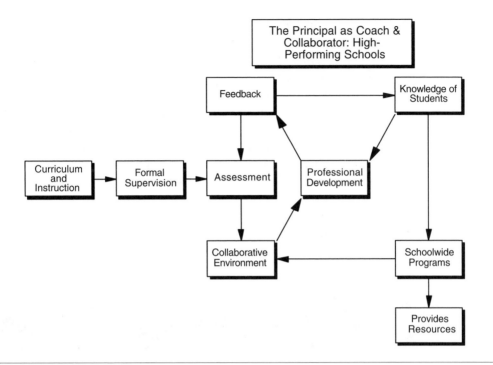

Figure 11.5

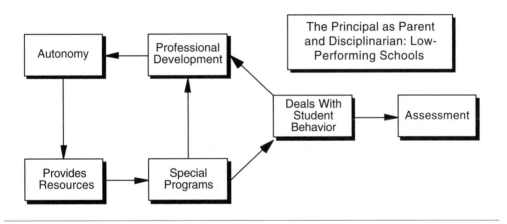

Figure 11.6

low-performing schools and as Coach and Collaborator in the high. A coach is responsible for a team, while a parent is responsible for individual children. Analogously, Knezek (2001) points out that the high-performing schools operated as systems (teams) in the truest sense; programs, knowledge of students, training, feedback and assessment, and collaboration all operate in the high-performing teachers' construction of their principal's supervision in a series of interlocking feedback loops that could have been designed by a management expert to follow the plan-do-assess-revise cycle.

The principal in the high-performing schools is seen by teachers as a coach and a collaborator in a "total quality school system," and the primary outcome (other than high student achievement) is seen to be resources (rather than a constraint or a driver, as is seen in many other contexts).

The principal in the low-performing schools is understood quite differently: Rather than resources being a logical outcome of a team effort, the principal is seen as the parent who disburses allowances to the children, and these children value their autonomy rather than seeing themselves as part of a team. Furthermore, the principal plays another important parental role, the disciplinarian (the affinity Deals With Student Behavior points toward this role). Finally, assessment is seen as an end in itself, rather than a component of a wider system that can contribute to student success.

CASE IV. EDUCATION ENTREPRENEURS: LEADERS AND FOLLOWERS

In a study of entrepreneurial leadership, Burrows (2002) used IQA to create a mindmap for a group of community college leaders who were considering (some with jaundiced eye) the "vertical extension" of their schools to four-year institutions. Burrows's issue statement is the very model of simplicity:

> Please close your eyes, relax, and focus your thoughts on the community college baccalaureate movement. Think back to when you first started considering the idea of extending the mission of the community college into the baccalaureate arena. What motivated your interest? What conflicting issues did you consider? Think about conversations you have had with both opponents and advocates. What thoughts, opinions, and concerns have emerged from these conversations? (p. 73)

Burrows then took the focus group through the IQA silent nominal and coding process, and followed up with interviews of the leaders on the affinities developed from the focus group. The composite mindmap of these community college leaders is reproduced in Figure 11.7.

Treading Water. Burrows (2002) characterized the first portion of the conventional leaders' mindmap as "Business as Usual," meaning that in striving to move their institutions toward baccalaureate degree–granting status, the "conventional" group understood the task to be not much different from any of the other challenges facing community colleges. Business as Usual involves "a cycle of struggling for limited state resources; networking with local, state, and federal agencies to supplement

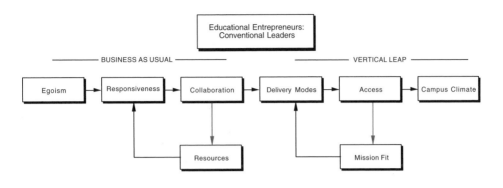

Figure 11.7

inadequate budget allocations; and keeping abreast of economic and social developments to remain responsive to one's constituency" (p. 181).

Going Ballistic. Burrows called the second portion of the conventional leaders' system "The Vertical Leap." Questions about mission fit, delivery modes, and the implications for student access are all raised in this portion of the system, suggesting that in the minds of these leaders, the vertical extension of their community colleges will indeed require a prodigious leap or a bootstrap from the ground of business as usual.

In an ingenious design twist, Burrows then conducted an IQA interview with the acknowledged visionary, an entrepreneur who advocated the vertical extension of community colleges in the state. This was the man who was both the intellectual and emotional force behind the entire movement, and who had indeed developed the legislation necessary to authorize the movement and who had shepherded it through the state legislature. How would the entrepreneur's mindmap, Burrows wondered, compare to his more conventional colleagues? Using the affinities developed by the focus group, Burrows guided the visionary through the IQA axial and theoretical coding process, then followed up with a debriefing session after a mindmap had been produced (shown in Figure 11.8).

Mavericks. Whereas the conventional leaders' mindmap suggests that a gravity-defying leap will be required, the system constructed by the entrepreneur reveals no such barrier. The first difference between the entrepreneur and the conventional leaders is one of omission: The entrepreneur adamantly refused to include Egoism in his system, and indeed were insulted at the suggestion that his leadership and interest were motivated by a personal agenda or a desire for aggrandizement or attention. More significant, the entrepreneur agreed with the other affinities but constructed a quite different system from his more conventional colleagues. For example, where his colleagues placed Mission Fit as an outcome (and a worry), the entrepreneur placed it as the primary driver of his

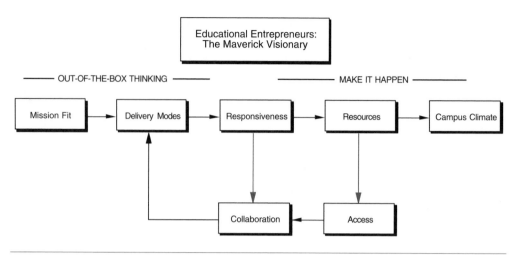

Figure 11.8

construction of the issues involved in the vertical extension of the community college. Burrows, commenting on this affinity, observes that "Just as legendary pioneer Samuel Maverick refused to brand his calves or confine them to his San Antonio ranch, [the entrepreneur] has refused to brand himself or his college with a mission that restricts their potential to move beyond their comfort zone. For this, and the perception that he is egocentric and a loner among his peers, [the entrepreneur] has often been referred to as a maverick—a label that has never bothered him" (2002, p. 185).

The Essence of Entrepreneurship. Burrows, in continuing her interpretation of the mindmaps, also comments on the relative placement of Resources in the two systems, observing that to the entrepreneur, resources are more of an outcome than a driver (see a similar result in the Knezek [2001] study). Burrows quotes Stevenson (1999) as describing entrepreneurship as an approach to management that involves the pursuit of opportunity regardless of the resources currently controlled. The IQA map of this entrepreneur, as contrasted to that of his more conventional peers, quite clearly is consistent with this understanding of entrepreneurship.

CASE V. RURAL COMMUNITY VISIONING

Gray (2003), after observing that many rural areas of the United States are economically distressed and that two-thirds of the country's comprehensive community colleges are located in rural areas, used IQA to investigate the potential role of community colleges in rural community development. Gray conducted focus groups and interviews of two constituencies, local community college presidents and rural community development specialists. The mindmaps of these two are presented in Figures 11.9 and 11.10.

Planning and Doing. Note that the mindmaps of the two constituencies suggested to Gray that the presidents constructed the issue of community development as a planning model, while the community developers constructed the same issue in terms of implementation. How best to link the planning capabilities of the community colleges with the implementation skills of the development specialists? Was there a natural link between the two? the investigator wondered. Gray (2003) found this link in the "Results/ Characteristics" affinity of the presidents and the "Characteristics" affinity of the community developers. The two affinities were, in fact, essentially the same thing, which suggested that the two systems could be pasted together, as shown in Figure 11.11.

Pasting Systems Together. Having found a potential for dialogue between the two groups, Gray then noticed that the "Leadership" affinity appeared in both systems. Envisioning a common source of leadership for the two constituencies, she merged the two Leadership affinities to produce the integrated mindmap shown in Figure 11.12.

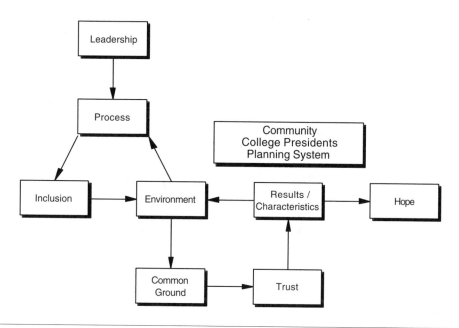

Figure 11.9

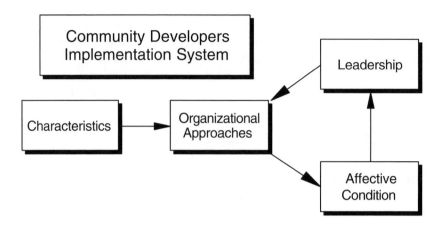

Figure 11.10

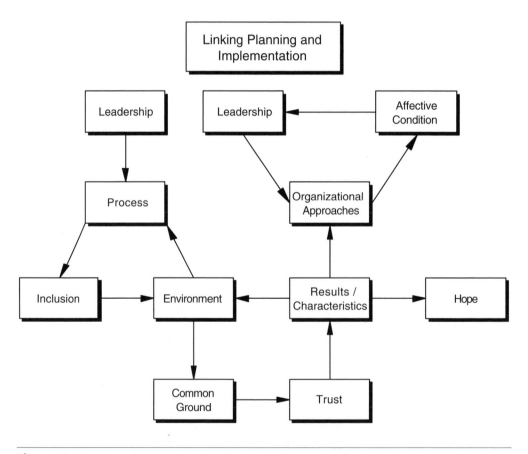

Figure 11.11

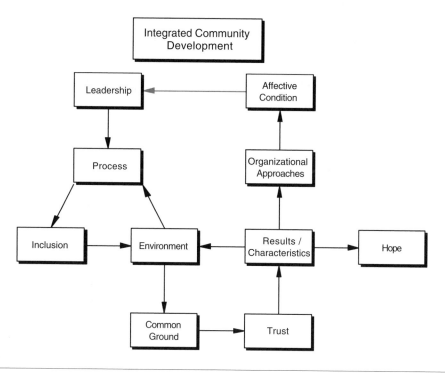

Figure 11.12

Vision and Hope. Gray, at this point in the study, is obviously much more than a stenographer or passive recorder of the "facts," but rather is moving toward the construction of a theory that, like all good theories, is the result of interaction between the researcher and the data. Gray added a link of her own between Affective Condition (the feeling of depression and hopelessness in the community) and Leadership in order to complete the feedback loop. This link, she hypothesized, would occur when the leadership was encouraged to continue their development efforts, as people in the community started seeing the results of those efforts (a classic interaction between leaders and followers).

Loops. Although she had not originally thought of the project in such terms, Gray realized at this point in the study that hers was fundamentally a study of what leadership theorists call "vision." Using the participants' theoretical codes to illustrate the nature of the links between affinities, she partitioned the integrated mindmap according to function—vision planning and vision implementation; further, she exploited IQA theory suggesting that feedback loops have functions and therefore can be named. She named the two feedback loops within the vision-planning system Community Agency (a term not referring to a particular institution but to any agent or driving force or instrument for action) and Community Capacity, and the loop inside the implementation system she named Implementation. The vision-planning and implementation systems, with illustrations of the links and the named feedback loops, can be seen in Figures 11.13 (page 413) and 11.14. (page 414)

Zooming Out. As a last step, our community development theorist substituted the names for the feedback loops to produce a high-level or, in IQA terms, a zoomed-out representation of community development visioning, shown in Figure 11.15, page 414.

Generalizing the Theory. Finally, Gray suggested that this system, when generalized beyond the narrow context of rural community development, can be conceived as a general model for planning, implementation, and evaluation, as seen in Figure 11.16, page 415.

A Spiritual Outcome. Gray's (2003) theory argues that hope[3] is the primary outcome of the system and identifies the dialectical process that can transform despair to hope. Gray reviews the literature on hope and makes the connection to her topic:

> Community members who do not believe in the possibility of changing things for the better act within their self-imposed limitations. Unfortunately, when rural people face challenges at every turn, hope is fragile. Hope reflects the mental set in which we have perceived the mental willpower and waypower to get to our destination [which is] consistent with the concept of Community Capacity defined in this study. As strange as it may seem, hope evolves only out of despair. Hope does not arise otherwise. Recognizing the fragile nature of hope, community college presidents interviewed in this study believe community colleges are often the only opportunity for hope in rural communities. Therefore, they become a major player in building hope for community survival. (pp. 187–188)

The rural community visioning study offers some comfort to those who have concerns that IQA methodology is too mechanical, too quantitative, too positivistic to capture the real essence of human concerns. "Vision" is such a concept; nevertheless, vision emerges rather naturally as a course of the study. "Hope" or faith is another spiritual quality, and yet, if the methodology is to be trusted, it is the primary outcome of the study. In the hands of the right investigator, IQA can help articulate such difficult constructs with power and eloquence.

CASE VI. THE GRADUATE SCHOOL EXPERIENCE

The rural development visioning study illustrates how systems from different constituencies may be integrated into a more comprehensive one. IQA

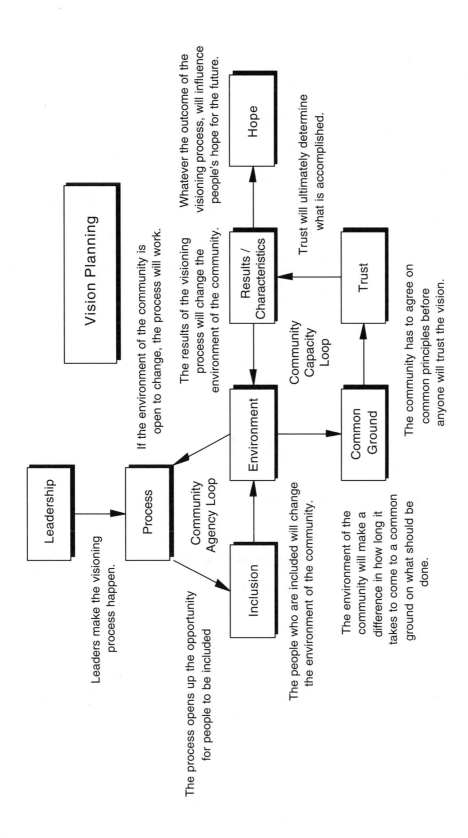

Figure 11.13

413

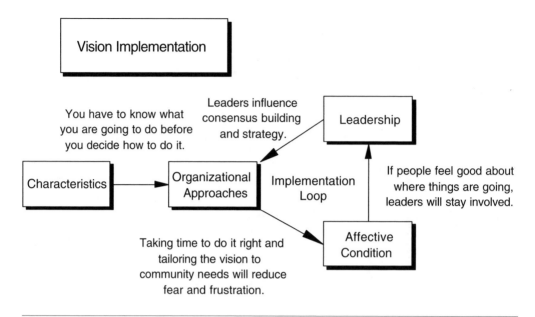

Figure 11.14

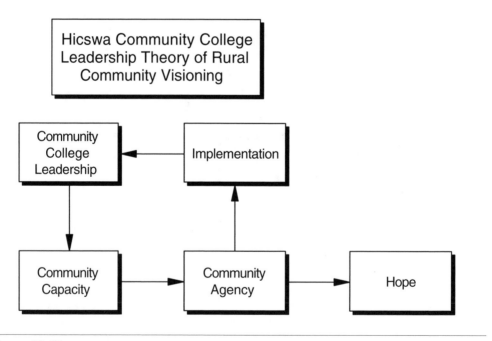

Figure 11.15

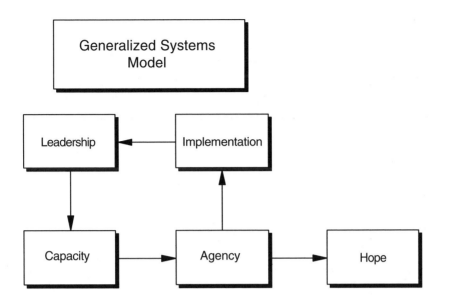

Figure 11.16

also makes it possible to integrate different but related systems from the same constituency to create a "MetaSID." Consider the following example:

Issue 1: Classroom Dynamics. Our study of graduate students in the classroom (the one used as a case study in this book) produced a picture, or a theory if you will, of the dynamics of at least one kind of classroom. This system is reproduced once more here, in Figure 11.17, page 416.

Issue 2: Campus Dynamics. In another similar graduate class (similar enough that the authors felt confident that they represented the same constituency), the issue was broadened from the classroom to the life of the graduate student "on-campus." In a guided imagery form of the issue statement, students were asked to reflect on their graduate school experience not only in their present class but with respect to all aspects of their interactions with the graduate school. The IQA process yielded the mindmap shown in Figure 11.18, page 416.

Issue 3: Off-Campus Dynamics. A third group, again representative of the constituency of graduate students at the University of Texas at Austin, was asked to consider a final variation on the graduate school experience issue: We asked them to tell us about their life outside of school; their mindmap is shown in Figure 11.19, page 417.

A simple conceptual "distance" model suggested these three variations of the same issue (the graduate school experience), as shown in Figure 11.20, page 417.

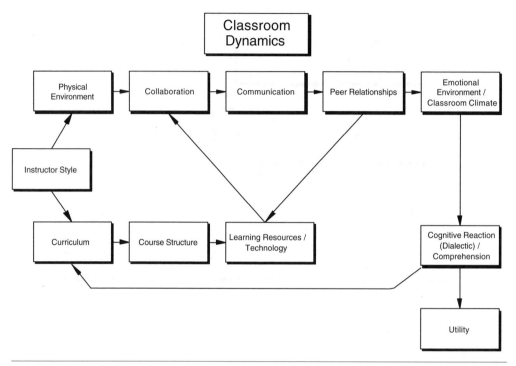

Figure 11.17

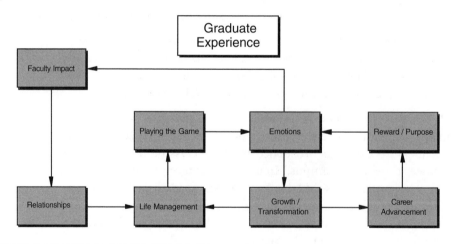

Figure 11.18

Pasting Again. A search for similarities among the mindmaps is rewarded almost immediately with the discovery that "Relationships" is common to all three. What, we wondered, would be the implications of a metaSID in which "Relationships," as suggested by the three independent mindmaps, was a nexus? Assuming that the three "Relationships" affinities could be represented as a single one, the rules for rationalization produce a system

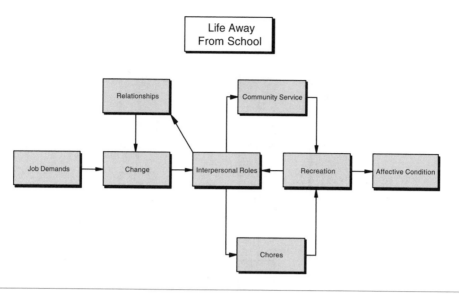

Figure 11.19

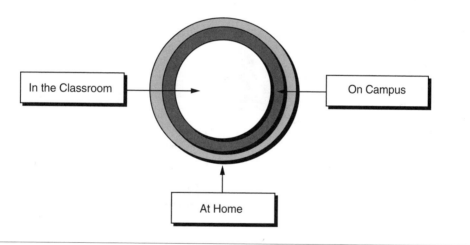

Figure 11.20

that represents the totality (or at least a totality as circumscribed by the authors' original conception) of the graduate school experience from the student's point of view, as seen in Figure 11.21, page 418.

MetaSIDs. This metaSID represents a theory of the graduate school experience; the single most compelling implication of this theory is the importance of relationship management. If the results of these IQA studies are an indication, it seems that graduate school is not all that different from the workplace or home. The reason graduate school can be so

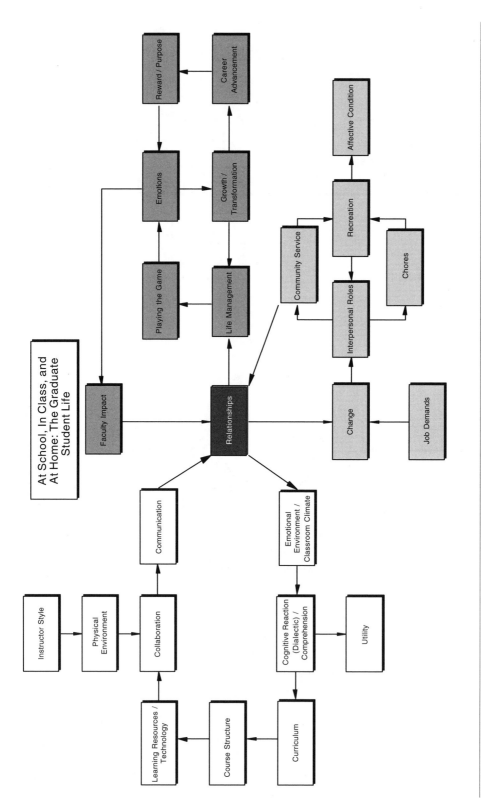

At School, In Class, and At Home: The Graduate Student Life

Figure 11.21

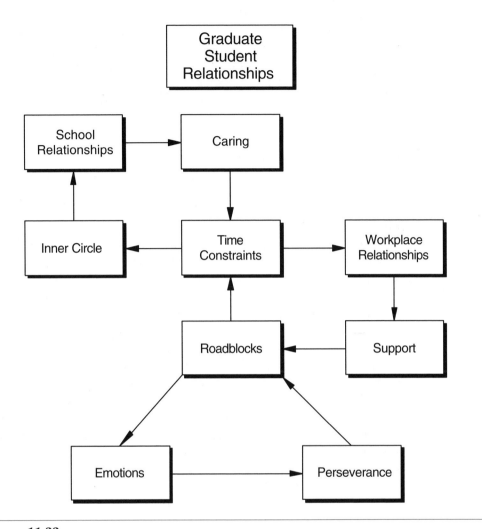

Figure 11.22

stressful is similarly highlighted by the metaSID: The graduate student is at the intersection, relationshipwise, of three different and often competing streams of demands.

Recursing Yet Again. IQA theory suggests that we can zoom in on any affinity to describe the nature and interaction of its components. The placement of Relationships as a pivot for the subsystems making up the graduate school experience cries out for such a study. Accordingly, Robole (2003) conducted a study zooming in on the Relationships affinity. A preliminary version of the mindmap created by her work is shown in Figure 11.22.

A more complete analysis of the Relationships SID must await the full review of Robole's 2003 study, but her preliminary results support the interpretation of the overall graduate student experience SID that management of relationships, rather than intelligence, or scholarship, or any of a host of other factors, may be the most important factor determining success in graduate school, at least for "ordinary" students in that Perseverance is an important outcome of the Relationships mindmap.

A Final Theoretical Sidebar. The last example, interpretation of (written) text, leads into perilous territory. A complete exploration of literary theory is beyond both the scope of this work and the capabilities of the authors, but some comments situating IQA within some broader intellectual contexts are now in order.

Systems consist of elements and relationships, but IQA attempts to represent the wholeness of the system rather than just the characteristics of the individual parts. Moreover, systems have the potential of change or self-regulate through the mechanism of feedback. These facets of IQA, as well as its advocacy of comparisons as a primary hermeneutical tool, all reflect the influence of de Saussure's (1907/1965) structural linguistics as well as Levi-Strauss's (1966) anthropological investigations into the structure of myth.

Certain poststructural concepts also play a leading role in shaping the form of IQA methodology. Foucault's (1972, 1984, 1994) analyses of the relation of power, knowledge, and discourse are manifested in the IQA notion of a constituency, and Derrida's (1974) and other postmoderns' contention that every text exists only in relation to other texts is taken seriously (if not dogmatically) by the methodology in its insistence on comparisons and fidelity to the discourse of the subject. The technique of zooming in and out is consistent with the poststructural suspicion of totalizing or essentialist approaches as well.

We have argued that quantitative and qualitative approaches to research have more in common than the extreme proponents of either school care to recognize. In a broader context, we also suggest that there are also communalities between the structuralists and poststructuralists, and this communality can be found when one considers that both views are all about *differences*. De Saussure (1907/1965) highlights the difference between signifier and the signified as well as the arbitrary nature of the relationship between them, leading one quickly to a conclusion that much of reality is socially constructed. One methodological implication of this understanding is IQA's reliance on focus groups and analysis designed to understand how realities are socially constructed. Levi-Strauss (1966), in his analysis of the structure of myths, suggests that mythical thought progresses from awareness of oppositions toward their resolution, thus identifying one of the major themes of IQA analysis, which is that of the dialectic. Derrida's (1974) deconstruction is based on not only a systems viewpoint but on the principle that all structures have a center and are further typified by binary pairs or oppositions. In his critique of Western philosophy, Derrida concludes that one element of the pair is always subordinated to the other on some scale of value; in making this claim, Derrida may have taken a step too far (consider the examples in the discussion of dialectics in Chapter 1); nevertheless, the IQA emphasis on the dialectical nature of elements of systems is at the very least an indirect result of Derridian thought. Lastly, Foucault's suggestion that knowledge, or the production of discourse, is a process of selection, distribution, and control mediated by power leads one back again to the meaning of differences.

CASE VII. TEXT ANALYSIS

Reading the Times. With our *bona fides* briefly established, we now proceed to the last case, a demonstration of using IQA to analyze written discourse. IQA is more than just focus groups and interviews; the skills and tools associated with axial and theoretical coding provide one with a way of thinking. As just described, IQA tries to make sense out of words. As an introduction to IQA as a way of thinking, a newspaper article of no special importance (Zernike, 2001), but which nonetheless was judged to be well written and rich in concepts, was identified and emailed to members of the class. A beginning group of IQA students was asked to read "School Dress Codes" for homework. In class, they were asked to read the article once more. Cards were passed out to the class, and students were asked to reflect back on the article and record any thoughts they had about it. Very quickly, many cards were generated. These were taped on the wall and an affinity analysis was conducted, in which the class identified 10 themes (affinities). Next, the class was given an Affinity Relationship Table (ART), and each member was assigned several affinity pairs and asked to go back into the article and find quotes that indicated a relationship between assigned pairs of affinities, indicated by the author's words. After this stage, while the students were on break, the authors used the IQA rules for rationalization to draw a SID that reflected the students' analysis of Zernike's article. The system in Figure 11.23 awaited students when they took their seats after the break.

With very little training in the formal procedures of IQA, the class had constructed a cogent representation one person's (the author of the article) analysis of a complex issue. After facilitating a discussion of the implications of this system, we took the class a step farther so that they could begin to understand how interpretation is an interaction between the reader and the text. Each class member was given another ART, but this time students were asked to create theoretical codes reflecting how *they* believed the affinities related, never mind the argument made by the author of the article. The results were compiled and run through the Pareto Protocol. Figure 11.24 is the group's perception of the issue.

The resulting systems were similar in drivers and outcomes, but the topological placement of loops within the two systems was different. The

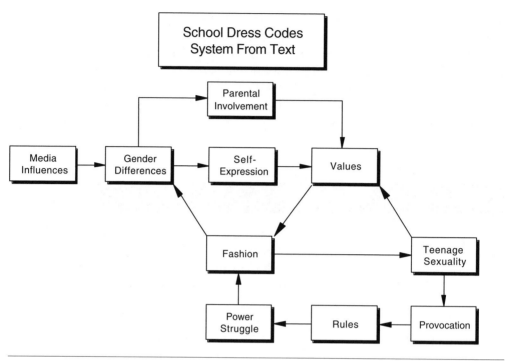

Figure 11.23

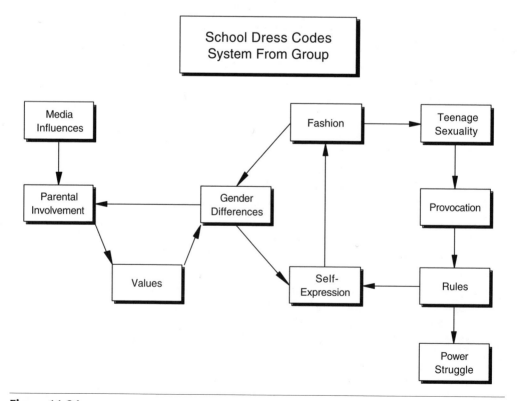

Figure 11.24

differences in the systems are those of an individual telling a story in the way journalists are trained to write versus 20 readers coming to consensus on the issues and systematically organizing their thoughts. The group's system is a "smoother" representation of the phenomenon than the author's, which reflects what one infers was a bit of a struggle to present her argument. The point we were trying to make with the students is that it is not so much that the group's system is "better" than that of the original article, but simply that it is so very hard to look at a blank piece of paper and begin to tell a story. Having a system to work within provides us with some structure and rules to make a better and stronger case.

One can conceive of using IQA to map the great concepts of literature. For example, imagine drawing a system to help explain, simplify, contrast, and synthesize the complex discourses of Aristotle, Thomas Jefferson, and Alexis de Tocqueville on democracy. Consider the possibilities of a group of scholars around the globe (or, even better, different ideological groups) collaborating electronically to analyze the meaning of a work—identifying affinities and submitting theoretical codes to be compiled into a consensus system in a process that is public and transparent to all participants. Similarly, social and political issues, which by their very nature are ill-defined, could be clarified by convening (either physically or electronically) different constituencies vis-à-vis the issue to construct their own representations of the issue and to use as a basis for dialogue and possible synthesis, rather than the recrimination, demonization, and conflict that characterize so much public discourse.

Notes

1. The interviewer was, of course, one of the authors, but he could easily have been the other one.

2. The women reacted to the men's presentation of their own construction of power with cynical smiles and knowing glances, but they did not, in contrast to the men, overtly criticize the men's system—possibly because the most powerful people in the classroom (the instructors) were both men.

3. Theologians might argue that what the focus groups identified as "hope" is more like faith: The Apostle Paul surely understood the dynamics of transformational leadership and vision when he wrote in Hebrews II:1 that faith "is the substance of things hoped for, the evidence of things not seen."

Afterword

A Brief History of the Text

This work is theoretical, but not of the armchair variety. Rather, it results from years (since 1993) of sustained development and field-testing against theoretical, operational, and pedagogical criteria. The authors have presented IQA as the methodology in doctoral-level qualitative research courses, each time revising and extending both the theory and practice of IQA according to the informal and formal evaluations of the course and concepts. Indeed, the book's primary case study is just such an evaluation. Students brave or foolhardy enough to try a new approach to qualitative research have conducted numerous studies using IQA. Selected summaries of these studies, along with methodological comments, are included in the book.

A Play in Three Acts

F. Scott Fitzgerald pungently observed that there are no second acts in American lives. In contrast, the first and third acts of the story of qualitative research are less well developed than the middle. Our students have complained over the years of the barren plots in the qualitative methods field, especially when they struggled with writing the first act: design, and the third: analysis and interpretation. Many of the books in this field are *about* qualitative research, but they do not have much to say about how *to do* qualitative research. To the extent that the "how" issue is addressed, many books speak to observation or interview methodology, or data collection in general, but are relatively silent about analysis. Furthermore, many texts have even less to say about the mysterious process of designing qualitative studies, a shortcoming also evident in the quantitative arena.

Despite strenuous attempts to distance themselves from the dreaded positivist paradigm, many authors still (perhaps unthinkingly) erect an

425

unnecessary epistemological barrier between the observer and the observed. Whatever its empirical tradition (anthropology, sociology, critical theory, or the like), much of the literature presumes that it is the sole responsibility of the researcher to make sense of the "data." Member checking aside, much of the literature takes the stance that the hermeneutical function is best left to professionals and that the *subject* or *participant* has, at most, a passive role in the whole enterprise.

Mathematical Revolutionaries

Mathematicians have long understood the rules of a game called "Turn the Assumption on its Head." For example, Bolyai and Lobachevsky (apparently independently and simultaneously) wondered what a system of geometry would look like if it rejected Euclid's fifth postulate. Their work led to revolutionary systems of non-Euclidean geometry, and indirectly to an explosion of new algebras. But in their enthusiasm for the new geometries, mathematicians did not demand that all rulers, tape measures, maps, plats, architectural plans, and blueprints be confiscated and burned. Plane geometry and trigonometry books were allowed to remain on library shelves, and teachers of these subjects were not forced into intellectual ghettoes outside the mathematical pale.

Like Bolyai and Lobachevsky, Lincoln and Guba in 1985 asked what would happen if the assumptions underlying positivism were turned on their heads and, as in mathematics, the results have been revolutionary. The revolution in educational research, however, has taken quite a different turn from that created by the non-Euclideans. It seems that those of us who care about educational research have not understood Lincoln and Guba's work with the same level of sophistication that informed the reception of the new geometries within the community of mathematicians. In the mid- to late 1970s, we were defending the "new paradigms" of postmodernism against a regime whose most fervent desire was to be more scientific than the scientists. Today, no savvy young educational researcher would ever be branded with the red "P" of Positivism, but that same savvy researcher quite often, in the authors' experience, is poorly trained in and has little tolerance for logic and systematic analysis. To be sure, we have seen dramatic change, but it seems reasonable to ask whether there has been progress.

Hegel suggested that history could be understood through the dialectic of thesis-antithesis-synthesis. We have seen the thesis of positivism almost overwhelmed in many quarters by the antithesis of postmodernism in the past 25 years. Perhaps now is that moment in Hegelian history, that *logos,* in which a synthesis can emerge.

References

Aristotle. *The Organon.*

Aquinas, Thomas. *Summa Theologica.*

Bann, E. F. (2001). *Effects of media representations of a cultural ideal of feminine beauty on self body image in college aged women: An interactive qualitative analysis.* Unpublished doctoral dissertation, University of Texas at Austin.

Ben-Yehuda, N. (1995). *The Masada myth: Collective memory and matchmaking in Israel.* Madison: University of Wisconsin Press.

Bogdan, R. C., & Biklen, S. K. (1992). *Qualitative research for education: An introduction to theory and methods.* Boston: Allyn & Bacon.

Burrows, B. A. (2002). *The vertical extension of Florida's community college system: A case study of politics and entrepreneurial leadership.* Unpublished doctoral dissertation, University of Texas at Austin.

Byrne, R. *www.tcd.ie/Psychology/Ruth_Byrne/mental_models/*

Campbell, D. T., & Stanley, J. C. (1963). *Experimental and quasi-experimental designs for research.* Chicago: Rand McNally.

Carley, K. (1997). Network text analysis: The network position of concepts. In C. W. Roberts (Ed.), *Text analysis for the social sciences* (pp. 79–100). Mahwah, NJ: Erlbaum.

Carley, K., & Palmquist, M. (1992). Extracting, representing, and analyzing mental models. *Social Forces* 70: 601–636.

Craik, K. (1943). *The nature of explanation.* London: Cambridge University Press.

Delta Associates (C. Kallendorf & J. Speer). (1995). Proprietary report on communications patterns, Austin, TX. *www.delta-associates.com.* Cited by permission of the authors.

Denzin, N. (1989). *Interpretive biography* (Qualitative Research Methods, Vol. 17). Newbury Park, CA: Sage.

Denzin, N. K., & Lincoln, Y. (Eds.). (2000). *Handbook of qualitative research* (2nd ed.). Thousand Oaks, CA: Sage.

Derrida, J. (1974). *Of grammatology* (G. C. Spivak, Trans.). Baltimore: Johns Hopkins University Press. (Original work published 1967)

Dewey, J. (1910). *Systematic inference: Induction and deduction.* Chapter 7 in *How We Think.* Lexington: D. C. Heath (1910): 79–100.

Emerson, R. W. (1841, repr. 1847). *Compensation essays, first series.* Referenced in *www.bartleby.com/66/2/19702.html.* Accessed November 1, 2003.

Emerson, R. W. (1860). *Worship. The conduct of life.* Referenced in *www.bartleby.com/66/58/21558.htm.* Accessed November 1, 2003.

Engels, F. (1984). *Anti-Dühring: Herr Eugen Duhring's revolution in science.* Chicago: Charles H. Kerr Publishing. (Original work published 1878)

Floyd-Bann, E. (2001). *Effects of media representations of a cultural ideal of feminine beauty on self body image: An interactive qualitative analysis.* Unpublished dissertation, University of Texas at Austin.

Fodor, J. (1975). *Language of thought.* New York: Thomas Crowell.

Foucault, M. (1965). *Madness and Civilization: A history of insanity in the age of reason* (R. Howard, Trans.). New York: Pantheon. (Original work published 1961)

Foucault, M. (1972). *The archeology of knowledge* (A. M. Smith, Trans.). New York: Pantheon. (Original work published 1969)

Foucault, M. (1977). *Discipline and punishment: The birth of the prison* (A. Sheridan, Trans.). New York: Vintage. (Original work published 1975)

Glaser, B. (1978). *Theoretical sensitivity.* Mill Valley, CA: Sociology Press.

Glaser, B. (1992). *Emergence vs. forcing. Advances in the methodology of grounded theory.* Mill Valley, CA: Sociology Press.

Glaser, B. G., & Strauss, A. (1967). *The discovery of grounded theory: Strategies for qualitative research.* Chicago: Aldine Publishing Co.

Gray, S. H. (2003). *The role of community college presidents in vision building for rural community development.* Unpublished dissertation, University of Texas at Austin.

Heidegger, M. (1962). *Being and time* (J. Macquarrie & E. Robinson, Trans.) New York: Harper. (Original work published 1927)

Houlgate, S. (1991*). Freedom, truth and history: An introduction to Hegel's philosophy.* London and New York: Routledge.

Hughes, R. (1988). *The fatal shore: The epic of Australia's founding.* New York: Vintage Books.

Husserl, E. (1965). *Phenomenology and the crisis of philosophy* (Q. Lauer, Trans.). New York: Harper & Row. (Original work published 1935)

Johnson-Laird, P. (1983). *Mental models.* Cambridge, MA: Harvard University Press.

Jonassen, D. H. (1995). *Operationalizing mental models: Strategies for assessing mental models to support meaningful learning and design-supportive learning environments.* HTML Paper: *www-cscl95.indiana.edu/cscl95/jonassen.html.*

Juran, J. M. (1988). *Juran on planning for quality.* New York: The Free Press.

Kauffman, J. M. (1993.) Places of change: Special education's power and identity in an era of educational reform. *Journal of Learning Disabilities* 27: 610–618.

Kayser, T. (1995). *Mining group gold.* New York: McGraw-Hill.

Kerlinger, F. (1985). *Foundations of behavioral research* (3rd ed.). Chicago: Holt, Rinehart & Winston.

Kitcher, P. (2002). *Science, truth, and democracy.* New York: Oxford University Press.

Knezek, E. J. (2001). *Supervision as a selected instructional leadership behavior of elementary principals and student achievement in reading.* Unpublished dissertation, University of Texas at Austin.

Kuhn, T. (1970). *The structure of scientific revolutions* (2nd ed.). Chicago: University of Chicago Press.

Laird, J. (2001). *An interactive qualitative analysis of health and student development in college freshmen.* Unpublished dissertation, University of Texas at Austin.

Lakoff, G. (1991). *Women, fire, and dangerous things.* Chicago: University of Chicago Press.

Lawrence-Lightfoot, S., & Hoffman Davis, J. (1997). *The art and science of portraiture.* San Francisco: Jossey-Bass.

Levi-Strauss, C. (1966). *The savage mind* (2nd ed.). Chicago: University of Chicago Press.

Lincoln, Y. S., & Guba, E. G. (1985). *Naturalistic inquiry.* Beverly Hills, CA: Sage.

McCoy, D. (1992). *IQA and instructional systems design.* Dissertation proposal, University of Texas at Austin.

Merleau-Ponty, M. (1967). *The structure of behaviour.* Boston: Beacon Press.

Patton, M. P. (2001). *Qualitative evaluation and research methods* (3rd ed.). Thousand Oaks, CA: Sage.

Poe, E. A. (1843). *The Black Cat. United States Saturday Post.* Referenced in *http://www.bartleby.com/66/39/44739.html.*

Polkinghorne, D. (1983). *Methodology for the human sciences.* Albany, NY: SUNY Press.

Robole, D. (2000). *Impact of primary relationships and individual attitudes on doctoral students' persistence.* Dissertation proposal, University of Texas at Austin.

Robole, D. (2003.) *Zooming in: An examination of the impact of primary relationships and individual attitudes on doctoral student persistence.* Unpublished dissertation proposal, University of Texas at Austin.

Rubin, A., & Babbie, E. (1993). *Research methods for social work* (2nd ed.). Pacific Grove, CA: Brooks/Cole.

de Saussure, F. (1965). *Course in general linguistics* (W. Baskin, Trans.) New York: McGraw-Hill. (Original work published 1907)

Seale, C. (1999). *The quality of qualitative research.* London: Sage.

Staggers, N., & Norcio, A. (1993). Mental models: Concepts for human-computer interaction research. *International Journal of Man-Machine Studies* 38: 587–605.

Stevenson, H. (1999). A perspective on entrepreneurship. In W. Sahlman, H. Stevenson, M. Roberts (Eds.), *The entrepreneurial venture* (2nd ed.), Cambridge, MA: Harvard Business School Press.

Strauss, A., & Corbin, J. (1998). *Basics of qualitative research* (2nd ed.). Thousand Oaks, CA: Sage.

Strauss, A., & Corbin, J. (Ed.). (1997). *Grounded theory in practice.* Thousand Oaks, CA: Sage.

Street, W. R. (1994). *A chronology of noteworthy events in American psychology.* Washington, DC: American Psychological Association.

Sutherland, S. (Spring 1990). Choose your method. *Nurses Notes* 22(2): 21.

Titscher, S., Meyer, M., Wodak, R., & Vetter, E. (2000). *Methods of text and discourse analysis.* London: Sage.

Wheatley, M. (1999). *Leadership and the new science: Discovering order in a chaotic world* (2nd ed.). San Francisco: Berrett-Koehler.

Wittgenstein, L. (1922). *Tractatus Logico-Philosophicus.* London: Routledge.

Zernike, K. (2001, September 11). "School dress codes vs. a sea of bare flesh." *The New York Times* Online.

Index

About the Authors

Dr. Norvell Northcutt is a Senior Lecturer in the Community College Leadership Program, Department of Educational Administration, University of Texas at Austin, where he teaches courses in quantitative and qualitative research methods and serves as research advisor on many dissertation committees in several graduate schools. In addition, he serves as Technical Advisor to the Community College Survey of Student Engagement (CCSSE) Project. After conducting a series of national research and development projects in adult functional literacy, for which he was an American nominee for the UNESCO world literacy award in 1977, Northcutt was named Director of Research for the Southwest Educational Development Laboratory. He then went to Austin Community College (ACC), where he taught math, statistics, and computer science while serving as Director of the college's administrative computing system and as Director of Analysis for ACC's Office of Institutional Effectiveness.

Dr. Danny McCoy is a multimedia instructional systems designer and qualitative researcher who specializes in full life cycle development of technology-integrated instruction. He is a Multimedia Instructional Designer and Military Trainer with Northrop Grumman Mission Systems at the Battle Command Training Center at Fort Hood, Texas. He also serves as a consultant with McCoy Multimedia, a research and instructional technology group. He has been designing multimedia courses since 1995, and has developed secondary- and graduate-level courses as well as corporate and private sector training. Dr. McCoy coteaches an advanced qualitative research graduate course (IQA) at the University of Texas at Austin and provides IQA workshops around the country.